This book is dedicated to anyone who agrees with more than five of the following statements:

1. Francois Truffaut, Alain Resnais, and Jacques Rivette are the coolest film directors ever.

2. There's never really been a better song than "Idiot Wind," by Bob Dylan.

3. Someone really should open up a better restaurant or bar near the offices of *Book Magazine* where Lucy, Jerome, Kristin, Eric, and Bill could get something not completely revolting for lunch.

4. Beate is the coolest woman on the planet.

5. Someone should really turn Joseph Conrad's *Chance* into a movie.

6. The Coq d'Or bar at the Drake Hotel features the best club sandwich in Chicago.

7. Nine out of ten indie filmmakers really want to sell out and do Coke commercials with really cool effects.

8. People working behind the counter at most artsy video stores have bad attitudes.

9. Baseball really hasn't been as interesting since Richie Allen retired.

10. Writing guidebooks is not quite the glamorous profession that some mammals might perceive it to be.

Contents

Introduction

The introduction to the third edition of this book will certainly look a lot different than the introduction to this version. I'm certain of it. It's something about where you are in the process of making a film that changes your perspective on what a festival is and what it's for. I wrote the first edition in the middle of heavy-duty editing of a film while trying to find all the festivals to submit to. That's how the book started—because there was no one single resource where one could go and find out about virtually every festival in the world to decide which ones to enter.

This edition was written once that film had gotten a distribution deal, which allows for some greater perspective. Once you're looking at festivals from a distance, you see more of what they're about. You don't get pissed because your film didn't get accepted. You don't get angry because Lorenzo Lamas got a career achievement award. You grow to understand that most festivals are for audiences foremost and for filmmakers secondarily. You realize that just because a film festival accepts the new Al Pacino movie for its opening night and not the shoestring indie made by your buddy, that doesn't mean the festival is somehow corrupt. You realize, truth be told, that when it comes right down to it you'd rather see that Al Pacino movie anyway.

The best festivals are the ones that combine the best of both worlds—making those new discoveries that can vault new, undiscovered filmmakers from absolute obscurity to semi-obscurity, while keeping the audiences happy by showing them the movies they wouldn't see otherwise, whether they're directed by Joe Eszterhas or Joe Schmo.

In this edition, we provide you with updated listings of more than 500 film festivals around the world. Some, like the Kudzu Film Festival and the Fort Worth Festival, are brand-new. Some have bitten the dust. We've also talked to some more festival directors who tell us a little bit about how films get chosen and what festivals are looking for. We've included a list of the best movie theaters in the world, so you can catch up on the best of world cinema even when there's not a festival in town. Also new is a brief list of tips for the filmmaker who wants to submit to festivals.

Important Note Do not view these listings as the Bible. We've tried to be as up-to-date and diligent as possible, but festivals are changing their deadlines and their guidelines and their dates and locations all the time. Some festival deadlines list only the month when they occur. This is because of often-changing deadlines. Always phone first.

The third edition of this book will be written, most likely, during a heavy-duty editing process for the next feature film. But even when that film's edited and scored and it's having its premiere, I might well be wandering the streets looking for that next Wim Wenders movie. Or at least something with Al Pacino. Won't you?

Tips for the Filmmaker When Submitting to Festivals

1. Just because a festival calls you out of the blue and asks you to submit your film, don't become overjoyed. There are a number of festivals out there (which shall remain nameless) that make a lot of money off festival entry fees. The more entries they get, the more money they make. Be cautious and only submit to the festivals that you truly feel are appropriate.

2. Do not submit your film to a festival before you feel it's truly done (edited, mixed, and so forth). Don't think that the person viewing your film will automatically make allowances and understand that "all those problems will be taken care of in postproduction." Better to miss the deadline and send in your film a year late than regret having an unfinished, unpolished product rejected.

3. Do not grouse that a lot of films seem to be accepted to certain festivals because of connections the filmmakers and producers have to members of the festival juries or boards. You're not paranoid. It's true. But that's the way the politics work sometimes. Better to start making your own connections and have other filmmakers grouse about you.

4. Don't take rejection personally. Not being selected for a film festival doesn't mean your film sucks (maybe it does, but that's not the point). All it means is that on one particular day, some volunteer who was watching the first 15 minutes of it along with the first 15 minutes of two dozen other films didn't find a reason to pass it upstairs to the next viewer.

5. Don't view a film festival as the thing that will make or break your career. A few careers have been made at Sundance, but not a lot. Take a more hang-loose approach to it. Even Antonioni has trouble getting his films screened or distributed these days.

6. Don't spend a lot of money on press materials and fancy posters. Most people won't even see them before they watch your film to consider it.

1 Best of the Fests

A Completely Biased Guide to the Sixteen Festivals Worldwide That Are Worth the Trip

Art Film Festival

Where Trencianske Teplice, Slovak Republic
When One week in late June
Background Art Film, which refreshingly views cinema as an art form rather than as a commodity or advertising tool, was founded in 1993 in this vibrant spa town with the intention of supporting narrative and documentary art films as well as films dealing specifically with artistic media. The most recent jury was helmed by the brilliant French writer and director Alain Robbe-Grillet. Said former jury chairman Krzysztof Zanussi: "We see the state of crisis of the arts in the world generally. Thus, we see a festival of art films as necessarily reflecting that crisis. Out of this state of confusion and depression, we see the creation of some films suitable only for use as prison punishment. On the other hand, springing out of the same confusion and depression we see the ideas of the prize-winning films as offering some hope. Many look back to the deep roots of humanity; others look forward to the future." Films out of competition are screened in the following categories: British Film Day (a presentation of Scottish films organized in cooperation with the British Council Bratislava), French Film Day (a presentation of the Centre Pompidou), Arte (a selection of made-for-TV art films), Czech Day at Art Film (a presentation of Czech films), and Heritage of Our Era (a series of documentaries from Central and Eastern Europe).
Major Award Winners Best Film: *Love Is the Devil*, by John Maybury; Best Cinematography: John Mathieson, *Love Is the Devil*; Golden Key Award for Documentary: *Voyage*, by Christian Boustani; Silver Key Award: *The Legends and Morytates of Ladomirova*, by Peter Kerekes; Bronze Key Award: *Georges Rousse: Light and the Ruins*, by Gilles Perru; Best Short: *Melody of the Street*, by Diana Groo
Films About 100 live-action and animated features
Noteworthy Celebrity Sightings Sophia Loren, Jiri Menzel, Gina Lollobrigida, Peter Greenaway

Tickets Free!
How to Enter For more information contact:
    Art Film Festival
    Konventna 8
    811 03 Bratislava
    Slovak Republic
    Telephone 011.42.7.531.9481
    Fax 011.42.7.531.1679
    E-mail festival@artfilm.sk
    Web www.artfilm.sk
Entry Deadline April

Berlin International Film Festival

Where Berlin, Germany
When Two weeks in mid-February
Background This is an indescribably huge festival that has been around since 1951 and features such a wide spectrum of films that there is truly something for everyone. The most recent festival boasted the premiere of the Bono-Wim Wenders-Mel Gibson collaboration *The Million Dollar Hotel*. Everybody who's anybody premieres his work here. Lifetime achievement awards and tributes tend to have an irritatingly pseudo-Hollywood or Agatha Christie-movie feel to them, honoring the likes of Lauren Bacall and Kim Novak—though 2000 did somewhat better, with a tribute to Jeanne Moreau and a screening of Tony Richardson's adaptation of Jean Genet's *Mademoiselle*. But hell, it's bigger than Sundance, it's better than Venice, and it's cooler than Cannes. (Now if they could just get the cuisine in order in this city, they just might have something here.) The festival jury was most recently headed by Andrzej Wajda and Gong Li.
Major Award Winners Golden Bear: *Magnolia*, *Sense and Sensibility*, *The People vs. Larry Flynt*; Silver Bear for Runner-Up Film: *Vive l'Amour*, by Trai Ming-Liang, *The Million Dollar Hotel*, by Wim Wenders; Best Actor: Denzel Washington, *Hurricane*, Leonardo DiCaprio, *Romeo & Juliet*
Films About 250 features and shorts
Tickets $7.50–$12 per individual screening; $150 pass to all screenings; call 011.49.30.25.4892
How to Enter For more information contact:
    Berlin International Film Festival
    Potsdamer Strasse 5
    10785 Berlin
    Germany
    Telephone 011.49.30.25.4890
    Fax 011.49.30.48.9249
    E-mail info@berlinale.de
    Web www.berlinale.de
Entry Deadline November

Cannes International Film Festival

Where Cannes, France

When Two weeks in mid-May

Background They say that Cannes is Cannes. This is about as apt and concise a description as I can come up with. You can criticize it, say it's a pain in the ass, say it's all hype, say that if given your druthers you'd really prefer not to have your hotel room down the hall from Mel Brooks's (particularly after seeing *Dracula: Dead and Loving It*), say that half of what's shown here is trash, say that you're sick of the hawkers trying to shove promotional information in your face even though you don't have enough money to buy dinner let alone the Korean distribution rights for their movie. But after all is said and done, it's still Cannes. It's still along the Mediterranean. And as they said about *The Great Santini*, you may love it, you may hate it, but you'll never forget it. Founded now more than 50 years ago, it's the place where everything screens, where everybody goes, were even if you can't find a film screening in an official center, you're sure to find it projected against the wall of some sharpie's hotel room for prospective buyers. Films are screened in the official competition, Un Certain Regard (noncompetitive showcase of work), Directors' Fortnight, plus a spotlight on some of the best work from French filmmakers.

Major Award Winners Palme d'Or for Best Picture: *Rosetta*, by Luc and Jean-Pierre Dardenne; Grand Jury Prize: *L'Humanité*, by Bruno Dumont; Best Actor: Emmanuel Schotte, *L'Humanité*; Best Actress (tie): Severine Caneele, *L'Humanité*, and Emilie Dequenne, *Rosetta*. Best Director; Pedro Almodóvar, *All About My Mother*; Best Screenplay: Youri Arabov, *Moloch*; Palme d'Or for Best Short Film: *When the Day Breaks*, by Wendy Tilby and Amanda Forbis; Jury Prize for Short Film: *Stop*, by Rodolphe Marconi, and *So-Poong*, by Song Ilgon

Noteworthy Celebrity Sightings Got an hour? I'll give you a list.

Tickets Variable. Contact French film office in New York at 212.832.8860.

How to Enter For more information contact:

Cannes Film Festival
99, Boulevard Malesherbes
75008 Paris
France
Telephone 011.33.1.45.61.66.00
Fax 011.33.1.45.61.97.60
E-mail festival@cannes.bull.net
Web www.cannes-filmfestival.com

Entry Deadline March

Chicago International Film Festival

Where Chicago, Illinois

When Two weeks in mid-October

Background What a difference a couple of years make. Once on rocky financial ground, the festival lived in a sort of limbo for a while, programming largely safe choices. But recently Chicago has gotten its act together to become one of the more excitingly programmed events around. Founded in 1967 by Michael Kutza, the festival has had a difficult history. Still the festival premieres more than 100 films annually and has gained fame for jump-starting the careers of many previously little-known filmmakers, including Martin Scorsese, whose *Who's That Knocking at My Door* captured a Gold Hugo at the first festival in 1967. Some of the coolest films I've ever seen premiered here, including Franco Maseli's *Codice Privata* and Jacques Rivette's *Haut/Bas/Fragile*. The 1999 fest featured a wonderful array of films including *Set Me Free*, *Ma Petite Entreprise*, *The Dream Catcher*, *My Best Fiend* and the hilariously Woody Allen-esque *Rien Sur Robert*. Of course, there are some duds (as in all festivals), and one could probably do better than *Mansfield Park* for an opening night feature. But like a baseball player who comes from hitting .216 to .307, this festival deserves some award as comeback player of the year. Recent honorees include Lauren Bacall, Gregory Peck, Ray Harryhausen, John Frankenheimer, and Morgan Freeman. Films are screened at the Water Tower Theatres and Chicago's jewel of a cinema, the Music Box Theatre.

Major Award Winners Gold Hugo for Best Film: *La Maladie de Sachs*, by Michel Deville; Silver Hugo for Best Film: *Not of This World*, by Giuseppe Piccioni; Silver Hugo for Best Actor: Benoit Poelvoorde, *The Carriers Are Waiting;* Silver Hugo for Best Actress: Hilary Swank, *Boys Don't Cry*; Best First Feature Film: *The Love of Three Oranges*, by Hung Hung; Best Documentary: *American Hollow*, by Rory Kennedy; Best Short Subject: *Acide Animé*, by Guillaume Breaud

Films Thirty-five films presented in official competition; approximately 15 shown in showcase of American independents; approximately 50 shown in showcase of new international cinema

Noteworthy Celebrity Sightings Jodie Foster, Jennifer Beals, Andy Davis

How to Enter Send VHS dub, entry form, and $150 entry fee to:
Cinema/Chicago
32 W. Randolph Street
Chicago, IL 60601
Telephone 312.425.9400
Fax 312.425.0944
E-mail filmfest@wwa.com
Web www.chicago.ddbn.com/filmfest

Entry Deadline August

Flanders International Film Festival

Where Ghent, Belgium
When Twelve days in mid-October
Background Founded in 1974 as a student film festival, the Flanders fest now plays host to more than 70,000 spectators every year as it continues to focus on the impact of music on film, awarding the Georges Delerue prize annually for the best use of music in a film. The Delerue competition is only open to fiction films. As we have been told: "A biographical film about Schubert or Jim Morrison is not eligible for competition." Tributes and retrospective programs include an official selection of competing films, Filmspectrum (a panorama of world cinema), tributes, film classics (a recent program featured a selection of American films from the McCarthy era), and a selection of Belgian films, along with seminars. Films that have received their premieres here have included *Stop Making Sense*, *Crossroads*, and Jean-Luc Godard's *Detective*. A recent spotlight paid tribute to Irwin Winkler and the Ghent Opera House, and the Palais des Beaux Arts featured concerts of the scores of Stephen Warbeck (*Shakespeare in Love*) and Elliott Goldenthal (*Interview with a Vampire*).

Major Award Winners Best Film: *Cyclo*, by Tranh An-Hung; Best Music: Thon That Thiet, *Cyclo*
Films 150 feature films and 80 shorts
Noteworthy Celebrity Sightings Amanda Plummer, Christopher Lee, Jocelyn Pook (!), Peter Wolf, Sandra Bullock, Sydney Pollack, Peter Greenaway, Christopher Hampton, Stephen Frears
Tickets 100–300 BF per individual screening; 500 BF per day pass
How to Enter For more information contact:
>Internationaal Filmfestival van Vlaanderen
>Kortrijksesteenweg 1104
>9051 Ghent
>Belgium
>Telephone 011.329.269.28.78
>E-mail filmfestival@glo.be
>Web www.filmfestival.be
Entry Deadline August

Locarno International Film Festival

Where Locarno, Switzerland
When Ten days in early August
Background Founded in 1946, this is one of the best international film festivals around. Held in a lovely town at the base of the Alps along Lake Maggiore and focusing mainly on first and second features, the festival also showcases a wide range of Swiss and European cinema along with retrospectives that in recent years have included Hitchcock, Jean-Luc Godard, Clint Eastwood, and Youssef Chahine. One of the more interesting features in recent years was the so-called Film of a Lifetime section, in which major directors were asked to choose films that had been poorly received but influenced them greatly. Woody Allen chose Sidney Lumet's *The Hill*, Abel Ferrara chose Allen's *Zelig*, John Carpenter picked Orson Welles's *Chimes at Midnight*, David Lynch opted for Stanley Kubrick's *Lolita*, and Kathryn Bigelow chose Sam Peckinpah's *The Wild Bunch*.
Major Award Winners Golden Leopard for Best Film: *Mr. Zhao*; Silver Leopard: *The Adoptive Son*, by Aktan Abdikalikov, and *Marian*, by Petr Vaclav
Films About 250 features
Noteworthy Celebrity Sightings Atom Egoyan, Ken Loach, Kathryn Bigelow, Bernardo Bertolucci, Laurence Cote
Tickets 10–17 Fr per individual screening; 250 Fr for entry to all films.
How to Enter For more information contact:
>Locarno International Film Festival
>Via della Posta 6
>6600 Locarno
>Switzerland
>Telephone 011.41.91.756.21.21
>Fax 011.41.91.756.21.49
>E-mail info@pardo.ch
>Web www.pardo.ch
Entry Deadline May

Montreal World Film Festival

Where Montreal, Quebec, Canada
When Late August through early September
Background Though Toronto is the most famous festival in Canada, the Montreal festival features a breathtaking array of films. This marathon of all film festivals offers so many films that St. Catherine Street is closed down to accommodate pedestrian cinephiles. The festival bills itself as "the largest publicly attended film festival in the Western world." Maybe so. Screenings take place in downtown Montreal at Le Parisien (480 St. Catherine Street), Places des Arts (175 St. Catherine Street), Complexe Desjardins (St. Catherine Street West and Jeanne-Mance), and the Imperial Cinema (1430 Bleury Street).
Major Award Winners Grand Prix of the Americas: *Color of Paradise*, by Majid Majidi (Iran)
Films About 400
Noteworthy Celebrity Sightings Claudia Cardinale, Alain Delon, Clint Eastwood, Jeanne Moreau
Tickets CA$7.50 per individual screening; CA$200 "9-to-5" pass gains admittance to all screenings between 9 A.M. and 5 P.M.
How to Enter For more information contact:
    Festival des Films du Monde
    1432, Rue de Bleury
    Montreal, PQ H3A 2J1
    Canada
    Telephone 514.848.3883
    Fax 514.848.3886
    E-mail ffm@Interlink.net
    Web www.ffm-montreal.org
Entry Deadline July

New York Film Festival

Where New York, New York
When Two weeks in late September and early October
Background Few major festivals are smaller than the New York festival, but few are better. Founded in 1963, the festival is not the place to find a huge array of quirky underground foreign films and U.S. indies, but it is the locus for probably the best of these categories. Major film artists who are notoriously shy about publicity show up here. Major films from master filmmakers who, for some reason, can't get U.S. distribution wind up here. The New York festival has presented the U.S. premieres of Alexei Guerman's *Khroustaliov, My Car!*, Michelangelo Antonioni's *Beyond the Clouds*, Emir Kusturica's Cannes-winning *Underground* and Leos Carax's *Les Amants de Pont Neuf*. Rediscovered or reconstructed classics (the *Rolling Stones' Rock 'n' Roll Circus*) are often presented here for the first time in decades. One expects class and elegance from a festival sponsored by Grand Marnier. The festival is also sponsored by the Film Society of Lincoln Center, and screenings are held at Alice Tully Hall (1941 Broadway), the Walter Reade Theater (165 W. 65th Street), and the Ziegfeld Theater (141 W. 54th Street).

Major Award Winners Noncompetitive
Films Only about 50, with a focus on features
Noteworthy Celebrity Sightings Milos Forman, Mike Leigh, virtually every other film-maker at one time or another
Tickets About $12 per individual screening, though tickets vary from screening to screening
How to Enter One of the only American festivals—and certainly the most prestigious —that does not accept entry fees for film submissions. Cool. For more information contact:

Film Society of Lincoln Center
70 Lincoln Center Plaza
New York, NY 10023-6595
Telephone 212.875.5638
Fax 212.875.5636
E-mail filmlinc@dti.net
Web www.filmlinc.com/nyff

Entry Deadline July

Pordenone-Le Giornate del Cinema Muto

Where Pordenone, Italy
When One week in mid-October
Background One of the coolest film festivals running. Period. Dedicated solely to the art of silent cinema, this festival, founded in 1982 by La Cineteca del Friuli (a film archive in Gemona) and the Cinemazero Film Club in Pordenone, turns this northern Italian town into a heavenly meeting place for cinema buffs, film scholars, and archivists. Screening rare silent films in the nearly 100-year-old Teatro Cinema, the festival programs retrospectives of the likes of Mack Sennett, Louis Lumière, and Max Fleischer, even 100-year-old kinetoscopes of prize fighters. The festival, now headed by film historian David Robinson, combines the ardor of the amateur film enthusiast with the rigorous attention to detail of the film historian, presenting tons upon tons of little-seen work from the dawn of cinema. The festival has recently screened a passel of Krazy Kat cartoons, as well as works by Gregory LaCava, Cecil B. DeMille, and "unknown American silent comedians." One recent retrospective, honoring the Edison Motion Picture Company, showed all surviving work from the company from 1890 through 1900. Other retrospectives have included Italian comedians of the teens, early Scandinavian cinema, and German film production before Caligari. Anyone who thinks silent film means only Buster Keaton, Mary Pickford, and Charlie Chaplin is in for quite a surprise.
Major Award Winners Noncompetitive
Films More than 500
Noteworthy Celebrity Sightings Ken Rive, a childhood star of German and British silents
How to Enter For more information contact:

Le Giornate del Cinema Muto
La Cineteca del Friuli
Via Osoppo 26
33013 Gemona UD
Italy

Telephone 011.39.432.980.458
Fax 011.39.432.970.542
E-mail pp.lj@proxima.conecta.it
Web 194.184.27.63/gcm

Rotterdam International Film Festival

Where Rotterdam, Netherlands
When Two weeks in late January and early February
Background Featuring approximately 1,000 film screenings, the Rotterdam festival is one of the biggest, one of the best, and one of the most creatively programmed. Over the course of the festival, the city becomes host not only to a slew of world and Dutch premieres and great focus programs but also to intriguing lectures, showings of avant-garde films with live music accompaniment, a children's film festival, and related exhibits in area museums. Hundreds of noteworthy films in a variety of genres premiere here every year, including, in recent years, Wim Wenders's short film *A Trick of the Light*; Raul Ruiz's *Three Lives and Only One Death*; Robert Frank's music video for Patti Smith, *Summer Cannibals*; and Alain Tanner's *Fourbi*. One of my favorite features is a series called "Exploding Cinema," a group of lectures and screenings about multimedia projects and other aspects of twenty-first-century cinema. Author Douglas Rushkoff and director Peter Greenaway have been featured in this series. Recent retrospectives have included a tribute to Hong Kong production company Golden Harvest, and a series called "Fake," which focused on fake documentaries (including Peter Jackson's *Forgotten Silver*, Rob Reiner's *This Is Spinal Tap*, Albert Brooks's *Real Life*, and Bruce Macdonald's *Hard Core Logo*, along with 45 others), as well as retrospectives of the works of Russia's Oleg Kovalov, France's Alain Cavalier, and Korea's Jang-Sun Woo. Another cool aspect of the Rotterdam fest is the Hubert Bals Fund, which it established to give support to emerging filmmakers from developing countries. The fund contains nearly half a million dollars and gives individual grants of up to $50,000 per project. Screenings are held in the Pathé Theatre on Schouwburgplein with seven screens.
Major Award Winners Tiger Award for Best Film: *Last Holiday*, by Amir Karakulov, *The Day a Pig Fell into the Well*, by Hong Sang-Soo, and *Robinson in Space*, by Patrick Keiller; Moviezone Award: *Buffalo '66* by Vincent Gallo; Citroen Audience Award: *Celebration*; Fipresci Prize: *Suzaku*, by Kawase Naomi; KNF Prize: *Irma Vep*, by Olivier Assayas; and Netpac Award: *2 Duo*, by Siwa Nobuhiro
Films More than 600 features and shorts
How to Enter For more information contact:
International Film Festival Rotterdam
Netherlands
P.O. Box 21696
3001 AR Rotterdam
Telephone 011.31.10.890.9090
Fax 011.31.10.890.9091
E-mail iffr@luna.nl
Web www.iffrotterdam.nl
Entry Deadline October

San Francisco International Film Festival

Where San Francisco, California
When Two weeks in late April and early May
Background Founded in 1957, this was the first American film festival to showcase international cinema, but since it started more than 40 years ago, it was the first to do a lot of things. Unlike a lot of the American film festivals, which seem to be about hype more than film and about getting Anne Bancroft to attend more than attracting serious film enthusiasts, this festival takes movies seriously. That's why you'll see flicks such as Alain Resnais' wonderful *Same Old Song*; restored versions of *Gigi* and *A Hard Day's Night*; and even more excitingly, three silent films by Czech director Gustav Machaty. Other films that have premiered here include Aleksandr Sokurov's *Whispering Pages* and Philippe Garrel's *The Birth of Love*. Recent retrospectives have paid homage to the work of Robert Kramer and Manoel de Oliveira.
Films About 150 features
Noteworthy Celebrity Sightings Jim Jarmusch, Peter Greenaway
Tickets $7.50 per individual screening
How to Enter For more information contact:
    San Francisco International Film Festival
    1521 Eddy Street
    San Francisco, CA 94115
    Telephone 415.929.5000
    Fax 415.921.5032
    E-mail sfiff@sfiff.org
    Web www.sfiff.org
Entry Deadline December

Seattle International Film Festival

Where Seattle, WA
When Three weeks in late May and early June
Background Probably the biggest film festival in the United States, with more than 140,000 folks showing up, this is also one of the best and most adventurous, offering screenings in the following categories: Contemporary World Cinema, New Directors' Showcase, Children's Film Fest, Tribute Section (e.g., Bertrand Tavernier), Archival Presentations (Dreyer's Ordet, Frank Capra's *The Matinee Idol*, and Todd Browning's *The Unknown*, scored by the Alloy Orchestra), Short Film Showcase, Best of the Northwest, and, best of all, the Secret Festival, which shows a grab bag of films that supposedly can't be seen anywhere else (lost films, works in progress, films tied up with legal problems). There's also a cool program called "Fly Filmmaking," in which three directors are given 800 feet of film, equipment, a crew, and five days to shoot, edit, score, and present a finished film. All attendees are required to take an "oath of silence," a contractual agreement pledging to never discuss the films included in the festival (which, legend has it, has never, ever been broken). Intriguing recent premieres have included Olivier Assayas's *Late August, Early September*, Deepa Mehta's *Earth*, and John Sayles's *Limbo*. Revivals have included Eisenstein's *Potemkin* and a 1959 Otto Preminger film of *Porgy and Bess*. On the less intriguing side, recent premieres have included *The Dinner Game* and (ouch) *Austin Powers: The Spy Who*

Shagged Me. There is even an auction of foreign film posters every year. Screenings are held at five locations including the Egyptian (801 E. Pine Street), Harvard Exit (807 E. Roy Street), King Cat (2130 Sixth Avenue), Broadway Performance Hall (1625 Broadway), and Guild 45th (2115 N. 45th Street). The Valley Drive-In also features an all-night tribute to the drive-in movie theater.

Major Award Winners Golden Space Needle for Best Film: *Run Lola Run*, by Tom Tykwer; Best Director: John Sayles, *Limbo*; Best Actor: Rupert Everett, *An Ideal Husband*; Best Actress: Piper Laurie, *The Mao Game*; Best Documentary: *Buena Vista Social Club*, by Wim Wenders; Best Short Film: *12 Stops on the Road to Nowhere*, by Lay Lowi; American Independent Award: *Dead Dogs*, by Clay Eide; New Directors Showcase Award: Patrice Toye, *Rosie*

Films More than 150 features and 70 shorts

Noteworthy Celebrity Sightings Nick Nolte, Bruce Willis, Mel Gibson, Gus Van Sant, Wallace Shawn, Adrienne Shelly, Minnie Driver, Sandra Bernhard

Tickets $7 for individual screening; $350 for full-series pass; tickets: 206.325.6150

How to Enter

> Seattle International Film Festival
> 911 Pine St. #607
> Seattle, WA 98101
> Telephone 206.464.5830
> Fax 206.264.7919
> E-mail mail@seattlefilm.com
> Web www.seattlefilm.com

Entry Deadline March

Telluride Film Festival

Where Telluride, Colorado

When Labor Day weekend

Background Tucked away in a Colorado ski town where Butch Cassidy and the Sundance Gang used to hang out with the Hole-in-the-Wall Gang, Telluride is now populated by vacationing Hollywood types and doctors with timeshare condos. Films are shown in five theaters, including a 250-seat opera house where Sarah Bernhardt once performed and in the Abel Gance Open Air Cinema (cool). The festival is noteworthy for being one of the only ones I can think of that shows films at an altitude of 9,000 feet. Founded in 1974, the Telluride Film Festival has grown into one of the more prestigious and idiosyncratic festivals in the country, converting the burg with a population of 1,500 into Hollywood east. The festival prides itself on hosting premieres and, with the exception of fascinating revivals and rereleases, does not generally show any film that has appeared elsewhere in the United States. One of the coolest things about the festival is that because it is so small, it doesn't offer comp tickets. Even Roger Ebert pays his own way. The festival is also notoriously secretive, not announcing its program information until the opening day. More than 7,000 attend each year.

Films Only about 35 films are shown here, and over the years, premieres have included Todd Solondz's *Happiness*, David Lynch's *Blue Velvet*, Wim Wenders's *Paris, Texas*, and Jim Jarmusch's *Stranger than Paradise*. That is to say, competition is tough.

Noteworthy Celebrity Sightings Werner Herzog, Andrei Tarkovsky, Clint Eastwood, Gloria Swanson, Peter Greenaway

Tickets $10 for individual films; $450 for festival ticket passes, which allow admission to all films at all times

How to Enter For more information contact:

> Telluride Film Festival
> 53 S. Main Street, Suite 212
> Hanover, NH 03755
> Telephone 603.643.1255
> Fax 603.643.5938
> E-mail tellufilm@aol.com

Entry Deadline July

Toronto International Film Festival

Where Toronto, Ontario, Canada

When Ten days in mid-September

Background What people remark on when they return from the Toronto Film Festival, founded in 1976, is how clean the city is. And though they're talking about the streets, they could be talking about the festival itself—smoothly run, predictably programmed. No surprises. Films getting the most attention in recent years tend to be high-profile American and European ones getting some prime publicity before their North American releases. These include Sam Mendes's *American Beauty*, Peter Kassovitz's *Jakob the Liar*, Scott Hicks's *Snow Falling on Cedars*, Kevin Smith's *Dogma*, Woody Allen's *Sweet and Lowdown*, and Alan Rudolph's *Breakfast of Champions*. With such a reputation to uphold, there is little room to concentrate on smaller or quirkier films that don't have any kind of name or distribution company attached to them, though there have also been recent premieres such as Youssef Chahine's *The Other*. Anyway, the festival, in addition to gala events and premieres of soon-to-be-cineplexed movies, presents films in the following categories: Perspective Canada (Thom Fitzgerald's *The Hanging Garden*, Mina Shum's *Drive, She Said*), Contemporary World Cinema, Planet Africa (Gaston Kabore's *Budd Yam*, Don Letts and Rick Elgood's *Dancehall Queen*, and, most intriguingly, Midnight Madness). A recently added category called The Masters showcases the works of major established directors including the likes of Jean-Luc Godard, Lars von Trier, and Michelangelo Antonioni. The festival appears on a whopping 16 screens in downtown Toronto.

Major Award Winnners International Critics' Award: *Shower*, by Zhang Yang; People's Choice Award: *American Beauty*, by Sam Mendes; Film Discovery Award: *Goat on Fire and Smiling Fish*, by Kevin Jordan

Films More than 300

Noteworthy Celebrity Sightings Jean-Luc Godard, Ralph Fiennes, Robin Williams, Mia Farrow, Diane Keaton, Robert Duvall, Walter Matthau, Kenneth Branagh, Sting

Tickets CA$11 per individual screening.

Festival Hotline 416.968.3456

How to Enter For more information contact:

> Toronto International Film Festival

16th Floor
2 Carlton Street
Toronto, ON M5B 1J3
Canada
Telephone 416.967.7371
Fax 416. 967.9477
E-mail tiffg@torfilmfest.ca
Web www.bell.ca/filmfest
Entry Deadline June

Valladolid International Film Festival

Where Valladolid, Spain
When Nine days in late October
Background Since it began in 1956, this festival—held in the capital of Spain under King Philip II, 120 miles northwest of Madrid, where Cervantes, Columbus, Ferdinand, and Isabella all lived for some time—has had a reputation for jump-starting the careers of major directors in Spain, including Bergman, Fellini, Wajda, and Buñuel. During the reign of Franco, the festival was noteworthy for showing films that otherwise would have been banned under the fascist regime. In 1975, *A Clockwork Orange* received a belated premiere here. The governmental repression has died down, and it is difficult to maintain a scandalous or outspoken reputation in light of that. Nevertheless, the festival continues to seek the controversial and the extraordinary in programming its films. Retrospectives and tributes of late have covered Australian, German, Polish, Chinese, and Canadian cinema. The festival offers The Official Section (a panorama of current international cinema) and Time of History (documentary films). About 80,000 attend annually. Screenings are held in nine separate locations, including the National Polychromatic Sculpture Museum. Cool. Recent tributes have featured Carl Dreyer, Nanni Moretti, and Czech animation.
Major Award Winners Golden Spike for Best Film: *La Promesse*, by Luc and Jean-Pierre Dardenne; Best Actor: Max von Sydow, *Hamsun*; Best Actress: Eleni Alexandraki, *A Drop in the Ocean*
Films About 200 features, shorts, and documentaries
Noteworthy Celebrity Sightings Arthur Penn, Atom Egoyan
How to Enter For more information contact:
    Valladolid International Film Festival
    P.O. Box 646
    47080 Valladolid
    Spain
    Telephone 011.34.83.305700
    Fax 011.34.83.309835
    Web www.seminci.com
Entry Deadline June

Venice Film Festival

Where Venice, Italy

When Ten days in early September

Background If Cannes is Cannes, then Venice is Venice, and personally, I'll take Antonio's gondola over Jean-Pierre's motorbike every time. It seems hardly fair that Venice should have such an excellent, huge festival, since even if they were showing *Beavis and Butt-head* movies over and over again on Lido, there still would be more than enough reason to go. Venice premiered *Eyes Wide Shut* and *Fight Club* and has offered a tribute to cinematographer Christopher Doyle and a Satyajit Ray retrospective. Films are screened in an international competition section as well as Venetian Nights (a showcase of excellent international cinema). The festival also features a panorama of Italian films, and tons of documentaries, shorts, and cartoons. Well, that said, this is the oldest film festival in the best location, and it has many of the best movies. Is there anyone in his right mind who wouldn't want to go?

Major Award Winners Silver Lion: *The Wind Will Carry Us*, by Abbas Kiarostami; Special Prize for Direction: Zhang Yuan, *Seventeen Year*; Best Film out of Competition: *Being John Malkovich*; Best Actor: Jim Broadbent, *Topsy-Turvy*; Best Actress: Nathalie Baye, *A Pornographic Affair*; Best New Actor: Nina Proll, *Northern Skirts*; Award for Social and Civil Commitment: Marion Vernoux, *Empty Days*; Golden Lion for career achievement: Jerry Lewis

Noteworthy Celebrity Sightings Maggie Cheung, Tom Cruise, Cindy Sherman

Films About 180

Tickets From $3 to $19 for individual screenings

How to Enter For more information contact:
La Biennale di Venezia
54 Mostra Internazionale d'Arte Cinematografica
Lungomare Marconi
30124 Venice
Italy
Telephone 011.39.41.521.8878
Fax 011.39.41.522.7639
E-mail das@labiennale.com

Entry Deadline June

2 North American Film Festivals

The Good, the Bad, the Ugly, and the Just Plain Strange

Abbitibi-Temiscaminique International Film Festival

Where Rouyn-Noranda, Quebec, Canada
When Last week in October.
Background Founded in 1982, the festival offers a medium-sized selection of shorts and features and quite a bit of animation. Devoted solely to films by Canadian filmmakers and films receiving their Canadian commercial premieres ("exceptional excuses notwithstanding"), the festival has premiered such works as David Cronenberg's *Crash* and Roger Frappier's *Cosmos*. Though there is no theme per se here the festival likes to bill itself as a romantic one concentrating on love stories, seducing its viewers with its Don Juan-esque programming and boasting that it may well be called "the charmer of autumn." The festival is housed in the small town of Rouyn-Noranda (population 35,000), about 400 miles away from Montreal, and screenings are held in the 723-seat Theatre du Cuivre and the 350-seat Cinema Paramount. About 15,000 attend annually.
Films About 20 features, 30 shorts, and 30 animated shorts
Noteworthy Celebrity Sightings Denys Arcand, Billie August, Claude Lelouch, Margot Kidder, Pierre Richard
How to Enter For information contact:
    Festival de Cinema International en Abbitibi-Temiscaminique
    215, Avenue Mercier
    Rouyn-Noranda
    Canada
    Telephone 819. 762.6212
    Fax 819.762.6762
    E-mail fciat@sympatico.ca
Entry Deadline September

AFI Los Angeles International Film Festival

Where Los Angeles, California
When Last week in October
Background Founded by the American Film Institute, the festival offers a dramatic competition, a showcase of low-budget features by first-time directors, a panorama of world cinema, and a noncompetitive presentation of short subjects. The festival does a good job of mixing the predictable (*Breaking the Waves, Looking for Richard*) with the best of American independents and foreign films. Previous tributes have honored the careers of Gena Rowlands, Louis Malle, and Anjelica Huston and provided retrospectives of Asian and Mexican cinema. One of the annual highlights is the all-night movie marathon, which has shown once-scandalous films like *Bob & Carol & Ted & Alice, Butterfield 8, Kiss Me, Stupid, The Group,* and *Myra Breckenridge* until the wee hours of the morning. Screenings are held at the GCC Galaxy Theatre (7021 Hollywood Boulevard), Mann's Chinese Theatre (6925 Hollywood Boulevard), and Laemmle's Monica Theatre (1332 Second Street). The festival, which recently paid tribute to Spanish Language movies from Spain and Latin America, is held in conjunction with the free AFI Video Festival.
Films About 100 features plus shorts
Noteworthy Celebrity Sightings Michelangelo Antonioni, Emily Watson, Holly Hunter
Tickets $8.50 per individual screening; $6 matinee; $300 AFI Fest Pass allows entrance into all screenings
Festival Hotline 323.520.2000
How to Enter Send entry fee ($40 for features, $30 for shorts), VHS dub, and rudimentary entry form to:

> AFI Los Angeles International Film Festival
> 2021 N. Western Avenue
> Los Angeles, CA 90027-1657
> Telephone 323.856.7600
> Fax 323.467.4578
> E-mail afifest@afionline.org
> Web www.afionline.org/afifest

Entry Deadline June (early deadline), August (final deadline).
Fact Programmers at the L.A. Film Festival are getting serious swag from film supplicants desperate to get their work noticed: one guy sent along with his film a care package of a batch of coffee, a vial of Clear Eyes and some No-Doz. Other, less imaginative types simply offered sex or cash.

American Indian Film Festival and Video Exposition

Where San Francisco, California
When Ten days in early November
Background Founded in 1975, the festival presents competitions in the following categories: documentary feature, documentary short, commercial feature, live short subject, animated short subject, public service, music video, and industrial film. The festival screens at San Francisco's Palace of Fine Arts and the AMC Kabuki 8 Theatres.
Films About 50

How to Enter Send entry form, $50 entry fee, and video to:
American Indian Film Festival
333 Valencia Street, Suite 322
San Francisco, CA 94103
Telephone 415.554.0525
Fax 415.554.0542
E-mail indianfilm@aifsf.com
Web www.aifisf.com
Entry Deadline August

Ann Arbor 16 mm Film Festival

Where Ann Arbor, Michigan
When One week in mid-March
Background Devoted to independent and experimental 16 mm film, the Ann Arbor
Film Festival features animation, documentary, cinema verité, narrative, experimental, and personal documentary. The festival states as its goal the promotion of
cinema as art and sponsors a touring festival of winning films. Screenings are held
at the Michigan Theater. The festival awards a total of $11,000 in cash prizes each
year in so many categories that one wonders whether individual filmmakers can
expect to get more than 11 bucks. Categories include: Best Michigan Filmmaker
Award for Excellence and Creativity in Cinematography, the Old Peculiar Award for
High Regard for Film as a Creative Medium, Liberty Street Video Award for the
Best Gay/Lesbian Issues Film, the Award for Narrative Integrity, and so forth. If
nothing else, a festival of experimental 16 mm film offers quite a few eye-opening
titles, such as Mike Sloat's *Hieronymous Bosch Burger*, Zack Stiglicz's *God the Pugilist*,
The 13th Protocol, and Helen Stickler's *Andre the Giant Has a Posse*.
Major Award Winners Best Film ($2,000): *The Shanghaied Text*, by Ken Kobland
Films About 100 short films
Tickets $6 per individual screening; $10 for evening of screenings; $35 for festival
pass good for all screenings
Ticket hotline 313.668.8397
How to Enter Send entry fee ($32 for U.S. contestants, $37 foreign), VHS dub and
entry form to:
Ann Arbor Film Festival
P.O. Box 8232
Ann Arbor, MI 48107
Telephone 313.833.2323
Entry Deadline February

Asian American International Film Festival

Where New York, New York
When Two weeks in late July and early August
Background Founded in 1978 and sponsored by the New York City–based Asian
Cine Vision, this is the oldest Asian American film festival, screening 16 mm and
35 mm movies in New York and sponsoring a North American tour for the films
chosen in its festival. Films are screened at Florence Gould Hall in the French

Institute/Alliance Française in Manhattan, Brooklyn Heights Cinema in Brooklyn, and the American Museum of the Moving Image in Queens. The festival was one of the first to introduce American audiences to the work of such artists as Mira Nair and Wayne Wang.

Films About 60 films
Major Award Winners Noncompetitive
Noteworthy Celebrity Sightings Ang Lee, Mira Nair
Tickets Varies depending on venue
How to Enter Send VHS dub (no entry fee) and entry form to:
    Asian American International Film Festival
    Asian Cine Vision
    32 E. Broadway
    4th Floor
    New York, NY 10002
    Telephone 212.925.8685
    Fax 212.925.8157
Entry Deadline March

Aspen FilmFest

Where Aspen, Colorado
When Last week in September
Background Unlike the many film festivals that are geared toward filmmakers and industry professionals, this one is geared toward the public, screening films that one wouldn't normally see at the local cineplex in Aspen. The films shown here concentrate on Colorado filmmakers and art house fare along the lines of *Snow Falling on Cedars*. Films that have premiered here include *Getting to Know You*, by Lisanne and Tristine Skyler. A recent tribute featured Bob Rafelson. Screenings are held at the Crystal Theatre and the Wheeler Opera House. Not to be missed alongside the FilmFest is Aspen's culinary sampler, appropriately named FoodFest.
Noteworthy Celebrity Sightings Bob Rafelson, Peter Bogdanovich
How to Enter Aspen FilmFest
    110 E. Hallam Street, Suite 102
    Aspen, CO 81611
    Telephone 970.925.6882
    Fax 970.915.1967
    E-mail info@aspen.com
    Web www.aspenfilm.com
Entry Deadline July

Athens International Film and Video Festival

Where Athens, Ohio
When First week in May
Background This festival, founded in 1973, features mainstream films as well as 16 mm film work and video. Filmmakers compete for prizes in a variety of categories.
Major Award Winners Best Narrative Features: *A Short Wait Between Trains*, by Rick Williamson; *Family Attraction*, by Brian Hecker; and *Lock and Key*, by Kisi Imani

Cameron; Best Documentaries: *Sacrifice*, by Ellen Bruno, and *Future Remembrance*, by Tobias Wendl

Noteworthy Celebrity Sightings Bridgett M. Davis, Herb E. Smith, Stephen Bognar, Michael Powell, Barbara Hammer

How to Enter Send entry fee ($25), VHS dub and entry form to:
Athens International Film and Video Festival
P.O. Box 388
75 W. Union Street
Room 407
Athens, OH 45701
Telephone 740.593.1330
Fax 740.597.2560
E-mail filmfest@ouvaxa.cats.ohiou.edu
Web www.cats.ohiou.edu

Entry Deadline February

Atlanta Film and Video Festival

Where Atlanta, Georgia

When First week in June

Background Founded in 1987 by the IMAGE Film and Video Center and originally part of Atlanta's Arts Festival, the festival has premiered the works of many American filmmakers who went on to great fame and fortune. Most notably, Steven Spielberg won an award for his first film, *Amblin*. Screenings of such films as *Run Lola Run* and *American Gypsy* are held at AMC Theatres (3500 Peachtree Road NE), the Carter Center (435 Freedom Parkway) and the IMAGE film and Video Center (75 Bennett Street NW in the TULA Arts Complex).

Major Award Winners Grand Jury Award: *Double Life of Ernesto Gomez Gomez*, by Gary Weimburg; Southeastern Mediamakers' Award: *Burning Questions*, by Mishael Porembski; Best Narrative Feature: *Killing Joe*, by Mehdi Norowzian; Best Animated Film: *Roadhead*, by Bob Sabastian and Tommy Pallotta

Noteworthy Celebrity Sightings Spike Lee, Roberto Rodriguez, Jim Sikora, Julie Dash

Tickets $7.50 per individual screening; $150 for pass with access to all screenings and other festival events.
Ticket Hotline 404.352.4225

How to Enter For more information contact:
Atlanta Film and Video Festival
c/o Image Film and Video Center
75 Bennett St., NW
Suite N–1
Atlanta, GA 30309
Web www.imagefv.org/afvf/home.html

Entry Deadline January

Atlantic Film Festival

Where Halifax, Nova Scotia, Canada

When Last week of September

Background Founded in 1980, the festival had inauspicious beginnings, having been financed with money made from screenings of *The Rocky Horror Picture Show*. Even so, the festival has grown year by year, showcasing work from around the globe as well as from Newfoundland, New Brunswick, Prince Edward Island, and Nova Scotia. With a large selection of short and feature films from Canada (including one of my favorite titles of all time, *As They Drove Away She Shouted "So Long, Kiss My Ass"*), the Atlantic Festival generally shows premieres and revivals, all of which tend to have some sort of Canadian reference point. These include screenings of *Canadian Bacon* (starring Toronto's John Candy), a revival of Michael Powell's 1941 U.K. feature *49th Parallel* (concerning six survivors of a U-boat trekking across Canada), and many other features culled from the vaults of the National Film Board of Canada. Films generally fall into the categories of Atlantic Focus (regional filmmaking), Canadian Perspectives (more regional films), International Perspectives (not-so-regional films), Screenscene (a showcase for films by, for, and about youth), and The Late Shift (horror, B-movies, and other late-night fare). The festival screens at the Art Gallery of Nova Scotia (1741 Hollis), Halifax Main Branch Library (5381 Spring Garden Road), Oxford Theatre (6408 Quinpool Road), Park Lane Cinemas (5657 Spring Garden Road), the Sir James Dunn Theatre Dalhousie Arts Centre (University Avenue), and Wormwood's Cinema (2112 Gottingen Street). In conjunction with the festival, there are also a number of seminars that have treated such topics as "What's The Buzz? Tell me What's a-Happening," "International Co-Productions," and a "Hands On! Animation Workshop." Films that have shown here include *The Divine Ryans* and *New Waterford Girl*

Major Award Winners Best Canadian Feature: *New Waterford Girl*; Best Canadian Short: *When The Day Breaks*, by Wendy Tilby and Amanda Forbis; Best Nova Scotia Produced Film: *New Waterford Girl*; People's Choice Award: *One More Kiss*, by Vadim Jean

Films About 100

Noteworthy Celebrity Sightings Michael Moore, *The Blair Witch Project* producers Gregg Hale and Robin Cowie

Tickets $8 prescreening; $75 for silver festival pass entitling holder to access to all films

Ticket Hotline 902.422.6965

How to Enter Send entry form and fee (amount varies depending on length and category) to:

Atlantic Film and Video Festival
1541 Barrington Street, Suite 326
Halifax, NS B3J 125
Canada
Telephone 902.422.3456
Fax 902.422.4006
E-mail agg81@gfn.cs.dal.ca or aff@screen.com or AG881@chebucto.ns.ca
Web www.screen.com/atlanticfilm

Entry Deadline June

Austin Film Festival

Where Austin, Texas

When One week in early October

Background One of the best things about this festival is that it is not beholden to any major or semi-major studio, so no big-budget flicks with Sean Penn, Parker Posey, and Lili Taylor posing as "indies" to attract the art house crowd. Held in the groove capital of Texas, the festival, founded in 1994, places an emphasis on screenwriters, holding a screenwriting competition and conference in conjunction with the festival screenings, and awarding the Writer's Award for the best film in competition. However, the recent rosters of writers, including *Lethal Weapon's* Shane Black and *The Client's* Akiva Goldsmith, makes one wonder whether the scribes were chosen for their literary merit or their box office clout. To be fair, a number of writers of excellent scripts (Mardik Martin, *Raging Bull*, and Frank Pierson, *Dog Day Afternoon*) have turned up as well. Screenings are held at the Paramount and Dobie Theaters.

Noteworthy Celebrity Sightings Wes Craven, Tobe Hooper, Robert Townsend

How to Enter Send VHS dub, $35 entry fee, and entry form to:

Austin Film Festival
1600 Nueces, Suite 101
Austin, TX 78701
Telephone 800.310-FEST or 512. 478.4795
E-mail austinfilm@aol.org
Web www.austinfilmfestival.org

Entry Deadline August

Avignon/New York Film Festival

Where Avignon, France, and New York, New York

When One week in mid-April in New York and the last week of June in Avignon

Background Founded by the French American Film Workshop, the festival offers $125,000 in prizes to young French and American filmmakers and tries to introduce the young Americans to French audiences and vice versa. The festival also offers panel discussions and screens films in New York at the Alliance Française (55 East 59th Street). In previous years, there have been tributes and homages to directors, such as Marcel Carn, Richard Brooks, and John Sayles.

Major Award Winners 21st Century Filmmaker Awards: Geoffrey Sharp, *Slings and Arrows*; Camille de Casabianca, *Madame Petlet's Fabulous Destiny*; Didier Fontain, *En Garde Monsier*; Jo Andres, *Black Kites*

Films About 20 features and retrospectives

Noteworthy Celebrity Sightings John Sayles, Maria de Medeiros, Paul Schrader

Tickets $8 per individual screening

How to Enter For more information contact:

French American Film Workshop
10, Montée de la Tour
30400 Vlleneuve-les-Avignon
France
Telephone 011.33.90.25.9323
Fax 011.33.90.25.9324

or

French American Film Workshop
198 Avenue of the Americas
New York, NY 10013
Telephone 212.343.2675
Fax 212.343.1849

Entry Deadline February (New York); April 25 (France)

Banff Mountain Film Festival

Where Banff, Alberta, Canada
When One weekend in early November.
Background "The Banff Mountain Film Festival is one of the greatest if not the greatest film festival on mountaineering matters in the world." So says Sir Edmund Hillary, and if he doesn't know, who would? While many festivals pride themselves on being graced by the presence of Clint Eastwood et al., the Banff festival, founded in 1975, boasts that it has been attended by Chris Bonington, the first British man to ascend the North Wall of the Eiger and the first to ascend the Ogre in the Karakoram Himalayas and the Chisel, the Ivory Tower, and the Needle in Greenland. Films and videos are screened in the 1,000-seat Eric Harvie Theater and the more intimate 250-seat Margaret Greenham Theater on the campus of the Banff Centre. The festival is attended annually by 55,000 outdoors enthusiasts and tours a series of its best films to more than 100 locations across North America and Europe.
Major Award Winners Grand Prize for Best Film ($2,000): *Behind the Ice Wall*, by Harriet Gordon and Peter Getzels; Best Film on Climbing, Mountain Sports, Mountain Culture, and Mountain Environment: *The Tsaatan: The Reindeer Riders*, by Boréales; Best Film on Climbing: *San Valentin*; Best Film on Mountain Sports: *Snowboard*, by Alessio Viola; Best Film on Mountain Environment and People's Choice Award: *Mountain Gorilla: A Shattered Kingdom*; Special Jury Award: *Canada's Legacy*, by Peter McAllister
Noteworthy Celebrity Sightings Sir Chris Bonington, Walter Bonatti, Catherine Destivelle, Alex Lowe
Tickets $88 for a pass to all screenings
Festival Hotline 800.298.1229
How to Enter Send VHS dub and entry fee to:
    Banff Festival of Mountain Films
    P.O. Box 1020
    Station 38
    Banff, AB T0L 0C0
    Canada
    Telephone 403.762.6125
    Fax 403.762.6277
    E-mail mff@banffcentre.ab.ca
    Web www.banffcentre.ab.ca
Entry Deadline September

Black Maria Film and Video Festival

Where Jersey City, New Jersey, and elsewhere
When January to June, depending on location
Background Named for Thomas Edison's 19th-century laboratory Black Maria (so named for its resemblance to a paddy wagon), which contained one of the first-known movie studios, the film and video festival was founded in 1981 as an open international competition for independent, noncommercial film- and video makers. And true to its goal of noncommercialism, very little if anything that has ever been seen here ever shows up at your local cineplex. Selected films tour the

country, concentrating mainly on the East Coast, though the tour occasionally reaches the Midwest, the West Coast, and Canada as well.

Major Award Winners The festival grants tons of awards in several categories, splitting $2,500 in the Juror's Choice category, $2,000 in Juror's Citation, and $1,000 in Director's Choice. A selection of the titles of some of these films might give a hint as to the content of the festival: *Class Struggle in Palo Alto, Bontoc Eulogy, Zimbabwe Wheel,* and *Death by Design.*

Films Works of 100 minutes or less shown in 35 mm, 16 mm, 8 mm, and video formats

How to Enter Send entry form, entry fee ($35 for works up to 30 minutes, $45 for works between 31 and 100 minutes), and film either on VHS or 16 mm to:

    Black Maria Festival
    c/o Department of Media Arts
    Jersey City State College
    203 West Side Avenue
    Jersey City, NJ 07305

Entry Deadline November 16

Boston Film Festival

Where Boston, Massachusetts
When Ten days in mid-September
Background Founded in 1985, this respectable, if not altogether imaginatively programmed, fall festival screens at the Sony Copley Plaza Theaters and the Kendall Square Cinemas. Films that have premiered here include *The War Zone, Tumbleweeds, Snow Falling on Cedars, The General, Reservoir Dogs, Gods and Monsters, Mute Witness, Drunks, Palookaville,* and *The City of Lost Children.*
Films About 50
Major Award Winners Offers awards for career excellence. Winners have included Kenneth Branagh and Vanessa Redgrave.
Noteworthy Celebrity Sightings Eric Bogosian, Bob Goldthwait
Tickets $7.50 per individual screening; $65 per ten screenings
How to Enter For more information contact:

    Boston Film Festival
    P.O. Box 516
    Hull, MA 02045
    Telephone 781.925.1373
    Fax 781.925.3132
    Web www.bostonfilmfestival.org

Entry Deadline July

Boston International Festival of Women's Cinema

Where Boston, Massachusetts
When April and May
Background Founded in 1991, the festival screens at Boston's excellent Brattle Theater, holds panel discussions, and provides workshops conducted by major

women directors. Among films that have premiered here are Agnes Varda's *101 Nights*, Lisa Apramian's *Not Bad for a Girl*, and Fine Torres's *Celestial Clockwork*.
Films 22 features and 12 shorts
Noteworthy Celebrity Sightings Claire Denis, Mina Shum, Allison Anders
Tickets $7 per individual screening
How to Enter For more information contact:
    Boston International Festival of Women's Cinema
    40 Brattle Street
    Cambridge, MA 02138
    Telephone 617.876.0838
Entry Deadline March

Boston Jewish Film Festival

Where Boston, Massachusetts
When Ten days in mid-November
Background Screening films that explore themes of Jewish culture, heritage, and history or are of particular interest to the Jewish community for one reason or another, this festival, founded by the Filmmakers Collaborative, presents a showcase of narrative, documentary, animated, and experimental works. The festival also sponsors panel discussions; a recent one focused on the role of Switzerland in the Holocaust. One of the more intriguing titles to show here in recent years was *Let There Be Light*, in which God becomes a screenwriter and can't get Hollywood to produce his script. Films are screened at the Warwick Theatre in Marblehead, the Museum of Fine Arts in Boston, and the Coolidge Corner Theatre in Brookline. About seven thousand attend annually.
Major Award Winners Noncompetitive
Films About 30 features
Noteworthy Celebrity Sightings Liv Ullmann, Gila Almagor, Mordecai Richler, Jan Schutte, Elijah Moshinsky, Susanne Bier
Tickets $6–$9 per individual screening
How to Enter For more information contact:
    The Boston Jewish Film Festival
    1001 Watertown St.
    West Newton, MA 02465-2104
    Telephone 617.369.3770
    E-mail info@bjff.org
    Web www.bjff.cyways.com
Entry Deadline June 1

Brandon Film Festival

Where Brandon, Manitoba, Canada
When One week in mid-March
Background Founded in the mid-1960s at Brandon University, the festival still screens at the Evans Theatre in the university's library arts building and is noteworthy for being the second most interesting festival in Brandon. The most interesting, of course, is the International Pickle Fest, in which people compete in "pickle

putting" and pickle judging. Everything from a series of Canadian shorts to Bruce MacDonald's *Hard Core Logo* has been shown. There is a tendency here to mix works of Canadian directors with mainstream U.S. art house fare along the lines of Al Pacino's *Looking for Richard* and Nicholas Hytner's *The Crucible*.

Films Twelve features plus shorts and programs of commercials

How to Enter For more information contact:

Brandon Film Festival
Box 21084, West End P.O.
Brandon, MB R7B 3W8
Canada
Telephone 204.727.9704

Entry Deadline Late November

Breckenridge Festival of Film

Where Breckenridge, Colorado

When Four days in mid-September

Background Hey, any film festival that has film critic Jeffrey Lyons on its board of directors has to be doing something right. Right? No comment. Actually, Lyons, despite spending aeons hosting his dopey syndicated radio spot "The Lyons' Den" and sparring with the likes of Michael Medved and Neal Gabler, has still maintained a respectable reputation (no small accomplishment), and so does the film festival for which he serves as M.C. Founded in 1979, the festival, two hours west of Denver in a 140-year-old Victorian mining town, screens and offers awards in the categories of drama, comedy, documentary, and alternative cinema. Films that have received their premieres here include Terry George's *Some Mother's Son*, Charles Matthau's *The Grass Harp*, and *The Joy Luck Club*. The slightly irritating thing about the festival is that it insists on differentiating in its schedule between movies that feature celebrities and movies that don't, so crap such as Garry Marshall's *Nothing in Common* and James Bridges' *Urban Cowboy* get a big C for celebrity next to them, and other, more interesting flicks such as Miranda Smith's *My Father's Garden* take a backseat. If you're not fond of the selection of films, there's always the nearby forty-mile bike path and a municipal golf course designed by the Golden Bear himself, Jack Nicklaus. Films are screened at seven venues including River Walk (Park and Main streets), Ten Mile Room (Village at Breckenridge), Colorado Mountain College (103 S. Harris Street), Backstage (Village at Breckenridge), Town Hall (150 Ski Hill Road), and the Lake Twin 1 and 2 in the Dillon Mall.

Films About 55 features

Noteworthy Celebrity Sightings Eva Marie Saint, Alan Arkin, Peter Fonda, Rip Torn, James Earl Jones, Jonathan Demme

Tickets $6 for individual screenings

How to Enter For more information contact:

Breckenridge Festival of Film
Riverwalk Center
P.O. Box 718
150 W. Adams Street
Breckenridge, CO 80424
Telephone 970.453.6200

Fax 970.453.2692
E-mail filmfest@brecknet.com
Web www2.colorado.net/bff/home.html
Entry Deadline June

Canyonlands Film and Video Festival

Where Moab, Utah
When Three days in early April
Background This festival, founded in 1995, focuses, like many others, on indie film and video and provides a certain down-home feeling. Films are placed in the following categories: environmental/social/documentary issues, drama, experimental, children/youth, comedy, animation, Westerns, Southwestern regional, and student-produced. There is also a category for outdoor-adventure films that concentrate on mountain biking and river running. But the films are hardly the show when one can step out of screenings and go camping, hunt for dinosaur bones and ancient Indian relics, visit the Red Rock Desert, or even (ick) go on a winery tour. Screenings are held at the historic Star Hall on Center Street and the intriguingly named Slickrock Cinemas on Kane Creek Boulevard. But never fear—even if the small-town surroundings get you lost, the festival operators tell us, "Moab's a small town, and people are friendly with offering directions."
Films About 20
Tickets $6 per individual screening; $10 per evening
How to Enter Send entry form, VHS dub, and entry fee ($30 for 35 mm, $24 for 16 mm, and ½- and ¾-inch video) to:
> Canyonlands Film and Video Festival
> 435 River Sands Road
> Moab, UT 84532
> Telephone 801.259.9135
> E-mail cfvf@moab-utah.com
Entry Deadline February 1

Carolina Film and Video Festival

Where Greensboro, North Carolina
When One weekend in mid-March
Background Both students at UNC-Greensboro and indie filmmakers showcase their films at this fest, and the festival has a rather hip, unpretentious college town feel to it. May I quote from the most recent statement of philosophy given to us by the festival's organizers? "Entering a film festival takes a lot of *cojones*. One is mailing hundreds of hours of blood, sweat, and toil to a room full of people living on coffee and adrenaline. It is a leap of faith that maybe this tape will go in the VCR and be the one, the film to blow everyone away. It's a big risk, putting one's work out like that, sealing one's heart and soul with the sticky strips on a Fed-Ex mailer. Therefore, with great fanfare, this festival is a salute to all the student and independent filmmakers." The festival has promised to screen the "most skewed voices" of filmmakers around the country. The festival is composed primarily of shorts and has included over the past few years Peter Gilbert's *Vietnam: Long Time Coming*; Ken

Rosenburg's *A Judge Judges Mushrooms* (a documentary about an eighty-six-year-old judge whose hobbies include mushrooms), Jeff Balis's *Aluminum Samurai* (described as "one man's battle with mass conformity, density, and Verona halogen lamps"), and Etang Inyang's *Badass Supermama* (a personal documentary about the significance of blaxploitation star Pam Grier). The festival has an annual motto/theme (1998's was "Urban Legends"; 1997's was "Redeploy your Schemata"). Featured guest speakers have included Janos Kovacsi and Annabelle Sheehan.

Films About 42 shorts

How to Enter Send $25 entry fee to:
    Carolina Film and Video Festival
    Broadcasting/Cinema Division
    100 Carmichael Building
    P.O. Box 26170
    UNC-Greensboro
    Greensboro, NC 27412
    Telephone 336.334.4197
    Fax 336.334.5039
    E-mail cfvf@uncg.edu
    Web www.uncg.edu/cbt/cfvf

Entry Deadline February

Carrousel International du Film de Rimouski

Where Rimouski, Quebec, Canada

When One week in late September

Background Billing itself as the only Francophone fest for children in America, the festival also offers workshops in which kids can help create a short film and participate in classes and workshops with film professionals. One of the cooler aspects is the festival's Summer Camp Cinema, which allows young adults ages 16 to 20 to work together on scripting, filming, and producing a three-minute short.

Major Award Winners Best Film: *Belma*, by Lars Hesseholdt; Best Short: *Histoire du Chat et de la Lune*, by Pedro Serrazina; Best Actress: Emina Isavic, *Belma*; Best Actor: Jarl Karjayse, *Trop Fatigué*, *Pour Hair*

How to Enter For more information contact:
    Cinema Lido
    Galeries GP
    92, 2e rue Ouest
    Rimouski, PQ
    Canada
    Telephone 418.722.0103
    Fax 418.724.9504
    E-mail cifr@quebectel.com

Cascadia Festival of Moving Images

Where Powell River, British Columbia, Canada

When Last week of May

Background Founded by the Cascadia Society of Moving Images in 1982, this festival of student films and videos screens the works of everyone from fourth graders on up. The festival is part of the British Columbia Festival of Arts. Awards are given in categories of Independent Film and Video, British Columbia Student Films (grades four through ten), 11th- and 12th-grade students, and post-secondary students. Films are shown in 16 mm film and VHS and 8 mm video formats at Powell River's Patricia Theatre.

Major Award Winners Best Early Intermediate Production: *Kinderaddicton*; Best Late Intermediate Production: *AIDS-PSA*; Best Graduate Production: *Beautiful Girl*; Best Post-Secondary Production: *Victim Eyes*

Tickets: $5 per individual screening

How to Enter Send entry fee ($25 for indies, $20 for postsecondary students, $15 for 11th- and 12th- graders; $10 for younger students) and entry form to:

> Cascadia Festival of Moving Images
> Stargate Connections, Inc.
> 6450 Roberts Street, Suite 347
> Burnaby, BC V5G 4E1
> Canada
> Telephone 604.886.3269
> E-mail BCFA@canisle.net

Entry Deadline April

Central Florida Film and Video Festival

Where Orlando, Florida

When Ten days in late September and early October

Background Despite the fact that the winner of the Best of Show award here receives a HammerCam award, which the festival boasts was created by the artist who designed the NCAA Dick Butkus Award, this is still an excellent spot to check out as yet unknown U.S. indie filmmakers. Perhaps because this festival is over-shadowed by the glitzier Florida fests or perhaps because cash prizes range from only $100 to $500, this festival remains one of the better-kept secrets of the Florida film fest scene. And it's probably better off that way.

Major Award Winners Best of Show: *In the Time of Angels*, by David Anderson; Best Narrative Film: *Decade of Love*, by Kurt Voelker; *Wake Up Call*, by Will Horton, and *Parking*, by James Morrison; Best Documentary: *Jane: An Abortion Service*, by Kate Kirtz, *All of It*, by Jacob Bricca, and *My Father's Garden*, by Miranda Smith

Films About 140 features and shorts

How to Enter Send entry fee ($40 for features, $30 for shorts) and entry form to:
Central Florida Film and Video Festival

> 15½ N. Eola Drive, Suite 5
> Orlando, FL 32801
> Telephone 407.895.4999
> Fax 407.839.6045
> E-mail festival@cffvf.org
> Web www.cffvf.org

Entry Deadline July

Charlotte Film and Video Festival

Where Charlotte, North Carolina
When First week of May
Background The Charlotte fest has premiered Zeinabu Davis's *Mother of the River*; Melissa Hacker's documentary about the Kindertransport, *My Knees Were Jumping*; and Mary Harron's *I Shot Andy Warhol*. It took 1999 off, but word has it that it's on the way back. Screenings will be held at the Light Factory.
Films About 50 films
How to Enter Send VHS dub, $30 entry fee, and entry form to:
    Charlotte Film and Video Festival
    Mint Museum of Art
    2730 Randolph Road
    Charlotte, NC 28207
    Telephone 704.337.2019
    Fax 704.337.2101
    E-mail film@mint.uncc.edu
Entry Deadline March

Chicago International Children's Film Festival

Where Chicago, Illinois
When Eleven days in mid-October
Background Describing itself as "Cannes for Kids," CICFF is the largest competitive festival of kids' movies in the United States. Even though it screens most of its films at Facets Multimedia (1517 W. Fullerton Ave.), which despite being one of Chicago's best art house cinemas also has one of the worst sound systems in town, the festival presents an excellent array of national and international shorts and features. Recent screenings have included *The Wind in the Willows*, featuring the voices of Vanessa Redgrave, Alan Bennett, and Michael Palin, and Nick Park's *A Grand Day Out*. The best aspect of the film festival is its intelligently programmed features, which don't shy away from difficult issues. The festival also conducts children's workshops led by professional actors and directors. One of the best of these is Dream Screen, in which tots can create their own animated films. The fest also screens a selection of shorts and feature-length films at nearby Children's Memorial Hospital. And in case you were dreadfully worried about your children associating with that awful riffraff of big bad Chicago, the folks at the fest assure us that "87 percent of adults attending the festival have at least one college degree, and all are concerned about the value and quality of programs shown to children." Comforting, isn't it? About 12,000 attend the festival annually.
Films 150 feature films and videos
Noteworthy Celebrity Sightings Martha Plimpton, Lester Holt, Maggie Daley (Da First Lady of Chicago)
Tickets $4 per individual screening
How to Enter For more information contact:
    Chicago International Children's Film Festival
    c/o Facets Multimedia
    1517 W. Fullerton Avenue
    Chicago, IL 60614

Telephone 773.281.9075
Fax 773.929.5437
E-mail kidsfest@facets.org
Entry Deadline June

Chicago International Film Festival

See Best of the Fests

Chicago Latino Film Festival

Where Chicago, Illinois
When One week in early April
Background This is an excellent festival, arguably the best-run one in Chicago. It continues to quietly showcase a fascinating array of films from major and unknown directors. Screening films at the less-than-comfy Facets Multimedia (1517 W. Fullerton Avenue) and the more upscale and slightly more boring Water Tower Theatres (175 E. Chestnut Street) the festival, founded in 1984, offers Chicago residents their only opportunity to see excellent movies from South America, Spain, and Portugal. Films that have received their premieres here include Camilio Luzuriaga's *Between Marx and a Naked Woman* and Daniel Gruener's *All of Them Witches*. Retrospectives have included a special program on "Spanish Civil War and the Aftermath" (which included Ken Loach's *Land and Freedom*) and tributes to the work of Tomás Gutiérrez Alea and Leon Hirzman. This is not a pretentious, star-studded affair. It's just a serious, well-programmed fest. About 25,000 attend. 1999's fest featured a tribute to one of the treasures of Spanish cinema: Carlos Saura.
Major Award Winners Audience Choice Award: *Guantanamera*, by Tomás Gutiérrez Alea; Runner-up for Audience Choice: *A May-December Affair*, by Carlos Galettini; Emerging Filmmaker Award: Carlos Da Silva, *Dying to Go Home*
Films About 100 films and videos
Tickets $7.50 per individual screening; $70 festival pass buys admission to all festival events
How to Enter For more information contact:
Chicago Latino Film Festival
c/o Columbia College
600 South Michigan Avenue
Chicago, IL 60605
Telephone 312.431.1330
Fax 312.360.0629
Entry Deadline February

Chicago Lesbian and Gay International Film Festival

Where Chicago, Illinois
When Ten days in November
Background Any festival that screens primarily at the Music Box Theater, one of the last remaining art house gems in Chicago, has to have something going for it.

Founded in 1981, the Chicago fest, also known as "Reeling," is a very strong festival of shorts, features, documentaries, and experimental works. Films that have premiered here in recent years include Rose Troche's *Bedrooms and Hallways*, Hettie McDonald's *Beautiful Thing*, Julie and Gretchen Dyer's *Late Bloomers*, and Peter Litton's *The Art of Cruising Men*. A recent feature at the fest was called *Up Yours, Tonto! Homosexual Subtexts in Pre-Stonewall Westerns*. It also featured a tribute to noted grump George Cukor (*"You with the flag! Siddown!"*).

Major Award Winners First Place Narrative: *Paulo and His Brother*; Second Place: *Chocolate Babies*; Third Place: *Better Late*; First Place Documentary: *There Is No Name For This*; Second Place: *You Don't Know Dick: Courageous Voices of Transsexual Men*; Third Place: *Anything Boys Can Do*; First Place Experimental/Animation: *essential things*; Second Place: *Forever*; Third Place: *Fistfull*.

Films About 50 features plus shorts programs

Tickets $5–$7 per individual screening; $75 for admission to all screenings

How to Enter For more information contact:

Chicago Filmmakers
Attn: Reeling
5234 N. Clark St., 2nd Floor
Chicago, IL 60640
Telephone 773.384.5533
Fax 773.384.5532
E-mail reeling@filmmakers.org
Web www.chicagofilmmakers.org/reeling

Entry Deadline July

Chicago Underground Film Festival

Where Chicago, Illinois

When One week in August

Background It may not be the biggest festival in Chicago, but it's certainly the least predictable. A sort of cross section of the New York Underground Film Festival, Slamdance, and a sci-fi convention, this fest screens everything from great unsung indie features to splatter-tripe to excellent experimental shorts and documentaries. The festival claims no political agenda ("We're just about the films") and proclaims, "If you think your film is underground, it probably is"—all of which makes this the most refreshingly offbeat film event in Chicago. Recent festival highlights have included *Please Kill Klaus Kinski*, *Raping Private Spielberg*, *Searching for Carrie Fisher*, *Perfect Blue*, *Suckerfish*, and documentaries about the Chicago music scene and Nick Cave. Tributes have focused on Nick Zedd, George Kuchar, and John Waters. Films screen at the skeevy-but-charming Village Theater (1548 N. Clark Street). Dedicated to "the defiantly independent filmmaker."

Films About 135 shorts, 16 features, and 14 documentaries

Award Winners Lifetime Achievement Award to Melvin Van Peebles

Noteworthy Celebrity Sightings John Waters, Vaginal Cream Davis, and Jim Sikora

Tickets $8 per individual screening

How to Enter Send VHS dub, entry fee ($25 for shorts, $35 for features), and rudimentary entry form to:

CUFF
3109 N. Western Ave.
Chicago, IL 60618
Telephone 773.327.FILM
Fax 773.327.3464
E-mail info@cuff.org
Web www.cuff.org/sub/cuffguide.html
Entry Deadline April
Fact A barbecue fundraiser for the Chicago Underground Film Festival served vegetarian roast pig.

Cinecon

Where Glendale, California
When Labor Day weekend
Background This is a great place for nostalgia and cinema history buffs. Films recently screened include Raoul Walsh's *The Loves of Carmen* and *The Monkey Talks*; *Two Señoritas from Chicago*, featuring Ann Savage; *The Mirror*, starring Mary Pickford; *Sagebrush Tom*, with Tom Mix; *His Glorious Night*, directed by Lionel Barrymore and starring John Gilbert; Ernst Lubitsch's *Eternal Love*, starring John Barrymore; *The Good Companions*, starring John Gielgud and Edmund Gwenn; *Mexicali Rose*, with Barbara Stanwyck; and Frank Capra's *So This Is Love*. Special retrospectives have featured a commemoration of the Hollywood blacklist, featuring a panel of blacklisted Hollywood actors and writers; a tribute to Linda Darnell; and a series of films shot at Balboa Studios, a silent film studio on Long Beach. A 1999 tribute featured Francis Boggs, who operated the first movie studio in Los Angeles and was murdered in 1911.
Major Award Winners Noncompetitive
Noteworthy Celebrity Sightings Stanley Kramer, Kathryn Grayson, June Havoc, Ronald Neame, Anita Page, Robert Wise
Tickets $20 for a single-day pass; $100 gains admittance to all events
How to Enter Not applicable
For more information contact: www.mdle.com/classicfilms/cinecon
Entry Deadline Not applicable

Cinefest: The Sudbury Film Festival

Where Sudbury, Ontario, Canada
When One week in mid-September
Background Founded in 1989 in Sudbury, which is known primarily as a mining town, the festival draws approximately 25,000 people per year for its screenings of largely Canadian but also European and American cinema. The festival has premiered such works as *Jesus of Montreal*, *Canadian Bacon*, and *Margaret's Museum*. Screenings are held at the Sudbury Theatre Centre and City Centre Cinemas.
Major Award Winners Best International Film: *The White Balloon*, by Jafar Panahi; Best Canadian Film: *Le Confessional*, by Robert LePage

Films About 100 features, shorts, and documentaries
Noteworthy Celebrity Sightings Clement Vigo
How to Enter Send rudimentary entry form with biographical information and VHS dub to:
 Cinefest
 218-40 Elm Street, Suite 218
 Sudbury, ON PC3 1S8
 Canada
 Telephone 705.688.1234
 Fax 705.688.1351
 Web www.cinefest.com
Entry Deadline August

Cinequest San Jose Film Festival

Where San Jose, California
When First week in February
Background San Jose's Cinequest, founded in 1991, prides itself on being a maverick film festival. It gives awards to maverick films and pays tributes to maverick filmmakers, and though its award for "maverick spirit" is sponsored by oh-so-mainstream Apple Computer, the festival has been quite effective in discovering and showcasing quality U.S. premieres overlooked by other festivals. Screenings are held at Camera Three (288 S. Second Street) and United Artists Pavilion (201 S. Second Street).
Major Award Winners Best First Feature Film: *All Men Are Liars*, by Gerard Lee, and *Jerome's Secret*, by Phil Comeau; Maverick Spirit Award: *Fiesta*, by Pierre Boutron; Best Documentary: *Personal Belongings*, by Steven Bognar; Audience Favorite Choice Award: *The Scottish Tale*, by Mackinlay Polhemus, *Follow the Bitch*, by Julian Stone, and *The Other Side of Sunday*, by Berit Otto Nesheim
Films Approximately 100 features and shorts
Noteworthy Celebrity Sightings Neil Jordan, John Covert, Jennifer Jason Leigh, John Harriman, Robert Wise
Tickets $7 for individual screenings; $195 for a VIP Festival Pass allowing admission into all films
Festival Hotline 408.955.5033
How to Enter Send VHS tape, press kit with synopsis, biographies, black-and-white stills, $25 entry fee, and official entry form to:
 Cinequest
 P.O. Box 720040
 San Jose, CA 95172-0040
 Telephone 408.995.6305
 Fax 408.995.5713
Entry Deadline October
Fact Award for overuse of the word "maverick" goes to Cinequest San Jose, which had five different "maverick" showcases. Must be all them crazy Silicon Valley types.

CineVegas Las Vegas Film Festival

Where Las Vegas, Nevada

When One week in early December

Background Las Vegas is pretty much a film set anyway, so it deserves as good a fest as other cities. Since it's still pretty much in its infancy, it's hard to see how this one's going to turn out (especially given that CineVegas, the organization that runs it, has a *Baywatch* producer on its board). But it's trying, showing some domestic indies such as Timothy Hutton's *Digging to China* and Peter Masterson's *The Only Thrill* and having Whit Stillman head up a filmmaker's panel. Film programs include French Kisses (French indies), Rebels With a Cause (U.S. indies), and A Walk on the Wild Side (cult and sci-fi). Lest it get too uppity, though, it's staying true to its Vegas roots: there's a celebrity golf tournament, a poolside trivia contest, and documentaries such as *Mob Law: A Film Portrait of Oscar Goodman, Las Vegas Attorney*.

Films 50 or so

How to Enter Send VHS dub, fee ($50 or $25 for students) and entry form to:
CineVegas
Polo Towers, Polo Plaza, Suite 204
3745 Las Vegas Boulevard South
Las Vegas, NV 89109
Telephone 702.477.7530
Fax 702.477.7533
E-mail cinevegas@aol.com
Web www.cinevegas.com

Entry Deadline October

Cinevent Classic Film Convention

Where Columbus, Ohio

When One week in late May

Background Founded in 1968, this is one of the best locations for film geeks of all persuasions, screening classic and seldom-screened films and offering an annual vintage poster art auction and other assorted posts for trading memorabilia. About 1,000 people attend annually. Though not quite the classy and exciting event that Pordenone's Days of Silent Cinema festival is, Cinevent has nevertheless reintroduced audiences to such odd gems as *The Woman Men Yearn For*, starring Marlene Dietrich; a silent *Dr. Jekyll and Mr. Hyde*, starring John Barrymore; and the 1944 *Christmas Holiday*, starring Deanna Durbin and Gene Kelly. The festival's organizers tell us that it's Columbus, Ohio's longest-running classic film festival. Oh, really?

Major Award Winners Noncompetitive

Tickets $20 registration fee

How to Enter For more information contact:
Cinevent
P.O. Box 13463
Columbus, OH 43213
Telephone 614.229.3555

E-mail steve@cinevent.com
Web cinevent.com
Entry Deadline Not applicable

Cleveland International Film Festival

Where Cleveland, Ohio
When Mid-March
Background Any festival that hosts a seminar titled "Is Hollywood Killing the Movies?" and then plugs screenwriter Joe Eszterhas (*Showgirls, Basic Instinct*) as its featured opening-night guest has to be a bit schizophrenic. But for this city, which has hardly ever been seen in the past as the epicenter of cutting-edge culture, the festival does make an effort to step out in its selection of films, boasting the Family Film Festival, Ten Percent Cinema (which focuses on gay and lesbian themes), and Pan-African images (a collection of films from and about communities), as well as the usual lineup of American independent and foreign films. Recent screenings have included *The Language of Kickball, Edge of Seventeen, Chillicothe, Out of Season,* and *Hellhounds on My Trail: The Afterlife of Robert Johnson.* Sponsored by the Cleveland Film Society, screenings are held at Tower City Cinemas. Over the years, the CIFF has premiered such films as *Berlin Alexanderplatz* and *Eight Men Out* and hosted retrospectives of the careers of Charlie Chaplin and Audrey Hepburn. The festival tends to be rather jingoistic about hometown filmmakers: the entry form specifically asks about Cleveland connections. Five-hundred-dollar cash awards are offered in the following categories: Best Short, Best Student Short, Best Ohio Short, Best African American Short, Best Women's Short, and Best Documentary Short.
Major Award Winners Previous winners of the Roxanne T. Mueller Award for Best Film include: *Shall We Dance?,* by Masayuki Suo; *Fiddlefest,* by Allan Miller; *The Sum of Us,* by Kevin Dowling and Geoff Burton; *Backbeat,* by Iain Softley; and *Into the West,* by Mike Newell.
Films Approximately 80 features plus more than 80 shorts
Noteworthy Celebrity Sightings Hampton Fancher, Bob Gosse, Jerry Blumenthal, Daniel MacIvor, Heidi van Lier, Robert Mugge, David Lee Wilson, Joe Eszterhas, Janet Leigh, Peter Falk, Frank Capra
Tickets $7.25 for evening shows; $4.50 for matinees; $125 festival pass provides access to all screenings except opening and closing nights
Ticket Orders 216.623.FILM
How to Enter Send entry fee ($50 for features, $35 for shorts under 45 minutes) plus form to:
Cleveland International Film Festival
The Cleveland Film Society
2510 Market Ave.
Cleveland, OH 44113-3434
Telephone 216.623.0400
Fax 216.523.0103
Web www.clevelandfilm.org
Entry Deadline November

Interview with

David Wittkowsky

executive director of the Cleveland

Film Society, which presents the

Cleveland International Film Festival

AL Do you have a specific process by which you choose films?

DW We certainly have a process, one that's sort of developed over the years. I don't know that there's anything magical about it or even scientific. It's largely subjective, but it's the role of the artistic staff to make the decisions that lead to the program presented in the film festival. We travel to film festivals, usually starting in the late summer running through January, and see as many films as we can on the festival circuit. We also have a call for entries that brings in a number of films for consideration on videotape, and we keep an eye on the trades to see what's being reviewed and getting good coverage that we can pursue and check out, and we have colleagues at various festivals around the world and around the country with whom we stay in touch as well. We all seem to be such a collegial group. For festivals like ours, festival directors tend to be very cooperative and helpful, because we're all just trying to run a good program and not necessarily competing for the same audience.

AL Sometimes you're competing for the same films, though.

DW We sometimes are, and I don't usually encounter a situation where if I need information about a film, someone won't give it to me because they don't want me to get it. Admittedly, there may be people I am not calling because I don't think I could get information from them, but there are a lot of people who I can call.

We have a general outline of the kind of program we're trying to put together. Our festival is presented in a number of different sections, the largest of which is our world tour, but we also have a program of family films, of new films from Eastern Europe, documentaries, American independents, and so on, and I'm watching for films to fill slots in those sections and films that just make for a strong program overall. I don't think I choose films much differently than anyone else would if they took this job. Of course, having seen as many films as I have and having the experience I've had in programming for so many years, I perhaps have a better sense of what will make a more balanced program than others might, but it really is not neurosurgery.

AL Are there occasionally films you love that for some reason you feel won't make a balanced film festival?

DW That occasionally happens. Earlier on, there were films that I just loved that I was committed to putting in the film festival regardless, and sometimes that worked out really well and sometimes there was just no response to those films at all, so while I might have a personal reaction in favor of a certain film, I will occasionally investigate or give special thought to my own reaction before making a decision for the festival. On the other hand, there are often films that I see that I'm not enamored of, and I'll have to give a thought to that as well, even though I may not have loved the film. Even though it might not have struck me as a particularly wonderful film, it may in fact be quite strong, and I didn't connect with it, and it might be that our audience might think it's wonderful, so it's not always programming just for me.

AL What would make you think that something was worth showing even though it didn't strike you? Stars? A well-known director?

DW Not that, actually. It's not about a director, because oftentimes a good director who's made great films in the past might, well, make a dog, and I'm always going to judge a film on its own merits and not on the history of the director. If everybody is saying how much they loved a particular film and it's colleagues whose opinions I respect and I'm out in left field thinking, "It didn't do much for me," if I didn't actually hate the film I would give it some additional thought. Sometimes my opinion is running against the grain, and it's so strong that I'll absolutely refuse to put a film in the festival, but that's not usually the case.

AL Has there ever been a film about which you put your foot down and said, "Absolutely not," and it turned out to be a great success?

DW I'm certain that that has happened. I don't know that I could call one to mind. There is no doubt that's the case. I can think back to *The River's Edge*, a film that wasn't really available to us because of the timing of our festival and the timing of the film's release. But I had seen it in a festival somewhere else and didn't like it at all. Later that year it was finally released, and it had a great critical response. Everybody loved it. So I said, there must be something there that I just didn't get at the time, or maybe I was having a bad day or a bad morning. So I went through the trouble of going back to see the film and had the exact same response, so that was the end of that. Had it been available for the festival, would I have tried to put it in? I'm not sure.

AL Do you become jaded over the years after hundreds and hundreds of films? Do you have less patience?

DW I have always loved movies, and so I kind of feel like I'm the luckiest guy in the world having the job that I have, because I get to not only work in the film business in one particular fashion, but I get to travel to film festivals around the world and just watch a lot of movies. And I was just saying to somebody this morning that, even though I may be at the Montreal Film Festival for 10 days and have seen six films a day, that last evening before I'm going home, I'm sitting in a movie theater at 9:30, and the lights go down, and the credits come up on the screen, and I'm still filled with excitement and anticipation, because it could be anything, and it could be brilliant, and I just love that moment of anticipation. So I'm not jaded about the moviegoing experience, even though I go to a lot of movies every year—and in really intense doses, too, the way festivals provide. But I probably have become less patient with films that I think are familiar, derivative, films I've seen in one form or another in the past. I don't hesitate to walk out if I feel that after a half an hour, a film just isn't appropriate for our festival or there's nothing I'd be interested in. There was a time early on when I was convinced that even though I didn't like the first half hour, there was a possibility that the last 10 minutes would have some redeeming feature, so I better sit through the whole thing. I no longer feel that way.

AL Are you usually sitting near the back of the festival?

DW Not necessarily, but I always try to get on an aisle.

AL Can you break down where, percentage-wise, the films you program come from? Blind submissions? Festivals? Recommendations?

DW If there's a majority, it would be from festivals that we go to, because I see so many films at other festivals. This year, before our next festival, I will have been to the Jerusalem festival, Montreal, Toronto, Vancouver, London, and Sundance, with the possibility of a weekend trip here or there, and that's usually 30 to 40 films per festival. And I'm not usually just shooting in the dark at those festivals, either. Watching films that I've read or heard good things about before I get there. There's some guessing. There's some discovery going on, but I try to go as informed as possible, so I make the best use of my limited time. So as a result, I see an awful lot of great films at those festivals, and those are the ones that I start pursuing for our lineup every March. Then the films that I pursue because I've read good things about them or films that have been submitted for our consideration, those all take a backseat to the festival method. Another piece of that puzzle is that the latter method involves watching films on videotape, and festivalgoing involves seeing films on the big screen, and there is no comparison.

AL Do you tend to try and see everything that's sent to you, or do you have to put it before a screening committee first to deal with the bulk?

DW We use a couple of different methods. We have a screening committee for shorts. This year we'll probably see 400 or so short films, and we have a committee of about a dozen people, all of whom are in the arts, who take it upon themselves to sit through the films that are submitted. For feature films, I watch those, and I serve as the front-line screening committee. Oftentimes, I will just say yes or no all by myself and be done with it, and other times, there'll be films that I then pass on to others for additional opinions.

AL You go home with a big stack every day?

DW Yep. I don't watch all of them. My typical method is to watch a half an hour of what comes in, and I understand from other festival directors that that's really generous. Oftentimes there are festivals that will watch only five to ten minutes of a film and either put it on the yes pile, the no pile, or the maybe pile. I try to watch for 30 minutes and then put it on the no pile or the maybe pile. And with the kinds of films that are being submitted, often by first-time directors, there are a number of submissions that definitely go to the no pile right away.

AL What sends something so quickly into the no pile?

DW All the standard things. Weak script. Production values aren't always the issue. I can often overlook weak production values, because a filmmaker might not have the financial resources to have as polished a production as might otherwise be possible. But bad acting, bad script, completely familiar plotlines, that sort of stuff.

AL Do you program films that have major distribution deals?

DW Yes, we do. If the films have not played in greater Cleveland, we will often include them in our festival if they are available, and we do that for a couple of reasons. Sometimes films that have commercial distribution might still never come to Cleveland or might not come for a long time. That's less true today than it was a while ago, because today Cleveland is a terrific film town. We have nine art house screens plus the Cleveland Cinematheque, which runs a program four nights a week, plus the Cleveland Museum of Art, which runs three nights a week, and those go on year-round, plus the film festival with 70 features. It's a great film town, so it's less likely today that if a film has commercial distribution it won't come to Cleveland. But once upon a time, there was the question whether films would come through or not. Today if we're showing films that have commercial distribution, (a) they have not yet shown in Cleveland, and (b) we might be using them because they are solid films, they've been reviewed perhaps nationally, and those film lovers in Cleveland who've been reading *The New York Times* or the film trades have read about them and are eager to see them and will offer a high-profile element to the film festival that might be immediately appealing to the film lover who gets our program guide three weeks before the festival starts, looks through the whole thing, and then actually recognizes a couple of titles, rather than be hit by an 80-page program guide in which they recognize absolutely nothing. It helps to serve as a warm-up for people who've been eager to see some films that have already opened in New York and L.A. or took the top prize at Cannes or Berlin. We use four screens, and we program from noon to midnight.

AL Are there any festivals out there that do a particularly good job or ones that you look to for those that you'll take back to Cleveland?

DW Yes. There are a handful of very strong film festivals and the programming of which I really admire and is in line with what we're doing here. Sometimes festivals are really good, but it just isn't the same situation as what Cleveland has, and so, while I might go to them if I were a film lover, I don't necessarily look to them for the programming work that I'm doing. But certainly the festivals that I go to, I choose to go to because I think they're applicable and good, and that includes Toronto, Vancouver, London, and Sundance. And then there are festivals that I can't get to but whose program guides I always look at, and that would include festivals like Mill Valley and Portland.

AL Does every festival director want to make a movie at some point?

DW I can honestly say that no, not every festival director wants to, because I do not fancy myself a filmmaker in any way.

Dallas Video Festival

Where Dallas, Texas
When Late March
Background And you thought television was just a bastardization of an art form, not an artistic medium in itself. Well, maybe you didn't. Maybe it's just me, and I don't get cable. Founded by the Video Association of Dallas in 1987, the DVF has provided one of the strongest selections of video screenings nationwide. Presenting a vast spectrum of films at the Dallas Theatre Center, the festival's programs range from the experimental (*Dance of Darkness*, Edin Velez's documentary of the macabre dance form Butoh) to excellent straight documentaries (Susanne Ofteringer's *Nico Icon*) to the intelligent and socially conscious (Kim Flores's feature film *Little Voices*, about a Dallas rape survivor). Retrospectives and spotlights have featured the work of Marlon Riggs, Ernie Kovacs, M. C. Escher, and Steve Allen. In addition, the festival presents video and animation workshops for children and a hands-on selection of interactive CD-ROMs (e.g., *Adventures of the Smart Patrol* featuring Devo). For those

who can't get out of the house, local channel 13 and cable channel 27 broadcast a series of the best programs from the festival on television. The festival also hosts a series of lectures on television that have included University of Texas at Austin professor Sandy Stone's "Good TV Is Dangerous as Hell," and film critic John Lewis's "Please Engage Brain Before Opening Mouth."

Major Award Winners Ernie Kovacs Award (given to seminal figures in the world of TV): Joel Hodgson, *Mystery Science Theater 3000* and *The TV Wheel*

Films Hundreds of videos in a variety of categories

Noteworthy Celebrity Sightings Allen Funt, Marlon Riggs, Steve Allen

Tickets $10–$15 for a day pass; $25 for an all-festival pass good for all events.

How to Enter Send entry fee ($20), VHS dub, and entry form to:

Dallas Video Festival
1405 Woodlawn
Dallas, TX 75208
Telephone 214.999.8999
Fax 214.999.8998
E-mail bart@videofest.org
Web www.videofest.org

Entry Deadline July

Davon Johnson's Annual Fall Film Festival

Where Denver, Colorado

When One weekend in September

Background Essentially a one-man operation founded in 1993 by irrepressibly self-promoting Denver documentary filmmaker, actor, and man-about-town Davon Johnson, this small festival gets credit for American ingenuity if not for comprehensiveness. Taking over the City Spirit Cafe (1434 Blake Street), Johnson devised this festival for filmmakers like him who had been denied entry to the Denver Film Festival. Showing a handful of films on video and focusing on independent women filmmakers and the works of African American directors, Johnson has attracted Emmy Award-winning performers and cineasts to his storefront fest.

Major Award Winners Noncompetitive

Films About 10

Noteworthy Celebrity Sightings Eriq LaSalle, Davon Johnson (of course)

Tickets $5

How to Enter Send VHS dub to:

Davon Johnson
3055 Kearney Street
Denver, CO 80207
Telephone 303.377.2517
E-mail dfilm@majordomos.com

Entry Deadline Variable

Interview with

Davon Johnson

founder of the one-man operation known as

Davon Johnson's Annual Fall Film Festival,

an alternative to the Denver Film Festival

since 1993

AL What made you decide to start your own festival?

DJ Just seeing how some of the bigger festivals are running things here in the States. They seem geared only to make money. You send in a $25 entry fee, and your film doesn't even get in. You can't constantly have your cake and eat it, too. But when you know you got a good project and your film doesn't get in, it's kind of bogus and stuff, and I just wanted something for independent filmmakers.

AL So you think that a lot of the festivals out there really aren't for independent film-makers?

DJ They're not. They're truly not. You look at some of the films that get in, and you can say, "How is that independent?" You look at the cast, you look at the crew, and you say, "That's an independent film? That looks like a big-budget Hollywood film." And they attach the word "independent" to it.

AL What's an independent film to you?

DJ Independent film to me is a guerrilla crew—a very small crew that works on it for the sheer pleasure and love of it. Same thing with the cast. Something that just barely gets made by the skin of its teeth.

AL Is that how you've made your films over the years?

DJ Yeah, I've made my films through contributions from physicians. I work in a hospital part-time. I get money sometimes from my doctor friends who help me make my films.

AL And would you call your festival a guerrilla festival as well?

DJ No, the festival is definitely a one-man thing, but it's really nice. I got a good deal here in downtown Denver. The festival is basically for independents who are trying to get their work out there and are tired of being rejected by some of the bigger festivals like Sundance and in New York and all across the country.

AL What are you looking for when you look at films?

DJ I'm just looking for quality. It doesn't really matter and stuff as long as it's good intent, nothing bad. Anything. I don't charge an entry fee. I give awards out.

AL Do you show some of your stuff?

DJ Yeah, I've been showing synopses of all five films I've directed through my own company.

AL Have you been to any of the other festivals around?

DJ I've been to a small one in California, just a showcase for filmmakers and a big one in Brussels in '92.

AL Have you ever been to, say, Sundance, to check it out?

DJ No, I sent a film there, and it was rejected. They kept my entry fee, and they didn't even send me my tape back. And if you don't have contacts in making your dubs, it can be expensive making dub tapes. Sending your film and tapes out gets really expensive. You'd like for your film to be accepted, because that's gratifying, but when you don't get accepted and they have your entry fee and they don't even send your tape back, it's like you're totally left out, and you're out the price of the dub of the tape, you don't have your film no more, and you're out of a check, you know?

AL Do you make anything off the festival?

DJ No, not really. Just to cover my expenses. That's all I want to do. I'm not interested in making money. I even paid the filmmakers last year a rental fee for their film. I lost money last year, actually.

AL Have you approached the Denver festival with your work?

DJ I had a film in there in '92, but I don't have anything to do with them anymore. I always wanted to do my own film festivals, but my dealings with them gave me more energy and boost to do my own. The first time I did a 16 mm film, they had the nerve not to take it even though I knew them personally and had done a good deal of volunteer work for them. They took some crap from some other local filmmakers, and I'm like, "Hey, that's not cool."

AL Do you think that by charging these fees some of the festivals are trying to shut out filmmakers like you who can't afford to enter?

DJ In a way, they are. And in a way, I don't think it's about that so much as it's about just making money. Charging that kind of money? Come on. One hundred fifty bucks? One hundred? How can you afford to pay that? Because by the time you get through post-production and finish your film, you're exhausted. You're exhausted physically and financially, unless you've got some rich mom or dad funding your films, which I don't. I'm broke today, because I funded all my films, but it's gonna pay off. . . . My film festival is for true independent filmmakers, people who have a strong passion to make movies and who are being turned away by the big film festivals. They could definitely come and see me, because my doors are open. I bet you could never guess what the license plates say on my car.

AL Davon Johnson?

DJ No, they say "CINEMA." That's how strong a passion I have.

AL What kind of car are you driving?

DJ A '96 Honda Civic.

Denver International Film Festival

Where Denver, Colorado

When One week in late October

Background Founded in 1978, the festival is an odd but alluring mix of the very predictable, major-market "art films" (*Shine*, *Looking for Richard*, *Michael Collins*), offbeat American independents and documentaries, and cool revivals rarely seen on the big screen (Buster Keaton's *The Cameraman*, Jean Renoir's *The Rules of the Game*, Billy Wilder's *Ace in the Hole*). The festival also offers a similarly contradictory selection of tributes that have included John G. Avildsen, Tony Curtis, Charles Burnett, and Chuck Jones all in one year. But to its credit—and the city's detriment—Denver never seems quite so alive as when the festival is here. Special screenings and retrospectives have included an Israeli film series as well as the Denver debut of Kieslowski's Decalogue series and tributes to filmmakers Dorota Kedzierzawska and Mweze Ngangura. Recent films shown here include Sydney Pollack's *Random Hearts* (which was followed by a black-tie reception), *Snow Falling on Cedars*, *The Big Brass Ring*, *The Acid House*, *Kadosh* and *American Movie*. Screenings are held at Bluebird Theatre (3317 E. Colfax), New Media Expo Hall (Turnhalle at the Tivoli), and mostly at the AMC Tivoli Theatres (Ninth and Auraria Parkway).

Major Award Winners Lifetime Achievement Award: James Coburn; John Cassavetes Award: Barbara Kopple

Noteworthy Celebrity Sightings Sydney Pollack, James Coburn, Leonard Maltin

Films More than 150

Tickets $7.50 regular; $6 students and seniors

Telephone 303.830.8497

Hotline 303.321.FILM

How to Enter Send entry form, $25 entry fee, and VHS film copy to:

Denver International Film Festival
1430 Larimer Square, Suite 201
Denver, CO 80202
Telephone 303.595.3456
Fax 303.595.0956
E-mail dfs@denverfilm.org
Web www.denverfilm.org

Entry Deadline August

Interview with

Ron Henderson

of the Denver International Film Festival

CB How do you come up with your programs?

RH Each year, the Denver festival combs the globe in search of the best of new international cinematic works. The festival program tends toward the eclectic and away from the thematic, with an emphasis on films that would not normally play theatrically in Denver. Between 60 and 75 guest film artists introduce their works and engage audiences in dialogue each year. Because Denver is more a community festival and less an industry event, filmmakers have no business to do (except for working the media) and are free to stand up in front of an audience and bathe in its appreciation. Consequently, Denver has a far-reaching "festival-friendly" reputation with filmmakers. The city of Denver, which rests one mile above sea level at the foot of the majestic Rocky Mountains, lays claim to having the second largest filmgoing audience per capita in the United States. These cinema lovers not only get (naturally) high on the altitude—and on life—but on their annual feast of film as well. I program the festival in the following ways: I attend a number of international film festivals each year looking for new films. This year, I attended Sundance, Rotterdam, Berlin, Taos, and Cannes. We also send out a call for entries, which this year produced approximately 800 unsolicited entries—shorts, features, fiction, and documentary. I also utilize an international program advisory group, which recommends films from around the world. In addition, I subscribe to Film Finders, which tracks new independent productions worldwide, and I read the trades and independent film magazines on a regular basis. And finally, we solicit a few high-profile art films from the various speciality distributors before they are released theatrically. Every effort is made to strike a balance in our annual survey of the "best of world cinema," in our mix of cutting-edge feature fiction and documentary selections, as well as quality short subjects and experimental works. The festival also pays tribute to established and emerging film artists, showcasing retrospectives of their works; presents restored prints of rediscovered archival treasures, and a critics' choice programs of lost or forgotten films which deserve a second look.

CB Do you see any trends in filmmaking?

RH Yes, I see trends every year—mostly genre and personality driven. Tarantino, slacker, relationship, and coming-of-age themes—all clones of successful originals, which become formulaic rip offs. Disappointing, for sure, but trend does—or should—serve as a persistent wake-up call for both festival programmers and distributors to be on the lookout for so-called independent films which are no more than a warmed-over calling card to Hollywood. Our programmatic instincts are to embrace the risk-taking film artist who has a good story and tells it well and whose vision is bold and original, and to reject the warmed-over, formulaic fare which seems to be, at the moment at least, pervasive.

CB Do you see all the films yourself?

RH I share the preview process with several staff members, but I still see between 500 and 1,000 films a year—but not necessarily the entire film.

CB If you don't like a film, will you turn it off?

RH Yes, I do turn off a film after 15 minutes if it is judged, for whatever reason, not appropriate for festival consideration.

CB Any advice for filmmakers?

RH What I would say to a filmmaker who submits his or her film to the Denver festival is not to take a rejection personally. The very fact that they completed a film is commendable. We reject many decent films which deserve to be seen by a larger audience. There are many reasons for this. Although I would not try to talk anyone out of submitting a film, I would caution that the medium-length (20 to 45 minutes) narrative films are the most difficult to program.

CB How has the festival changed? In the early years, the Denver festival struggled financially.

RH The Film Society has added a number of niche festivals during the year and now has a major presence throughout the calendar year adding value for our sponsors and our members. Today the festival is financially healthy and growing in terms of programs, membership, audience and corporate support. The festival's reputation within the international film community is also strong, which is reflected in our ability to acquire highly acclaimed films, on a consistent basis, for our various festivals.

CB What are some of the highlights of your tenure at Denver?

RH In the early years, the Denver festival was on the vanguard of introducing Eastern European cinema to the region—and, outside of New York, the nation. We continued that tradition during the glasnost years of the late '80s–early '90s by bringing scores of films and filmmakers to Denver from the former Soviet Union-previously banned works-and the Eastern European countries. The directors from "behind the wall" include Larisa Shepitko, Elem Klimnov, Marta Mezaros, Miklós Jacsó, Karel Kachyna, István Szabó, Károly Makk, Rajko Grlic, Emir Kusturica, Ivan Nitschev, Dusan Hanák, and Jirí Menzel, among others. I am most proud of the U.S. premiere, in 1989, of Krzysztof Kieslowski's towering 10-part *Decalogue*, with the great Polish director appearing in person. We brought it back to SRO audiences a few years ago on the anniversary of Kieslowski's death. That same year, with the endorsement of Gena Rowlands, we established the John Cassavetes Award, to be given annually to an American director for outstanding achievement in independent filmmaking.

CB Any films you're embarrassed that you showed?

EH Yes, I was particularly embarrassed—once. I took an opening night film unseen. It was an independent production called *O'Hara's Wife*, starring Ed Asner, Mariette Hartley, Jodie Foster, and Tom Bosley. Great cast. How could it be bad? It was horrible! But the audience forgave us because Ed Asner was our guest and elicited a lot of sympathy.

Edmonton Local Heroes International Screen Festival

Where Edmonton, Alberta, Canada
When First week of April
Background As much an industry convention as a film festival, Edmonton's festival, founded in 1986, has premiered many international and Alberta-based films while hosting dorkily named seminars ("Go! On Your Mark. Get Set!" "Butting Heads, Scratching Backs") concerning how to package film projects, how to find funding, and the relationship between producers and writers. Films that have received their premieres here include *Lumiére and Company*, *The War of the Buttons*, and *The Total Balalaika Show* shown in a midnight screening. Special screenings have included Tod Browning's *The Unknown* starring Lon Chaney and with a live score by the Alloy Orchestra. The festival also hosts an Alberta home-video competition in which "Camcorder Coppolas" and their five-minute opuses vie for a $500 gift certificate. Screenings are held at the Capitol Square Theatres (10065 Jasper Avenue), the Garneau Theatre (8712 109th Street), Timms Center for the Arts (87th Avenue and 112th Street), and the Princess Theatre (10337 82nd Avenue).

The National Screen Institute offers the Drama Prize, a 16-month professional development program to aid emerging filmmaking teams, each of which is given

$6,000 in cash and $5,500 in services toward refining and premiering a short film project.

Major Award Winners Canadian Broadcasting Corporation Award: *Through My Eyes*; CanWest Global System Award: *A Boy's Own Story*; Rogers Telefund Award: *The Trial of Stubby McPherson*; Telefilm Canada Award: *Tall*; Western International Communications Award: *Henry's Café*

Noteworthy Celebrity Sightings Werner Herzog, Costa Gavras, Paul Cox

Tickets $15 for opening night events; $6 for afternoon screenings; $10 for evening screenings; $150 for festival package

Ticket Hotline 403.421.4084

How to Enter For more information contact:
    2000 Local Heroes Edmonton Festival
    10159 108th Street
    Edmonton, AB T5J 1L1
    Canada
    Telephone 403.421.4084
    Fax 403.425.8098
    E-mail filmhero@nsi-canada.ca or jan-nsi@supernet.ab.ca
    Web www.nsi-canada.ca

Entry Deadline November

Empire State Film Festival

Where Various locations around New York state

When Mid-September through early October

Background Screens new works by indie film- and videomakers, including students, in different cities around New York state (Albany, Buffalo, Ithaca, and New York City). Kind of hard to figure out what's playing when and where, but it has a good selection of edgy experimental, narrative, and animated material: *Little Dark Poet*, *Atomic Tobacco*, and *The Canterbury Tales*.

Major Award Winners Noncompetitive

Films About 25

How to Enter For more information contact:
    Empire State Film Festival
    P.O. Box 1313
    Saratoga Springs, NY 12866
    Telephone 212.802.4679
    Fax 518.580.2328
    E-mail empirefilm@aol.com
    Web www.empirefilm.com

Entry Deadline July

Festival de Cinema Ste.-Thérèse/Ste.-Adéle

Where Ste.- Thérèse/Ste.- Adéle, Quebec, Canada

When Ten days in early October

Background Essentially a showcase for first- and second-time directors, the Quebec festival has premiered such works as *La Cri de la Soie*, by Yvon Marciano, and Laurent Chevalier's *L'Enfant Noir*. Screenings are held at the Cinema Pine (24, Rue Morin, Ste.-Adéle) and at College Lionel Groux (100, Rue Duquet, Ste.-Thérèse). Programs range from official competition in features, shorts, and young directors along with special presentations.

Major Award Winners Best Film: *Croix de Bois, Croix de Guerre*, by Marius Horst; Best Short: *Le Jour de Bain*, by Dominique De Rivaz.

Films About 60 features plus a program of shorts

How to Enter For more information contact:
Festival de Cinema International, Ste.-Thérèse/Ste.-Adéle
    34, Rue Blainville Ouest
    Ste.-Thérèse, PQ J7E 1W9
    Canada
    Telephone 514.434.0387
    Fax 514.434.7868
    E-mail festival@odyssee.net
    Web www.microtec.net/~festival

Entry Deadline July

Filmfest DC

Where Washington, D.C.

When Two weeks in late April and early May

Background Very little is unpredictable about this festival, which shows largely early premieres of so-called independents from the likes of Miramax, Fine Line Pictures, and Fox Searchlight. But in the nation's capital, what do you expect? Controversy? Recent screenings have included *The Red Violin*, Bernardo Bertolucci's *Besieged* and, more interestingly, Olivier Ducastel and Jacques Martineau's *Jeanne and the Perfect Guy*. Retrospective sections focus on a particular country (e.g., Italy), and the Global Rhythms section screens films with a musical bent (recent showings have included *Listening to You: The Who at the Isle of Wight Festival*, *Bob Marley: Live in Concert*, Wim Wenders' *Buena Vista Social Club*, *Duke Ellington on Film*, and a BBC-TV archive presentation of *The Little Richard Special*. DC's festival screens at the Cineplex Odeon Tenley (4200 Wisconsin Avenue NW), Cineplex Odeon Foundry (1055 Thomas Jefferson Street SW), and the Kennedy Center. The festival has premiered the restored version of Jacques Demy's *The Umbrellas of Cherbourg* as well as *The Red Violin* and *Buena Vista Social Club*.

Major Award Winners Audience Award for Best Film ($500): *Celestial Clockwork*, by Fina Torres; and *W. E. B. DuBois*, by Louis Massiah.

Films About 70 features and special programs of shorts

Noteworthy Celebrity Sightings Umm, Andrew Sarris

Tickets $7 per individual screening; festival hotline 202.628.FILM; available through ProTix 703.218.6500

How to Enter For more information contact:
    Filmfest DC
    P.O. Box 21396
    Washington, DC 20009

Telephone 202.274.6810
Fax 202.274.6828
E-mail FilmfestDC@aol.com
Web www.capaccess.org/filmfestdc
Entry Deadline February

Film Fest New Haven

Where New Haven, Connecticut
When One weekend in early April
Background The motto here is "You can't imagine what you'll see," a fitting enough motto if you're hosting a festival in Cannes or Brussels, but a bit overreaching when it comes to a little fest near Yale University, because if you've been to any other festival around the country, it won't take much imagination to figure out what you'll see. Founded in 1996, the New Haven fest has played host in its scant history predominantly to American indies, screening quite a few features that are seen nowhere else but here. No big-name Hollywood types. No blockbuster screening. No chance to nibble the celery stick out of Leslie Caron's Bloody Mary glass. Just a humble but intelligently chosen selection of offbeat films. The biggest films to premiere here were Stuart Gordon's *Space Truckers*, starring Dennis Hopper, and Michael Davis's American comedy *Eight Days a Week*. Others have included Michael Kantor's *Cornerstone* and art critic Faith Hubley's *Africa* and *Seers and Clowns*. Screenings are held at the Little Theater (1 Lincoln Street) and the Whitney Humanities Center.
Films 17 features and 46 shorts
Recent Award Winners Connecticut Filmmaker Award: Jeremy Leven
Tickets $5–$7 per individual screening
How to Enter For more information contact:
Film Fest New Haven
111 Clinton Avenue
New Haven, CT 06513
Telephone 203.865.2773
Fax 203.865.2773
E-mail film_fest_new_haven@compuserve.com
Web www.ourworld.compuserve.com/homepages/film_fest_new_haven
Entry Deadline January

Florida Film Festival

Where Maitland, Florida
When Two weeks in mid-June
Background Screening films at Maitland's Enzian Theatre, the festival plays host to only about 6,000 every year. In addition to Florida premieres, which have included *The Blair Witch Project*, John Sayles' *Lone Star*, Eric Rohmer's *Rendezvous in Paris* and Jacques Rivette's *Up/Down/Fragile*, the festival holds tributes and homages including a recent one devoted to the work of Rod Steiger.
Major Award Winners Grand Prize for Best Film: L. M. Meza, *Staccato Purr of the Exhaust*

Films About 60 features plus programs of shorts and cartoons
Noteworthy Celebrity Sightings Roger Corman, Steve Buscemi, Paul Newman, Oliver Stone
How to Enter Send entry fee ($30), VHS dub, and entry form to:
Florida Film Festival
Enzian Theatre
1300 S. Orlando Avenue
Maitland, FL 32571
Telephone 407.629.1088
Fax 407.629.6870
E-mail wgridley@enzian.org
Web www.enzian.org
Entry Deadline February

Fort Lauderdale International Film Festival

Where Fort Lauderdale, Florida
When Four weeks from mid-October to mid-November
Background Despite the fact that Blockbuster Entertainment is a proud sponsor of the film festival and despite the fact that Tony Curtis was a recent lifetime achievement award recipient (others have included Roger Corman, Jerry Lewis, Vincent Price, and Donald O'Connor), the Fort Lauderdale fest still has quite a bit of buzz as one of the best showcases for offbeat U.S. independents. Screenings are held in the AMC Coral Ridge movie theater. Any festival that shows *The Wizard of Oz* on its big screen for its children's mini-fest is OK in my book. In addition to its competition and children's fest, the festival also highlights American Independents, Florida Treasures, and Asian Films and presents a student film showcase. Screenings are also held at the AMC Mizner Park in Boca Raton, the AMC Sheridan in Hollywood, and the Blockbuster IMAX Theatre in downtown Fort Lauderdale. About 55,000 attend annually. Among recent screenings: *20 Dates, Motel, Left Luggage.*
Major Award Winners Best Film: *Shine*; Audience Award for Best Film: *Shine*; Best Director: Lars von Trier, *Breaking the Waves*; Best Actress: Emily Watson, *Breaking the Waves*; Best Actor: Noah Taylor, *Shine*; Best Foreign Film: *Sicario*, by Jose Novoa; Best Independent U.S. Film: *Sex and the Other Man*, by Karl Sloven
Films Approximately 100 features and documentaries plus shorts and a student film festival
Noteworthy Celebrity Sightings Kevin Spacey, Lynn Redgrave, Elisabeth Shue
Tickets $7 per individual screening
Festival Hotline 954.563.0500
How to Enter Send entry form, fee ($40 U.S. features, $30 U.S. shorts), and VHS dub to:
Fort Lauderdale International Film Festival
2633 E. Sunrise Boulevard
Ft. Lauderdale, FL 33304-3205
Telephone 954.563.0500
Fax 954.564.1206
Entry Deadline September

Interview with

Gregory von Hausch

president and executive director of the

Fort Lauderdale Film Festival

AL Can you go into some detail as to how you choose films?

GVH I'm not sure it's so unusual, but what we do is go on the festival circuit. We see a lot of films that have already played. We solicit through publications, the trade magazines such as *Moving Pictures, Hollywood Reporter, Variety,* and *Screen.* We take out full-page color ads. We have an Internet site that we advertise. While I'm at the festivals, I bring posters and entry forms. We also do direct mail to all of the film schools in the nation. Those are more or less the main ways that we seek films.

AL Can you pinpoint where the majority of the films come from?

GVH I would have said prior to last year that the majority of them come from other festivals. But last year, I think we had primarily unsolicited films that were just entered, that we didn't know about before we received them, and I'm not sure if that's because we've stepped up our marketing or because there's been more word-of-mouth about the festival.

AL Are you seeing a higher quality of work now from unsolicited submissions?

GVH Yeah. I am. I also see a preponderance of these Generation X films of kids lamenting why they're not doing what they really want to do. And if you took that flood of films out of the market, you'd have a really good ratio. But there are too many twenty-something kids making films who haven't stopped to think about the ways of the world. It's hard to make the great American novel. You have to have a little bit of experience behind you. And the same thing is true with filmmakers. But they're all so eager to have that first big film that somehow they're finding the money. In the '60s, kids were toiling off-Broadway or in little regional theaters writing plays, trying to get them performed or picked up by a theater troupe. And there was a wealth of theaters that did those, and that was a whole different ball game. But I think that the style of artist is now gravitating toward filmmaking. Everybody wants to make a film, and I think it's great. I think it's wonderful, but you get a lot of drivel, too.

AL So would your advice to twenty-something filmmakers wanting to make their first film be "Wait until you're 30"?

GVH No. You have to try and fail and all that, but with film it's such a dire consequence when you put $150,000 into a film and no one picks it up and maybe it's picked up by a couple festivals. That's a pretty tough bullet to bite. But I think short films are good to develop your craft rather than starting out with a feature, and some kids have it, but it's like any other art profession. Most of them don't. Think about the material. Stay true to what you really want to say. Move the audience. You go back to all those classic films, and they were about people, and that's so much more moving to me than about attitudes.

AL Do you watch everything that comes in?

GVH Yeah, I view all of the tapes. If something is really terrible in terms of production quality, if it doesn't move me in 35 minutes and I can see that there are no redeeming qualities to it, then I might not watch the whole thing. We have around 675 entries right now, and between that and going on the circuit, it's tough to see them all. I have long ago given up the idea that I have to watch films until the final frame.

AL Thirty-five minutes sounds pretty generous in comparison to some of the other festivals.

GVH Yeah, but we're charging an entry fee. It's not like I have an egg timer up there. We definitely want to give everyone a shot, and I have seen some films that start out great and go downhill. Very rarely do they start out terrible and turn out great.

AL Do you think young filmmakers have the wrong impression about film festivals, that they think the festivals are there to serve them?

GVH I think what they have to expect from our festival is this: We don't always show perfect movies. We show movies with flaws in them, and that's to their benefit. So if there's promise in your film, there's a really good shot that we're going to show it, bring you in, and have you get that experience of being reviewed, getting the audience reaction, and hopefully learning and honing your craft. That's what we're about while simultaneously educating our audience as to what independent film is all about, and as we do that, that movement is constantly being redefined, where you have people like Tarantino, who aren't really making independent films anymore, but they still represent the movement.

AL Do you program films that have already latched onto major distributors, or do you shy away from those?

GVH We do that to some degree. We have opened with *Shine*, and that fits into that scheme of things. We don't do that many of them. We might just use them to bookend the festival. Because you have 2000 people coming to opening night, you want to make sure that you're appealing to a wide segment of the audience.

AL How many entries do you get per year?

GVH Seven hundred, plus the things I go out and see that amount to about 40 to 45 percent of what we do.

AL So you have around 700 competing for about 50 slots?

GVH I would say so.

AL What festivals do you attend?

GVH I go to Sundance, Berlin, AFM, Cannes, Montreal, and Venice.

AL Are there festivals with program guides you look at?

GVH We have a pretty good group of friends. We work with the Puerto Rican Film Festival, Mill Valley, Denver, and Cleveland. That's my closest circle. We don't feel competition between us, though. When you're programming a festival, you do feel competitive. There is an incredible lust for being the first to do a film even if it's no good, but you're getting a premiere, and in doing so, you negate the reason for the festival, which is to promote the filmmaker and not the festival, and we've been pretty good about it. That's pretty lofty hyperbole, but we keep the filmmaker in our sights all along.

AL Have you seen changes in audience taste or sophistication?

GVH Oh yes. It's incredible. When I came on in 1989, the audience was so small. It was almost entirely American and Canadian independents, and now we're doing 50 percent European, and that has been refreshing, to get that appreciation from the audience to be able to do films from Asia and Bangladesh. We have 35 separate countries.

> People are also recognizing the filmmakers and seeing them grow. When I queue up in Montreal, I notice the audience there is so sophisticated. The pizza guy behind you and the secretary in front of you are so knowledgeable about film. They lust for movies, and I think it's terrific. We're not quite there yet, but we're making strides.

Fort Worth Film Festival

Where Fort Worth, Texas
When Five days in late October
Background Since everybody else in Texas gets a film festival (Houston, Dallas, Austin, etc.), I guess Fort Worth gets one too. While it purports to focus on "The Western," reviving greats such as *High Noon* and *The Good, The Bad and the Ugly*, as well as lessers such as *Westworld*, it's a loose sort of definition. It likes Texans, of course, bringing Wes Anderson in for a screening of *Rushmore* and James V. Hart to introduce *Dracula*, which he wrote (regardless of what Bram Stoker's estate says).
Noteworthy Celebrity Sightings Gregory Peck, Tippi Hedren, M. Emmet Walsh, Larry McMurtry
Films More than 50 features and shorts
How to Enter Send entry form to:
    Fort Worth Film Festival
    P.O. Box 17206
    Fort Worth, TX 76102-0206
    Telephone 817.915.9155
    Fax 817.390.7226
    E-mail fwff@fortworthfilmfest.com
    Web www.fortworthfilmfest.com
Entry Deadline July 15

Gen Art Film Festival

Where New York, New York
When One week in late April
Background Founded in 1996, this desperately hip festival, showcasing features, documentaries, and shorts by young filmmakers at the tony Lincoln Center and the Cineplex Odeon on 49th Street has the whiff of Upper West Side money about it, although it has premiered some pretty good features, including *The Darien Gap*, *Far Harbor*, and *Synthetic Pleasures*. Filmmakers presented must be between 18 and 35 upon the completion of their flicks. About 7,000 attend.
Major Award Winners Noncompetitive
Films About seven
Noteworthy Celebrity Sightings Leonardo DiCaprio, Mike Newell, Adam Horowitz, Edward Burns, Josh Hamilton
How to Enter Send $10 entry fee for short subject films (30 minutes or less in

length) or $20 for feature-length films (60 minutes or more) plus dub and entry form to:

Gen Art Film Festival
145 W. 28th Street, Suite 116
New York, NY 10001
Telephone 212.290.0312
Fax 212.290.0254
E-mail info@genart.org
Web www.genart.org

Entry Deadline February

Gravity-Free Film and Video Competition (Lucille Ball Festival of New Comedy)

Where Jamestown, New York

When One weekend in mid-September

Background It shouldn't come as any particular surprise that this somewhat depressing city housing a Lucy-Desi museum, featuring exhibits devoted to the history of Lucille Ball's humor and an exhibit concerning "Technological Innovation in the Work of Lucille Ball and Desi Arnaz," would also hold a film festival as part of its annual Lucille Ball Festival of New Comedy. Since 1989, the Gravity-Free Competition has been devoted to screening short comedies under 30 minutes in length.

Major Award Winners Winner of "People's Choice Award" receives $500 prize and plane ticket to Jamestown; $250 awards given in Family, International, and Late Night categories; winners include *How Dinosaurs Learned to Fly*, *A Straight Long Road*, *Good Night*, and *Blackfly*

Noteworthy Celebrity Sightings George Wallace, Paula Poundstone

Tickets $5 for a daily screening pass, which also entitles one to free entry at the Lucy-Desi Museum (yowzah!)

How to Enter Send short film (under 30 minutes) to:

Lucy-Desi Museum
212 Pine Street
Jamestown, NY 14701
Telephone 716.664.2465
Web www.lucy-desi.com

Entry Deadline June

Great Plains Film Festival

Where Lincoln, Nebraska

Background A compelling mixture of first-run Hollywood and independent art films (*Ulee's Gold*, *Career Girls*), indie shorts and documentaries, and films with a Nebraska flavor to them, the festival has paid tribute over the years to Peter Fonda, Sandy Dennis, and Joan Micklin Silver. Founded in 1992 by the director of Lincoln's Ross Theater, the festival (the first of its kind in the region) provides a welcome dose of cinematic culture in a city that tends to show only mainstream Hollywood tripe. Judges include Tony Bui and Chris Eyre (*Smoke Signals* and, rumor has it, a filmed adaptation of Peter Matthiessen's *In The Spirit of Crazy Horse*). Films are screened in the following categories: Films Made for Public Television, Dramatic Feature Films and Videos, Documentary Feature Films and Videos, Dramatic Shorts, and Documentary Shorts. Only entries by filmmakers from the Great Plains (Colorado, Iowa, Kansas, Minnesota, Missouri, Montana, Nebraska, New Mexico, North Dakota, Oklahoma, South Dakota, Texas, Wyoming, and the Canadian provinces of Alberta, Manitoba, and Saskatchewan) and (deep breath) films that relate to these regions are accepted. Screenings are held at the Mary Riepma Ross Theater.

Major Award Winners Grand Prize ($1,500): *The Life and Times of Allen Ginsberg*, by Jerry Aronson; Rainbow Award ($1,000 given to film by "marginalized" ethnic or racial minorities): *For Angela*, by Nancy Botkin; Best Dramatic Feature ($500): *Omaha (The Movie)*, by Dan Mirvish; Best Documentary Short ($250): *Everything I Saved I'm Sending*, by Camille Seaman, and *Flesh*, by Anthony Tenczar; Best Dramatic Short ($250): *Roswell*, by Bill Brown; Made for Public Television ($250): *I'll Ride That Horse*, by Doris Loeser, and *The Man Who Drew Bug-Eyed Monsters*, by Mel Bucklin and Bill Chvala

Films About 32 films and videos

Noteworthy Celebrity Sightings Peter Fonda, Les Blank

Tickets $6 for individual screening; $25 festival pass grants admittance to all screenings

Festival hotline 402.472.5353

How to Enter Send entry form, VHS dub, and entry fee ($25 for features, $15 for shorts) to:

> Great Plains Film Festival
> Mary Riepma Ross Film Theater
> University of Nebraska-Lincoln
> Lincoln, NE 68588-0302
> Telephone 402.472.9100
> Fax 402.472.2576
> E-mail dladely@unl.edu
> Web www.incolor.inetnebr.com/theater

Entry Deadline May

H. P. Lovecraft Film Festival

Where Portland, Oregon

When One weekend in early October

Background Probably the most specific festival in the states, the HPLFF offers a sampling of films dedicated to the spirit of H. P. Lovecraft. Screenings are held at 5th Avenue Cinemas (510 S.W. Hall), and titles in previous years have included: *The Neconomicon*, *The Outsider*, *The Music of Erich Zann*, and screenings of trailers from *Bride of Re-Animator*, *From Beyond Re-Animator*, *The Lurking Fear*, *Castle Freak*, and *The Resurrected*.

Major Award Winners Best H. P. Lovecraft Film Adaptation: *The Outsider*, by Andrew Hooks; Best Lovecraft Inspired Film: *McLaren*, by Ted Purvis; Best Lovecraft Kindred Spirit Film: *Reality Trip*, by Jason Forest

Tickets $6 for a Lovecraftian evening of films, trailers, and entertainment

How to Enter For more information contact:
HPL Film Festival
Beyond Books
610 S.W. Broadway, Suite 505
Portland, OR 97205
Fax 503.243.2479
E-mail festival@beyond-books.com
Entry Deadline August

Hamptons International Film Festival

Where East Hampton, New York
When Five days in mid-October
Background Yet another in the round of fests showing American indies in plush surroundings, the Hamptons fest rivals Sundance for indie buzz and cocktail party invitations. Founded in 1993, the festival, for better or worse, does take risks on first-time filmmakers and helps to vault them, if not to fame, at least to Sundance. With heavy-duty corporate sponsorship, the festival is an uneasy blend of gung-ho cinephilia and celebrity elbow-rubbing (Spielberg serves as a "special advisor"). On the plus side, recent festivals have premiered such works as Alex Cox's *Three Businessmen*, Srdjan Dragojevic's *Pretty Village, Pretty Flame*, and John Johnson's *Ratchet*, but also new directorial efforts by the likes of Richard Dreyfuss, Jeff Goldblum, and Rob Lowe. There is a Golden Starfish award for American indies.
Major Award Winners Best Film (Golden Starfish award): *Judy Berlin*, by Eric Mendelsohn; Best Documentary: *Night Waltz*, by Owsley Bowen; Best Short Film: *Moments of Doubt*, by Louis Pepe; Audience prize for best film: *Train of Life*, by Radu Mihaileanu
Films About 40 features
Noteworthy Celebrity Sightings Anjelica Huston, Jeanne Moreau
Tickets $7–$15 per individual screening; $350 gains access to all screenings
How to Enter For more information contact:
Hamptons International Film Festival
3 Newton Mews
East Hampton, NY 11937
Telephone 516.324.4600
Fax 516.324.5116
E-mail hiff@hamptonfest.org
Web www.hamptonfest.org
Entry Deadline August

Hawaii International Film Festival

Where Honolulu, Hawaii, and other locations on neighboring islands
When Two weeks in mid-November
Background You wouldn't necessarily expect to see great new films from Kazakhstan or Iran around Thanksgiving in Hawaii. But the festival, founded in 1981, has prided itself as being the American festival "where strangers meet." Screening films in more than 20 locations in Honolulu (check out the Varsity

movie palace, which looks straight out of 1960s Los Angeles, and Honolulu's Movie Museum), as well as on Kauai, Oahu, Molokai, and Maui, the festival pays special attention to features and documentaries made by Asians, Pacific Islanders, and Hawaiian filmmakers but also presents quite a few dollops of the works of other international and American filmmakers. Recent features at festivals have included tributes to United States and Chinese comic cinema and Korean film director Im Kwon Taek. Some films that one is unable to see at their venues for one reason or another are available for $3.95 on pay-per-view.

Major Award Winners The HIFF awards the ever-so-politically-correctly named Golden Maile Nominee for the feature and documentary film that best promotes cultural understanding; Best Hawaiian Film: *Red Turtle Rising*, by Jay April; Ohana People's Choice Awards include: Best Film: *Siam Sunset and in a Savage Land*; Best Documentary: *Surfing for Life*, produced by David Brown; and Best Short: *Peep Show*

Films More than 100 features and shorts

Noteworthy Celebrity Sightings Joan Chen, Rena Owen

Tickets Free, but $50 membership assures entrance to all screenings

How to Enter Send entry form and $25 to:
> Hawaii International Film Festival
> 700 Bishop Street, Suite 400
> Honolulu, HI 96813
> Telephone 808.528.3456
> Fax 808.528.1410
> E-mail hiffinfo@hiff.org
> Web www.hiff.org

Entry Deadline June

Heartland Film Festival

Where Indianapolis, Indiana

When One week in late October

Background Founded in 1991, the festival began with some rather safe choices (the world premiere of the rerelease of *Snow White and the Seven Dwarfs*) and a tribute to hometown boy Robert Wise. But it has grown into a noteworthy celebration of hometown Americana in cinema, premiering earnest and thought-provoking films from the so-called heartland. The festival's purpose is "to recognize and honor filmmakers whose work explores the human journey by artistically expressing hope and respect for the positive values of life." Nice work if you can get it.

Major Award Winners Offers Crystal Heart Awards and prizes of $10,000 and $20,000; recent winners include *Walking Across Egypt, Troublesome Creek: A Midwestern, No Easy Way, The Water Carrier, Jirohachi, Williams Syndrome: A Highly Musical Species,* and *Flowers for Charlie*

Films Only about 10 films shown, plus mainstream screenings, such as a recent showing of *101 Dalmatians* and an anniversary screening of *Hoosiers*

Noteworthy Celebrity Sightings Ellen Burstyn, Judge Reinhold, Sydney Pollack, Jeffrey Lyons, Karl Malden, Winston Groome (author of *Forrest Gump*)

Tickets $6 per individual film; $75 for an all-access pass

How to Enter All entries must be submitted on VHS and must be available to be screened in 16 mm or 35 mm during the festival. Send film plus $55 entry fee for feature films or $20 fee for short entries, made payable to Heartland Film Festival, along with 250-word synopsis, 250-word "visionary statement" about how the film meets the festival's purpose, two black-and-white stills, principal cast list, list of credits, and official entry form to:

Jeffrey L. Sparks
Heartland Film Festival
613 N. East Street
Indianapolis, IN 48202
Telephone 317.464.9405
Fax 317.635.4201
E-mail hff@pop.iquest.net
Web www.heartlandfilmfest.org
Entry Deadline July

Herland Film Festival

Where Calgary, Alberta, Canada
When Ten days in late March and early April
Background In conservative Alberta, the Herland fest shines out as a welcome slap-shot of politically correct politics in hockey country. Founded in 1989 by the Calgary Status of Women Action Committee and funded by the Canadian Council, Herland focuses exclusively on the works of Canadians and holds an Aboriginal Film and Video Night as well as a tribute to Cinematic Sistahs (films and videos by women of color). Works by Jewish women are also screened, and all filmmakers whose works are screened are paid a fee. To be considered, your film should be antiracist, antisexist, or anticlassist, preferably all three. Among films that have premiered here is *Earth*, by Deepa Mehta.
Films About 60 to 80 films and videos
Noteworthy Celebrity Sightings Persimmon Blackbridge, Maureen Bradley, Lorna Boschman
How to Enter For more information contact:

Herland Feminist Film Festival and Video Celebration
c/o Herland Planning Committee
CSWAC
233 12th Avenue SW
Calgary, AB T2P 0G9
Canada
Telephone 403.262.1873
Fax 403.262.4849
E-mail herland@cadvision.com
Entry Deadline September

Hispanic Film Festival

Where Miami, Florida
When Ten days in late April and early May
Background The only Spanish-language festival ever in Miami, the Hispanic fest, founded in 1996 by Jaime Angulo, started out with only about 20 films from the

United States and various Spanish-speaking nations and has already tripled in size. Screenings are held at nine separate auditoriums throughout Dade County.

Major Award Winners Offers Golden Egret awards for the usual categories

Films Between 60 to 70 films

How to Enter For more information contact:

Hispanic Film Festival
10700 S.W. 88th Court
Miami, FL 33176
Telephone 305.279.1974
Fax 305.279.1809
E-mail jangulo@hispanicfilm.com
Web www.hispanicfilm.com

Entry Deadline January

Hot Docs

Where Toronto, Ontario, Canada

When Four days in mid-March

Background Sponsored by the Canadian Independent Film Caucus, this mid-size documentary film festival provides an excellent overview of the state of contemporary documentary cinema. Films are screened at the excellent Bloor Cinema. A recent festival featured a tribute to Australian contemporary documentary films.

Major Award Winners Best Feature Length Documentary: *Bones of the Forest*, by Heather Frise and Velcrow Ripper; Best Political Documentary: *Haiti dans Tous Nos Rives*, by Jean Daniel Lafond; Best Arts Documentary: *Enigmatico*, by David Martin and Patricia Fogliatol; Best Biographical Documentary: *In My Own Time: Diary of a Cancer Patient*, by Joseph Viszmeg

Films About 50 documentaries

Tickets $5.35 per individual screening; $37.45 for unlimited access to screenings

How to Enter For more information contact:

Hot Docs
Canadian Independent Film Caucus
189 DuPont Street
Toronto, ON M53 1V6
Canada
Telephone 416.975.3977
Fax 416.968.9092

Hot Springs Documentary Film Festival

Where Hot Springs, Arkansas

When One week in mid-October

Background Somewhat of a preview to the Academy Awards, the festival (founded in 1992) screens a selection of films being considered for the Best Documentary Oscar along with classic documentaries. Screenings are held at the Malco Theatre (817 Central Avenue) and the Hot Springs Convention Center. Recent screenings include a tribute to *The Birds* and *Marnie* star Tippi Hedren, who brought her film *Life with Big Cats*. Others have included *Hitman Hart: Wrestling with Shadows*,

Himalayan Herders, and *Bingo! The Documentary.* The most recent festival was attended by more than 15,000 viewers.

Celebrity Sightings Tippi Hedren

Films About 70

Tickets $3 individual screenings, $10 day pass, and $50 festival pass

How to Enter Send $25 entry fee, form, and VHS dub to:
>Hot Springs Documentary Film Institute
>819 Central Ave.
>Hot Springs, AR 71902-6450
>Telephone 501.321.4747
>Fax 501.321.0211
>E-mail hsdff@docufilmfest.org
>Web www.docufilmfest.org

Entry Deadline April

Houston Gay and Lesbian Film Festival

Where Houston, Texas

When Ten days in May

Background Founded in 1997, the Houston G & L fest is the first in this city, which means that homoerotic entertainment will not have disappeared with the departure of the Oilers. Screenings are held at six locations: the Angelika Film Center, Aurora Picture Show, DiverseWorks, the Greenaway 3, the Museum of Fine Arts and Rice Media Center. Films that have played here include *Relax . . . It's Just Sex* and *Hallelujah.*

Films About 25

Celebrity Sightings Kelli Herd

Tickets Varies from theater to theater

How to Enter Check out the festival Web site:
>Web www.neosoft.com/~travism/filmfest.htm

Hudson Valley Film Festival

Where Poughkeepsie, New York

When First week of June

Background Ahh, Poughkeepsie! I can't recall whether the bumper stickers said City of Sun or City of Sin. I don't even know whether the best restaurant in town is still Napoli's pizza parlor, and the memories of the butter crunch sundaes at Sweet Blondie's ice cream shop are as distant as those of the Juliet Cinema, where we watched *Ishtar* and *The Best of Times.* But what remains is a quirky little festival whose star-studded honorary board shines out in distinctly strange contrast to the actual fare of the festival. On one hand, you have the board composed—almost absurdly—of everyone from Woody Allen to Armand Assante to Anjelica Huston to John Pierson to Paul Schrader to Martin Scorsese to Meryl Streep to John Travolta. And then you have the few small indie films, which are almost overshadowed by the festival's desire to become known as "Hollywood on the Hudson." The best aspect of the festival is that it features a selection of short films that are given original new scores by the Hudson Valley Philharmonic. The rest of the fest doesn't have all that much to write home about. With seemingly more panel discussions than actual films, the fest does a good job of seeking out the peculiar American indies (e.g., Sedat Pekay's *Walker Evans' America* and Dean Bivins's *The Electric Urn*) but seems to lean heavily on those that have some sort of name recognition, particularly in its star-powered screenplay reading series, for which the likes of John Heard and Angelica Torn turn out. Best of all, there's a drive-in night at the Roosevelt in Hyde Park. Films are screened at Vassar Brothers Institute in Poughkeepsie and at Upstate Films in quaint Rhinebeck (Sunday brunch, where is thy sting?). A recent tribute featured Andrew Bergman (*The In-Laws*, *Fletch*). Panel discussions over the years have featured the likes of Walter Bernstein, screenwriter Ron Nyswaner, and indie mogul John Pierson.

Films About six features plus shorts and a documentary

Noteworthy Celebrity Sightings Peter Falk, Beth Fargis-Lancaster, others too numerous to mention

Tickets $8 for individual screenings; $70 film pass gains entry to all screenings plus opening-night festivities

How to Enter For more information contact:
Hudson Valley Film and Video Office
40 Garden Street
Poughkeepsie, NY 12601
Telephone 914.473.0318
Fax 914.473.0082
E-mail hyfo@vh.net
Web www2.sandbook.com/sandbook/hvfo/festival.html

Entry Deadline March

Human Rights Watch International Film Festival

Where New York, New York, and other locations

When Two weeks in mid-June

Background Founded in 1990 by the human rights organization from which it draws its name, the festival concentrates on "the power of film to communicate across borders, both physical and ideological, and tell some of the most important stories of our time." It goes on to say, "The issues tackled in these films are never distant or abstract. They probe experience on the human level, authentically personalizing epic social events. In witnessing for human rights, these films also testify for other, enduring expressions of what is human." Recent films have dealt with such issues as the relationship between blacks and Jews, the Vietnam War, Chechen resistance, pacifist tax resisters, and the California educational system. Among the more recent features: *Regret to Inform* and *The Terrorist*. Screenings are held at New York's Walter Reade Theater at Lincoln Center (165 W. 65th Street).

Major Award Winners Noncompetitive, but it does offer lifetime achievement awards (one recent one went to Alan J. Pakula) and the Nester Almendros Prize (given in 1997 to Ingrid Sinclair for the film *Flame*, concerning two women growing up in Rhodesia)

Films About 20

Noteworthy Celebrity Sightings Jonathan Demme, Costa Gavras, Ron Silver

Tickets $8 per screening. Ticket Hotline/Box Office: 212.875.5601 or 212.875.5645

Telephone 212.290.4700
Fax 212.736.1300
How to Enter Send a VHS dub and entry form to:
Human Rights Watch
485 Fifth Avenue
New York, NY 10017
Telephone 212.972.8400
Fax 212.972.0905
E-mail hrwnyc@hrw.org
Entry Deadline December

Humboldt International Film and Video Festival

Where Arcata, California
When First week in April
Background The oldest festival run by students, HIFVF, based at Humboldt State University and founded in 1967, showcases student and independent films under 60 minutes. The festival screens at the Minor Theater, which is reportedly the oldest operational movie theater in the United States.
How to Enter Send entry form and $20–$40 entry fee (depends on length) to:
HIFVF
Department of Film, Theatre and Dance
Humboldt State University
Arcata, CA 95521
Telephone 707.826.4113
Fax 707.826.4112
E-mail filmfest@axe.humboldt.edu
Web www.humboldt.edu/~filmfest
Entry Deadline February 25

Idyllwild International Film Festival

Where Idyllwild, California
When Four days in early October
Background Founded way back in 1997, the festival, held in the midst of national forest and state wilderness where one can go hiking, rock-climbing, and mountain-climbing, seeks to imitate the success of other resort fests such as Telluride. Spectators are invited to explore Lake Fulmor, Lake Hemet, and Strawberry Creek while savoring the pleasures of independent American cinema.
Films About 30 features.
How to Enter Send entry form and VHS dub to:
Idyllwild Film Institute
P.O. Box 3319
Idyllwild, CA 92549
Telephone 909.659.7733
Fax 909.659.7735
Web www.filmcafe.com
Entry Deadline September

Indiana Film and Video Festival

Where Indianapolis, Indiana
When One weekend in July
Background Founded in 1989 by the Indiana Film Society, the festival showcases the works of filmmakers from Indiana and neighboring states Illinois, Kentucky, Ohio, and Michigan. "Midwestern artists bring a distinctive heritage and perspective to film and video," the folks over there tell us. Recent screenings have included *Marion*, a documentary about the lynching of two black men in the 1930s, and Jensen Rufe's intriguingly named *In Search of the Famous Hoosier Breaded Tenderloin*. Awards are offered in: Fiction, Documentary, Experimental, Music Video, and Animation, and winners in professional, amateur, and student categories vie for $8,000 in prizes. Screenings are held at the Jewish Community Center (6701 Hoover Road).
Tickets $10 per screening
How to Enter For more information contact:
　　Indiana Film Society
　　c/o Indianapolis Art Center
　　820 E. 67th Street
　　Indianapolis, IN 46220
　　Telephone 317.299.1800
Entry Deadline June

Insect Fear Film Festival

Where Champaign-Urbana, Illinois
When One weekend in August
Background "Yech" is about the best word to describe this festival. Well, yech to me, but probably not yech to the budding entomologist that crawls beneath all of us (or at least some of us). I normally resist quoting from press releases, but here it's impossible: "Each year more than 300 people of all ages gather in room 228 Natural History Building on the University of Illinois Urbana-Champaign campus to eat insect treats (chocolate-covered crickets—yum), play with live insects (the Madagascar hissing roaches are always a favorite), and watch really bad horror movies that feature insect monsters (for example, *Them* and *Mothra*). Yes, it's the annual Insect Fear Film Festival, a celebration of giant rubber bugs, low-production budgets, and an underhanded attempt to educate nonentomologists about the joys of insects. Now in its 12th year, the Insect Fear Film Festival was started in 1983 by entomology professor Dr. May Berenbaum and is organized yearly by a selfless band of entomology graduate students. Dr. Berenbaum introduces each film and points out the facts (rare) and fiction (abundant) about insects in each movie and explains such things as why Jeff Goldblum as *The Fly* couldn't walk on the ceiling (he's way too big) and what's wrong with the *Mantid's* attack style (mantises are quiet; this one sounds like a B-2 bomber). The recent Best of the Fest featured two mosquito movies: *Popcorn* and *Yellow Jack*." Sound like your scene? Go for it.
Tickets Free
How to Enter For more information contact:
　　University of Illinois
　　Department of Entomology

320 Morrill Hall
Urbana, IL 61801
Telephone 217.333.2910
Fax 217.244.3499
E-mail cerg0661@uxa.cso.uiuc.edu or d-lampe@uiuc.edu

Inside/OUT Lesbian and Gay Film and Video Festival of Toronto

Where Toronto, Ontario, Canada
When Ten days in late May
Background Screening at the Famous Players Paramount multiplex, the focus here is on Canadian gay cinema, although there are a number of major international features as well. The Australian documentary *Shinjuku Boys* has premiered here, as has *Love! Valour! Compassion!*, Susan Streitfeld's *Female Perversions,* and Midi Onodera's *kin Deep.* Local videomaker Steve Reinke has also enjoyed a retrospective of his work. Sometimes, though, the most eye-catching elements of the festival are the seminars, such as a recent one that discussed homosexual subtext in Yiddish film. The festival was founded in 1991. About 10,000 attend annually. Screenings are held at Cumberland Cinemas.
Major Award Winners Best Upcoming Film or Videomaker: Amy Gottlieb, *In Living Memory*; Best Canadian Film or Video: *Heaven or Montreal*, by Dennis Day; Audience Choice Award: *Watermelon Woman*, by Cheryl Dunye
Films About 170 features, shorts, and videos
Noteworthy Celebrity Sightings Arthur Dong, Kelli Herd
Tickets $8 per individual screening; ticket hotline: 416.925.XTRA
How to Enter For more information contact:
Inside/OUT Lesbian and Gay Film and Video Festival
401 Richmond Street W, Suite 216
Toronto, ON M5V 1X3
Canada
Telephone 416.977.6847
Fax 416.977.8025
Entry Deadline January

International Festival of Films on Art

Where Montreal, Quebec, Canada
When Second week of March
Background Founded in 1981, the festival takes a broad view of the word "art," comprising films that deal in painting, sculpture, architecture, design, crafts, fashion, decorative arts, museology, restoration, photography, literature, dance, music, theatre, and the art of cinema. Films are screened in six categories: Trajectories (a noncompetitive showcase of current films on art), Focus (a tribute to a particular artist), Reflections (a series of films created by rather than about, artists), Artificial Paradise (works related to cinema as an art form), Time Recaptured (commemorations and archival films), and the competition. Recent films have been shown

dealing with subjects as diverse as Bruce Nauman, Frantz Fanon, Bill Evans, Edward Steichen, I. M. Pei, and Henri Cartier-Bresson. Awards are for creativity, best portrait, best essay, best made-for-TV film, best media work, and best educational film. This is one of the most idiosyncratic and intelligently programmed North American festivals.

Major Award Winners *La Voix d'un Traducteur*, by Anne-Marie Rocher, and *Gabrielle Roy*, by the very talented Lea Pool

Films Approximately 160 features and shorts

Noteworthy Celebrity Sightings Nigel Finch

How to Enter Send $35 entry fee, rather demanding entry form, and documentation to:
International Festival of Films on Art
640 Saint-Paul Street W, Suite 406
Montreal, PQ H3C 1L9
Canada

Entry Deadline October

Internet Festival of Crud

Where Kent, Ohio
When One night in mid-April
Background "Making a 16 mm film is great, but who has the money?" So ask the organizers of the Crud festival, which solicits videos and "lowbrow" shorts for a 2½-hour annual screening at Kent State University. The annual budget for the fest runs about five bucks. As they say, "Punk and stupid is the key." All schlock is accepted, but anything with a UFO theme is especially sought. The festival is also known as the Punk Festival of Crud, and about 100 people attend. Wow!

Major Award Winners Noncompetitive, although entries accepted will be shown in Kent coffeehouses and punk bars and sold on a compilation videotape

Noteworthy Celebrity Sightings None

How to Enter Send VHS dub to:
Festival of Crud
MCS Building
Kent State University
Kent, OH 44242
Telephone 216.672.4004, ext. 491
E-mail dulm@mcs.kent.edu

Entry Deadline May

Iowa Independent Film and Video Festival

On hiatus

Israel Film Festival

Where New York, New York; Los Angeles, California; Miami, Florida; and Chicago, Illinois

When Early March in New York; early April in Los Angeles; early February in Miami; late April in Chicago

Background Founded in 1984, Israfest provides the viewer with a smattering of films highlighting the contemporary state of the Israeli film industry. The festival screens features, documentaries, TV dramas, and shorts. Among recent screenings, the festival has featured *Jewish Vendetta*, by Alexander Shatayev, and Avraham Heffner's *Laura Adler's Last Love Affair*.

Films About 30 films in a variety of categories

Noteworthy Celebrity Sightings Shimon Peres, Mia Farrow

Tickets $8.50 per individual screening; $35 for five films

How to Enter For more information contact:

Israfest Foundation Inc.
6404 Wilshire Boulevard, Suite 870
Los Angeles, CA 90048
Telephone 213.966.4166
Fax 213.658.6346
E-mail israelfest@earthlink.net
Web www.israelfilmfestival.com

Jackson Hole Wildlife Film Festival

Where Jackson Hole, Wyoming

When One week in late September in odd-numbered years

Background Established in 1991 and held in odd-numbered years, this is as much an industry seminar and get-together as it is a traditional film festival. Holding seminars on the future of television and the potential uses of HDTV as well as casual outdoor barbecues, the festival screens and offers awards for nature programming. A highlight is the National Geographic party. About 800 attend annually.

Major Award Winners Grand Teton Award: *Life in the Freezer: The Big Freeze*, BBC/National Geographic Television; Award for Innovation: *The Private Life of Plants*, BBC; Most Resourceful Film: *Fanamby, Conservation International*

How to Enter Send $75 entry fee, synopsis, VHS dub, and entry form to:

Jackson Hole Film Festival
P.O. Box AD
125 E. Pearl Street
Jackson Hole, WY 83001
Telephone/Fax 307.733.7376
E-mail jhfilmfestival@wyoming.com

Entry Deadline May

Kudzu Film Festival

Where Athens, Georgia

When Mid-October

Background A nifty, pretty new festival that looks to have a lot going for it. Screens a lot of more out-of-the-way indies such as Darren Stein's *Sparkler* and Myra Paci's

"*Girls Night Out.*" Has a strong local connection, trying to nurture the talent of a lot of filmmakers from the Southeast (R.E.M. even came on as a sponsor recently). Screenings are held at the historic Morton Theatre.

Award Winners Best feature: *The Eden Myth*, by Mark Edlitz; Best Short: *12 Stops on the Road to Nowhere*, by Jay Lowi; Best Animation: *Billy's Balloon*, by Don Hertzfeltdt; Audience Choice Award: *Man of the Century*, by Adam Abraham

How to Enter For more information contact:

    Prometheus X Productions
    P.O. Box 1861
    Athens, GA 30603
    Telephone 706.227.6090
    Fax 706.227.1083
    E-mail omni@prometheus-x.com
    Web www.prometheus-x.com

Entry Deadline August

Laguna Beach Film Festival

Where Laguna Beach, California

When Early October

Background A rather small festival screening at the Festival of Arts Forum Theater at the Festival of Arts (650 Laguna Canyon Road), the festival has offered premieres of *Lola and Bilidikid*, *Wrestling with Alligators,* and *Some Nudity Required*. The Laguna Festival has offered a number of seminars on everything from how to produce a short to how to distribute a horror film. The Festival offers one of the most conscientious when it comes to family values, even indicating which films have scenes of wine drinking and cigarette smoking for protective parents. Those who've attended have included Jon McIntyre, former road manager of the Grateful Dead. Hey man. Annual attendance is about 4,000.

Films About 12

Tickets $8 per screening; ticket info: 949.494.1313

How to Enter Send VHS dub, entry form, and fee ($20 for shorts, $35 for features) to:

    Laguna Beach Film Festival
    1235 N. Orange Grove, Suite 4
    Los Angeles, CA 90046
    Telephone 714.494.1313
    Fax 714.497.3568
    E-mail lainco@fia.net
    Web www.lagunafilmfestival.org

Entry Deadline March

Interview with

Paul Marchant

codirector, Kudzu Film Festival

CB How do you decide what to program?

PM We try for diversity. That's the most important thing. We know that not everyone is going to like every film we show, so if we program a wide variety, then everyone's going to like something. We look for the offbeat in terms of subject matter. They tend to be more from the U.S. We're not an independent festival, but we do look for an independent spirit. As long as it's good, we'll program it.

CB Do you go to a lot of festivals to find entries?

PM We have the Atlanta festival near here, but we have full-time jobs, so we're kind of tied down.

CB How do you screen all the entries? How many of them are you able to watch all the way through?

PM We have a selection committee of 11 people. They view them as a group and then vote by secret ballot. Most of the time they try to make it all of the way through the film.

CB Are there any films that you really regret programming?

PM We have a very short space to program; it's only a four-day event. We actually have a very good amount of films in our program.

CB Is there a film that you're really proud of having shown?

PM Last year we had the Grand Jury Winner, which was a film called *Brother Tied*, that was a highlight for everyone involved in the festival. Also last year *Sparkler* won the Audience Choice Award. This year we've got about two or three films that the audience will enjoy. Hopefully they'll enjoy.

CB Are there too many festivals going on right now? Do you have too much comepetition?

PM It actually very much determines what you program. I know that the Hamptons Festival and Austin are pretty close to us, but fortunately nobody has our exact dates. It is very hard to battle for the films sometimes.

CB Do you have any advice for filmmakers, such as something that would help them to get noticed by a festival?

PM Gotta grab you in the first 10 minutes. That's not to say we don't watch them all the way through. But especially with features, you've got to get them in the first 10 minutes. Each year we get films in a theme. Last year we had a lot of office comedies. This year we haven't seen a particular genre that came about. Little bits of dialogue here and there that connect.

CB Why did you start the festival?

PM Athens is known primarily for being a music town. We looked around the town and noticed that while there was a big film scene here, there was no showcase of films. The town itself dictated the need for it. We all love films. Got about 4,000 people last year with only 18 films. We have more shorts this year. We get funding from the city. We hope for a bigger audience this year.

CB The area needed a festival?

PM As far as Georgia was concerned, yes. Showing movies is really important for the American Southeast, especially for the indie market. Athens just opened an art house this year. That's been a long time in coming. The university programs good films. But there's never been an art house per se that catered to the college crowd.

CB What's the Kudzu film-viewing environment like?

PM We only screen at one venue, called the Morton Theatre; we couldn't conceive of a better venue to host a film. Built in 1910, burnt down in the 1950s, restored in the 1990s, full-on showcase. We have something kind of rare, in that the theater doesn't have a projector—we have to rent it.

CB Have you thought about expanding?

PM Four days is working for us right now. If we keep getting more submissions then maybe.

Lo-Con Short Film Festival

Where Beverly Hills, California
When Three days in late September
Background This festival of shorts screens in two rather self-explanatory categories: Under 15 Minutes and Between 15 and 30 Minutes. Among films that have screened here are *Uptown Dizzy* and Ari Gold's *Frog Crossing*.
How to Enter Send $10 entry fee and entry form to:
    lo-con.com
    289 S. Robertson Boulevard, Suite 250
    Beverly Hills, CA 90211
    Telephone 310.358.9962
    E-mail info@lo-con.com
Entry Deadline September 1

Long Island Film Festival

Where Stony Brook, New York
When Two weeks at the end of July and beginning of August
Background Held at the Staller Center at the University of Stony Brook on Long Island, the festival founded in 1984 by the Suffolk County Film Commission focuses on classic films as well as films by Long Island filmmakers. The festival has to be given credit for its prescience, highlighting the works of many then-unknown directors who went on to fame and sort-of fortune. These include Hal Hartley, Jim Jarmusch, Todd Haynes, and Bill Plympton, all of whom screened shorts here early in their careers. There are also seminars given by the likes of indie guru John Pierson and tributes that have included Lee Grant.
Films Thirty features and 30 shorts
Noteworthy Celebrity Sightings Brooke Smith, Lee Grant, John Pierson

Tickets Pass for all screenings, $40; call 516.632.7230
How to Enter For more information contact
　　　Long Island Film Festival
　　　P.O. Box 13243
　　　Hauppauge, NY 11788
　　　Telephone 800.762.4679 or 516.853.4800
　　　E-mail festival@lifilm.org
Entry Deadline June

Los Angeles Independent Film Festival

Where Los Angeles, California
When Five days in mid-April
Background Almost exclusively composed of American films making their L.A. pre-mieres, the festival, founded in 1995, has a pseudo-indie feel, screening the sorts of independents that feature William Hurt or Mary Stuart Masterson in key roles and Janet Jackson on the soundtrack. The festival also offers a series called *Actors Direct*, in which such screen gods as Sandra Bullock, Rob Lowe, and Richard Dreyfuss have premiered their work behind the camera. The festival screens at the Director's Guild (7920 Sunset Boulevard), Raleigh Studios (5300 Melrose Avenue), Paramount Studios (Studio Theatre), and the Martini Lounge (5857 Melrose Avenue). About 12,000 attend. The LAIFF also sponsors industry-related seminars covering such topics as "Working with Guilds and Unions on a Budget" and "40 Years of Indie Cinema" as well as parties sponsored by such movers and shakers as *Buzz* and *Details* magazine. Premieres have included George Hickenlooper's *The Big Brass Ring* and Philip Joanou's *Entropy*.
Films About 25 films and 35 shorts
Noteworthy Celebrity Sightings Gregory Hines, Gena Rowlands, Helen Hunt
Tickets $7.50 per individual screening; $185 Deluxe Founders Pass gains admit-tance to all screenings, parties, and gala events
How to Enter For more information contact:
　　　Los Angeles Independent Film Festival
　　　3580 Wilshire Boulevard, Suite 1660
　　　Los Angeles, CA 90010
　　　Telephone 323.937.9155
　　　Web www.laiff.com
Entry Deadline January

Making Scenes Gay and Lesbian Film Festival

Where Ottawa, Ontario, Canada
When Last week of April
Background Founded in 1982 as a strictly Canadian fest, the festival still focuses primarily on the works of Canadian filmmakers dealing with gay topics. Screening at the National Gallery of Canada in Ottawa, the festival has premiered such films as *Just a Little Crush*, *Boys in Love*, *Angels in the Dark*, and *Lesbian Tongues Untied*.
Films About 40 films

Tickets $8.50 per individual screenings; $65 fanatic pass gains admittance to all screenings and buys you a commemorative T-shirt
How to Enter Send VHS dub and entry form to:
Making Scenes
380 Sussex Drive
Ottawa, ON
Canada
Telephone 237.XTRA
E-mail scenes@fox.nstn.ca
Entry Deadline "Flexible"

Margaret Mead Film Festival

Where New York, New York
When One week in mid-November
Background Named for famed anthropologist Mead, who was an early user of film in her discipline and died in 1978, the festival takes special interest in screening "fake documentaries," as well as nonfiction anthropological and ethnographic films. Works that have screened here recently include *My Life as a Poster* and Peter Adair's *Holy Ghost People*.
Films About 10 films plus screenings of University of Southern California student films
How to Enter Send VHS dub and entry form to:
Margaret Mead Film and Video Festival
American Museum of Natural History
79th Street at Central Park West
New York, NY 10024
Telephone 212.769.5305
Fax 212.769.5329
E-mail meadfest@amnh.org
Web www.amnh.org/mead99
Entry Deadline May

Miami Film Festival

Where Miami, Florida
When First week of February
Background Founded in 1984 by the Florida Film Institute, the small but prestigious festival has paid particular attention to filmmakers of Hispanic heritage, having given Fernando Trueba's Academy Award–winning *Belle Époque* its U.S. premiere and showing virtually all the works of Pedro Almodóvar. There is a refreshing lack of pretension here—even the Q and A sessions, which get ponderous in most places, here are held outside in Bayfront Park, where filmmakers and audiences talk cinema while eating picnic lunches. All screenings are held in a restored movie palace, the Gusman Theatre for the Performing Arts in downtown Miami. More than 30,000 attend annually. Films that had their premieres here include Terry Gilliam's *Brazil* and the Coen Brothers' *Blood Simple*. (Blech. Yeah, I know everyone thinks they're brilliant, so I should probably shut up.)

Major Award Winners Noncompetitive
Films Approximately 25 films
Noteworthy Celebrity Sightings Abbas Kiarostami, Pedro Almodóvar, Atom Egoyan, Sylvester Stallone
Tickets Contact festival hotline: 305.377.FILM
How to Enter Send entry form, VHS copy, and entry fee to:
Miami International Film Festival
444 Brickell Avenue, Suite 229
Miami, FL 33131
Telephone 305.357.3456
Fax 305.577.9768
How to Enter November

Michigan Lesbian and Gay Film Festival

Where Madison Heights, Michigan
When One weekend in September
Background Founded in 1993 by South East Michigan Pride, the festival screens films annually for an audience of about 2,500 and bills itself as "the most exciting queer cinema weekend this side of Lake Michigan." Screenings are held at the AMC Abbey Theaters (Fourteen Mile Road and I-75) in Madison Heights. The Detroit area does not always get exposed to so-called queer cinema, and this is the best opportunity. Films that have premiered here include *Edge of Seventeen*, *The Jaundiced Eye*, *Bedrooms and Hallways*, Kelli Herd's *It's in the Water*, Ronnie Larsen's *Shooting Porn*, and Julia Dyer's *Late Bloomers*.
Major Award Winners Noncompetitive
Films Eight features and seven shorts
Noteworthy Celebrity Sightings Kelli Herd
Tickets $5–$7 per individual screening; $75 gains admission to all screenings
How to Enter Send VHS dub and entry form to:
Michigan Lesbian and Gay Film Festival
P.O. Box 1915
Royal Oak, MI 48068
Telephone 248.443.5029

Mill Valley Film Festival

Where Mill Valley, California
When One week in mid-October
Background Founded in 1978, MVFF is one of the more prestigious of the lower-profile U.S. film festivals, having premiered such films as *Shine*, *Bullets Over Broadway*, and *Salaam Bombay* and held tributes to many notable film directors including John Frankenheimer and Peter Weir. Screenings are held at the Sequoia Twin Theatres, a Masonic hall, and an outdoor art club in Mill Valley, as well as at art house cinema the Lark Theatre in Larkspur. The festival also hosts an interactive and new-media festival, which offers seminars and screenings of CD-ROMs and other examples of cutting-edge technology. Although the hundred films come from many places around the globe, more than 50 percent are American. There has

been a good collection of tributes (including one in 1999 to Gillian Armstrong) and revivals. Recent years have featured such revivals as *Seven Brides for Seven Brothers*, *Singin' in the Rain*, and the Jack Kerouac vehicle *Pull My Daisy*. A recent festival had two opening night films: *Ride With the Devil* and *Mansfield Park*.

Major Award Winners Noncompetitive

Films About 100 films from around the globe

Noteworthy Celebrity Sightings Alan Arkin, Amanda Plummer, Robert Altman, Jeanne Moreau, Hot Tuna

Tickets A Fast Pass that allows admittance to all films, videos, and programs costs only a cool $2,500. Those not quite as well-heeled may purchase individual tickets that vary in price from show to show; festival hotline: 415.380.0888

How to Enter Send $20 entry fee plus entry form to:
    Film Institute of Northern California
    38 Miller Avenue, Suite 6
    Mill Valley, CA 94941
    Telephone 425.385.5256
    Fax 415.383.8606
    E-mail finc@well.com
    Web Site www.finc.org or www.well.com/user/finc

Entry Deadline May

Milwaukee Gay and Lesbian Film Festival

Where Milwaukee, Wisconsin

When Two weekends in October

Background Though the Milwaukee fest was founded in 1988, its organizers tell us that its history is shrouded in mystery. There isn't anything particularly mysterious about the festival right now, though, although it does have its cool and idiosyncratic aspects. Coordinated by Great Lakes Film and Video and the University of Milwaukee Film Department, the festival screens films mainly at UWM's Union Hall but also has an outdoor experimental section as well, screening in the cold October air at a riverfront park.

Major Award Winners Noncompetitive, but votes for an audience choice award; Audience Choice Winner: *Hustler White*, by Bruce LaBruce

Films About 15

Noteworthy Celebrity Sightings Su Friedrich, Barbara Hammer, Bruce LaBruce ("We Love Bruce!" the festival's organizers tell us)

Minneapolis/St. Paul International Film Festival

Where Minneapolis, Minnesota

When Two weeks in mid-April

Background Founded in 1983 by the University of Minnesota Film Society, the festival still boasts an intellectual feel along with its stunningly diverse collection of films. The festival director even likes to throw around words like "Kierkegaard" while discussing a festival that has recently shown everything from Jean-Luc Godard's *For Ever Mozart* to Steven Soderbergh's *Gray's Anatomy*. The festival screens films in six locations, including the Historic State Theatre on Hennepin

Avenue, and offers an emerging filmmakers' competition in the categories of documentary short, narrative short, and feature film sponsored by Eastman Kodak Company. It also offers a Minnesota Spirit award for Minnesota-based or -oriented filmmakers. The fest offers an excellent selection of local, U.S., and world premieres, which stay away from the more predictable major "independent" studio releases and concentrate on the offbeat, the unusual, and the unsung. I didn't choose this for the Best of the Fests section, but it would be my first runner-up.

Major Award Winners Emerging Filmmaker Award ($500): George Ungar, *Champagne Safari*

Films About 120 features plus shorts programs

Tickets $6 per film; $100 for Gold Pass good for all screenings; festival hotline: 612.627.4430

How to Enter Send VHS dub and entry form to:
Minneapolis/St. Paul International Film Festival
2331 University Avenue SE, Suite 130B
Minneapolis, MN 55414-3067
Telephone 612.627.4431
Fax 612.627.4111
E-mail Fimsoc@gold.tc.umn.edu

Entry Deadline February

Montana Five Rivers Festival of Film

Where Missoula, Montana

When Late April and early May

Background One of the newer festivals in the United States (the first annual was held in 1998), this is not a showcase of new films, but rather a showcase of behind-the-scenes talent. The festival—founded by a University of Montana graduate and a former administrative director at Sundance and named for the Jocko, Blackfoot, Lochsa, Bitterroot, and Clark Fork rivers—is devoted to highlighting the contributions of such unsung cinematic heroes as gaffers and cinematographers. Among the works shown at the festival have been Gus Van Sant's *To Die For* and Wim Wenders's *Paris, Texas*.

Major Award Winners Noncompetitive

How to Enter Not applicable for new filmmakers. For more information contact:
Five Rivers Festival of Film
P.O. Box 1300
Missoula, MT 59806

Entry Deadline Not applicable

Montreal/New York International Nouveau Festival

Where Montreal, Quebec, Canada; New York, New York; and Juan-les-Pins, France

When Montreal: 10 days in early June; New York: one week in mid-June; Juan-les-Pins: one week in early July

Background Taking place in three separate cities, the festival is most impressive in Montreal, where it occupies five indoor and three outdoor screens. Recent tributes have featured the works of Gerard Philipe and Marguerite Duras and a festival of

Samuel Beckett films. The documentary *The Gate of Heavenly Peace* premiered here. Recent premiere screenings have also included *I Was a Jewish Sex Worker* and *Pushing Daisy*.

Major Award Winners Le Loupe D'Or for Best Film ($4,200): *En Avoir ou Pas*, by Laetitia Masson

How to Enter Send VHS dub and entry form to:
Festival du Nouveau Cinema de Montreal
3726, Boulevard St.-Laurent
Montreal, PQ H2X 2V8
Canada
Telephone 514.843.4725
Fax 514.843.4631
E-mail nouveaufestival@spherenet.com

Entry Deadline April

Montreal World Film Festival

See Best of the Fests

Mountainfilm in Telluride

Where Telluride, Colorado

When Three days in late May

Background Known to area residents as "Telluride's other film festival," this one speaks more to the town's previous history as a skiing and adventure capital where the San Juan mountain peaks reach 13,000 feet in the sky than a place to catch a glimpse of Nicolas Cage. Films screened at the Sheridan Opera House and the Nugget Theatre are new and relatively recent, dealing with mountains and mountaineering; adventure; Alpine people and culture; environmental preservation, protection, and education; and exploration of wild and remote locales. Recent titles have included *Fire on the Mountain*, *Cry of the Forgotten Land*, and *A Glorious Way to Die*. There is also a special program of children's cinema. For those who have grown tired of the movies, there are of course country trails, waterfalls, picnics, and outdoor seminars. Oh, and some skiing too.

Noteworthy Celebrity Sightings Hardly celebrities in the Hollywood or Cannes sense, nevertheless there are a great deal of folks who are well-known to the mountain-climbing world, including Greg Child, Bruno Engler, Alf Engen, and Maurice Herzog, the Frenchman who was the first to scale an 8,000-meter peak. Ken Burns also popped by recently.

Films About 50 films

Tickets $100 Sunshine pass includes admission to all films, seminars, and special events

Festival hotline 800.525.3455

How to Enter Send entry fee ($40), entry form, and VHS dub to:
Mountainfilm
Box 1088
300 S. Pine
Telluride, CO 81435

E-mail info@mountainfilm.org
Web www.mountainfilm.org.
Entry Deadline March

Movies on a Shoestring

Where Rochester, New York
When Four days in mid-May
Background According to the festival's organizers, it all started with a pun, taking its name from the by-now obsolete nickname of "shoestring gauge" given to 8 mm film. Founded in the late1950s and originally held at the Rochester Public Library, the aptly named festival is devoted solely to films under 40 minutes in length. This is also the only festival that takes the time and bother to give detailed critiques of all films entered (a lot claim they do that but rarely do). Films chosen for the festival receive a Shoestring Trophy, and as an added bonus, filmmakers who actually bother to show up to the fest get free T-shirts. Screenings are held at the Dryden Theatre of the International Museum of Photography at the George Eastman House in Rochester. About 2,000 attend annually.
Films About 40
Tickets Free, though donations are requested
How to Enter Send entry fee ($20) and VHS dub to:
    Movies on a Shoestring
    P.O. Box 17746
    Rochester, NY 14617
    Telephone 716.271.2116
    Fax 716.473.4490
    E-mail moas@juno.com or pdoering@frontier.net
    Web www.frontiernet.net/~pdoering/5MOAS/MOAS.html
Entry Deadline February

Moving Pictures Film Festival

Where Various spots in Canada
When Late February to mid-May, depending on location
Background Also known (quite rightly) as the Traveling Canadian Film Festival, the organizers of Moving Pictures declare only to have "high hopes, a few uncertainties, a borrowed van, a full tank of gas, and some great movies in tow" as they tour Canada screening such films as *Kissed* and *The Sweet Hereafter* where they may. The festival is dedicated to showcasing the works of Canadian filmmakers and has shown some excellent ones, including *Dance Me Outside* and *Margaret's Museum*. It has succeeded in gaining screenings in Nanaimo, Kamloops, Nelson, and Kelowna. Films are screened in Nanaimo's The Bay Theatre, Kamloops's The Northills Theatre, Nelson's Civic Theatre, and Kelowna's The Uptown Theatre.
Films About nine features
Noteworthy Celebrity Sightings Bruce Macdonald
Tickets. $6.50 for admission to individual screening; $15 for a three-film pass; $25 for a six-film pass; $35.00 for a festival pass to all nine films
How to Enter Send VHS dub and entry form to:

Moving Pictures Film Festival
1008 Homer Street, Suite 410
Vancouver, BC V6B 2X1
Canada
Telephone 604.685.8952
Fax 604.688.8221
Web www.multimedia.edu/~movepic/index.htm
Entry Deadline Not applicable

Nantucket Film Festival

Where Nantucket Island, Massachusetts
When One week in mid-June
Background Something of Kennedy family money and Sundance schmoozing oozes out of this new East Coast festival (founded in 1996) that hosts a screenwriting competition, Q and A sessions with filmmakers, and screenings of short and feature-length films in this resort town. Staged readings of screenplays by the likes of Mary Stuart Masterson and Craig Lucas (*Prelude to a Kiss*) have also provided part of the entertainment. Films screened here have included *Next Stop Wonderland*, Nicole Holofcener's *Walking and Talking*, the Brothers Quay's *Are We Still Married?*, and Christopher Munch's very pretty *The Color of a Brisk* and *Leaping Day*. Seminars include one in which low-budget filmmakers are matched with investors. And lest we forget, the festival reminds us that it is "Where Screenwriters Inherit the Earth."
Major Award Winners Screenwriting winner: Michael Almereyda, *Fever*
Films About 40 films
Noteworthy Celebrity Sightings Greg Mottola, R. J. Cutler, Rob Morrow, Winona Ryder
How to Enter For more information contact:
Nantucket Film Festival
P.O. Box 688 Prince Street Station
New York, NY 10012-0012
E-mail info@ackfest.org
Entry Deadline April

Nashville Independent Film Festival

Where Nashville, Tennessee
When One week in early June
Background Founded in 1969 and now held on the campus of Vanderbilt University, this festival's emphasis is on young filmmakers, though not necessarily students. An interesting mix of indies (*Decline of Western Civilization, Part III*, the premiere of *Desert Blue*, and a documentary on John Waters) are screened at Regal Cinemas' Green Hill Commons. About 7,000 attended the most recent fest, which featured such Nashville-produced films as *Existo* and *Films That Suck*.
Films About 180 films and videos
How to Enter Send VHS dub, entry forms, and entry fee ($35 for shorts, $50 for features) to:
Nashville Independent Film Festival
Attn: Michael Catalano

P.O. Box 24330
Nashville, TN 37202-4330
Telephone 6105.742.2500
Fax 615.742.1004
E-mail niffilm@bellsouth.net
Web www.nashvillefilmfest.org
Entry Deadline December

Native American Film and Video Festival

Where New York, New York
When One week in mid-April
Background Showcasing films about and by Native Americans, the festival is presented by the Film and Video Center of the National Museum of the American Indian in Harlem. Categories of films screened include Amazon Now; Hollywood Views; and new films, videos, and made-for-TV projects.
Films About 30
How to Enter Send VHS dub and entry form to:
Native American Film and Video Festival
Film and Video Center of the Museum of the American Indian
Broadway at 155th Street
New York, NY 10032
Telephone 212.283.2420
Fax 212.491.9302
Entry Deadline March

Newark Black Film Festival

Where Newark, New Jersey
When Summer
Background Founded in 1974, this small festival sponsored by Mobil Oil screens a small number of films at the Newark Museum (49 Washington Street), the Newark Public Library Auditorium (5 Washington Street), New Jersey Institute of Technology (99 Summit Street), Newark Symphony Hall (1020 Broad Street), and Hopewell Baptist Church (785 Dr. Martin Luther King Jr. Boulevard). Except for the winners of the annual Paul Robeson awards, the films here are rather of the mainstream variety and have included Spike Lee's *Get on the Bus*, Leon Gast's *When We Were Kings*, and Charles Burnett's *Nightjohn*, with special attention paid to films appropriate for children.
Major Award Winners Paul Robeson Award winners: Short Narrative: *Morningside Prep*, by Malcolm Lee; Feature Film: *The Keeper*, by Joe Brewster
Films About 10
Tickets Free
How to Enter Send entry fee ($25) and VHS dub to:
Newark Black Film Festival
Newark Museum
49 Washington Street
Newark, NJ 07101-0540

Telephone 201.596.6550
Fax 201.642.0549
Entry Deadline April

New Directors/New Films

Where New York, New York
When Three weeks in late March and early April
Background Founded in 1972 by the Film Society of Lincoln Center and the Museum of Modern Art, this film series at MOMA has long had the reputation of screening the cream of the crop of new works. Directors Alain Tanner, Wim Wenders, Atom Egoyan, and Steven Spielberg were first introduced to the American public here. More recent offerings have included Darren Aronofsky's π and David Williams' *Thirteen*.
Films 22 features
How to Enter For more information contact:
New Directors/New Films
Film Society of Lincoln Center
70 Lincoln Center Plaza
New York, NY 10023
Telephone 212.875.5638
Fax 212.875.5636
E-mail sbensman@filmlinc.com
Web www.filmlinc.com
Entry Deadline Ongoing

New England Film and Video Festival

Where Boston, Massachusetts
When Late March
Background Founded in 1975, this festival spotlights independent filmmakers in a variety of categories (see below). About 2,500 attend annually.
Major Award Winners Special Jury Award: *The Apple is Delicious*, by George Reyes; Best Animation: *Between the Lines*, by Benjamin Maxfield; Spirit of New England Award: *The Farmer's Wife*, by David Sutherland
Films 18 features
How to Enter Send VHS dub and entry form to:
New England Film and Video Festival
1126 Boylston Street #201
Boston, MA 02215
Telephone 617.536.1540
Fax 617.536.3576
E-mail bfvf@aol.com
Web www.newenglandfilm.com/festival/2000/entry.htm
Entry Deadline Not available

New Jersey International Film Festival

Where New Brunswick, New Jersey
When May through July
Background Though New Yorkers might scoff at the idea of New Jersey having the chutzpah to hold its own festival, this small festival with its sporadic screenings has nevertheless brought films from India, Vietnam, Europe, and Australia to the state, along with programs of independent American and specifically New Jersey filmmakers. Most of the films shown are those that have already done the bigger U.S. festivals (*Irma Vep*, *Female Perversions*, *When We Were Kings*). Nevertheless, it's a promising start, and in addition, the festival has presented a retrospective of the work of Kenneth Anger and more offbeat screenings, such as *Sick: The Life and Death of Bob Flanagan*, *Super Masochist* and *Twilight of the Ice Nymphs*.
Films About 40
Tickets $5 per individual screening
How to Enter For more information contact:
New Jersey Film Festival
c/o Rutgers Film Co-op/NJMAC
131 George Street
Rutgers University
New Brunswick, NJ 08901-1414
Telephone 732.932.8482
Fax 732.932.1935
E-mail njmac@aol.com
Telephone 908.932.8482
Web www.rci.rutgers.edu/nigrin
Entry Deadline Not available

New Orleans Film and Video Festival

Where New Orleans, Louisiana
When Ten days in mid-October
Background Founded in 1989 by the New Orleans Film and Video Society, the New Orleans fest bills itself as the independent's showcase, though a certain pecking order is established by screening Super-8, 16 mm, and low-budget 35 mm projects on a video projector in Cinema 16 (third floor of Southern Repertory Theater, 333 Canal Street), at Zeitgeist Theater Experiments (740 O'Keefe Street), and at Canal Place and larger-budget feature-length films with distributors at the Big House (Canal Place Cinema, 333 Canal Street). So, while the Big House has premiered such films as *Reservoir Dogs*, Wes Craven's *New Nightmare*, *Shine*, *The Wild Bunch*, *Microcosmos*, *Twelfth Night*, *Down By Law*, *Living in Oblivion*, *Red Rock West*, and *It's All True*, Cinema 16 on the third floor shows the cooler and more adventurous flicks such as Matthew Harrison's *Rhythm Thief*, Damon Leary's *Cookiepuss Rex*, Alan Arkin's *Samuel Beckett is Coming Soon*, and *Women and Their Tattoos*. There is a good representation also of New Orleans filmmakers at Cinema 16. In conjunction with the festival, there is also an annual film and video congress featuring seminars on funding and distributing indie films. At about the same time every year, Tulane University sponsors a Latino Film Program (www.nettown.com/alpo/nofilm).

Major Award Winners Ruth's Chris Steak House Judges Award: *Confessions of a Sexist Pig* by Sandy Tung
Films About 120
Noteworthy Celebrity Sightings John Waters, Geoffrey Rush
Tickets $3 for Cinema 16 screenings; $6 for big-picture screenings
How to Enter Send VHS dub and entry form to:
New Orleans Film and Video Festival
225 Baronne, Suite 1712
New Orleans, LA 70112
Telephone 504.523.3828
Fax 504.529.2430
E-mail society@neworleansfilmfest.com
Web neworleansfilmfest.com
Entry Deadline July

Newport Beach International Film Festival

Where Newport Beach, California
When Ten days in early April
Background The folks at the Newport Beach fest boast that they are located in the third most densely populated area in the country—Orange County. Some advertisement. But if the nearly 3 million neighbors don't get you down completely, the modest but well-programmed fest should perk you up. Screenings are held at the Edwards Cinemas, the University of California-Irvine, and, best of all, the 450-seat Balboa Theatre, which hails from the 1930s. Founded in 1996, the festival has featured a retrospective of five decades of comedy including *The Palm Beach Story*, *The Producers*, and *This Is Spinal Tap*.
Major Award Winners Jury Award: *Vukovar Poste Restante*, by Boro Draskovic; Audience Award: *A Weekend in the Country*, by Martin Bergman; Maverick Award: Bill Carter, *Miss Sarajevo*; Best Short Film: *Yellow Lotus*, by Tony Bui
Films One hundred features, shorts, and documentaries
Noteworthy Celebrity Sightings Vlade Divac
Tickets $6 per individual screening; $375 for an all-access pass
How to Enter Send entry fee ($35 for features, $25 for shorts) to:
Newport Beach International Film Festival
4000 MacArthur Boulevard, Suite 3000
Newport Beach, CA 92660
Telephone 714.851.6555
Fax 714.851.6460
Entry Deadline January

New York Comedy Film Festival

Where New York
When Five days in late October
Background Kid's films, Q and A session with the creators of *South Park* and *Bean*, a tribute to Richard Pryor, and a night of stand-up and short films accompanied by music from Grandmaster Flash. It actually does have it all! Plus, the festival

donates a lot to charity. World premieres of under-the-radar films such as *The Deli, Flushed,* and *Good Money* (Jerry Seinfeld's only feature appearance).

Films Over 50

Noteworthy Celebrity Sightings Ben Stiller, Harry Shearer

How to Enter For more information contact:

New York Comedy Film Festival
110 W. 57th Street
New York, NY 10019
Telephone 212.343.8449
Fax 212.343.9557
E-mail nycff@nycff.org
Web www.nycff.org

Entry Deadline Not available

New York Expo of Short Film and Video and Interactive Multimedia

Where New York, New York

When One weekend in November

Background Billing itself as the longest-running festival of independent short film and video and having offered early exposure to such directors as Spike Lee, Martha Coolidge, and George Lucas, the festival screens 16 mm, 35 mm, and Super-8, as well as CD-ROMs and Websites. A recent curator's choice section featured Chuck Jones' *Duck Amuck*. Films are screened at the Tishman Auditorium of the New School (66 W. 12th Street), while multimedia winners are presented at Cyberfeld's Internet Cafe.

How to Enter Send VHS dub, filmmaker's bio (30 words max—wow!), synopsis of film (25 words max—double wow!), description of work (75 words max), entry form, and $35 entry fee to:

New York Expo and Video
532 La Guardia Place, Suite 330
New York, NY 10012
Telephone 212.505.7742
Fax 212.873.1353
E-mail rswbc@cunyvm.cuny.edu

Entry Deadline July

New York Film Festival

See Best of the Fests

New York Gay and Lesbian Experimental Film and Video Festival

Where New York, New York

When Ten days in mid-November

Background Held in conjunction with Mix Brasil (Festival das Manifesta oes da Sexualidae), this fest bills itself as the oldest of its type in New York City and screens films in everything from 35 mm to Super-8 to interactive digital technology. Recently the festival has featured the works of Jean Genet, Todd Haynes, and Chantal Akerman, screening at the NYU Cantor Film Center (36 E. Eighth Street), the Knitting Factory (74 Leonard Street), and the Victoria Theater (235 W. 25th Street).
Films Hundreds and hundreds of features and shorts
Tickets $7.50 per individual screening; $20 for three screenings
How to Enter Send VHS dub, entry form, and $10 entry fee to:
New York Gay and Lesbian Experimental Film and Video Festival
341 Lafayette Street #169
New York, NY 10012
Telephone 212.539.1023
Fax 212.501.2309
E-mail mix@echonyc.com
Web www.echonyc.com/mix
Entry Deadline August

New York Independent Feature Film Market

Where New York, New York
When One week in September
Background More a zoological event than a bona fide festival of films, this ridiculously enormous spectacle resembles a ladies' night in a Bourbon Street bar where desperate filmmakers try by any means necessary to attract the attention of distributors to their independent film. Founded in 1979 by the Independent Feature Project, this marketplace premieres hundreds of completed features and works in progress annually and turns Greenwich Village into its party central headquarters as film companies, festivals, distributors, and the like attend parties, lectures, seminars, and only God knows what else. It becomes nearly impossible to tell the poseurs from the genuine articles as men in Italian suits gather in nearby cafés to talk pictures, three-picture deals, and who's picking up the check. A word to the wise: the Sundance party is not worth the wait outside. You're better off walking a mile and getting a knish. No matter how nasty it may seem to your digestive system at the time, it's still somehow easier to swallow. Ahem.
Major Award Winners Noncompetitive
Films About 250 narrative features, documentaries, shorts, and works in progress
Noteworthy Celebrity Sightings Austin Pendleton
Tickets $100 for a daily entry pass to see more finished and unfinished independent films than you would need to in a decade
How to Enter Send VHS film copy and $300 entry fee to:
The Independent Feature Project
104 W. 29th Street
12th Floor
New York, NY 10001
Telephone 212.465.8525
Web www.ifp.org
Entry Deadline July

New York International Festival of Lesbian and Gay Film

Where New York, New York
When Ten days in mid-June
Background Screening at the Public Theater (425 Lafayette Street) and the New York Film Academy (100 Eighth Street), the festival offers a decent, mid-sized selection of new and classic gay cinema with some cleverly programmed series. Special features have included a retrospective of Su Friedrich's work and so-called queer animation. Panel discussions and lectures are held in conjunction with the fest and have included "The Other Dyke TV," "Gay and Lesbian Images in TV," and "Alternative Sexuality in Popular Indian Cinema."
Films About 75 features
Noteworthy Celebrity Sightings Sasha Torres
Tickets Contact Telecharge: 212.239.6200
How to Enter Send VHS dub and entry form to:
New York International Festival of Lesbian and Gay Film
80 Eighth Avenue
New York, NY 10011
Telephone 212.807.1820
Fax 212.807.9843
E-mail newfest@idt.net
Web www.newfestival.com

New York International Independent Film and Video Festival

Where New York, New York
When April
Background Sponsored by the International Talent Network, the festival showcases photographers, sculptors, artists, painters, and photographers along with filmmakers. The festival is open to features, shorts, animation, documentaries, and multimedia projects in all formats. A screenplay competition is also offered. Films are screened at Le Bar Bat (311 W. 57th Street), the Mark Goodson Theater (2 Columbus Circle), and the International Talent Network offices (873 Broadway, Room 303). Not as discriminating as many other festivals, this is still the only one I know that will call you three times to ask whether you're still thinking of entering your film after you have requested information about it ("Just letting you know we extended our deadline again . . . "). Nevertheless, a number of intriguing shorts and animated features turn up here. By title, my favorites have been Eric Rosner's animated short *The Adventures of Walter Bong* ("Indeed," the NYIIFVF tells us, "there is help out there for those who are in need of weed!"); *Desi Remix Chicago Style*, Balvinder Dhenjan's documentary about an Indian disc jockey in Chicago; and Joe Humeres's *Hairball or Puke*?
Films About 150 shorts, features, and documentaries
How to Enter Send entry fee ($55 under 30 minutes, $95 over 30 minutes) and form to:
NYIIFVF
175 Fifth Avenue, Suite 2334
New York, NY 10010

Telephone 212.777.7100
Web www.nyfilmvideo.com
Entry Deadline August

New York Underground Film and Video Festival

Where New York, New York
When One week in mid-March
Background Gritty and subversive, if sometimes just endorsing provocation for its own sake, the NYUFF plays host to underground pioneers on the order of Nick Zedd, Richard Kern, and Jim Sikora. The festival has recently screened *Surrender Dorothy*, *Chickenhawk: Men Who Love Boys*, Larry Turner's *Tattoo Boy*, and Jim Sikora's *Bullet on a Wire*. Screenings are held at the New York Film Academy (100 E. 17th Street).
Major Award Winners Best Feature: *Tattoo Boy*, by Larry Turner; Best Short: *Farley Mowat Ate My Brother*, by Ken Hegan; Best Documentary: *Not Bad for a Girl*, by Lisa Apramian; Festival Choice Award: *Middletown*, by Philip Botti
Films About 100 features and shorts
Tickets $6 per individual screening
How to Enter Send $30 entry fee, entry form, and VHS dub to:
New York Underground Film Festival
225 Lafayette Street, Suite 409
New York, NY 10012
Telephone 212.925.3440
Fax 212.925.3430
E-mail filmfest@bway.net
Web www.nyuff.com
Entry Deadline January

Northampton Film Festival

Where Northampton, Massachusetts
When First week of November
Background For those who thought New England was a tad provincial comes a festival that is open only to filmmakers who come from Delaware, Maine, Maryland, Massachusetts, Vermont, New Hampshire, New Jersey, New York, Pennsylvania, Rhode Island, or the District of Columbia. In recent years, the festival has offered a tribute to John Braderman, and recent seminars have covered such topics as film financing and the art of film criticism. Recent screenings have included *The Corndog Man*, *Billy's Balloon*, *The Silent Clowns* (featuring the Alloy Orchestra), *Ride With the Devil*, and others. Panels have featured Errol Morris and James Schamus.
Major Award Winners Advocate Newspaper Journalism Award: *Holding Ground: The Rebirth of Dudley Street*, by Leah Mahan and Mark Lipman; Kodak Vision Award: *Halving the Bones*, by Ruth Ozeki Lounsbury; Best of the Fest: *The Blinking Madonna and Other Miracles*, by Beth Harrington
Films About 45 films, mostly shorts
Noteworthy Celebrity Sightings James Schamus, Errol Morris, Douglas Trumbull, and Harvey Fierstein

How to Enter Send $25 entry fee, entry form, and VHS dub to:
Northampton Film Festival
351 Pleasant Street
P.O. Box 137
Northampton, MA 01060
Telephone 413.585.3471
E-mail filmfest@nohofilm.org
Web www.nohofilm.org
Entry Deadline June

Northwest Documentary Film Festival

Where Seattle, Washington
When Three days in early November
Background Screening at the Rose Theater in the Seattle Art Museum, the festival offers a good selection of documentaries with an accent on filmmakers from the northwest United States.
Major Award Winners Best of Fest: *Tell the Truth and Run: George Seldes and the American Press*, by Rick Goldsmith
Noteworthy Celebrity Sightings Fred Marx, Terry Zwigoff, Ross McElwee, Ed Asner
Films Fifteen features, 10 shorts
How to Enter Send VHS dub, entry form, and $10 to:
Washington Commission for the Humanities
615 Second Avenue, Suite 300
Telephone 206.682.1770
Fax 206.682.4158
E-mail wch@humanities.org
Entry Deadline None provided

Northwest Film and Video Festival

Where Portland, Oregon
When Ten days in early November
Background Founded in 1974, the festival screens films made by residents of Alaska, British Columbia, Idaho, Montana, Oregon, and Washington and sponsors a Best of the Northwest touring cinema program for films chosen. A recent fest had Portland native Matt Groening selecting five films for special mention.
Films About 40 films
How to Enter Send VHS dub and $15 entry fee to:
Northwest Film and Video Festival
Northwest Film Center of the Portland Art Museum
1219 S.W. Park Avenue
Portland, OR 97205
Telephone 503.221.1156
Fax 503.294.0874
E-mail info@nwfilm.org
Web www.nwfilm.org
Entry Deadline August

Oakland Black Filmworks Festival of Film and Video

Where Oakland, California
When One week in September
Background Aside from showing films and videos concerning the black American experience, the festival also sponsors an international black independent film, video, and screenplay competition.
Major Award Winners Best Film ($1,000): *One Red Rose*, by Charlie Jordan and Michelle Barnwell
How to Enter Send VHS dub and entry form to:
    Oakland Black Filmworks Festival of Film and Video
    Black Filmmakers Hall of Fame
    P.O. Box 28055
    Oakland, CA 94604
    Telephone 510.465.0804
    Fax 510.839.9858
    E-mail bfhfi@aol.com
Entry Deadline June

Ohio Independent Film Festival

Where Cleveland, Ohio
When Six days in early November
Background A truly indie festival that focuses on little-seen domestic flicks such as *Punk: The Robert Young Story* and *Suicide, the Comedy*. Focuses on screenplays and acting, with workshops and readings.
Major Award Winners Best Screenplay Award: Chesley Chen, *Under the Coca-Cola Sign*
Tickets $5 for individual screening, $40 fest pass
How to Enter For more information contact:
    Ohio Independent Film Festival
    2258 W. 10th Street #5
    Cleveland, OH 44113
    Telephone 216.781.1755
    E-mail OhioIndieFilmFest@juno.com
    Web www.ohiofilms.com
Entry Deadline August

Olympia Film Festival

Where Olympia, Washington
When Ten days in mid-to-late October
Background Screening at the 1924 Capitol Theater, where many a Marx Brothers and Tom Mix film was seen way back in the day, the festival, founded in 1984, offers an interesting selection of old classics and new soon-to-be classics. Recent premieres have included Raul Ruiz's *3 Lives and Only One Death* as well as experimental films and videos by Northwest filmmakers. On the less serious side are the recent series of 3-D flicks including *Creature of the Black Lagoon* and a series of

midnight films including *Midnight Confidential*. The classic silent *Pandora's Box* was screened here with accompaniment by the Olympia Chamber Orchestra. One of the early highlights of the festival was the screening of the Talking Heads concert film *Stop Making Sense*, which was so well received that the last two reels were screened again after the end of the film. Recent features have included *Sprocket Ensemble, Amerikan Passport*, and *The Fourth*.

Films About 40 features

Noteworthy Celebrity Sightings Alison Anders, Crispin Glover, Russ Meyer, Lydia Lunch

Tickets $6 per screening; $50 buys admission to all screenings

How to Enter Send VHS dub, entry form, and fee (cost to be determined/most of the films in this festival are invited) to:

Olympia Film Festival
416 Washington Street SE, Suite 208
Olympia, WA 98501
Telephone 360.754.6670
Fax 360.943.9100
E-mail ofs@olywa.net
Web www.olywa.net/ofs/home.html

Entry Deadline August

Ottawa International Animation Festival

Where Ottawa, Ontario, Canada

When First week of October

Background Takes its animation seriously, even holding a workshop recently titled "Duck vs. Duck: A Study of Donald and Daffy." Founded in 1976 as the Canadian International Animation Festival, this is the world's second-largest animation festival next to Annecy. Recent retrospectives have included the work of Raymond Krumme, Israeli animation, and Warner Brothers and Disney cartoons. The festival also holds an animators' picnic and a de rigueur Great Pumpkin Carving Contest.

Major Award Winners Best Film Under 10 Minutes: *Joe's Apartment: Funky Towel*, by Chris Wedge; Best Film Between 10 and 30 Minutes: *The End of the World in Four Seasons*, by Paul Driessen; Best First Film: *The Saint Inspector*, by Mike Booth; Best Film: *Bird in the Window*, by Igor Kolyakou; Grand Prize: *The Wrong Trousers*, by Nick Park

Films About 125 films

Noteworthy Celebrity Sightings Pritt Parn

How to Enter Send VHS dub and entry form to:

Ottawa International Animation Festival
2 Daley Avenue, Suite 140
Ottawa, ON K1N 6R2
Canada
Telephone 613.232.8769
Fax 613.232.6315
E-mail aj899@freenet.carleton.

Entry Deadline July

Outfest: Los Angeles Gay and Lesbian Festival

Where Los Angeles, California
When Ten days in mid-July
Background Founded in 1982, it began in UCLA as the Gay and Lesbian Media Festival and Conference and has grown into Outfest, screening films at Directors' Guild of America, the Harmony Gold (350-seat house), and the Laemmle Sunset 5, a multiplex. Outfest shows mostly new films, but its best feature so far has been a show called "Guilty Pleasures," in which a celebrity chooses his or her guiltiest pleasure films. Clive Barker chose *Cleopatra*. Chastity Bono chose *Personal Best*. Julie Newmar chose *Some Like It Hot*. And best of all, Phranc chose the Dr. Seuss classic *The 5,000 Fingers of Doctor T*. A recent lifetime achievement award was given to John Schlesinger. Recent screenings have included *Valley of the Dolls*, *A Luv Tale*, and *Battle for the Tiara*.
Major Award Winners Grand Prize Documentary ($2,000): *Hide and Seek*, by Su Friedrich; Grand Prize Feature ($2,000): *Lilies*, by John Greyson; Audience Choice Outies, Narrative Feature ($500): *Fire*, by Deepa Mehta, and *Broadway Damage*, by Victor Mignatti; Audience Choice Outie, Best Documentary: *You Don't Know Dick*, by Candace Schermerhorn
Films 200 films and videos
Noteworthy Celebrity Sightings Julie Newmar, Clive Barker, Chastity Bono
Tickets $7 for matinees; $10 for evening screenings; $500 for out-passes for all screenings
How to Enter Send VHS dub, entry fee ($10 for shorts, $15 for under 30 minutes, or $20 for over 60 minutes), and entry form to:

> Outfest
> 8455 Beverly Boulevard, Suite 309
> Los Angeles, CA 90048
> Telephone 213.951.1247
> Fax 213.951.0721

Entry Deadline March

Palm Beach International Film Festival

Where Palm Beach, Florida
When One week in February
Background In an area that's known more for its shopping and resorts than its taste in cinema, this festival still manages to put on a fairly good mid-sized selection of European and American independent features. Despite the festival's proximity to Burt Reynolds, PBIFF has premiered Peter Gothar's *Vaska Easoff* and Jack Green's *Traveller*. More recent premieres have included Errol Morris' *Fast, Cheap, and Out of Control*. Tribute series have included Alfred Hitchcock and Anouk Aimée. And, as the festival is in Palm Beach, try not to miss out on the party at the Palm Beach Hilton and the black tie gala celebrations, unless, of course, you don't feel like going.
Films About 55 features plus shorts programs
Notable Celebrity Sightings Tommy Lee Jones, Anouk Aimée, William Friedkin
Tickets Contact ticket hotline: 561.626.1345
How to Enter Send VHS dub and entry form to:

Palm Beach International Film Festival
7108 Fairway Drive, Suite 235
Palm Beach Gardens, FL 33418
Telephone 561.626.1345
Fax 561.691.0335
Web www.pbfilmfest.org
Entry Deadline March

Palm Springs International Film Festival

Where Palm Springs, California
When Nearly three weeks in January
Background One of the larger West Coast festivals around, PSIFF has premiered such works as *Out of the Present* and *Eight Days a Week*. Lifetime achievement awards have gone to Richard Dreyfuss, Lauren Bacall, and Bill Conti. The festival also hosts a short film fest in the summer.
Major Award Winners Golden Palm Award for Best Short Film: *Mon Papa d'America*, by Daniel Hiquet
Films About 130 features
Noteworthy Celebrity Sightings Lauren Bacall, John Travolta, Roberto Benigni, Debbie Reynolds
Tickets $7 per individual screening; $250 for platinum pass gaining admittance to all screenings. Contact Festival Box Office: 619.778.8979
How to Enter Send VHS dub and entry form to:
Palm Springs International Film Festival
1700 E. Tahquitz Way #3
Palm Springs, CA 92262
E-mail filmfest@ix.netcom.com
Entry Deadline November

Philadelphia Festival of World Cinema

Where Philadelphia, Pennsylvania
When Twelve days in late April and early May
Background Though it's only been around since 1992, the Philadelphia festival has become one of the most extensive and intelligently programmed large festivals in the country, spotlighting talented and sometimes unknown filmmakers instead of aiming for the most noteworthy celebrity who has little else to do during the festival period. Screening films from 34 countries in nine different Philadelphia venues including the Painted Bride Art Center (230 Vine Street), the festival has presented series focusing on the African diaspora and director Ken Loach and the so-called Festival of Independents, concentrating on indie Philadelphia filmmakers. The festival also hosts a Set in Philadelphia screenwriting competition and a number of comprehensive, if somewhat arcane and provincial, film industry forums and seminars, many of which are rather yuckily named ("Work It Baby! A Guide to Presenting and Promoting Your Work"; "Writer's Survival Guide;" "Mission Possible"; and "Dissecting Frogs for Snakes: The Soundtrack"). Recent premieres have included *Black Cat, White Cat, Wounds, Drylongso,* and *My Family's Honor.*

Major Award Winners Set in Philadelphia Screenwriting Competition: *Angel Brothers*, by Eugene Martin
Films About 70 features and 60 shorts
Noteworthy Celebrity Sightings The Alloy Orchestra, Lina Wertmuller, Fridrik Thor Fridriksson, Spalding Gray
Tickets $7.50 for individual screenings; many package options
How to Enter Send $17 entry fee and entry form to:
>   International House of Philadelphia
>   3701 Chestnut Street
>   Philadelphia, PA 19104
>   Telephone 215.895.6571
>   Fax 215.895.6593
>   E-mail pfwc@ihphilly.org
>   Web www.libertynet.org/pfwc
Entry Deadline January

Philadelphia International Gay and Lesbian Film Festival

Where Philadelphia, Pennsylvania
When Twelve days beginning on the first Thursday after July 4
Background Founded in 1995 by Raymond Murray, the festival has quickly become one of the most extensive and well-attended of the country's many gay and lesbian fests. Films that have premiered here include *Trick*, *Better Than Chocolate*, *The Velocity of Gary*, *It's Elementary*, *Rescuing Desire*, *Lilies*, *Alive and Kicking*, *Defying Gravity*, and *Neptune's Rocking Horse*. Films are screened in the repertory cinema Theater of the Living Arts, the Prince Music Theater, and the Roxy Screening Room.
Major Award Winners Audience Award for Best Feature Film: *It's in the Water*, by Kelli Herd; Audience Award for Best Documentary: *Licensed to Kill*, by Arthur Dong; Grand Prize Winner: *Broadway*, by Victor Mignatti; Director's Award: *Fire*, by Deepa Mehta
Films About 200 features and shorts
Noteworthy Celebrity Sightings Clive Barker
Tickets $6.50 per individual screening; $55 for admission to 10 screenings
How to Enter Send VHS dub to:
>   TLA Entertainment Group
>   1520 Locust Street, Suite 200
>   Philadelphia, PA 19102
>   Telephone 215.790.1510
>   Fax 215.790.1501
Entry Deadline April

Portland International Film Festival

Where Portland, Oregon
When Two and a half weeks in February
Background Founded in 1975 by the Northwest Film Center in Portland, the festival has done an excellent job in recent years of turning up rare and precious cinematic jewels along with some good Portland art house premieres. Most exciting of all was

a recent screening of the 1912 *Richard III*, the oldest-known existing American feature film. Screening at the Film Center (1219 S.W. Park Avenue), Broadway Cinemas (Southwest Broadway at Main), the Guild Theater (Southwest Ninth and Taylor), and Cinema 21 (Northwest 21st and Hoyt), the festival has screened *Central Station*, *Black Cat, White Cat*, Stephen Soderbergh's *Gray's Anatomy*, Christopher Guest's *Waiting for Guffman*, and, on a less interesting note, Paul McCartney's short film about the Grateful Dead. A recent feature spotlighted contemporary Hispanic cinema. This is another runner-up for the Best of the Fests category.

Major Award Winners Audience Award: (tie) *Harmonists*, by Joseph Vilsmaier, and *My Name is Joe*, by Ken Loach; New Director: Tony Bui, *Three Seasons*; Best Short Film: *Flatworld*, Daniel Greaves

Films About 70 features plus a program of shorts

Tickets $6.50 per individual screening; $100 for an all-festival pass

How to Enter Send VHS dub, $25 (no form—cool!) to:
Portland International Film Festival
1219 S.W. Park Avenue
Portland, OR 97205
Telephone 503.221.1156
Fax 503.294.0874
E-mail info@nwfilm.org
Web ww.nwfilm.org

Entry Deadline October

Interview with

Bill Foster

director of the Portland International
Film Festival

AL How do you go about choosing films for your festival? Is there some sort of method to the madness?

BF Hmmm. I guess it's just watching all kinds of films. And after a while, you start to develop a sense of who are interesting filmmakers and what are interesting films. Every film festival is so different, because they all have particular roles they play in the ecology of the film business and they also are shaped by the community they're in, the time of year they're in, who else is exhibiting in that time frame in the same area. So it's a combination of the guiding aesthetic of the programmers and outside forces.

AL Out of the thousands of films, what causes one to leap out and grab your attention?

BF It could be the subject. It could be the style of the film. Hopefully, a combination. I guess if you get into real film-buff territory, you start to look at the film in the context of the artist's other work and whether or not it's interesting in that regard. There are all kinds of levels. It's very subjective.

AL You must see the widest spectrum of films, from brilliance to home video camcorder junk.

BF Yep.

AL Do you watch everything that comes in?

BF I don't, no.

AL Does somebody?

BF Yeah, somebody does.

AL If a feature is sent to you and it's obviously not working in your estimation, how long does it take to shut it off?

BF Five minutes.

AL Five minutes and you can tell?

BF Not every film, but some.

AL What do you see in the first five minutes? Production quality? Acting?

BF All that stuff. Maybe longer than five minutes. But if it doesn't get your attention or intrigue you right out of the chute, it's not gonna get there.

AL Has your patience decreased over the years? Did that five minutes used to be 35?

BF I think so. I think your patience grows shorter. I think that's inevitable. But hopefully your open-mindedness grows.

AL Open-mindedness grows while patience decreases? That's a cool mix.

BF I think the more you see, the more you're open to the possibilities that are out there and people are doing all kinds of things.

AL Are there any styles or trends in films that you're already sick to death of seeing?

BF Yeah. I think you're sick to death of seeing parent- and relative-funded calling card films. People make these glossy, high-budget shorts to have made them for all the studio guys to see, and in a year they'll be directing the Michelle Pfeiffer film. A lot of these glib, slick, lowest-common-denominator shorts with high production values and no reason for being other than being demonstration vehicles. I just think there's a surplus of those kinds of empty exercise films and a dearth of people being able to make more experimental things, and part of it has to do with public funding and fellowship money and NEA kinds of things, but we're seeing many more films made for the commercial market. You're seeing on one hand the slick, high-budget things, and on the low-budget things, you're seeing a lot of derivative *Clerks* and Tarantino and slacker films. Too many of those.

AL Has audience acceptance of art house films grown during your tenure?

BF Yeah. At least it has here. But nationally, they talk about foreign films as an extinct species. In some degree they've been supplanted by independent American films, which is a category that didn't really exist in a large way before.

AL Have you ever had films that you regretted programming, like, "I can't believe I programmed that?"

BF No. . . . Well . . . there's no particular film that I regret programming. You have films that inspire hoopla, like a good art film like (Godard's) *Hail Mary*, and a thousand Catholics circle the block with rosaries and candles.

AL But that's not something you regret.

BF No. You don't regret it, but on another hand, you have offended them. Or you have Vietnamese guys burning flags, because the North Vietnamese films are politically incorrect. Or last year we showed a Cuban film that had all right-wing Cuban types up in arms. Or another year you'd show *Strawberry and Chocolate*, and you have all the left-wing Cuban guys up in arms. Sometimes you relish those things, and sometimes you regret it.

AL Does every festival director want to make a feature film at one time or another?
BF I don't think so.

AL You wouldn't put yourself in that category?
BF I entertain it, but I'm not waiting to do that.

AL Are there other festivals that you look to or you really respect?
BF I think Toronto is an unbelievably great event. I think Rotterdam is relatively unheralded and really rich. I think Locarno has a lot of good things about it. Cannes is what Cannes is, and Venice is Venice, and Berlin is obviously a good film festival, but there are a lot of really good film festivals. It's really incredible.

Rough and Ruined Film Festival

Where Amsterdam, Netherlands; Vancouver, British Columbia, Canada; and Minneapolis, Minnesota
When One weekend in mid-July in Amsterdam, one weekend in late July in Vancouver, and one weekend in early September in Minneapolis
Background You can't accuse this festival of an excess of pretension. The festival, held in the three aforementioned groovy cities, is dedicated to showcasing the rejected works of filmmakers and advertises itself to up-and-coming (or down-and-not-coming) filmmakers as follows: "Are you a hopeless geek? Are you a helpless date? Are you having trouble paying your rent? Are you a full-time loser? Then the Rough and Ruined Film Festival wants you! We want subversion, humor, decadence, and bad taste!" That said—and leaving aside the fact that the festival says that it delights in "low-budget, home-made, trash, kitsch, or cult" films—this is one of the coolest small fests around, screening short films in nontraditional, "ruined" surroundings that have included old warehouses, abandoned textile factories, and shitty little bars. And aside from a host of unknown filmmakers, R & R has screened the first works of Aki Kaurismaki and Jim Jarmusch. My award for most intriguing film title and concept goes to Michael Wellenreiter's 1997 *Goats and Drugs and Rock 'n' Roll*, described as the story of a goat who leaves a rundown farm and teams up with a junky 1980 Buick Park Avenue in the decrepit big city. "They discover the joys of sex and teach a scummy heroin pusher a few lessons about the need for humility and compassion in a world gone to hell." Hey, if that ain't a great road movie, what is? A close runner-up would have to be Ken Egan's *William Shatner Lent Me His Hairpiece*: "An obsessed Star Trek fan battles William Shatner for possession of Shatner's alluring yet addictive magical hairpiece."
Films About 70 short films
Noteworthy Celebrity Sightings George Kuchar, Vito Rocco, Helen Stickler, Danny Plotnick, Joe Gibbons
Tickets Variable prices depending on location
How to Enter Send just your entry form, and you will be contacted:

Rough and Ruined Film Festival
c/o Red Eye Collaboration
15 W. 14th Street
Minneapolis, MN 55403
Telephone 604.708.5105
E-mail tee@rough-and-ruined.org
Entry Deadline February 28

Saguaro International Film Festival

Where Scottsdale, Arizona
When First week of May
Background Founded in 1994 by the Arizona Film Society, the festival is still a small one and not overly adventurous in its programming, although Arizona filmmakers do get a pretty good showcase here. In addition to its screenings in the AMC Arizona Center Theatres, the festival sponsors, in addition to its screenings, a two-day film school co-sponsored by Scottsdale Community College's film department, a seminar on screenwriting, and a Sunday brunch with the filmmakers (at least the filmmakers who stick around until Sunday). Noteworthy among previous screenings are the *Night of Black Independents*, featuring African American indie filmmakers, as well as Arizona premieres of Bryan Singer's first film, *Public Access*, and Peter Cohn's 1995 film *Drunks*, starring Richard Lewis, Dianne Wiest, Faye Dunaway, Spalding Gray, Parker Posey, and Amanda Plummer. That's some cast. Wonder what ever happened to it.
Major Award Winners Best Feature Film: *Running Time*, by Josh Becker; Best Short Film: *The Oval Portrait*, by Phillip A. Boland, and *Jimmy and Frank Rob a Bank*, by Scott Anderson; Best Documentary: *Calaveros*, by Denise Richards; Best Experimental Film: *A Refutation of Time*, by Dan Boord, Greg Durbin, and Luis Valdovino; Best Screenplay: *Golden Years*, by Scott Petri
Films About 15 features
Tickets $5; available from Ticketmaster: 602.784.4444.
How to Enter Send VHS dub, entry form, and $25 entry fee to:
Saguaro Film Festival
P.O. Box 9147
Scottsdale, AZ 85232
Telephone 480.970.8711
Fax 480.945.3339
E-mail filmz@primenet.com
Web extracheese.com/afs
Entry Deadline February

St. John's International Women's Film and Video Festival

Where St. John's, Newfoundland, Canada
When Four days in mid-October
Background Founded in 1989, this small festival shows a small selection of Canadian and American films by women directors, ranging from the little-known (*Hollywood Handshake* and *Ain't Gonna Pee in the Cup*, by Bianca Bob Miller) to the pretty well-known (Mary Harron's *I Shot Andy Warhol* and Rose Troche's *Go Fish*).

The festival usually has a particular focus, such as women living along the Atlantic Rim. Screenings are held at LSPU Hall and Avalon Cinemas.

Major Award Winners Noncompetitive

Films About 10 features and shorts

Tickets $8 per individual screening

How to Enter Send VHS dub and entry form plus film synopsis, photos of the film-maker, production stills, bios, lists of awards, other publicity materials (hey, that's quite a bit for a festival that shows 10 movies), and the $8 entry fee to:

St. John's International Women's Film and Video Festival
Program Committee
Box 984
St. John's, NF A1C 6C2
Canada
Telephone 709.754.3141
Fax 709.754.3143
E-mail daninef@plato.ucs.mun.ca

Entry Deadline June

St. Louis Film Festival

Where St. Louis, Missouri

When Ten days in early November

Background Nothing special about this film festival, but that's not necessarily a bad thing. No fancy tributes. No glitzy retrospectives. Hardly any archival presentations to speak of (although the fest has presented restored versions of *Around the World in Eighty Days* and *L'Atalante*, and *Metropolis* featuring the magnificent festival darlings the Alloy Orchestra). Just a strong mid-size selection of American independents and international films, not all of which have been already scooped up by major distributors. Sure, there have been the run-of-the-mill festival-en-route-to-big-screen flicks that have premiered here since the festival's 1992 founding (Al Pacino's *Looking for Richard*, Michael Winterbottom's *Jude*, Alan Taylor's *Palookaville*, Chris Newby's *Madagascar Skin*). But there also is a sophisticated selection of strong but lesser-known films, including Eric Rochant's *The Patriots* and Moufida Tlatli's *Silences of the Palace*. A recent special program featured a retrospective of black cinema from 1915 to 1965, including the film *The Bronze Buckaroo*. About 15,000 attend the festival annually, which screens films at the Tivoli Theatres, the Landmark Plaza Frontenac, and AMC West Olive 16.

Major Award Winners Best Film: *Betrayal*, by Radu Mihaileanu; Best First Feature: *Broken English*, by Gregor Nicholas; Audience Choice Award: *Shine*, by Scott Hicks

Films About 90 films

How to Enter Send VHS dub and entry form to:

St. Louis Film Festival
55 Maryland Plaza, Suite A
St. Louis, MO 63108-1501
Telephone 314.367-FEST
Fax 314.454-0540
E-mail info@sliff.org
Web www.sliff.org

Entry Deadline August

Delcia Corlew

managing director of the St. Louis

International Film Festival

CB What do you do as a managing director?

DC I'm involved in every aspect of the festival. This includes development and volunteers, planning the festival itself in terms of the venues. I also do some of the programming.

CB How do you decide what to program?

DC We have a wide range of films that we draw from—American independents, world cinema, and we do a lot of documentaries and short films, too. The way we make decisions is, our programming director and other people affiliated with us keep a very close eye and ear on what's going on at the other festivals through magazines, the Internet, and attending them. They know what's up-and-coming and what's hot. If there's a film attracting a lot of attention, we always try and get it.

CB Are there any films that you really regret programming?

DC Not that I'm aware of.

CB Is there a film that you're really proud of having shown?

DC One of the things that we are proud of is that we have a New Filmmakers' Forum. It's a competition aspect of the festival; we get entries from all over the world. Very often we will find that someone who presented a short in the program will then have a successful feature the second time around. One example is Tony Bui (*Three Seasons*), who showed his short film, *Yellow Lotus*, three or four years ago in the Forum. We invite the directors who go into competition to come here as our guests, and we present seminars and workshops. They usually go away feeling very good about their experience, after having had a chance to speak with industry people and network.

CB Are there too many festivals going on right now? Do you have too much competition?

DC In terms of scheduling, we're up against Tokyo and Fort Lauderdale. That can be a problem. But one thing that's good and bad in St. Louis is the sudden explosion of art houses. We like to pat ourselves on the back for having encouraged that with showing all of these foreign films. The theaters here now compete amongst themselves to show something that's been big at Sundance, and it's then harder for us to preview the film beforehand.

CB How do you screen all the entries? How many of them are you able to watch?

DC About six or seven people screen them individually. We always try and watch the whole thing unless it's really really bad. Sometimes you just have to turn it off.

CB Do you have any advice for filmmakers, such as something that would help them to get noticed by a festival?

DC Try to come up with an original script. We always see the same scenario over and over again. Send us something original.

St. Louis International Gay and Lesbian Film Festival

Where St. Louis, Missouri

When One week in mid-September

Background A long-running, slowly growing collection of lesbian/gay screenings in the heartland. Mixes mainstream material (*The Velocity of Gary*) with avant-garde (*Gendernauts*). Nothing terribly exciting here, like the city's other festival, but still a professional, worthwhile event.

Major Award Winners None

Films 30 shorts and features

Noteworthy Celebrity Sightings None

Tickets $6.50 per ticket

How How to Enter For more information contact:

    Saint Louis International Gay and Lesbian Film Festival
    PMB #388
    6614 Clayton Road
    St. Louis, MO 63117-1602
    Telephone 314.997.9846
    Fax 314.863.6993
    E-mail slilagff@aol.com
    Web www.slilagfilmfestival.org

Entry Deadline June

San Diego Film Festival

Where San Diego, California

When First week of February

Background If nothing else, this film festival features one of the more entertaining voice mail messages of any we've encountered. The screenings are announced by a woman who speaks as if she's talking on the phone with her best friend or a stoner buddy as she announces the intriguing foreign (i.e., *Dutch*) films that are screened here. "We don't want you coming in here in the rain for nothing but a cookie," quoth she when she was unsure of what films were being screened and whether they would arrive on time or not. "Tomorrow's up in the air," she observed on another occasion. Beyond that, a fairly respectable collection of foreign films.

Major Award Winners Patron's Award for Best Film: *Antonia's Line*, by Marleen Gorris; Festival Award for Best Film: *The Blue Villa*, by Alain Robbe-Grillet; Festival Award for Best Short: *That Sunday*, by David Zeff; Special Achievement Award for Best Screenplay: Roberto Sneider, *Two Crimes*; Special Achievement Award for Best Cinematography: Petr Hajda, *War of Colours*; Special Achievement Award for Animation: Sarah Watt, *Small Treasures*

Films Not available

Noteworthy Celebrity Sightings None

Tickets Not available

How to Enter Send VHS dub, $20 entry fee, and entry form to:

    San Diego Film Festival
    UEO, Dept. 0078

9500 Gilman Drive
UC San Diego
La Jolla, CA 92093-0078
Telephone 619.534.0497
Fax 619.534.7665
E-mail rbaily@ucsd.edu
Entry Deadline November

San Francisco International Asian American Film Festival

Where San Francisco, California
When The second week of March
Background Founded in 1982 by the National Asian American Telecommunications Association the SFIAAFF has gained a reputation as one of the most comprehensive and eclectic showcases for Asian cinema, refusing to shy away from controversial social or sexual politics, with recent festivals highlighted by outspoken gay filmmakers and brash "Gener-Asian Xers" along with a healthy dose of world premieres and showings of forgotten Asian classics. The SFIAAFF screens films at the AMC Kabuki 8 Theatres in San Francisco and the Pacific Film Archive in Berkeley. The festival has screened films from a ton of countries, including Bangladesh, Cambodia, Pakistan, and the Philippines. Among the more notable features shown recently are *Passing Through*, *Searching for Go-Hyang*, *Rabbit In The Moon*, *Sunrise Over Tiananmen Square*, *Chungking Express*, and *Mod Fuck Explosion*.
Major Award Winners Noncompetitive
Films Approximately 80 films and videos
Noteworthy Celebrity Sightings Joan Chen, Arthur Dong
Tickets $8 general admission for individual screenings; $7 for NAATA members
How to Enter NAATA accepts short, television, and feature-length films in 35 mm, 16 mm, and video formats. To enter, send video screener and $20 fee to:
NAATA, Call for Entries
346 Ninth Street
2nd Floor
San Francisco, CA 94103
Telephone 415.863.0814
Fax 415.863.7428
E-mail naata@sirius.com
Entry Deadline September

San Francisco International Film Festival

See Best of the Fests

Peter Scarlet

director of the San Francisco International Film Festival

AL How do you go about programming the festival?

PS There are actually two sections to the festival, if not three. The main section, for feature films, is invitational. I and two other colleagues program the festival, and we basically spend the year going out doing a lot of traveling and trying to put together a program of the latest work that is the most impressive to us, that moves us or touches us or makes us laugh or does something original in some unusual way. An emphasis for the festival is to limit the number of films that are already in commercial distribution, so that it's a festival that enables an American audience to discover things. Three-quarters of the films are either U.S. premieres or North American premieres. That's for feature films. In addition, we have a competitive section for shorts, for documentaries, for animated films, and for films made for television and experimental films. Those films are juried by upwards of 30 juries composed of filmmakers, film professionals, teachers of various sorts, and about 1,500 entries come from all over the world each year. We accepted unsolicited submissions for the feature film section, but frankly, we're not crazy about them.

AL Meaning?

PS Meaning we prefer to go out and find things.

AL So the chances of a filmmaker contacting you with a film you've never heard of before and then programming it are rather slim.

PS It's not to say that the submissions are not good, but generally our detective work is such that if there's quality stuff we probably know about it. Most of the unsolicited submissions are American independent films, at least lately, which is a buzzword for all sorts of things, and that's really not our prime focus. There are a lot of festivals doing that. Our prime focus is independent cinema from all over the world. And American films always occupy a good place, but not a major place in the program. We have probably the most eclectic and diverse program of any festival in North America, with the possible exception of Toronto. We want people to discover the world here.

AL Where is it that you find most of your films? Are there certain festivals that seed yours better than others?

PS Only to the extent that there are some we're able to get to more than others, both because of financial and calendar reasons. There are the big competitive festivals like Berlin, Venice, and Cannes. Then there are smaller, more specialized festivals that range from the festival in Italy in Pordenone that specializes in silent films and another one in Bologna that specializes in rediscovered work to a festival like the one in Nantes called the Festival des 3 Continents that shows exclusively work from Asia, Africa, and Latin America. I would say that those are the festivals that, to use your word, seed us. Those are the more important hunting grounds.

AL So what happens to your local wannabe Tarantino who sends you a film? Does it generally get viewed at all? Or do you have to look at material about it beforehand?
PS We used to try and ask for material first, and then we realized that it's the film, not the material, so we do try to look at everything that comes in.

AL Is there a screening committee who looks through it first?
PS Exactly, though one of us tries to look at it first.

AL Is it important for a film to have a distributor before being considered?
PS On the contrary. We try to limit the number of these films. There are some films that we like that then get bought, and by the time we devise the final program, we say, "Well, we don't want that many films in distribution." There are other festivals that have other opinions, but I feel that a film festival does not exist, particularly when it's a nonprofit institution, to simply publicize all the films that are going to be opening in town in the next six to 12 months, which is how some festivals operate.

AL Do distributors exert a certain amount of pressure, or do they try to?
PS Distributors are in the business to try to exert pressure. But there are a number of factors to keep in mind. A festival can help a film. A festival can hurt a film. One of the dangers in the business is that the release of a film can destroy it if the wrong kind of publicity happens, and by that I don't just mean someone saying, "This film is a piece of shit." I mean the critics can go bananas over it, write everything about it, and then when the film opens in distribution a month later, the papers, in effect, say, "Screw it. We already wrote about that." So that you have to be very careful and work both with the press and with the distributor to make sure that the audience can discover the film at the festival, but you don't want the audience to then be gone when the film opens commercially.

AL Over the years has there been any particular film that you have premiered that you're particularly proud of?
PS Well, my answer takes two forms. There are the films that had their world premieres here that now everybody and their uncle knows, and it's great to know that they started here, from Jonathan Demme's *Stop Making Sense* to Errol Morris's *The Thin Blue Line* to Spike Lee's *She's Gotta Have It*. The list goes on and on of films that began their careers here, and that gives you a nice warm fuzzy feeling. There are other films that were obscure when we showed them and are still obscure. I would say those spark equal feelings of pride—for example, the work of an Armenian filmmaker named Arthur Peleshian, who has made only short films and who when I first saw his work, when he was still in the Soviet Union, most of his work had been banned, and a lot of it had been destroyed, and he had been imprisoned. We finally got him out and showed his work here in 1990 and programmed five of his short films, and the audience went bananas. The response for his film was the second-most popular program in the festival—that, given that they were short films, was really remarkable. They've been shown all over the world now, and he is recognized as a great contemporary filmmaker.

AL With the explosions of festivals and everybody vying for the rights to give world premieres, has that caused troubles?
PS Yes. It's become a real problem. Festivals in some way have begun to supplant more traditional exhibition sites, because there are fewer theaters showing foreign work and independent work across the United States now with the growth of big companies,

multiplexes that are just showing the same-old-same-old. A lot of festivals have sprung up and will continue to spring up that both attempt to serve an audience that may want to see other films and can't in their neighborhood multiplex. There's the Judy Garland-Mickey Rooney syndrome of "Gee, wouldn't it be nice to fix up the old barn and put on a show?" And then there's always an element of civic boosterism in some of the smaller festivals that say, "Well, great! We'll get some stars in here! Great!" And there are an awful lot of half-assed festivals being run around the country now, being run around the world, particularly in this country.

AL The half-assed ones are those that are more interested in getting the glitterati to attend their festival?

PS Or that don't understand that there's a lot of damned hard work, and it's hard work that's not necessarily what the public cares about. There are enormous technical requirements. There are enormous logistical requirements, and unless you have the resources, the dedication, and the willingness to work for that kind of thing and the infrastructure to do it, you're gonna get a half-assed festival.

AL Do you have to offer any specific enticements or inducements to films to make them choose to premiere at San Francisco instead of Joe Schmo Festival?

PS Fair question. In part because we're in San Francisco, that's often inducement enough. It's not like we're in City X. If it's a film in distribution, there's always the whole issue of the release pattern and the release date of the film, and very often there are films we can't show simply because the distributor doesn't want to do anything with them until the fall or the film hasn't yet been bought and the producer doesn't want to have any screenings in North America until they see if they have a deal. Invariably we try to bring in the director of the film and to put that person up for a few days, unless the filmmaker doesn't want it, to arrange that there be a press screening or make it available to the press. We also cover the shipping costs of the film.

AL Which can probably get pretty steep.

PS You're talking a feature film coming in from some distant part of the world. None of this is cheap.

San Francisco International Lesbian and Gay Film Festival

Where San Francisco, California
When A week and a half in June
Background Not entirely surprising for San Francisco, but this is probably the hugest festival of gay and lesbian films nationwide. Founded in 1976, the festival screens films such as Jim Fall's *Trick* and Lukas Moodysson's *Show Me Love* from more than 20 countries at the Victoria Theater and Roxie Cinema.
Major Award Winners Dockers Khakis First Feature Award ($10,000): *Head On*, by Ana Kokkinos; Audience Award for Best Documentary: *Living With Pride: Ruth C. Ellis at 100*, by Yvonne Welborn; Frameline Award: Stanley Kwan
Films More than 200 features and shorts
How to Enter Send VHS dub and entry form to:

SFLGFF
346 Ninth Street
San Francisco, CA 94103
Tel: 415.703.8650
Fax 415.861.1404
E-mail info@frameline.org
Web www.frameline.org
Entry Deadline February

San Francisco Jewish Film Festival

Where San Francisco, California
When One week in mid-July
Background Founded in 1981, the SFJFF now hosts annual audiences of 34,000, screening an assortment of Jewish-interest films and presenting seminars on such subjects as "Emigration and the Arts." Particular attention is paid to films by San Francisco filmmakers and to the concept of rethinking the meaning of Judaism and Jewish film. The festival screens at the UC Theatre in Berkeley and on Stanford's Palo Alto campus. Films that have screened here include *Khroustaliov, My Car!*, *The Nasty Girl,* and *The White Rose*, plus documentaries about Isaak Babel, Hank Greenberg, and Phillip Roth.
Films About 37
Tickets $7.50 per individual screening; $65 for all films
How to Enter Send VHS dub and entry form to:
SFJFF
346 Ninth Street
San Francisco, CA 94103
Telephone 415.621.0556
E-mail jewishfilm@aol.com
Web www.well.com/user/ari/jff or www.sfjff.org
Entry Deadline Mid-March

San Juan Cinemafest

Where San Juan, Puerto Rico
When Third week of March
Background Founded in 1989, the Cinemafest still bills itself as the oldest such festival in Puerto Rico and has premiered such films as *Cinema Paradiso*, *Jesus of Montreal*, *The Crying Game*, and *Farewell My Concubine*. The festival is, not surprisingly, focused on Spanish-language cinema, with more than half of its features coming from South America and Spain. Tributes have been paid to such artists as Luis García Berianga and Tomás Gutiérrez Alea. Held in the capital of Puerto Rico, the festival offers screenings at the island's largest theaters—the Plaza Theaters—as well as at more scenic and idiosyncratic spots such as public squares and nearby university campuses.
Major Award Winners Though it claims to be noncompetitive, the Cinemafest nevertheless offers a special award from the Film Critics Association and an audience award for the best film in the world cinema section. There is also a Caribbean

competition that awards a carved wooden statuette called the "Pitirre Prize" in fiction, documentary, and animation categories. Recent winners include: *Sixteen-oh-sixty* (Caribbean Competition) and *Yo Sod, Del Son a La Salsa* (Prize of the Public)
Films About 90 films
How to Enter Send video dub to:
San Juan Cinemafest
Edificio Miramar Plaza, Oficina 703
954 Avenue Ponce de León
San Juan, PR
00907
Telephone 787.721.6125
Fax 787.724.4187
E-mail JMV333@aol.com
Entry Deadline Late August

San Luis Obispo International Film Festival

Where San Luis Obispo, California
When First week in November
Background Along with holding a competition for documentary films, the festival, founded in 1993, represents a puzzling combination of the classy and the tacky. On the classy and intriguing side, the film has held tributes to the work of Hitchcock and George Cukor, silent films as well as screenings of great (if not too surprising) films such as *From Here to Eternity*, *To Kill a Mockingbird*, *Sunset Boulevard*, and (I think it sucks, but it's a classic) *Rebel Without a Cause*. Less meritorious (at least to these cynical eyes) is the festival's tendency to offer panel discussions and Q and As with the likes of Noah Wyle from *ER* and writers for such shows as *Moonlighting* and *Duckman*. The films screen at the Downtown Centre Cinemas (888 Marsh Street), the Palm Theatre (817 Palm Street), and the Art Deco Fremont Theater (1025 Monterey).
Noteworthy Celebrity Sightings Stanley Kramer, Jonathan Winters
Tickets $5 per individual screening
Festival hotline 805.546.FILM
How to Enter Send $30 entry fee, VHS copy, and entry form to:
George Sidney Independent Film Competition
San Luis Obispo International Film Festival
P.O. Box 1449
San Luis Obispo, CA 93408
Telephone 805.546.FILM
Fax 805.781.6799
E-mail slofilmfest@slofilmfest.org
Web www.slofilmfest.org
Entry Deadline August

Santa Barbara International Film Festival

Where Santa Barbara, California
When One week in mid-March

Background Founded in 1986, the SBIFF began as a humble fest, premiering such features as *My Beautiful Laundrette* and paying tribute to New Zealand filmmakers and the late Robert Mitchum. Over the years, the festival has grown in scope, attracting about 25,000 annually and featuring well-attended panels and tributes, although some of the tributes have left a wee bit to be desired. (A gala tribute to Teri Garr? A salute to the work of Chazz Palminteri? A modern master award to Michael Douglas?) The festival also sponsors the Peter Stark Screenwriting Competition, awarding a grand prize of $5,000 for best screenplay.

Major Award Winners Burning Vision Award: *The Power of Kangwon Province*, by Hong Sang-soo; Best Foreign Film: *The Powder Keg*, Boran Paskaljevic; Audience Choice Award: *Roadkill*, by Matthew Leutwyler; Insight Award for Best Documentary: *Death: A Love Story*, by Michelle LeBrun

Films About 125 features.

Noteworthy Celebrity Sightings Sally Field, Corbin Bernsen, Beau Bridges, John Lithgow, Shelley Winters

Tickets $7 per individual screening

How to Enter Send VHS dub, entry form, and $40 entry fee to:
Santa Barbara International Film Festival
1216 State Street, Suite 710
Santa Barbara, CA 93101
Telephone 805.963.0023
Fax 805.962.2523
E-mail sbiff@west.net
Web www.west.net/~sbiff

Entry Deadline December

Seattle International Film Festival

See Best of the Fests

Seattle Lesbian and Gay Film Festival

Where Seattle, Washington

When Ten days in late October and early November

Background Founded by Three Dollar Bill Cinema (as in "queer as a . . . "), which hosts queer rock shows as well, Seattle's fest is one of the better and more provocative gay fests around, showing such films as *Queer as Folk* and *The Secret Life of Homos*. Recent premieres include *The Story of a Bad Boy*, featuring Julie Kavner, and the Hong Kong film *Portland Street Blues*. Panel discussions have included "Educating Our Youth: Teaching Anti-Homophobia in the Schools."

Tickets $7.50 for individual screenings; festival hotline: 800.965.4827

How to Enter Send VHS dub and entry form to:
Seattle Lesbian and Gay Film Festival
Three Dollar Bill Cinema
1122 E. Pike Street #1313
Seattle, WA 98122-3934

Telephone 206.323.4274
Fax 206.323.4275
E-mail filmfest@drizzle.com
Web www.seattlequeerfilm.com
Entry Deadline Not available

Short Attention Span Film and Video Festival

Where San Francisco, California
When Late September
Background True to its name, this West Coast festival, founded in 1992, accepts films that are two minutes or less in length and shows them back to back for two hours in San Francisco's Victoria Theater. Selected pieces are broadcast afterwards on the syndicated program Weird TV.
Major Award Winners Noncompetitive
How to Enter Send $5 entry fee plus VHS sub to:
    Short Attention Span Film and Video Festival
    P.O. Box 460316
    San Francisco, CA 94146
    E-mail sasfvf@aol.com
Entry Deadline August 15

Shorts International Film Festival

Where New York, New York
When One weekend in early November
Background Founded in 1997, the festival screens films under 40 minutes in length. The festival is dedicated to bringing back the concept of showing short films with mainstream feature films (a concept whose time has come, despite my horrifying memories of a 20-minute short called *Gone Fishing* that played before *The Concert for Bangladesh*) and screens animated, comic, dramatic, experimental, foreign, and student shorts, offering $2,000 in prizes to the best director in every category. The festival screens at the Sony Lincoln Square Theatres (Broadway and 68th Street). The jury, with members including Edie Falco and Aida Turturro, have awarded prizes to such films as *Sorrow's Child* and *A Soccer Story*.
Noteworthy Celebrity Sightings Taylor Hackford, the Coen brothers, Jim Jarmusch
How to Enter Send VHS dub, $25 entry fee, and entry form to:
    Shorts International Film Festival
    101 E. Second Sreet
    New York, NY 10019
    Telephone 212.343.9598
    Fax 212.343.1416
    E-mail info@shorts.org
    Web www.shorts.org
Entry Deadline September

Sinking Creek Film and Video Festival

Where Nashville, Tennessee
When One week in late November
Background Founded in 1969 and now held on the campus of Vanderbilt University, this festival emphasizes young filmmakers, though not necessarily students. Films are screened in the 350-seat Saratt Student Center of Vanderbilt.
Films About 75 films and videos
How to Enter Send VHS dub and entry fee ($30 for shorts and $60 for features) to:
> Sinking Creek Film and Video Festival
> 1250 Old Shiloh Road
> Greenville, TN 37743
> Telephone 615.322.4234
> E-mail daviesme@ctrvax.vanderbilt.edu

Entry Deadline April

Slamdance Film Festival

Where Park City, Utah
When Last week in January
Background Founded in 1995 as a tonic to the cliquish and Hollywoody image of Sundance, Slamdance has gained a sort of cliquey atmosphere of its own. Screenings are held in one single, overbooked ersatz theater in the Treasure Mountain Inn where movies are shown from 8 A.M. until the wee hours of dawn. Slamdance also hosts an annual screenplay competition.
Major Award Winners Grand Jury Prize for Best Feature Film: *Chi Girl*, by Heidi van Lier; Grand Jury Prize for Best Short: *Harry Knuckles and the Treasure of the Aztec Mummy*, by Lee Demarbre and Ian Driscoll; Best Black-and-White Film: *Angryman*, by David Baer; Audience Award for Best Drama: *Man of the Century*, by Adam Abraham; Audience Award for Best Short: *12 Stops on the Road to Nowhere*, by Jay Lowi; Spirit of Slamdance Award: *Herd*, by Mike Mitchell
Films About 45 features, shorts, and documentaries
How to Enter Send VHS, director's filmography, and entry fee ($50 over 40 minutes; $35 under 40 minutes) to:
> Slamdance Film Festival
> 6381 Hollywood Boulevard #520
> Los Angeles, CA 90028
> Telephone 310.466.1786
> Fax 310.466.1784
> E-mail mail@slamdance.com
> Web www.slamdance.com

Entry Deadline November

Solstice Film Festival

Where Boonville, California
When Three days in June
Background Founded in 1997 amid the fruit orchards, sheep ranches, and wineries

of Anderson Valley, California, this young festival has yet to develop a full identity and a complete slate of films. But with the unlimited popcorn offered with the all-access pass, the Solstice fest has taken a great leap in the right direction.

Films About five features

Noteworthy Celebrity Sightings Les Blank, Treat Williams

Tickets $10 per individual screening; $100 for admittance to all screenings and unlimited popcorn

How to Enter Send VHS dub and entry form to:

Solstice Productions
Box 451
Boonville, CA 95419
Telephone 707.895.2333
Fax 707.895.2665

Entry Deadline Not available

Sundance Film Festival

Where Park City, Utah

When Ten days in mid-January

Background Every filmmaker I know has a connection to Sundance. They all know the festival director or someone who worked for the festival director or someone who bumped into the festival director on a drunk, stupid evening. But somehow, none of their films ever got in. That's the kind of festival this is. It's like the popular cheerleader in high school: everybody knows her or knows somebody who knows her, but she still winds up going to the prom with some hunky asshole from New Trier. And despite all the hype, you've really got to wonder about a film festival that honors both R. W. Fassbinder and Tim Robbins at the same time, and no matter what they say about careers being made at Sundance, it's amazing how many films screen here and are never heard from again. Screenings are held at 13 theaters including Robert Redford's Sundance Resort. Just as Cannes will always be Cannes and Venice will always be Venice, Sundance will always be Sundance, and that's not necessarily a good thing. But if you're looking to see and be seen, to get some good skiing in, to catch a glimpse of Robert Redford, and maybe, just maybe, cram into a screening room (grumble, grumble, grumble), there's no better place I know of to do it. This is a festival that started out with the right idea but somehow became a victim of its own success. Now, if you want to see where the scene is happening, you're better off in Austin, though I hear the skiing's terrible.

Major Award Winners Grand Jury Prize (Documentary): *Long Night's Journey into Day*; Special jury prize: *The Ballad of Ramblin' Jack*, by Aiyan Elliott; Audience Award (Feature): *Two Family House*, by Raymond DeFelitta; Audience Award (documentary); *Dark Days*, by Marc Singer; Audience Award (world cinema): *Saving Grace*, by Nigel Cole; Best Ensemble: *SongCatcher*; Best Individual Performance: Donal Logue, *The Tao of Steve*; Best Cinematography: Tom Krueger, *Committed*

Films About 125 features and 60 shorts

Noteworthy Celebrity Sightings Plenty

Tickets $7–$10 per individual screening; $2,500 pass gains access to all screenings for a five-day screening

How to Enter Send VHS dub and entry form to:

Sundance Film Festival
P.O. Box 16450
Salt Lake City, UT 84116
Telephone 801.328.3456
Fax 801.575.5175
Web www.sundancechannel.com/festival
Entry Deadline Early October

Super Super-8 Fest

Where San Diego, California
When Three days in mid-September
Background Dedicated to the noble task of preserving the sadly dying form of Super-8 cinema, the San Diego-based festival screens animation and shorts by current filmmakers. But coolest of all, the fest screens old Super-8 oddities like travelogues, cartoons, and (my favorite category) garage sale finds. The best of the festival tours theaters on the West Coast.
How to Enter Send VHS dub to:
Super Super-8 Fest
3841 Fourth Avenue #207
San Diego, CA 92103
Telephone 619.544.9223
Fax 619.534.7315
Entry Deadline August

SXSW Film Festival

Where Austin, Texas
When One week in mid-March
Background Long known as one of the top spots for discovering new music talent, the South by Southwest film festival has an indie flavor and reputation that has surpassed even that of the far-more-ballyhooed Sundance festival. The festival has screened a collection of video shorts chosen by the Dallas Video Association, a retrospective on Monte Hellman, George Hickenlooper's *The Low Life*, Morgan J. Freeman's *Desert Blue*, and Greg Mottola's *Daytrippers* and has premiered John Sayles's *Lone Star* and *Ghost in the Shell*. The festival holds screenings at the Dobie, Paramount, Union, and Village theaters.
Films About 30 features, 12 documentaries, and five programs of short films.
Tickets Contact festival hotline: 800.966.SHOW
How to Enter Send VHS dub, entry form, and $20 entry fee to:
SXSW Film and Video Competition
P.O. Box 4999
Austin, TX 78765
Telephone 512.467.7979
Fax 512.451.0754
E-mail sxsw@sxsw.com
Web www.sxsw.com
Entry Deadline December

Interview with

Angela Lee

senior coordinator of the SXSW Film Festival in Austin, Texas

CB How long has the festival been around?
AL The first SXSW Film Festival took place in 1994.

CB When did you join it?
AL I started as a volunteer theater manager the inaugural year and have been around ever since.

CB How do you go about programming the films? How do you decide on the mix?
AL We have around 40 prescreening judges who watch the submissions on VHS as they come in. Each of these prescreeners tends to concentrate on a particular category (Narrative, Documentary, Animation, Experimental, or Music Video). The prescreeners send us critiques of the videos, and depending on the critique, the video either gets passed on to another prescreener or taken out of the running. It's rare that something gets knocked out in the first round. If the video is still in the running after three or four viewings by prescreeners, it goes on to a programmer who will decide if it makes the final cut. On average, each video gets watched two or three times by two or three different people. Ultimately, toward the end of our selection process, we hold a meeting to program each of the categories. All of the programmers (about eight of us) sit down with all the videos that are still left in the running and decide what the final lineup will be.

CB How many films do you personally look at?
AL If I don't sleep between September to February, 500 to 600 (shorts and features combined).

CB When you have so many entries, do you have a chance to look at everything, or sometimes do you just have to turn it off after 15 minutes to save time?
AL Everything gets looked at, and nothing gets taken out of the running after only a few minutes. Almost everyone involved in programming SXSW is an active filmmaker, so we give the films that are submitted to us the same consideration we would like our films to get.

CB Do you see a lot of trends in the entries? One year it's Tarantino ripoffs, the next it's horror movies, and so on?
AL Yes. This year the themes seem to be the millennium [and] "found footage" films á la *The Blair Witch Project.* Tarantino is also perennially popular.

CB What kind of advice would you give somebody who was sending a film to you?
AL Don't spend a lot on promotional materials. Let your work speak for itself. Instead of spending money on promotional materials, you should invest in getting the best transfer of your work possible. Don't rush to finish your project just because you want to have it done by the submission deadline. It's better to submit something you're completely happy with than to submit a rough cut that's not really

representative of your work. Please don't subject a festival to a barrage of press releases and phone calls once you've submitted your work. A common misconception is that the more film festivals your film has played at, the greater your film's chances are of being programmed again. This actually works against you (no festival wants to play a film that everyone's seen already).

CB How important are good presentation materials? Will an expensively packaged film catch your eye before the one that gets dropped off in a paper bag?

AL Packaging has no bearing whatsoever over our programming decisions. Usually, the packaging and promotional materials are separated from the actual video before the video reaches the programmers anyway. SXSW prefers minimal packaging and materials.

CB SXSW is obviously much more than a film festival. Is it difficult to keep focus on film with all the music/new media activities going on?

AL No. Sometimes I regret that we aren't able to enjoy the music/new media events, we're so focused on film.

CB Why do you think the festival's been a success?

AL Austin, Texas, is a great town. Filmmakers and participants have a great time when they come here. We have had a tremendous amount of support from the local and national film community, for which we're very grateful. We've been lucky to have some great films come through. I also think that people enjoy coming to SXSW because it's a very intimate and friendly festival.

CB Have there been any films you programmed that you are particularly proud of?

AL Yes. *In the Company of Men, Sonic Outlaws, American Job, Men with Guns, Lone Star.*

CB Any that you're particularly embarrassed of?

AL No.

CB If you could have made any movie in history, what would it be?

AL *Harold & Maude.*

Taos Talking Picture Festival

Where Taos, New Mexico
When Four days in mid-April
Background Fast gaining a reputation as one of the most innovatively programmed of the indie festivals, Taos is also the only festival that offers five acres of land to the winner of its innovation award. Seeking to foster a film community in Taos, the festival seems to think that a great way to do this is to make sure that filmmakers relocate here, and what better way than to give them the land to do it? Films tend to lean toward the American indie scene, and many of them take their cue from the Southwestern atmosphere of Taos. The festival, in this town where everything has a name that uses the word "sagebrush," "pueblo," or "canyon" in it, annually gives the Howard Hawks Storyteller Award, which honors a visionary filmmaker or film professional. Another award is given to maverick film performers. Award winners

have included Philip Kaufman and Louis Gossett Jr. Then there's the Taos Land Grant Award that gives five acres to promising filmmakers. There are also intriguing panel discussions and forums, such as a recent one that concerned product placement in films. Films are screened at the Storyteller Cinemas (110 Old Talpa Canyon Road) and the Taos Convention Center Forum (121 Civic Plaza Drive).

Films About 120 features, shorts, and documentaries

Noteworthy Celebrity Sightings Greer Garson's friends

How to Enter Send entry fee ($25 for films 30 minutes and under, $35 for films over 30 minutes) and VHS dub to:

> Taos Talking Pictures Festival-Submission
> 7217 NDCBU
> 1337 Gusdorf Road, Suite F
> Taos, NM 87571
> Telephone 505.751.0637
> Fax 505.751.7385
> E-mail ttpix@taosnet.com
> Web www.ttpix.com

Entry Deadline January

Interview with

Kelly Clement

director of programming and cofounder,

Taos Talking Pictures Festival

AL How does the festival go about programming films? What's the process?

KC I think our main source is our call for entries. We do a mass mailing to about 200 filmmakers in our database, so that call goes out, and we start getting submissions from September right up until our deadline, which is in January, and last year we got over 700 submissions from that call for entry that completely overwhelmed us. We weren't prepared at all for that.

AL What happens when you get so many entries? Do you have a chance to look at everything?

KC Well, what I do is form juries of media professionals and die-hard movie buffs here in the community of Northern New Mexico for different sections—documentaries; short films; short narrative that is, a narrative film 20 minutes to an hour long; and features, and then sometimes we form juries for animation and experimental— and these juries are usually about five people, and they choose their top picks and give them back to me, and then I usually watch all the top picks of all the juries.

AL So how many are you personally going through?

KC Me personally? Oh, God. I'd say I look at about a third to a half of them. I monitor all the submissions, and even if one doesn't make it through the jury process, if I see the synopsis or the bios or something that deserves attention, I'll give it that attention.

AL There are some festival directors out there who say, "I'll give it about 10 minutes, and if it doesn't hit me, it goes in the "no" pile." Is that how it has to work sometimes?

KC Yeah, I'm afraid so. There are just too many. There's too much to look at when you know from watching the first 10 to 15 minutes that it's not going anywhere. And that's not always true. Sometimes it picks up or develops, but it's pretty safe to say that in the first 15 minutes you can generally tell where it's going, the style, the pace, the characters, and you can usually tell if it's something that's appropriate.

AL So a filmmaker had better grab you in that opening 10 minutes.

KC I'm a filmmaker myself, and I've been on the other side of it, too. I've had to struggle with that.

AL How has viewing all these films changed your approach to filmmaking?

KC Well, I haven't done anything for the last four years as far as filmmaking. I have a documentary in the works, but I'd say the main influence if I were to go out and make my own feature right now would be not to rely on the trends. I see so many Tarantino-inspired films, low-budget, first-time director films, that it's just numbing. I would say that you should just try to be as fresh and original as you can.

AL What sort of mistakes do people make in approaching your festival? Are there things that people do wrong when sending you a film?

KC I would just say probably that a lot of people don't really read the entry requirements, and that's one thing. Every festival has its own set of entry requirements, and usually you can look through them and go cross-eyed reading the fine print and regulations. But when you're getting 700 entries, you really need some consistency, and that's what those regulations are designed to do. It's great when people do a little bit extra, labeling their tapes with the title on the spine and things like that. That really helps the selection committee and the programmer.

AL Are flashy press materials important? Do filmmakers need to catch your eye with their package?

KC I see the whole range of that, and yeah, they might initially catch my eye and make me thumb through it. I read through all the synopses, and if there's a synopsis that appears just typed on a 3-by-5 card that sounds intriguing, that's as good as a huge, flashy packet.

AL You do want a professional presentation too, though, don't you? You don't want people scrawling in crayon.

KC Yeah. A professional presentation is very important to us.

AL And somebody who fills theirs out like a doofus will wind up at the bottom of the pile?

KC Yeah. I'd say so.

AL Have there been any films that you've programmed that you're particularly proud of?

KC Yeah. Well, I think the first year we showed a film called *My Family* by Gregory Nava that was very important to the community. We actually gave Gregory Nava our first Cineaste Award for promoting dialogue between cultures, and we liked the film and thought it was good, but we didn't really know it was going to have the kind of impact it did on the community, which is a majority of Hispanic population here. The mayor of Taos presented the award to Gregory Nava at the screening, and he got up and he just broke down crying for five minutes before he could give the award, because the experience that was presented in that film was so much his experience and many of the people in this community.

AL Has there ever been a film that made you say, "I'm sorry this premiered here. Whoops, I made a mistake."

KC Oh, yeah. Every year there are a couple of them. My big challenge is striving for a balanced program so you have enough drama, enough comedy, enough over-the-edge films, and sometimes in doing that, looking for that balance, I might compromise a little bit. Every once in a while that kind of fizzles on you. We've only been doing this for a few years, so the personality of the festival is still emerging. We didn't set out with a real distinct personality, and we didn't even know what our audience wanted. We had a concept.

AL What does the audience want?

KC Now they want eclectic programming. They want to see things they've never seen before, and there's a real interest in foreign films.

AL Do you run films picked up by major distributors?

KC Yeah, but they're definitely in the minority. But we try to get major releases for our opening and closing night films, and every once in a while I also go to other festivals like Toronto, and I usually go to Telluride and Sundance and Rotterdam. And so sometimes the films that we see at those festivals and want to program very badly get picked up in between the time we initiate the process and the time we screen, so sometimes we get major distribution films by default. But we don't really ly actively go out and call Miramax and ask, "What've you got that's new?" We don't actively do that.

AL Are there certain themes or issues that get your attention more than others?

KC Of course we have the Native American film showcase that we present every year, so we're looking for the best work produced by Native American filmmakers and with Native American subject matter, and we also look for films that have been made by Latino filmmakers, just because one of our missions is to present those. But those are sidebar events. Our theme is primarily storytelling.

Téléscience

Where Montreal, Quebec, Canada

When Ten days in late October

Background Films about bugs. Films about frogs. Films about the North Pole, forests, Albert Einstein, the Ebola virus, salamanders, and newts. Like a 10-day-long episode of *Nova* on PBS, Quebec's science film festival is the best festival in the world I know for science and nature films, where you can even see films with titles such as *Contraceptive for Seal*. Screenings are held at the Cinéma du Café Électronique (514.849.1612). About 20,000 attend.

Major Award Winners Nortel Grand Prize: *The Saga of Life: The Unknown World*, by Mikael Agaton; Best Quebec Scientific Film: *Toutatis*, by Catherine Fol; Nortel Award for Scientific Excellence: *The Man Who Colors Stars*, by David Taylor; Award for Excellence in Television: *Meet the Real Penguins*, by Lloyd Spencer Davis; Excellence in Scientific Popularization: *A Hole in Fred's Head*, by Emma Walker; Best Scientific Research Film: *Blood Vessels: The Carrier of Life*, by Junichiro Takeda

Films About 200 creepy-crawly features

Tickets $5 per individual screening; $30 for pass to all screenings

How to Enter Send VHS dub, $50 entry fee, and entry form to:

Téléscience
15, rue de la Commune Ouest
Montreal, PQ H2Y 2C6
Canada
Telephone 514.390.1117
Fax 514.982.0064
E-mail festival@artech.org
Web cite.artech.org/festival

Entry Deadline May

Telluride Film Festival

See Best of the Fests

Texas Film Festival

Where College Station, Texas

When One week in mid-February

Background Run by the MSC Film Society of Texas A & M, this festival is devoted to highlighting the work of contemporary American independents. Aside from a great deal of mediocre American indie fare, the festival has screened Luke Greenfield's *Alive and Kicking* and John Sayles's *Lone Star*.

Major Award Winners Noncompetitive

Films About 15 films

Noteworthy Celebrity Sightings John Landis

Tickets $3 per individual screening

Festival hotline 409.845.1515

How to Enter Send VHS dub and entry form to:

Texas Film Festival
Memorial Student Center
Box J-1
College Station, TX 77844
Telephone 409.845.1515
Fax 409.845.5117

Entry Deadline December

Toronto International Film Festival

See Best of the Fests

Toronto Jewish Film Festival

Where Toronto, Ontario, Canada
When One week in early May
Background "You don't have to be filmish." So goes the motto of this festival founded in 1993 and dedicated to reflecting Jewish cinema's diversity. Films are screened at Toronto's Bloor Cinema and have included *Florentine*, by Eytan Fox, and *Kalinka Maya*, by Eitan Londner.
Major Award Winners Noncompetitive
Films About 100
Tickets $8 per individual screening; $75 for a festival pass
Festival hotline 416.324.8600
How to Enter Send VHS dub and entry form to:
    Toronto Jewish Film Festival
    33 Prince Arthur Avenue
    2nd Floor
    Toronto, ON M5R 1B2
    Canada
    Telephone 416.324.8226
    Fax 416.324.8668
    E-mail tjff@interlog.com
Entry Deadline February

UFVA Student Film and Video Festival

Where Philadelphia, Pennsylvania, and various other places across the country, including Austin, Texas; New York, New York; Los Angeles, California; Oshkosh, Wisconsin; Providence, Rhode Island; and Indianapolis, Indiana
When Various times during the year
Background Founded in 1993, the UFVA festival has fast become the largest student festival in the country, offering $9,000 in prizes and sponsoring a yearlong nationwide tour of winning films. Celebrities have been called in to help with the judging, and these have included Bill Plympton and Susan Seidelman.
Major Award Winners First Prize in Animation: *Genre*, by Don Hertzfeldt; First Prize in Documentary: *Ollie's Army*, by Brett Morgen; First Prize in Experimental Film: *First Love Second Planet*, by David Munro; First Prize in Narrative Film: *John*, by Marni Banack.
Films About 37 films
Noteworthy Celebrity Sightings The ubiquitous John Pierson
How to Enter Send VHS dub, entry form, and $15 entry fee to:
    NEXTFRAME/UFVA
    Department of Film and Media Arts
    Temple University
    Philadelphia, PA 19122
    Telephone 800.499.UFVA
    Fax 215.204.6740
    E-mail ufv@avm.temple.edu
    Web www.temple.edu/nextframe
Entry Deadline May

United States Super-8 Film and Video Festival

Where New Brunswick, New Jersey
When Two days in February
Background Devoted to Super-8 as well as S-8 and Hi-8 video, this Rutgers University–based festival also sponsors an international tour for films accepted into its festival. Recent screenings have included *The Collegians Are Go!*
Films About 80 films
Tickets $4 per individual screening
How to Enter Send VHS dub, $30 entry fee, and entry form to:
    United States Super-8 Film and Video Festival
    Rutgers Film Co-op
    NJMAC
    Program in Cinema Studies
    108 Ruth Adams Building
    Douglass Campus
    Rutgers University
    New Brunswick, NJ 08903
    Telephone/Fax 908.932.8482
    E-mail NJMAC@aol.com
Entry Deadline January

USA Film Festival

Where Dallas, Texas
When One week in late April
Background Leaving aside the Joe Bob Briggs at Midnight series, which features late-night screenings of *Texas Chainsaw Massacre*-style horror, the USA fest nevertheless offers a good overview of American independent cinema. Founded in 1971 at Southern Methodist University as the Screen Generation Film Festival, the festival began with rather provocative fare including Ralph Bakshi's *Fritz the Cat* and Andy Warhol's *L'Amour* but quickly mainstreamed itself with its program of Great Screen Actor retrospectives honoring the likes of Charlton Heston, Kirk Douglas, and Shirley MacLaine. More recent tributes have included Sydney Pollack, Robert Altman, Paul Schrader, Betty Comden, Tommy Lee Jones, Paul Mazursky, and Cyd Charisse. The festival also hosts a national short film and video competition and a Kidfilm Festival in January, which has screened a tribute to Daffy Duck as well as *The Phantom Tollbooth*, *The Wizard of Oz*, and *Pufnstuf: The Movie*. Screenings are held at the AMC Glen Lakes Theatres (9450 North Central Expressway) and General Cinema Northpark (8950 North Central Expressway).
Major Award Winners Best Fiction Film: *Spark*, by Garret Williams; Best Documentary: *Breathing Lessons: The Life and Work of Mark O'Brien*, by Jessica Wu; Best Experimental Film: *Swallow*, by Elisabeth Subrin; and Best Animation: *I Am the Happy Idiot*, by Sofia Núñez, and *Where Do Cows Go?*, by Ed Gavin
Films About 100 features and shorts
Noteworthy Celebrity Sightings John Waters, Frank Oz, Richard Dreyfuss, Martha Coolidge, Mia Farrow, Liza Minelli

Tickets Call Hotline: 214.821.NEWS
How to Enter Send $40 entry fee, entry form, and VHS copy of short film (under sixty minutes) to:
> USA Film Festival
> Artistic Director
> 6116 N. Central Expressway, Suite 105
> Dallas, TX 75206
> Telephone 214.821.6300
> Fax 214.821.6364
> E-mail usafilm@mistraldg.com
> Web www.usafilmfestival.com

Entry Deadline February

Vancouver International Film Festival and Trade Forum

Where Vancouver, British Columbia, Canada
When Last week of September through first week of October
Background Founded in 1982, the festival is one of the largest and best in Canada, hosting 130,000 spectators annually. Special focuses are offered on Canadian and American independent cinema, and films are divided into the following categories: Canadian Images; Dragons and Tigers: The Cinemas of East Asia; The Best of Britain; Cinema of Our Time; Nonfiction Features; Archival Series; and Walk on the Wild Side. Over the years, the festival has paid tribute to SCTV and to Krzysztof Kieslowski, among others. Screenings are held at the Caprice (965 Granville Street), the Judge MacGill (800 Robson Street), the Pacific Cinémathéque (1131 Howe Street), the Plaza (881 Granville Street), the Ridge (3131 Arbus Street), and the Vancouver Centre (650 W. Georgia Street). In conjunction with the festival, VIFF also presents a trade forum that features roundtable discussions and seminars about motion picture financing, how to break into the system, and other somewhat predictable topics.
Major Award Winners Air Canada Award for Most Popular Film: *Breaking the Waves*; Federal Express Award for Most Popular Film: *Fire*
Films About 175 features and 50 shorts
Noteworthy Celebrity Sightings Andrea Martin, Dave Thomas, Harold Ramis, Catherine O'Hara
Tickets $7.50 per individual screening; $75 for admission to all documentaries; $200 pass grants entrance to all screenings
Festival Hotline 604.685.8352
How to Enter Send VHS dub and entry form to:
> VIFF
> 1008 Homer Street #410
> Vancouver, BC V6B 2X1
> Canada
> Telephone 604.685.0260
> Fax 604.688.8221

Entry Deadline July

Victoria Independent Short Film and Video

Where Victoria, British Columbia, Canada

When Three days in early April

Background In this British Columbian film fest, entries are restricted to 30 minutes and under in pretty much all genres. Of late, the festival, which screens at the University of Victoria, has been daring and eclectic in its programming touching on the political, environmental, and experimental. Films in recent years have included a documentary about ostrich farming in British Columbia and another documentary about Vancouver's Yuppi Puppy dog day-care facility. Alongside the films, the festival also hosts seminars on diverse topics that have included forums on the making and marketing of independent films and how new technologies affect independent video.

Major Award Winners Best of Fest (Juror's Choice Award): *House of Cards*, by James Fry; Gold Shortie for Best Narrative Film: *Full Service*, by Todd Armitage; Silver Shortie for Runner-Up Narrative Film: *Major Tom*, by Sjon Johnson; Gold Shortie for Best Documentary Film: *Francisco Sionil Jose: A Filipino Odyssey*, by Arthur Makosinski; Gold Shortie for Best Animated Film: *Blinds*, by Sean Mahoney; Best Experimental Film: *Nocturne*

How to Enter Send $10 entry fee, VHS dub, and entry form to:

    Victoria Independent Short Film and Video Festival
    F-1322 Broad Street
    Victoria, BC V8W 2C9
    Canada
    Telephone 250.384.0184
    Fax 250.385.3327
    E-mail randomrd@islandnet.com

Entry Deadline February

Virginia Film Festival

Where Charlottesville, Virginia

When Four days in late October

Background Founded in 1988, this festival, which used to be known as the Virginia Festival of American Film, focuses on the American landscape and the mythos of the American dream—Westerns, road pix, documentaries about the Grand Canyon. Think Sam Shepard crossed with John Ford and bald eagles and you get the general idea. It has a different theme each year (1998's was "Cool," 1997's was "Caged!" etc.). The festival also holds a screenwriting competition stipulating that all three winners of the $500 cash awards must include Virginia locations in 75 percent of their films ("So yeah, the inside of that house in my film, that was in Charlottesville. No, honest!").

Noteworthy Celebrity Sightings John Lurie, Roger Ebert

How to Enter Send VHS dub and $30 entry fee to:

    The Virginia Film Festival
    109 Culbreth Road
    Charlottesville, VA 22903
    Telephone 804.982.5277
    Fax 804.924.1447

E-mail filmfest@virginia.edu
Web www.virginia.edu/~vafilm
Entry Deadline July

Wine Country Film Festival

Where Glen Ellen, California
When Late July and early August
Background *USA Today* called this "one of the 10 best film festivals in the USA," and if *USA Today* says it, you've got to be a little bit suspicious. In all fairness, though, despite the praise of the Hostess Twinkie of newspapers, this is still quite a good showcase for foreign films, American independents, and retrospectives. Programs include "The Arts in Films" and "Films of Commitment." Screening in theaters in Napa and Sonoma Valley and, best of all, on outdoor screening facilities at the Rutherford Hill and Viansa wineries, this is a cozy and enjoyable festival, and cool features such as *The Space Between Us*, *Kabloonak*, and *Manhattan Merengue* have screened here. On the downside, though, lifetime achievement awards given out to the likes of Teri Garr, Dudley Moore, and Michael York make one stop and pause. Better have been the tributes to Anthony Quinn, Gregory Peck, and Nastassia Kinski. (Hey, I'd give her any award she wanted if she showed up to my festival. Hell, I'd give her 10 awards if she came to visit for Sukkoth.)
Major Award Winners Gaia Award: *Baraka*; First Feature Director's Prize: *Colpo di Luna*, by Alberto Simone; Special Mention: *The Stars Fell on Henrietta*, by James Keach; Runner-up: *Tokyo Cowboy*, by Kathy Gareau; Audience Prize: *The Ride*, by Jan Sverák, and *Sopyonje*, by Im Kwon-taek; Best Short Film: *Le Baton*, by Ron Byron
Films About 100 films
Noteworthy Celebrity Sightings Gregory Peck, Nastassia Kinski, Dennis Hopper, Nicolas Cage
How to Enter Send VHS dub, $30 fee and entry form to:
　　Wine Country Film Festival
　　12000 Henro Road, Box 300
　　Glen Ellen, CA 95442
　　Telephone 707.996.2536
　　Fax 707.966.6964
Entry Deadline April
　　E-mail wcfilmfest@aol.com
　　Web www.winecountryfilmfest.com

WorldFest Flagstaff

Where Flagstaff, Arizona
When Mid-November
Background Formerly based in Charleston, South Carolina, WorldFest champions American and foreign indies. Along with these screenings, the festival has also featured a Panorama of French Cinema in cooperation with the French government. Despite its pared-down schedule of screenings, the festival still does offer awards for a cornucopia of categories including music videos, trailers, TV commercials,

public service advertisements and Web-sites, as well as short and full-length features and documentaries.

Major Award Winners Best Feature Film: *Kabloonak*, by Claude Massot; Gold Special Jury Award: *Jerome's Secret*, by Phil Comeau; *Microcosmos*, by Claude Nuridsany and Marie Perennou; *Shiloh*, by Dale Rosenbloom; and *Sling Blade*, by Billy Bob Thornton; Best Independent Feature: *All Men Are Mortal*, by Ata de Jong; Best First Feature: *Ed's Next Move*, by John Walsh; Best Foreign Film: *Red Cherry*, by Ye Ying; Best Television Commercial: "Pepsi/Wile E. Coyote," by Kathleen Helppie-Shipley

Films About 35 features

Noteworthy Celebrity Sightings Ralph Bakshi, Jonathan Demme, Oliver Stone, John Frankenheimer

Tickets $200 silver screen pass gains admission to all screenings including opening-night gala

How to Enter Send VHS dub and entry form to:
WorldFest Flagstaff
International Film and Video Festival
P.O. Box 56566
Houston, TX 77256-6566
Telephone 803.723.7600
Fax 713.965.9960
E-mail worldfest@aol.com
Web www.vannevar.com/worldfest

Entry Deadline September

WorldFest Houston

Where Houston, Texas

When Ten days in mid-April

Background Part marketplace, part film festival, part excuse to wear deck shoes and attend a cocktail party, this fest, founded in 1968, is difficult to get a handle on, boasting so many different categories for screenings, ranging from advertising to experimental to industrial to animation, that one almost feels as if one's attending an industry convention instead of a film festival. Up until the late 1970s, the festival hadn't been able to even maintain a steady home. It started in 1968 and moved to the Virgin Islands before winding up here. Screenings are held at Houston's Meyerland Plaza (Loop 610 South at Beechnut). The best and worst aspects of the festival are the retrospectives of major directors, which routinely show the works of great masters—but not enough of them, such as the recent Akira Kurosawa tribute (three films) or 1996's tribute to 100 years of Spanish filmmaking (four films). The fest recently adopted the slogan "Small is beautiful." Intriguingly, it is the festival where Steven Spielberg and George Lucas first received awards for filmmaking. Recent screenings have included Tony Bui's *Three Seasons*, Leonard Ricagni's *The Life Jacket Is Under Your Seat*, and Dachin Hsu's *My American Vacation*.

Major Award Winners Grand Award: *For Roseanna*, by Paul Welland; Gold Special Jury Award: *Kabloonak*, by Claude Massot; Best Short Subject: *Yellow Lotus*, by Tony Bui; Best TV Production: *Smoke Alarm: The Unfiltered Truth About Cigarettes*; Best Music Video: "Have We Forgotten What Love Is?" by Crystal Bernard

Tickets $5 for matinees; $7.50 for evening shows

Festival hotline 713.965.9955
How to Enter Send entry fee (it varies and can get quite high depending on your category) to:
WorldFest Houston
Entry Director
2700 Post Oak Road, Suite 1798
Houston, TX 77056
Telephone 713.965.9955
Fax 713.965.9960
E-mail worldfest@aol.com
Web www.worldfest.org
Entry Deadline February

World Population Film/Video Festival

Where Various places
When Various times
Background As the world's population approaches an estimated 6 billion, this high-minded touring video and film competition has been developed for college and secondary students to address issues raised by the human population explosion. Student filmmakers, judged by population experts, environmentalists, and other filmmakers, compete for $10,000 in cash prizes as they consider ecology, environmental studies, science, anthropology and other related topics. Winning films occasionally are screened on MTV, VH-1, Turner Broadcasting, and public television.
Major Award Winners First Prize, secondary school: *Wetland Neighbors*, Students of Oregon Episcopal School; First Prize, college: *Brian within Reach*, by Brian Beltech
Films Approximately 25
How to Enter Send VHS film copy and entry form to:
World Population Film and Video Festival
46 Fox Hill Road
Bernardston, MA 01337
Telephone 800.638.9464
Fax 413.648.9204
E-mail info@wpfvf.cof
Web www.wpfvf.com
Entry Deadline June 15

Yorkton Short Film and Video Festival

Where Yorkton, Saskatchewan, Canada
When Four days in mid-May
Background Founded in 1950, the festival has had an up-and-down history, its headquarters having once been destroyed in a fire. Today the festival is limited to Canadian filmmakers, who compete for the Golden Sheaf, which despite its name is actually made of bronze. Awards are given in countless idiosyncratic categories including best film exploring race relations, best music video, best public affairs video, and so forth. Films that have screened here include *Second Date*.

Major Award Winners Best Performance: Randy Houston, *The Feeler*; Best Comedy: *Royal Canadian Air Force*, by Perry Rosemond; Best Drama: *L'Affaire Nogaret*, by Johanne Prégent

Noteworthy Celebrity Sightings Norman Jewison

How to Enter Send VHS dub and entry form to:
> Yorkton Film Fest
> Golden Sheaf Awards
> 49 Smith Street E.
> Yorkton, SK S3N H4
> Canada
> Telephone 306.782.7077
> Fax 306.782.1550
> E-mail yorktonshortfilm@hmt.net

Entry Deadline March

More North American Festivals

These are not complete listings. For more information on any of these festivals, write or call for details.

Adirondack Silent Film Festival
P.O. Box 489
Lake Placid, NY 12946
Telephone/Fax 518.576.2063
E-mail naj@kvvi.net
Web www.adirondackfilm-society.org

African Diaspora Film Festival
535 Cathedral Parkway, Suite 14B
New York, NY 10025
Telephone 212.749.6020
Fax 212.316.6020
E-mail artmattan@africanfil.com
Web www.africanfilm.com/festival
Annual festival held during the first two weeks of December in New York, New York.

American Motion Picture Society Film and Video Festival
P.O. Box 4034
Long Beach, CA 90804-0034
Entry Deadline August 1
Founded in 1930 (wow), this is a pretty inclusive festival that, aside from everything else, devotes a category to teenage filmmakers working in 16 mm or 8 mm.

Arizona International Film Festival
P.O. Box 431
Tucson, AZ 85702-0431
Telephone 520.628.1737
E-mail azmac@azstarnet.com
Web www.azstarnet.com
Entry Deadline February 6
Annual festival held for 10 days in mid-April in Tucson, Arizona.

Aspen Shorts Festival
110 E. Hallam, Suite 102
Aspen, CO 81611
Telephone 970.925.6882
Fax 970.925.1967
Web www.aspenfilmfest.org
Entry Deadline December 15

Baltimore Film Festival
c/o Baltimore Museum of Art
10 Art Museum Drive
Baltimore, MD 21218
Telephone 410.235.2777
Fax 410.235.3111
Annual festival held in April in Baltimore, Maryland.

Berkeley Video Festival

2054 University Ave., Suite 203
Berkeley, CA 94704
Tel: 510.843.3699
Fax 510.843.3379
E-mail vid3699@aol.com
Annual festival held in late February
and early March. Formerly known as
the East Bay Video Festival.

Bermuda Film Festival

Festival Hotline 441.293.FILM
E-mail bdafilm@ibl.bm
Entry Deadline December 1
Annual festival held the first week of
May in Bermuda.

Birmingham International Educational Film Fest

Student Video Expo
P.O. Box 2641
Birmingham, AL 35291-0665
Telephone 205.250.2711
Fax 205.933.9080

Black Harvest Film Festival

The Film Center
School of the Art Institute
280 S. Columbus Drive
Chicago, IL 60603
Entry Deadline May 15
Excellently curated selection of contemporary black cinema held every year for one week in mid-July.

Border Film Festival

Festival passes $25
Annual festival held the first week of
November in Las Cruces, New Mexico.
Telephone 505.526.2226

Canadian International Annual Film Festival

25 Eugenia St.
Barrie, ON L4M 1P6
Canada
Telephone/Fax 705.733.8232
E-mail ciaff@canada.com
Web ciaff.org
Entry Deadline June 1

Cancún Film Festival

Festival Internacional Cinematográfico
de Cancún
Calzada de Tlalplan 1838
Col. Country Club CP
04220 DF
Mexico
Telephone 011.5298.689.0812
Fax 011.5298.689.0988
Entry Deadline October
Annual festival taking place for one week
in late November and early December.

Certamen Internacional de Cine

Apertado 171
Guadalajara 19080
Mexico

Columbus International Film and Video Festival

Film Council of Greater Columbus
3701 N. High St., Suite 204
Worthington, OH 43085
Telephone/Fax 614.841.1666
Entry Deadline July 1
Annual festival taking place in mid-
October, focusing on Latin American
and Caribbean filmmakers.

Cucalorus Film Festival

P.O. Box 2763
Wilmington, N.C. 28402
Telephone 910.343.5995
Fax 910.762.8572
E-mail cucalorus@mailcity.com
Web site www.cucalorus.org

Dances with Films

Dances with Films
Warner Hollywood Studios
1041 N. Formosa
Pickford Building, Room 203
West Hollywood, CA 90046
Telephone 323.850.2929
Fax 323.50.2928
E-mail info@danceswithfilms.com
Web www.danceswithfilms.com
Entry Deadline May 15
Annual festival held in Los Angeles in
late July.

European Union Film Festival
c/o The Film Center
Columbus Drive and Jackson Boulevard
Telephone 312.443.3733
Web www.artic.edu/saic/art/filmcntr
Annual festival of films from all coun-
tries in the European Union, held in
February.

Far North Film Festival
#4-4807 49th Street
Yellowknife, NT X1A 3T5
Canada
Telephone 403.873.4262
Fax 403.873.3654
A festival dedicated to promoting film-
makers from the circumpolar world.
Held for a weekend in late November in
Yellowknife in the Northwest
Territories.

Festival Cine Latino
346 Ninth Street
Second Floor
San Francisco, CA 94103
Telephone 415.553.8135
Fax 415.863.7428
E-mail cineaccion@aol.com
Entry Deadline May

Festival Silence Elles Tournent
Telephone 514.845.2821
E-mail eltourne@Mlink.net
Web www.vir.com/~amazines/
    amazones.html
Annual festival focusing on women
directors (Patricia Rozema, Mira Nair,
and others) held for one week in
October.

Film Arts Festival
346 Ninth Street
2nd Floor
San Francisco, CA 94103
Telephone 415.552.8760
Fax 415.522.0882
E-mail festival@filmarts.org
Web www.filmarts.org
Entry Deadline July
Annual festival held in late October and
early November.

Filmfront National Student Film and Video Festival
206 P.A.B.
University of Utah
Salt Lake City, UT 84112
Telephone 801.328.2428
Entry Deadline October

Floating Film Festival
15366 17th Ave., #441
White Rock, BC V4A 1T9
Canada
Telephone 604.531.7462
Fax 604. 987.8715
Web site www.cinepad.com/fff.html

Global Africa International Film and Video Festival
900 Fallon Street
9th Floor
Oakland, CA 94607
Telephone 510.464.3253
Fax 510.464.3418
Entry Deadline March

Guadalajara Film Festival
Av. Alemania 1370
Col. Moderna
Guadalajara 44190 Jalisco
Mexico
Telephone 523.812.1523
Fax 523.811.1882
E-mail muestra@cencar.udg.mx
Annual festival taking place for one
week in March.

Hollywood Black Film Festival
Hollywood Black Film Festival
1620 Centinela Ave., Suite 204
Inglewood, CA 90302
Telephone 310.348.3942
Fax 310.348.3949
E-mail info@hbff.org
Web www.hbff.org
Entry Deadline August
Annual festival in Inglewood,
California; in late February or early
March.

Hollywood Film Festival
433 North Camden Drive, Suite 600
Beverly Hills, CA 90210
Telephone 310.288.1882
Fax 310.475.0193
Entry Deadline June 1

Hometown Video Festival
The Buske Group
30001 J Street, Suite 28
Sacramento, CA 95816
Telephone 916.441.6277
Fax 916.441.7670
Entry Deadline March

Hong Kong Film Festival
The Film Center
School of the Art Institute
280 S. Columbus Drive
Chicago, IL 60603
Telephone 312.443.3737
Annual festival of Hong Kong films held at Chicago's Art Institute.

International Student Film Festival
International Student Film Festival
721 Broadway, Room 11043
New York, NY 10003
Telephone 212.998.1795
Fax 212.995.4063
Web www.nyu.edu/pages/intlfest
Entry Deadline By invitation only

International Student Film Festival
Film Festival Committee
Citadel Theatre
9828-101A Avenue
Edmonton, AB T5J 2L6
Canada
Entry Deadline April

Los Angeles Asian Pacific American Film and Video Festival
Visual Communications
263 S. Los Angeles Street, Suite 307
Los Angeles, CA 90012
Telephone 213.680.4462
Fax 213.687.4848
E-mail viscom@vc.apnet.org
Held in May in Los Angeles.

Louisville Film and Video Festival
c/o Speed Art Museum
2035 S. Third St.
Louisville, KY 40208
Telephone/Fax 502.896.2146
E-mail lfvf@artswatch.org
Web www.artswatch.org/LFVF.html
Entry Deadline August 2

MadCat Women's International Film Festival
MadCat Women's International
Film Festival
937 Fell Street
San Francisco, CA 4117
Telephone 415.436.9523
Fax 415.934.0642
E-mail alionbear@earthlink.net
Entry Deadline Late July
This festival, held one night each week in September, features films of all genres made by women from all over the world. Screenings have included Doris Wishman's *Bad Girls Go to Hell*.

Maine International Film Festival
10 Railroad Square
Waterville, ME 04901
Telephone 207.861.8138
Fax 207.872.5502
E-mail info@miff.org
Web www.miff.org
Entry Deadline April
Annual festival held in mid-July.

Marin County National Film Competition
Marin County Fair and Exposition
Fairgrounds
San Rafael, CA 94903
Telephone 415.499.6400
Entry Deadline May

Martinique Caribbean Film and Video Festival
77, Route de la Folie
97200 Fort de France
Martinique
Telephone 011.596.70.2381

Fax 011.596.63.2391
Annual festival held in June.

Maui Film Festival
P.O. Box 669
Paia, HI 96779
Telephone 808.579.9996
Fax 808.579.9552
E-mail mauifilmfestival@mauifilm
    festival.com
Web www.mauifilmfestival.com
Entry Deadline March 30
Annual festival held in June.

Moondance Film Festival
970 Ninth St.
Boulder, CO 80302
Telephone 303.545.0202
E-mail mermaid7cs@aol.com

Muestra del Cine Mexicano
University of Guadalajara
Avenue Vallarta, No. 2181 SJ CP
44140, Jalisco
Mexico
Annual festival taking place for one
week in mid-March.

N.A.P. Video Festival
New Arts Program
P.O. Box 0082
173 W. Main Street
Kutztown, PA 19530
Telephone/Fax 610.683.6440
Entry Deadline December 16
A mobile festival held in various spots
on the East Coast during the spring and
summer. Dedicated to screening the
best in narrative, experimental, and
documentary films on VHS, the festival
screens in New York and in
Philadelphia, Reading, and Lehigh,
Pennsylvania.

National Educational Film and Video Festival
655 13th Street
Oakland, CA 94612-1220
Telephone 510.465.6885
Fax 510.465.2835
E-mail nemn@aol.com

National Latino Film and Video Festival
El Museo del Barrio
1230 Fifth Avenue
New York, NY 10029
Telephone 212.831.7272
Fax 212.831.7927

New Frontiers Film Festival
IFCO
2 Daly Ave. Arts Court
Ottawa, ON K1N 6E2
Canada
Telephone 613.569.1789
Fax 613.563.4427
E-mail info@cyberus.ca
Web www.cyberus.ca/~ifco
One week in mid-November.

NO DANCE Film & Multimedia Festival
703 Pier Avenue, #675
Hermosa Beach, CA 90254
Telephone 310.939.6269
Fax 310.374.0134

Northern Lights International Film and Video Festival
1101 Cordova Street
Building 2, Suite 322
Anchorage, AK 99501
Telephone 907.274.6962
Fax 907.277.7925
Entry Deadline August 1
Super-8, 16 mm, and video festival
dedicated to Arctic traditions, culture,
and wildlife, held annually in mid-
September in Anchorage.

Palm Springs International Short Film Festival
1700 E. Tahquitz Cyn Way
Palm Springs, CA 92262
Telephone 619.322.2930
Fax 619.322.4087
E-mail filmfest@ix.net.com
Entry Deadline May

Palo Alto French Film Festival
Spargenburg Theatre
780 Arastradero Road
Palo Alto, CA 94306
Tickets $7

Telephone 510.601.8932
Web www.paff.org

Peachtree International Film Fest
140 First Union Plaza
999 Peach Tree Street NE
Atlanta, GA 30309
Telephone 770.729.8487
Fax 770.263.0652
Annual festival held in early November.

Philadelphia Independent Film and Video Festival
P.O. Box 11657
Philadelphia, PA 19116
Telephone 215.522.8787
E-mail wropro@msn.com
Entry Deadline January 15
Annual festival of features, shorts, documentaries, experimental films, music videos, and student films held for one week in late March. The festival promises that no accepted entry will be censored. Well, it is in Philadelphia after all.

Pittsburgh International Lesbian and Gay Film Festival
P.O. Box 110224
Pittsburgh, PA 15232
Telephone 412.232.3277
E-mail pilgf@trfn.clpgh.org
Web www.pilgff.org

Portchester Film Festival
630 Gramatan Avenue
Mount Vernon, NY 10552
Annual Super-8 film festival.

Portland Jewish Film Festival
Northwest Film Center
1219 S.W. Park Avenue
Portland, OR 97205
Telephone 503.221.1156
Fax 503.294.0874
E-mail info@nwfilm.org
Web site www.nwfilm.org
Entry Deadline November

Rainy States Film Festival
1136 13th Avenue
Box C
Seattle, WA 98122-4405

E-mail chip@halcyon.com
Entry Deadline December
Held for four days in mid-February, the festival concentrates on films made for under $500,000 by filmmakers who hail from Washington state, Alaska, Oregon, and British Columbia, Canada.

Rhode Island International Film Festival
Mailing Address: P.O. Box 162
Newport, Rhode Island 02840
Telephone 401.847.7590
Fax 401.861.4445
Office Address: 55 Bradford Street, Suite 300
Providence, RI 02903
E-mail flicksart@aol.com
Annual festival held for a week in August.

Rocky Mountain Women's Film Festival
255 Laurel Oak Court
Colorado Springs, CO 80906
E-mail dbkvi@aol.com
Entry Deadline June
Annual festival held for a weekend in November.

San Antonio Cine Festival
Guadalupe Culture Arts Center
1300 Guadalupe Street
San Antonio, TX 78207-5519
Telephone 512.271.3151
Fax 512.271.3480
Annual festival taking place in August

San Diego International Film Festival
Telephone 619.558.3456

San Diego Underwater Film Festival
San Diego Underwater Film Festival
P.O. Box 82782
San Diego, CA 92138
Telephone 909.676.8986
Entry Deadline Not available
Founded in 1964, this festival sponsored by the San Diego Underwater Photographic Society has included films with titles like *Drift Kelp: Tales of Life*, *Let's Go Diving*, *California Fish Part I*, *Aqua Expressions*, *Island Alchemy*, and

that much-discussed sequel *California Fish Part II*. Films are shown in conjunction with exhibits of underwater photography.

San Francisco Environmental Film Festival
Good First
398 60th Street
Oakland, CA 94618
Telephone 510.654.4400
Fax 510.654.4551
E-mail foodfirst@igc.apc.org

Santa Clarita International Film Festival
Telephone 805.257.8989
Entry Deadline November 1
Annual festival held for one week in mid-February in Santa Clarita.

Sierra Club Film and Video Fest
Telephone 212.391.6801
Fax 212.391.7508
E-mail festinfo@sierrafilmfest.org
Festival of nature films screened in late May at the New School in New York City.

Silver Images Film Festival
9848 W. Winchester Avenue
Chicago, IL 60643
Telephone 773.881.6940
Web www.terranova.org
Annual festival of films dealing with issues concerning the elderly. The festival screens at the Field Museum, Loyola University, Facets Multimedia, and other locations throughout the city.

Silver Lake Film Festival
2658 Griffith Park Boulevard
Los Angeles, CA 90039
Entry Deadline Late June
Annual festival held in mid-September.

Slice of Life Film and Video Showcase
Documentary Resource Center
106 Boalsburg Road
P.O. Box 909
Lemont, PA 16851
Telephone 814.234.1945
Fax 814.234.0939

Entry Deadline April
Annual festival held for three days in mid-July.

South Carolina Paddlesports Film Festival
4720 Portobello Road
Columbia, SC 29206
Telephone 803.777.9181
E-mail cbrennecke@aol.com
Web www.columbiasc.com

St. Barts Caribbean Film Festival
Telephone 212.989.8004
Fax 212.727.1774
E-mail jpharris@ritz.mordor.com

Sun Valley Documentary Film Festival
Sun Valley Center for the Arts
P.O. Box 656
Sun Valley, ID 97205
Telephone 208.726.9491
Fax 208.726.2344
E-mail mwitt@micron.net
Web site www.sunvalleyid.com/svcenter

Tacoma Tortured Artists Film Festival
Telephone 888.202.5827
Fax 253.627.1525
E-mail TacomaFilm@aol.com
Web www.clubseven.com
Entry Deadline July 31
Annual festival held in mid-September.

Temecula Valley International Film Festival
TV Chamber of Commerce
27450 Ynez Road, Suite 104
Temecula, CA 92591
Telephone 909.699.6267
Fax 909.695.5126
Web www.tviff.com
Annual festival held in mid-September focusing on romantic comedies. Recent winners include Best Foreign Film Award: *Shergar*; Best Documentary: *Vietnam: Long Time Coming*; Best Short Film: *Opie Gone Mad*; Best Animation: *1,001 Nights*; Best Feature Film: *Scrapbook*.

Three Rivers Film Festival
Pittsburgh Filmmakers
477 Melwood Ave.
Pittsburgh, PA 15213
Telephone 412.681.5449
Two-week film festival held in conjunction with Three Rivers Arts festival.

Two Rivers Native Film and Video Festival
The Native Arts Circle
1443 E. Franklin Avenue, Suite 7D
Minneapolis, MN 55404
Telephone 612.870.7173
Fax 612.870.9327
Entry Deadline October
Annual festival taking place in
November.

U.S. Comedy Arts Festival
2049 Century Park E., Suite 4200
Los Angeles, CA 90067
Telephone 310.201.9595
Fax 310.201.9445
E-mail film@uscaf.com
Web www.uscaf.com
Entry Deadline December 1
Annual festival held in mid-Febraury.

West Virginia International Film Festival
Telephone 304.342.7100
Fax 304.776.8469

E-mail haynespam@aol.com
Web www.wviff.org
Entry Deadline August 1
Annual festival held for 10 days in early
November in Charleston, West Virginia.

Women in Film International Film Festival
6464 Sunset Boulevard, Suite 900
Hollywood, CA 90028
Telephone 213.463.6040
Fax 213.463.0963

**Women in the Director's Chair International
Film and Video Festival**
941 W. Lawrence Avenue
Chicago, IL 60625
Telephone 773.907.0610
Web www.widc.org
Annual festival of films directed by
women.

World Animation Celebration
30101 Agoura Court, Suite 110
Agoura Hill, CA 91301
Telephone 818.991.2884
Fax 818.991.3773
Annual festival held the last week of
March in Agoura Hill.

3 European Film Festivals

Europa Europa, Zooropa Zooropa

Alès Film Festival

Where Alès, France
When Ten days in mid-March
Background Founded in 1983, the mid-sized festival provides a good selection of tributes, retrospectives, and French premieres. Seeking, as the folks at the Alès fest tell us, to "wed cinematographic heritage with recent film trends," the festival screens films based on the theme of "itinerances," films about wandering—road movies, travel films, films about exile—and has screened films in this tradition from the likes of Agnes Varda, Alain Tanner, Claire Denis, and Aki Kaurismaki. The festival also hosts a competitive program of short films and a festival of 15 films for children. Young folks between 14 and 20 can work at the Faites Votre Cinéma workshop, especially designed for disadvantaged youth to develop a screenplay and shoot it. About 10,000 attend annually.
Major award winners Noncompetitive
Noteworthy Celebrity Sightings Solveig Dommartin, Sandrine Bonnaire, Ben Gazzara, Henri Alekan, Samuel Fuller
How to Enter Send VHS dub and entry form to:
Festival Cinéma d'Alès
    Mas Bringer
    Rue Stendhal
    France 30100 Alès
    Telephone 011.33.1466.30.24.26
    Fax 011.33.1466.56.87.24
    E-mail itinerances@wanadoo.fr
    Web www.itinerances.fr.st
Entry Deadline Not available

Alpe Adria Cinema International Film Festival

Where Trieste, Italy

When One week in mid-June

Background Founded in 1988, this festival held in the border town of Trieste is devoted to showcasing the cinema of so-called Middle Europe, including films from Poland, Hungary, the Czech Republic, Slovakia, Germany, Austria, Slovenia, Croatia, Switzerland, Bulgaria, Albania, and Yugoslavia. Initially known as "Meetings with Cinema of Central and Eastern Europe," the festival selects 13 films from the aforesaid countries for its official section and has presented retrospectives on Middle European cinema. One particular retrospective featured a focus on the avant-garde and experimental, paying close attention to Slovenian modern art movements.

Major award winners Noncompetitive

Noteworthy Celebrity Sightings Jan Sverak, Jelena Rajkovic, Ivan Salaj, Miran Zupanic

How to Enter Send VHS dub and entry form to:
Via S. Rocco
1 Via della Pescheria, 4
34100 Trieste TS
Italy
Telephone 011.39.40.311.153
Fax 011.39.40.311.193

Entry Deadline Not available

Amalfi Screens on the Bay

Where Amalfi, Italy

When First week of October

Background Also known as "Cartoons on the Bay," the festival is mostly focused on animation but has its cool, idiosyncratic aspects as well, such as opportunities for children to play in Amalfi's *Toy Village*, an exhibition of old magazines, and even "la Pellicola da salvare," in which an old cartoon is restored during the week of the festival.

Major Award Winners UNICEF Award for Best Cartoon: *The Sun Is a Yellow Giraffe*, by Elmer Diktonius; Special Mention for Technical Innovation: *Brambly Hedge*, by Brian Little; Special Mention for the Best Script: *Dexter's Laboratory*, by Gennady Tartakovsky; Silver Pulcinella for the Best TV Movie: *Testament: The Bible in Animation*, by Alda Ziablikova; Silver Pulcinella for the Best Series for Infants: *Percy the Park Keeper*, by Geoff Dunbar; Silver Pulcinella for the Best Series for Teenagers: *Kablam*, by R. Mittemthal, W. McRobb, and C. Viscardil; Silver Pulcinella for All Audiences: *The Lion King's Timon and Pumba*, by T. Craig and E. Houchins; Silver Pulcinella for the Best European Series: *The Sun Is a Yellow Giraffe*, by Elmer Diktonius; Golden Pulcinella for the Best Series of the Year: *Link*, by Tapani Knuutila; and Golden Pulcinella for the Best Character of the Year: *Rotten Ralph*, by John Matthews

How to Enter Send VHS dub and entry form to:
Screens on the Bay (Amalfi)
Sacis
Via Tel.uada 66
00195-Rome RM

Italy
Telephone 011.39.6.374.981
Fax 011.39.6.372.3492
E-mail masella@mail.sacis.it or gianandrea@mail.sacis.it
Entry Deadline Not available

Amsterdam International Documentary Film Festival

Where Amsterdam, Netherlands
When 10 days in late November and early December
Background This is one of the most elaborate and diverse festivals of documentary films, spanning the globe with an amazing selection of features. Founded in 1987, the IDFA holds a competition for documentary films and one for videos. It also hosts a Reflecting Images section, featuring documentaries out of competition; Top 10 (a selection of favorite films chosen by a noted figure in the film biz); Highlights of the Lowlands (a selection of the best recent Dutch documentaries); First Appearance (featuring first- and second-time filmmakers); and Platform (films from developing countries). Each year the festival invites the directors of national film institutes to select series of films from their countries. Recently, the fest has dedicated screenings to the atrocities of Srebrenica, including the film *A Cry from the Grave*. Other screenings have included the Dutch documentaries *Crazy* and *God Is My Co-Pilot*. In previous years, screenings have been presented by the Hungarian Film Institute, the National Film Archive of India, the Israel Film Archive, the Japan National Film Center, Latvia's International Centre of Cinema, and many others. The festival also holds seminars and forums on documentary financing. About 50,000 attend each year.
Major Award Winners Best Film: *Atman*, by Pirjo Honkasalo; Silver Wolf Award for Best Film: *Mr. Behrman: Life Dream Death*, by Andreas Voigt; Special Jury Award: *The Typewriter, the Rifle, and the Movie Camera*, by Adam Simon; Audience Award for Best Film: *Blue Eyed*, by Bertram Verhaag; and *Away Matches*, by Puck de Leeuw; Jan Vrijman Fund: *Sowing Seeds*, by Avic Illagen and *Married to the Gods*, by Shyamal Sengupta
Films About 175 documentaries
How to Enter Send VHS dub and entry form to:
DFA
Kleine-Gartmanplantsoen 10
1017 RR Amsterdam
Netherlands
Telephone 011.31.20.627.33.29
Fax 011.31.20.638.53.88
E-mail info@idfa.nl
Web www.idfa.nl
Entry Deadline August

Art Film Festival

See Best of the Fests

Austrian Film Days

Where Vienna, Austria
When First week of October
Background One of the best aspects of this festival is its program of Partner Presentations. Here's how it works: the festival chooses a filmmaker and a film for its program and allows that filmmaker to present a European film of his or her own choice. Writer/director Reinhard Jud has shown an early work of Emir Kusturica, while Peter Patzak chose the work of Russian-born Pavel Lungin. In addition to this section, the festival offers programs of new Austrian works, Austrian and European avant-garde works, shorts, educational films, and a strange but intriguing selection of revivals. One of the most eye-catching features of recent years was the Austrian premiere of 1968's Otto Preminger comedy *Skidoo*, featuring Groucho Marx in his last film role as a gangster in the world of hippies and psychedelia. The festival also offers a self-explanatory section of Weird Cinema and has offered retrospectives of the works of Peter Kern and Margareta Heinrich.
Major Award Winners Best Film ($15,000): *Malli: Artist in Residence*, by Peter Zach
Films Around 100 total features and shorts
Noteworthy Celebrity Sightings Emir Kusturica, János Szász, Robert-Adrian Pejo
Tickets 75 S per individual screening
How to Enter Send VHS dub and entry form to:
Austrian Film Days
Columbusgasse 2
1100 Vienna
Austria
Telephone 011.43.1.60.40.126
Fax 011.43.1.60.20.795
E-mail 101645.3204@compuserve.com
Entry Deadline Not available

Balticum Film and TV Festival

Where Svaneke, Denmark
When One week in early June
Background Screening films in the 173-year-old Ronne Theater, the oldest theater in Denmark, the festival is dedicated primarily to films from Denmark, Estonia, Finland, Germany, Latvia, Lithuania, Poland, Russia, and Sweden. Tributes have included Swedish director Hans Alfredson and a retrospective of Latvian films. Recent screenings include *Eisenstein*, *Wednesday*, and a cartoon called *Die Hard*. There is also a children's festival and film-pitching seminars, and the festival even offers a babysitting service. In addition, the festival screens at the Kino Gudhjem.
Major Award Winners First Prize for Best Documentary: *Bread Day*, by Sergey Dvortsevoy; Second Prize: *White Sky*, by Susanne Helke and Virpi Suutari; Press Jury Prize: *Amateur Photographer*, by Dariusz Jablonski; Third Prize: *A Real Brian*, by Carsten Fromberg; Best Documentary: *Bread Day*, by Sergey Dvortsevoy
Noteworthy Celebrity Sightings Mike Leigh
Films About 53 features, documentaries, shorts, and cartoons

Tickets 30 DKr per individual screening; 275 DKr for admittance to screenings
How to Enter Send VHS dub and entry form to:
    Balticum Film and TV Festival
    Baltic Media Centre
    Skippergade 8
    Svaneke 3470
    Denmark
    Telephone. 011.45.70.202002
    Fax 011.45.70.202001
    E-mail balticmediacenter@bmc.dk
    Web http://www.dk-web.com/bbf/index.htm
Entry Deadline January

Barcelona International Exhibition of Gay and Lesbian Films

Where Barcelona, Spain
When Last week of November and first week of December
Background Founded in 1995 by Casa Lambda, the festival shows a great deal of contemporary world gay and lesbian cinema under the rubric "Pink and Purple." The festival also features retrospectives, such as a recent one called "Stonewall," which paid tribute to the most militant films of the 1990s, and homages to famous gay artistic personalities, such as a recent one to Jean Genet, which was highlighted by the screening of Genet's rare *Un Chant d'Amour*. It is estimated that around 6,000 attend annually.
Major Award Winners Best Short: *Achilles*, by Berry Purves; Audience Award for Best Short: *Trevor*, by Peggy Rajski; Best Film: *Sister My Sister*, by Nancy Meckler, and *Stonewall*, by Nigel Finch
Films About 40
Noteworthy Celebrity Sightings Patrice Chereau
How to Enter Send VHS dub and entry form to:
    Exhibition of Gay and Lesbian Films
    C/ Ample, 5
    08002 Barcelona
    Spain
    Telephone 011.34.3.412.74.76
    Fax 011.34.3.412.72.72
Entry Deadline August

Belfort International Film Festival

Where Belfort, France
When Last week of November
Background You've got to prefer the European concepts of festivals over the American ones. While American festivals nearly always tell you that their main goal is to link distributors with new filmmakers or to increase the audience base of the endowment for their not-for-profit, festivals such as this one declare their goals as "allowing the discovery of a new talent" and "to defend a certain ideal of the

cinema." Located near the Vosges mountain range, this festival focuses on young filmmakers, accepting only first-, second-, or third-time features, documentaries, and shorts (no longer than 12 minutes).

Major Award Winners Grand Prix du Jury-Prix du Public: *Y Aura-t-il de la Neige a Noël*, by Sandrine Veysset; Prix du Public: *La Mémoire Est-elle Soluble dans l'Eau?*, by Charles Najman; Grand Prix du Jury: *Reprise*, by Hervé LeRoux

How to Enter Send VHS dub and rudimentary entry form to:
Entrevues-Festival du Film
Direction des Affaires Culturelles
Hotel de Ville
90020 Belfort
France
Telephone 011.33.84.54.24.43
Fax 011.33.84.43.25.26

Entry Deadline October

Bilbao Festival of Documentary and Short Films

Where Bilbao, Spain

When One week in late November

Background Bilbao is not only a land praised in a great Kurt Weill-Bertolt Brecht song; it's also the home of one of the world's oldest festivals of shorts and documentaries. Founded in 1958 as the Festival Internacional de Cine Documental y Cortometraje de Bilbao, the festival is dedicated to the motto of "understanding between men [and women, one might presume] through pictures." Films accepted are generally under 30 minutes, though the rules may be stretched under special circumstances.

Major Award Winners Grand Prize for Best Film (400,000 ptas): *Fridge*, by Peter Mullan

How to Enter Send VHS dub and entry form to:
Bilbao International Festival of Documentary and Short Films
Colón de Larreategui, Vizcaya 37-4
48009 Bilbao
Spain
Telephone 011.34.4.424.55.07
Fax 011.34.4.424.56.24

Entry Deadline September

Birmingham International Film and TV Festival

Where Birmingham, England

When Last two weeks of November

Background Founded in 1985 by film director/producer Roger Shannon, the festival is not exactly a trailblazer in terms of film exposition, but it's quite good for a mid-size festival. Screening at Electric Cinema, MAC, Odeon Cinema, Piccadilly Cinema, and the Arcadian Center, the festival mainly concentrates on movies that will soon get greater releases throughout England and highlights from the Venice and Cannes festivals. Films that have screened here include such yawns as *Flirting with Disaster*, *Basquiat*, and *Kansas City*. Better are the less predictable series of retrospectives, which have included the works of Ken Loach, Humphrey Jennings's war films, and films by Peter Watkins.

Major Award Winners Noncompetitive
Films About 50 feature films
Noteworthy Celebrity Sightings Lynda LaPlante
Tickets £4.25 per screening; £70 gains admittance to all screenings
How to Enter Send VHS dub and entry form to:
    Birmingham International Film and TV Festival
    Central Television
    Broad Street
    Birmingham
    UK
    B1 2JP
    Telephone 011.44.121.634.4213
    Fax 011.44.121.634.4392
    Web www.centralcyberco.uk/filmfest
Entry Deadline July 1

Bitola Film Camera Festival

Where Skopje, Macedonia
When First week of October
Background The only major film festival in Macedonia, the Film Camera fest has premiered works as disparate as *Seven*, *Antonia's Line*, and Walter Koepp's *Cold Homeland*. In keeping with the camera theme, the festival has hosted film retrospectives of the works of famed directors of photography, as well as a series of children's and animated films.

Major Award Winners Noncompetitive
Films About 20 features
How to Enter Send VHS dub and entry form to:
    Film Camera Festival
    Vardar-Film 8 Mart 4
    91000 Skopje
    Macedonia
    Telephone 011.389.91.117527
    Fax 011.389.91.211811
    Web www.ultra.com.mk/manaki/programs.html
Entry Deadline Not available

Brest Short Film Festival

Where Brest, France
When One week in mid November
Background Aside from being a noteworthy spot for roast chicken, since 1986 Brest has also been the capital for screenings of eccentric short films, especially in the "Brest Off" program during its shorts festival. Brest Off has been known to arrange

films under peculiar subject headings such as "sowing one's wild oats," "love's fever," and "road movies." Short films, by the festival's definition, are under 52 minutes, one minute for every week of the year. About 20,000 attend.

Major Award Winners Grand Prix European Film: *Soldier's Bride*, by Vilka Tzouras; Grand Prix French Film: *Little Fish Killer*, by Alexandre Gavras; Jury Special Mention: *Greenmonkey*, by Rob Sprackling

Films About 40 short films in competition, 170 total

Tickets 35 F per individual admission; 250 F for an all-festival pass

How to Enter For more information contact:
Festival du Court Métrage de Brest
40, rue de la République
B.P. 173
29269 Brest
France
Telephone 011.33.98.44.03.94
Fax 011.33.98.80.25.24
E-mail film.festival@brest.com
Web www.film-festival.brest.com

Entry Deadline August

Brighton Arts Film Festival

Where Brighton, England

When Three weeks in May

Background Held in conjunction with the Brighton Arts Festival, an ultra-cool art fair with theater programs and art exhibits, the film fest here offers very cool retrospectives of classic cinema and silent films. The festival has screened Ernst Lubitsch's *Lady Windermere's Fan*; Sergei Eisenstein's *Strike!*; and Harold Lloyd's *The Freshman*, with an original score by Carl Davis. One recent cool retrospective featured British and French films from the 1960s, including Lindsay Anderson's *If* and Luis Buñuel's *Belle de Jour*.

Major Award Winners Noncompetitive

Films About 50

Tickets £3.50 per individual screening

How to Enter Send VHS dub and entry form to:
Brighton Arts Festival
21-22 Old Steine
Brighton
UK
BN1 1EL
Telephone 011.44.1273.713.875
Fax 011.44.1273.622.453

Entry Deadline Not applicable

Brno 16 (Brnênská Sestnáctka)

Where Brno, Czech Republic

When Four days in mid-October

Background Devoted primarily to short films, the Czech republic festival, founded in 1959, holds a competition honoring works in the categories of amateur works, student works, and works by freelance filmmakers. The festival, though it seems to be more enthusiastic about traditional narrative structures, seems to attract some of the most out-there and bizarre international filmmakers, many of whom come from the United States. Marek Najbrt's *The Invention of Beauty* concerns a robot who cannot stop singing, while Ruben Smillow's *Hard Eyes* deals with a girl who is trapped by animated camera lenses. Films are screened in Brno's White House.

Major Award Winners First Prize: *The Invention of Beauty*, by Marek Najbrt; Gold Medal: *Hard Eyes*, by Ruben Smillow, and *Lucia*, by Pedro Ballesteros; Silver Medal: *Excuse Me*, by Csaba Bereczki, and *The Brave Schoolgirl*, by Czech Nekrofilm; Bronze Medal: *The Lost Street*, by Marko Wilms

Films 43 in the competition; 16 shown out of competition

How to Enter Send $15 entry fee, entry form, and video to:
Brno 16
Kulturní a informacní centrum mêsta Brna
Radnická 4
658 78 Brno
Czech Republic
Telephone 011.420.5.4221.6139
Fax 011.420.5.4221.4625

Entry Deadline August

Brussels Animated Film and Cartoon Festival

Where Brussels, Belgium

When Twelve days in early February

Background Founded in 1982, the festival screens animated shorts and features in the 900 seat Auditorium 44 and, best of all, in the Botanic Cultural Center, which has been transformed from a botanical garden into two state-of-the-art cinemas. The festival, in addition to traditional cartoon fare, screens the best of multimedia work, computer animation, and special effects. Works including Enzo d'Alo's *The Blue Arrow* and (argh) *Space Jam* have screened here. There is a late-night series that features Beavis and Butt-head-style material and also retrospectives that have included one on Sarah Ann Kennedy and one on the Aargh! Studio.

Major Award Winners Noncompetitive except for People's Choice Award: *Noel Gourmand*, by Corinne Kuyl

Films About 100 flicks

Tickets 200 FB for adult tickets; 140 BF for children's tickets

How to Enter Send VHS dub and entry form to:
Le Festival du Dessin Animé
Rue de la Rhétorique 19
1060 Brussels
Belgium
Telephone 011.32.2.534.41.25
Fax 011.32.2.534.22.79
E-mail folioscope@skynet.be
Web www.awn.com

Entry Deadline November

Brussels International Festival of Fantasy, Thriller, and SF Films

Where Brussels, Belgium
When Two weeks in mid-March
Background Old film and television actors don't die; they just turn up in weird B-movies that show up on late-night cable and at the Brussels International Festival of Fantasy, Thriller, and Sci-fi Films. Founded in 1983, the festival plays host every year to about 50,000 spectators, who get the opportunity to see classic sci-fi films (*Forbidden Planet*), cutting-edge contemporary cinema (Neil Jordan's *In Dreams* and Kim Ji-won's *The Quiet Family*), and a hell of a lot of schlock. Few other festivals as large and well-attended as this one afford the viewer the opportunity to munch down on popcorn and see James Belushi and Rob Lowe in *Living in Peril*, Karen Black in *Crimetime*, Corbin Bernsen in *The Dentist*, or even a German film titled *The Killer Condom*. Half the show goes on outside the cinema in the variety of strange events held here, including the Bal des Vampires, a grotesque masked ball held at midnight on the first Saturday of the festival.
Major Award Winners The Raven: *Lawn Dogs*, by John Duigan; Audience Prize: *Over My Dead Body*, by Rainer Matsutani
Films More than 100 features, plus about 50 shorts
Noteworthy Celebrity Sightings Parker Posey, Robert Englund, Alan Parker, Luc Besson, Herbert Lom, Rod Steiger, Roger Corman, Patrick MacNee, Terry Gilliam
How to Enter Send VHS dub and entry form to:
　　Brussels International Festival of Fantasy Films
　　Avenue de la Reine 144
　　1030 Brussels
　　Belgium
　　Telephone 011.32.2.201.17.13
　　Fax 011.32.2.201.14.69
　　Web www.bifff.org
Entry Deadline January

Brussels International Film Festival

Where Brussels, Belgium
When Ten days in late January
Background Founded in 1974, this is yet another excellent festival in a city that probably has more of them than it deserves. There is a focus here on Belgian features and shorts, but a good selection of Euro-features are screened here as well.
Major Award Winners Best Film: *Theory of Flight*, by Paul Greengrass; Best Actor: Om Puri in *My Son the Fanatic*; Best Actress: Anita Kuskowska, *NIC*
Films About 100 features and 150 shorts
How to Enter Send VHS dub and entry form to:
　　International Film Festival
　　Chausseé de Louvain 50
　　1210 Brussels
　　Belgium
　　Telephone 011.32.2.218.53.33

Fax 011.32.2.218.18.60
E-mail infoffb@netcity.be
Web ffb.cinebel.com
Entry Deadline October 31

BUFF Children's Film Festival

Where Malmö, Sweden
When One week in the middle of March
Background Founded in 1984, BUFF (Barnoch Ungdomsfilmfestivalen) is one of the more cheerful and comprehensive of the children's fests held around the globe. Not just an incidental to a larger fest giving the kids something to do while Mom and Dad see the new Godard essay film, the festival concentrates on the art of children's cinema with the dutifulness of a school librarian. Refreshingly, the festival does not treat children like morons. There are some tough issues discussed in the international cinema here alongside the goofy cartoons, such as in the Israeli film *There Was No War in '72*, the controversial Norwegian *Dangerous Waters* ("Thirteen-year-old Hector has one gnawing thought: has he made his mother pregnant?"), and the Danish film *Blomsterfangen* about a father and son who meet for the first time in years in prison. Some of the more evocative titles in recent years have been Antonia Ringbom's *The Sun Is a Yellow Giraffe*, Clas Lindberg's *My Friend: The Sheik*, and Stellan Olsson's *Fleas Bark Too, Don't They?*
Major Award Winners Mostly noncompetitive, but does give out honorary awards; Honorary Award Winners (25,000 SKr) for outstanding feats for children and youth films: Jannik Hastrup and Per Ahlin
Films About 150 feature films and shorts
Tickets Free with $4 festival pass
How to Enter Send VHS dub and entry form to:
    BUFF Malmo Children and Youth Film Festival
    Box 179
    201 21 Malmö
    Sweden
    Telephone 011.46.40.30.7822
    Fax 011.46.40.30.5322
    E-mail buff@kajen.com
    Web www.kajen.com/buff
Entry Deadline December

Cambridge International Film Festival

Where Cambridge, England
Background Founded in 1977, the Cambridge fest began with major screenings from major directors (Kurosawa's *Dodeska-den*, Visconti's *Conversation Piece*, Rosi's *Illustrious Corpses*) along with some American dreck (*The Bad News Bears*). Over a 20-year period, the festival has continued its apparent policy of showing good if not particularly risky art house fare and archival presentations. Retrospectives of the work of Philip Kaufman, Krzystof Kieslowski, and Buster Keaton have been held, along with premieres of movies by Woody Allen, Quentin Tarantino, and

John Sayles. There are no unpleasant surprises, but there are not many surprises in general. Films are screened at the beautiful Cambridge Arts Cinema and the not-bad-but-nothing-to-write-home-about Cambridge Arts Theatre. Films that have premiered here include Lars von Trier's *The Kingdom*, Bertrand Tavernier's *Fresh Bait*, Jacques Rivette's *Jeanne la Pucelle*, and Patricia Rozema's *When Night Is Falling*.

Major Award Winners Noncompetitive

Films About 70 features

Noteworthy Celebrity Sightings Helen Mirren, Wim Wenders, Agnieszka Holland

How to Enter Send VHS dub and entry form to:

>Cambridge Film Festival
>8 Market Passage
>Cambridge
>United Kingdom
>CB2 3PF
>Telephone 011.44.1223.578.917
>Fax 011.44.1223.578.929
>E-mail festival@cambarts.co.uk

Entry Deadline May

Camerimage

Where Torún, Poland

When One week in late November and early December

Background We forget from time to time that film is a visual art and that cinematography, when in the hands of a master, can create images as brilliant, beautiful, and evocative as what artists splatter on canvas. Here in Poland, where that truism has not been forgotten, cinema professionals and the amusingly named TUMULT Foundation have gathered to create a festival that honors these true movie artists. Honoring the likes of Sven Nykvist and other such luminescent luminaries with the Golden Frog for Life Achievement, this film festival of the art of cinematography takes a serious, intelligent, and critical look at the oft-forgotten art of cinema. Films entered into competition have included James Ivory's *Howard's End*, Jane Campion's *The Piano*, Chen Kaige's *Farewell My Concubine*, Peter Greenaway's *The Baby of Macon*, Joel Schumacher's *Falling Down*, and Kai Wessel's *Das Sommeralbum*. Additional cool events have included concerts of movie music, including a live performance of the score to Francis Ford Coppola's *Dracula*. The most recent festival, whose jury was helmed by Mike Leigh, honored cinematographer Remi Adefarasin. About 45,000 attend annually.

Major Award Winners Golden Frog: *Elizabeth,* by Remi Adefarasin; Silver Frog: *Jude,* by Eduardo Serra; Bronze Frog: *Shine,* by Geoffrey Simpson; Audience Award: *Breaking the Waves*, by Robby Muller

Films 60 features, 30 shorts

Noteworthy Celebrity Sightings Vittorio Storaro, Agnieszka Holland, Paul Schrader, Vittorio Storaro, Haskell Wexler, John Schlesinger

How to Enter Wait for a response after sending a letter to:

>Camerimage
>Rynek Nowomiejski 28
>87-100 Torun

Poland
Telephone 011.48.56.248.79
Fax 011.48.56.275.95
Web www.ascomp.torun.pl/camerimage
Entry Deadline September

Cannes International Film Festival

See Best of the Fests

Cartoombria International Festival of Animation Film

Where Perugia, Italy
When One weekend in late November
Background Founded in 1995, this festival in a medieval Italian city screens cartoons in the neoclassical Theatre Pavone. The comprehensive festival screens everything from feature films and TV serials to animated drawings, logos, advertising spots, and experimental videos. Retrospectives have included tributes to Katsuhiro Otomo, Federico Vitali, and Osamu Tezuka.
Major Award Winners Noncompetitive
Films About 25 films in a variety of categories
Tickets 3,000–5,000 L
How to Enter Send VHS dub and entry form to:
 Cartoombria International Festival of Animation Film
 Umbria Spettacolo Foundation
 via Bontempi 25
 06122 Perugia PG
 Italy
 Telephone 011.39.75.572.6764
 Fax 011.39.75.572.6768
Entry Deadline September 18

Cattolica International Mystery Film Festival

Where Cattolica, Italy
When Last week of June
Background If awards were given for the coolest supplementary material provided by a festival, it would have to go hands down to the Cattolica Mystery Film Festival. The festival, founded in 1980, doesn't just put out a program book to talk about the films in its festival; it puts out a book. Like a book. Like a serious book that would cost twice the price of this one at Barnes & Noble. And what is contained in said book? Not only descriptions of films and thought-provoking illustrations but scholarly essays by Andrè Breton and Raymond Queneau and thought pieces on film history. Perhaps this is to be expected from an excellent and challenging festival like this one, which is directed by a Bologna professor of semiology, a respected publisher, and a film critic instead of the usual amalgamation of stars and monied folks. Which makes you wonder how such a lame-ass film as *Mother* managed to show up

at the festival recently. Leaving that aside, the festival boasts an incredible array of films related to mysterious and mystical themes. Aside from films in competition, the festival has recently held retrospectives of films relating to themes of transcendence (Satyajit Ray's *Devi*), surrealism (Buñuel's *The Exterminating Angel*), the devil (Charles Laughton's *Night of the Hunter*), reincarnation (*An American Werewolf in London*), and the mysterious land of Cairo (*The Purple Rose of Cairo*; Michael Curtiz's *The Egyptian*; and *Abbot and Costello Meet the Mummy*). Films are screened at the Cinema Lavatoio, Teatro della Regina, and Ridotto del Teatro.

Major Award Winners Best Film: *What I Have Written*, by John Hughes
Films About 75 features
How to Enter Send VHS dub and entry form to:
    Centro Culturale Polivalente
    Piazza Nettuno 1
    47033 Cattolica RN
    Italy
    Telephone 011.39.541.968.214
    Fax 011.39.541.958.137
    E-mail mystfest@cattolica.net
Entry Deadline May

Cinanima International Animation Film Festival

Where Espinho, Portugal
When One week in early November
Background Founded in 1976, the animated film festival (founded by the NASCENTE Cooperative Society with Cultural Purposes and the town hall of Espinho) screens a wide selection of animated features and offers awards in 10 different categories (cartoons under six minutes, cartoons between six and 13 minutes, cartoons between 13 and 26 minutes, animated title sequences, and so forth).
Major Award Winners Grand Prize for Best Film: *Nyurka's Bath*, by Oxana Cherkasova; Best Film under Six Minutes: *L'Égoïste*, by Jean Loup Felicioli; Best Film between Six and 13 Minutes: *Sarajevo*, by Stjepan Niharjevica; Best Film between 13 and 26 Minutes: *Small Treasures*, by Sarah Watt; Best Film between 26 and 52 minutes: *Puss in Boots*, by Garri Berdin; Audience Prize: *La Grande Migration*, by Yuri Tcherenkov
Films About 100 films
How to Enter Send VHS dub and entry form to:
    Cinanima
    Apartado 43
    Rua 62, 251
    4501 Espinho
    Portugal
    Telephone 011.351.2.724.611
    Fax 011.351.2.726.015
Entry Deadline August

Cinema dei Ragazzi

Where Pisa, Italy
When One weekend in mid-November
Background Dedicated to showcasing children's cinema, this festival also holds seminars on matters crucial to the industry, such as one recent one concerning images in children's films and violence. The festival also allows youngsters the opportunity to meet the directors of showcased movies. Films premiered here include *The Blue Arrow*, by Enzo D'Alo. The festival screens at the Odeon Cinema and the Cinema Arsenale.
Major Award Winners Noncompetitive
How to Enter For more information contact:
    E-mail cinekid@alfea.it
Entry Deadline Not available

Cinéma du Réel

Where Paris, France
When Ten days in mid-March
Background There can be little wrong with a film festival that takes place in the world's best art museum, the Centre Georges Pompidou, which combines Dr. Seussian surroundings with some of the greatest expositions of modern art to be found anywhere in the world. The festival, founded in 1979 by the Ethnographic Film Committee, pays tribute to documentary cinema dealing with ethnographic and sociological topics. Aside from a competition section that screens approximately 30 films from various spots around the globe, the festival also focuses on certain regions including the Baltic States, Iran, and Australia.
Major Award Winners Prix du Cinéma du Réel (50,000 Fr): *16 S. Barkhor Street*, by Duan Jinchuan; Special Jury Prize: *Jenseits des Krieges*, by Ruth Beckermann; Best Short: *Spring*, by Valdas Navasaitis; Joris Ivens Prize: *Bye Bye Babushka*, by Rebecca Feig
Films About 70
Noteworthy Celebrity Sightings Chantal Akerman, Nagisa Oshima, Frederick Wiseman
Tickets 27 Fr per individual screening
How to Enter Send information about film (synopsis, technical details, but no cassette) to:
    Cinéma du Réel
    BPI 25, rue de Renard
    75197 Paris
    France
    Telephone 011.33.1.44.78.44.21
    Fax 011.33.1.44.78.12.24
    E-mail cinereel@bpi.fr
    Web www.bpi.fr
Entry Deadline November

Cinemagic International Film Festival for Young People

Where Belfast, Northern Ireland

When Ten days in late November and early December

Background Founded in 1990 and held in the Nerve Centre, Northern Ireland's first major multimedia arts center, Cinemagic not only shows films for youth but also involves kids in the process, allowing them to exhibit their own films, select festival films, and invite major filmmakers to conduct workshops for them. Jim Sheridan (*My Left Foot, In the Name of the Father*) and Helen Mirren have taught master classes here. Twenty films are shown in competition and are judged by a jury of young folks. Films that have screened here range from the predictable (*Babe, A Little Princess, The Wizard of Oz*) to the less predictable (Jafar Panahi's *The White Balloon*). Some of the more refreshing aspects of the festival are its willingness to show highly intelligent films (e.g., *Henry V*) and to tackle social issues by presenting films and featuring film series dealing with racism and ethnicity, holding workshops on the topics plus showing such films as *Hoop Dreams* and *Where the Spirit Lives*. Retrospectives on Canadian and Australian cinema have also been held.

Films About 70

Major Award Winners Best Film: *Exhuming Mr. Rice*, directed by Nicholas Kendall, starring David Bowie; Best Short Film: *Humdrum*

Noteworthy Celebrity Sightings Helen Mirren, Jim Sheridan, Ralph Fiennes, Peter Postlethwaite

How to Enter Send VHS dub and entry form to:

>Cinemagic
>4th Floor
>38 Dublin Road
>Belfast
>United Kingdom
>VT2 7HN
>Telephone 011.44.1232.311.900
>Fax 011.44.1232.319.709

Entry Deadline July

Cinemalia

Where Beauvais, France

When One week in mid-March

Background Woof. Founded in 1991, this festival is mainly concerned with the images of animals in movies and Charlton Heston. Well, sort of. Actually, aside from focusing on animal movies, the festival has held a number of tributes and retrospectives, including the works of Robert Wise and Tony Curtis and, of course, Mr. Heston. And since Heston was in *Planet of the Apes*, it sort of all makes sense.

Major Award Winners Noncompetitive

Films About 25

Noteworthy Celebrity Sightings Chuck Heston, Tony Curtis

How to Enter Send VHS dub and entry form to:

>Les Amis du Cinéma
>32, rue Carnot

BP-40230
60002 Beauvais
France
Telephone 011.33.1.44.48.81.30
E-mail cinemalia@cci-oise.fr
Web www.cci-oise.fr/cinemalia
Entry Deadline Not available

Cinémas d'Afrique

Where Angers, France
When One week in mid-April
Background In Angers, the Cinémas d'Afrique festival is held in conjunction with a citywide African festival featuring conferences, art exhibitions, and concerts. Founded in 1987, the festival screens a handful of films by African filmmakers and celebrates the diversity of the vast continent. The films' directors are in attendance for screenings
Major Award Winners Noncompetitive
Films About eight features and 10 shorts
Tickets 30 Fr per individual event
How to Enter For more information contact:
    Cinémas d'Afrique
    3 bis quai Gambetta
    49100 Angers
    France
    Telephone 011.33.241.20.08.22
    Fax 011.33.241.20.08.27
Entry Deadline March

Cinéma Tout Écran

Where Geneva, Switzerland
When One week in mid-September
Background One of the more interesting aspects about this Swiss festival is that it tends to highlight the television work of major directors. So rather than seeing Woody Allen's latest film, you get to see what he did for network television (*Don't Drink the Water*). Over the past years, TV work by Jean Renoir and Satyajit Ray, of all people, have also been screened, as have works by Stephen Soderbergh and Tom Cruise (!).
Major Award Winners Grand Jury Prize: *Little Criminals*, by Stephen Surjik; Geneva Cinema Prize: *The Making of Maps*, by Endaf Emlyn; Runner-up: *L'Inconnu*, by Ismael Ferroukh
Films About 100
How to Enter Send VHS dub and entry form to:
    Geneva Association for Independent Cinema
    Maison des Arts du Groutli
    Rue du General DuFour 16
    CP 5305

1204 Geneva 11
Switzerland
Telephone 011.41.22.321.85.54
Fax 011.41.22.329.68.09
E-mail info@cinema-tout.ecran.ch
Web www.amg.ch/cinetoutecran/cte.html
Entry Deadline July

Ciné-Passion

Where Aubagne, France
When One week in late November
Background Not to sound too hippie-ish, but peace and love are the themes here. Things get mushy from time to time, but not too much so, considering that the festival has also paid close attention to the films of Michael Winterbottom and Jane Campion and also, oddly enough, has held a tribute to the work of actor Christopher Lee. The festival screens at the Cinema Palace (Avenue Loulou Delfieu) and the Cinema Pagnol (Cours Marechal Foch). Films that received their premieres here include Campion's *Portrait of a Lady* and Winterbottom's *Jude*.
Major Award Winners Passion d'Or (Amour Passion): *Le Cri de la Soie*, by Yvon Marciano; Passion d'Or (Film Decouvert): *ID*, by Philip Davis; Passion d'Or (Short Film): *Ada Sait Pas Dir Non*, by Luc Pagés; Best Actor: Reece Dinsdale, *ID*; Best Actress: Lola Gans, *Les Nuits Blanches*
Noteworthy Celebrity Sightings Christopher Lee, Sophie Barjo
Tickets 30 Fr per individual screening; 250 Fr for 10 screenings
How to Enter Send VHS dub and entry form to:
Ciné-Passion
23, avenue des Goums
13400 Aubagne
France
Telephone 011.33.1442.03.95.27
Fax 011.33.1442.03.47.06
E-mail g-lartigot@lcm.fr
Entry Deadline Not available

Cinewomen Film Festival

Where Norwich, England
When Four days in early November
Background Founded in 1980 and located about 100 miles outside of London, this is the only English festival dedicated to films by women. Scholarly seminars take their place alongside films and have included a University of Pennsylvania professor of English's seminar on "constructions of female aggression and violence in Marleen Gorris's *A Question of Silence* and John Dahl's *The Last Seduction*" and University of East Anglia lecturer Pam Cook's seminar on "mimicry and pastiche in the work of Kathryn Bigelow." The accent here is on shorts, and the festival spotlights British independent shorts, but it also screens premieres of features from

Greece, Israel, Canada, and the United States. Films are screened at Cinema City, Norwich's regional theater.

Major Award Winners Best Film (£1,000): *From A to D*, by Janie Walken

Films About 25

Tickets A payment of £50 grants you admission to everything the festival has to offer.

How to Enter Send application form and VHS dub to:

Cinewomen
Cinema City
St. Andrew's Street
Norwich
United Kingdom
NR2 4AD
E-mail j.h.morgan@uea.ac.uk

Entry Deadline June

Clermont-Ferrand Short Film Festival

Where Clermont-Ferrand, France

When Nine days in late January and early February

Background One of the major festivals of short films in the world, the CFSFF boasts that nearly 100 attend annually. Among films that have premiered here are George Hickenlooper's *Some Call It a Sling Blade* and Peter Capaldi's *Franz Kafka's It's a Wonderful Life*.

Major Award Winners Grand Prix for Best Short Film (20,000 Fr): *Ma Place su le Trottoir*, by Phillipe Pollet-Villard

Films About 75 shorts

How to Enter Send VHS dub and entry form to:

Clermont-Ferrand Short Film Festival
26, rue des Jacobins
63000 Clermont-Ferrand
France
Telephone 011.33.473.92.65.73
Fax 011.33.473.92.11.93
E-mail info@clermont-filmfest.com
Web www.clermont-filmfest.com

Entry Deadline October

Cologne Feminale Women's Film Festival

Where Cologne, Germany

When First week in June

Background Founded in 1983 by female film scholars, the festival offers films that meet some or all of the following criteria: questioning traditional images of women, opposing sexism in media, fighting for political change, conceiving of feminist utopias, and experimenting with content and form. The festival offers contemporary films (many are German, especially from the North Rhine–Westphalia region), a focus on female animators, and intriguing retrospectives such as recent ones on

Ida Lupino, American avant-gardist Maya Deren, and German director Helke Sander. Thematically arranged festival series have included documentaries by women in war and crisis regions and filmmakers in the Israeli-Palestinian conflict. In conjunction with the film screenings, panel discussions, networking meetings, and seminars deal with such topics as women's role in the film industry. About 18,000 attend yearly. The festival screens at the VHS Forum, the Broadway Theater, and the Filmpalette.

Major Award Winners Noncompetitive

Films About 260

Noteworthy Celebrity Sightings Helke Sander

How to Enter Send VHS dub and entry form to:

Feminale Women's Film Festival
Maybachstr. 111
50670 Cologne
Germany
Telephone 011.49.221.130.0225
Fax 011.49.221.130.0281
E-mail feminale@t-online.de
Web www.dom.de/filmworks/feminale

Entry Deadline June

Copenhagen Film Fest

Where Copenhagen, Denmark

When One week in mid-September

Background Founded in 1991, this festival pretty much takes over the film scene for the week, screening in about 11 theaters. There is a strange mix of the arty and the commercial, with films as disparate as *Latcho Drom* and *Go Fish* on one side and *Pocahontas* and *Waterworld* on the other. Spotlights focus on world cinema as in a recent tribute to Pedro Almodóvar and Spanish cinema.

Major Award Winners Asta Award (30,000 DKr): *Korea*, by Cathal Black

Films About 30 features

How to Enter Send VHS dub and entry form to:

Copenhagen Film Festival
Vesterbrogade 35A, 3
1620 Copenhagen
Denmark
Telephone 011.45.33.252501
Fax 011.45.33.255756
E-mail fside@datashopper.dk

Entry Deadline June

Cork International Film Festival

Where Cork, Ireland

When One week in mid-September

Background Founded in 1956 and directed by Mick Hannigan, this is the oldest film festival in Ireland, paying special attention to short films and films from

Ireland as well as the usual selection of global cinema. Sponsored by Murphy's Irish Stout, the festival has been known, like a Chippendale's performer, to boast that it "shows everything." Screenings take place in the cavernous 1,000-seat Cork Opera House (Emmet Place), the 100-seat Triskel Arts Centre (Tobin Street) in the Triskel Cafe, the intimate art house Kino Cinema (Washington Street), and the Grand Café (English Market, Princes Street). The festival offers quite a good selection of European films, although the selection of American films is generally predictable, sticking to those with major distributors, except in the quirky documentary section. Among the special features are the Documentary Panorama, Irish Showcase, and Tribute Programs.

Major Award Winners Best Irish Short Film: *Patterns*, by Kirsten Sheridan; Best Black-and-White Film: *The Letter*, by Michel Gondry

Noteworthy Celebrity Sightings Alison Anders

Films More than 150 films, 100 of which are shorts

Tickets £2.50 for individual screenings; £50 for passes for all shows

How to Enter No entry fee. Send VHS preview tape to:
Cork International Film Festival
10 Washington St.
Cork City
Ireland
Telephone 011.353.21.27.17.11
Fax 011.353.21.27.59.45
E-mail ciff@indigo.ie
Web www.corkfilmfest.org

Entry Deadline July

Créteil International Festival of Women's Films

Where Créteil, France

When Ten days in late March and early April

Background Although some festivals devoted solely to specific categories of filmmakers can be rather limited and noncomprehensive, this one, founded in 1979, is one of the best of its kind, featuring a broad range of films by female filmmakers from around the globe and a wide array of categories. Aside from the main competition, in which 10 features, 10 documentaries, and 30 shorts are screened, the festival also features retrospectives of major female directors (Maria Luisa Bemberg was one recently honored), a portrait of an actress (Carole Bouquet is one example), tributes to African filmmakers, and even films for teenagers.

Major Award Winners Prizes are quite generous—up to 25,000 Fr for best feature film; Best Feature Film: *Longue Vie*, by Larisa Sadilouz; Special Jury Prize: *Xiu Xiu*, by Joan Chen; Best Documentary: *Naisenkaari*, by Kiti Luostarinen

Films More than 200 features and shorts

How to Enter Send $15 entry fee, VHS dub, and entry form to:
A.F.I.F.F.
Maison des Arts
Place Salvador Allende
94000 Créteil
France
Telephone 011.33.149.80.38.98

Fax 011.33.143.99.04.10
E-mail filmsfemmes@wanadoo.fr
Web www.gdebussac.fr/filmfem
Entry Deadline December

Croatian Film Festival Pula

Where Pula, Croatia

When Three days in early August

Background Preceded by a giant fireworks display and a great ceremonial raising of flags, the Pula festival, founded in 1954, offers the most comprehensive program of Croatian cinema to be found anywhere in the world. Films screen in the hall of the Istraian National Theatre. The festival screens Croatian dramas, shorts, and animated films.

Major Award Winners Golden Arena for Best Director: *How the War Started on My Island*, by Vinko Bresan; Golden Arena for Best Actress: *Recognizing*, by Natasa Dorcic; Golden Arena for Best Actor: *The Seventh Chronicle*, by Rene Medvesek

Films About 20 features plus shorts and animated programs

Noteworthy Celebrity Sightings Richard Burton, Liz Taylor, Sophia Loren

How to Enter For more information contact:
E-mail lorelos@pu.tel.hr
Web www.pu.carnet.hr/kultura/festival/fhf/edojela_nagrada.html

Entry Deadline Not available

Deauville Festival of American Films

Where Deauville, France

When September

Background One of the few festivals around that organizes its festivals around themes instead of whatever eclectic criteria a certain festival director happened to have one particular year, the Festival du Cinema Américain has held tributes and screenings in previous years centered around the themes of Hollywood Goes to War, Jazz in Film, and New York in Film and, of course, Michael Caine. Yet if there is a focus here, it seems to be honoring glitterati and hobnobbing with celebs rather than actually celebrating cinema. The festival boasts of Deauville's lovely mayor ("probably the prettiest elected official in the country," the festival tells us), who is famous for her "charm, wit, and perfect command of the English language," as well as the food, the wine, the boardwalk, and, of course, the casinos and hotels that inspired the likes of Proust and Flaubert. About 180,000 allegedly attend. *Analyze This*, *Face/Off*, *Ride With the Devil* and *The Cider House Rules* have received their premieres here, and tributes have focused on Maurice Jarré and Clint Eastwood. *The Dram Catcher*, by Ed Radtke, also appeared here recently.

Major Award Winners Prix Special: *Sunday*, by Jonathan Mossiter; Jury Prize: *In the Company of Men*, by Neil LaBute

Films About 50

Noteworthy Celebrity Sightings Steven (if you have to ask "Steven who?" do you really think you should be reading this book?), Spike Jonze, Ang Lee, Gore Vidal, Elie Wiesel, Whoopi Goldberg, Liam Neeson, Mario Vargas Llosa

How to Enter Send VHS dub and entry form to:
Deauville Festival of American Films
40, rue Anatole France
92594 Levalois Perret France
Telephone 011.33.1.41.34.20.33
Fax 011.33.1.41.34.20.77
E-mail jlasserre@le-public-systeme.fr
Entry Deadline July
Fact The Deauville festival recently gave its Literary Prize to Mary Higgins Clark.
Fingers are crossed hoping that Danielle Steel will not be far behind.

Dinard Festival du Film Britannique

Where Dinard, France
When First week of October
Background Since 1989 the festival has been devoted to bringing out the Brit in
Brittany, serving the pressing needs of all of those who venture to Dinard and want
to see the latest Merchant-Ivory film. The festival has feted Merchant and Ivory as
well as Ken McMullen. Ken Loach's *Carla's Song* and Peter Greenaway's *The Pillow
Book* have premiered here. The best parts of the festival have been the retrospec-
tives, which have included early mysteries, such as Alfred Hitchcock's *Young and
Innocent* and *The Lady Vanishes* and George Cukor's *Gaslight*.
Major Award Winners Best Film: *Human Traffic*, by Justin Kerrigan; Special Jury
Prize: *Following*, by Christopher Nolan; Audience Prize: *Fanny and Elvis*, by Kay
Mellor; Golden Hitchcock Award: *Jude*, by Michael Winterbottom
Films About 30
How to Enter For more information contact:
Association du Festival du Film Britannique
2, Boulevard Féart
35800 Dinard
France
Telephone 011.33.299.88.19.04
Fax 011.33.299.88.67.15
E-mail fest.film.britan.dinard@wanadoo.fr
Entry Deadline Not applicable

Dortmund Women's Film Festival

Where Dortmund, Germany
When One week in mid-March
Background Held every other year, the "Femme Totale" film festival screens women's
films based on one particular theme. Past themes have included Power and Violence
in Films Made by Women, Films by Soviet Women, New Technologies/Female
Luddites, Uncanny Pleasures, and The Subversive Power of Laughter. Founded in
1986 by the Femme Totale Association, the festival resembles a major art exhibition
as much as it does a film festival, with its major concentration on thematic integrity
and dedication to cinema history. The festival is composed primarily of new films by
women filmmakers, but it also features tributes to major female directors (Kathryn

Bigelow) and provides neat retrospectives of little-known women in film history, such as a recent tribute to editor and screenwriter Alma Reveille, who worked most notably with Hitchcock, assistant directing Hitchcock's *The Lodger* and *The Pleasure Garden* and scripting his *Young and Innocent*. The festival also offers intriguing seminars as opposed to the usual how-to-make-it-in-showbiz BS. Such seminars have included "The Portrayal of Murderous Mothers in the Popular Cinema," "Female Detectives in Early Cinema," "The Suspense Content of Sounds," and "Scream If You Can: No Looking and Monstrous Femininity."

Major Award Winners Noncompetitive

Films About 150 films

Tickets 9 DM per individual screening; 80 DM for a festival pass

How to Enter Send VHS copy and entry form to:

> Femme Totale e.v.
> c/o Kulturbüro Stadt Dortmund
> Kleppingstr. 21-23
> 44122 Dortmund
> Germany
> Fax 011.49.231.50.251.62
> E-mail 106212.3237@compuserve.com or femmetotale@compuserve.com
> Web www.inter-net-work.de

Entry Deadline November

Douarnez Festival de Cinéma

Where Douarnez, France

Background One of the more interesting and politically aware festivals in France, the Douarnez fest focuses on marginalized and oppressed peoples around the globe. Concentrating each year on a specific country, festival sponsors debate cultural imperialism, oppression, and so forth alongside an excellent and comprehensive selection of films. Over the years Irish, Indian, Scottish, Aboriginal, Latin American, and African American cinema have been featured.

Major Award Winners Noncompetitive

How to Enter For more information contact:

> Douarnez Festival de Cinema
> 26, rue Duguay-Trouin
> BP 206
> 29172 Douarnez
> France
> Telephone 011.33.12.98.92.09.21
> Fax 011.33.12.98.92.28.10
> E-mail fdz@wanadoo.fr

Entry Deadline Not applicable—film submission is by invitation only

---

Dublin Film Festival

Where Dublin, Ireland

When Ten days in mid-April

Background Although the Dublin surroundings might be reason enough to attend, the films that screen here are hardly an unpredictable lot. Screening at five theaters, including the Irish Film Centre, the Ambassador, the Savoy, the Screen, and the UC1, the festival has featured *Smoke Signals* and *Beirut*. There is an annual "surprise" film screened, but it is up to you to judge whether Mike Nichols and Elaine May's *The Birdcage* is much of a surprise. On the plus side are the retrospectives, which in recent years have included an homage to Terry Gilliam. Sponsored by Miller Genuine Draft.

Major Award Winners Noncompetitive
How to Enter Contact:
    Dublin Film Festival Ltd.
    1 Suffolk Street
    Dublin 2
    Ireland
    Telephone 011.353.1.67.92.937
    Fax 011.353.1.67.92.939
    E-mail dff@iol.ie
    Web www.iol.ie/~dff
Entry Deadline November 1

Dublin Lesbian and Gay Film Festival

Where Dublin, Ireland
When Four days in early April
Background A small selection of gay-themed films are screened at the Irish Film Centre, 6 Eustace Street, Temple Bar, which features not only plush screening facilities but a full bar and restaurant. The festival also screens outdoors at Meeting House Square, where more than 1,000 attend. There's a good selection here, with such films as Billy Hollywood's *Screen Kiss* and Stanley Kwan's *Hold You Tight*, not to mention a "Robert Aldrich campfest."

Major Award Winners Noncompetitive
Films 22 features and lots of shorts
Tickets £2–£4
How to Enter Send VHS dub and entry form to:
    Dublin Lesbian and Gay Film Festival
    Outhouse
    6 S. Williams St.
    Dublin 2
    Ireland
    Telephone 011.353.1.672.7211
    Fax 011.353.1.679.1306
    E-mail dublinlesbiangayfilm@ireland.com
    Web www.iftn.ie/dublingayfilm
Entry Deadline June 1

Edinburgh International Film Festival

Where Edinburgh, Scotland

When Two weeks in mid-August

Background Ahh, Edinburgh. Home of delicious veggie "cruncheez" that you can snack on until dawn, home of noisy pubs, and home to one of the coolest and oldest film fests around. Founded in 1947, the festival has welcomed and honored virtually every major figure in cinema at one point or another, giving lifetime achievement awards to the likes of Fred Zinneman and Carol Reed. John Huston and Orson Welles have sat on the honorary board. Woody Allen's *Annie Hall*, Steven Spielberg's *E.T.*, and Abel Gance's reworked *Napoleon* were premiered here. Retrospectives have been held on Raoul Walsh, Douglas Sirk, Stanley Donen, and Wim Wenders. There are exceedingly cool archival presentations here, including Cecil B. DeMille's 1915 *Carmen* shown on an outdoor screen. And a recent animation retrospective paid tribute to Russian filmmaker Yuri Nornstein, who was declared by the festival to be the best animator of all time. As John Huston said, "It's the only film festival worth a damn." Around 50,000 people attend.

Major Award Winners Michael Powell Award for Best British Film (£2,000): *The War Zone*, by Tim Roth; Standard Life Audience Award: *Buena Vista Social Club*, by Wim Wenders

Films About 300 films

Noteworthy Celebrity Sightings Sean Connery, Cary Grant, Dusan Makaveyev, Jim Jarmusch, Jane Campion, Bill Forsyth, Lillian Gish, Bernardo Bertolucci, dozens of others

Tickets £5–£10 per individual screening; $250 for pass to all screenings; festival hotline: 011.44.131.228.4051

How to Enter Send VHS dub and entry form to:
Edinburgh International Film Festival
88 Lothian Road
Edinburgh
United Kingdom
EH3 9BZ
Telephone 011.31.228.4051
Fax 011.44.131.229.5501
E-mail info@edfilmfest.org.uk
Web www.edfilmfest.org.uk

Entry Deadline May

Fact Edinburgh is the longest continually running festival in the world.

European First Film Festival of Angers

Where Angers, France

When Ten days in late January

Background Founded in 1989 in this Loire Valley city with 250,000 inhabitants, the festival is one of the best opportunities to see the work of new, soon-to-be-established European filmmakers, holding a competition among 54 "Noveaux Noms" alongside tons of other shorts and student films. Out of competition, the festival holds many screenings and tributes, including a recent retrospective of Eric

Rohmer's work. What makes this festival excellent is that its retrospectives are comprehensive. Not just dragging out three or four flicks and calling it a tribute, the festival featured almost every damn thing Rohmer has ever done (which if you ask me is too much, but that's hardly the point). Award winners in previous years have introduced France to a variety of important filmmakers including England's Nick Park (*A Grand Day Out*), France's Cedric Klapisch (*Chacun Cherche Son Chat*, *Un Air de Famille*), Jim Sheridan (*My Left Foot*), and Danny Boyle (*Shallow Grave*, *Trainspotting*). Forty thousand or so turn out each year.

Major Award Winners Grand Jury Prize for Best European Feature: *Bolshe Vita*, by Ibolya Fekete, and *Lepa Sela Leop Gore*, by Srdjan Dragojevic; Audience Award for Best European Feature: *Lea*, by Ivan Fila, and *Some Mother's Son*, by Terry George; Best Screenplay: *La Bouche de Jean Pierre*, by Lucille Hadzihalilovic, and *En Apparence*, by Olivier Zimmerman; Best Short Film: *Lap Rouge*, by Lodewijk Crijins

Films About 110 features and shorts

Noteworthy Celebrity Sightings Agnieszka Holland, Claude Chabrol, Fanny Ardant

How to Enter Send VHS dub and entry form to:
Premiers Plans a Angers
23, rue de la Roe
49100 Angers
France
Telephone 011.33.1.42.71.53.70
Fax 011.33.1.42.71.47.55
E-mail premiersplans@wanadoo.fr
Web www.anjou.com/premiersplans

Entry Deadline November

European Student Film Festival

Where London, England

When One day in late November

Background Though this is a major and serious film festival, I especially like the rating system used by to jurors of this festival, which rates films as follows: High Quality = 6, Exciting = 5, Professional = 4, Standard = 3, Bad = 2, Very Bad = 1, and Appalling = 0.

Major Award Winners Best Student Film: *Plastering the Cracks*, by Gavin Gordon-Rogers

Films About 15 short films

How to Enter Send VHS dub and entry form to:
Festival Organiser
11 Holbein House
Holbein Place
London
United Kingdom
Swi W8NH
Fax 011.44.171.259.9278
E-mail kohle@mail.bogo.co.uk
Web www.bogo.co.uk.kohle/pearl.html

Entry Deadline Not applicable

Fantasporto

Where Oporto, Portugal
When Last week of February
Background Held in Portugal's second-largest city near the Atlantic, Fantasporto provides a bizarre but intriguing juxtaposition of standard groovy art films from the United States, Europe, and Asia with a definite fixation on horror and fantasy films. Few other festivals would program *Shine* alongside *Hellraiser IV: Bloodline*, but that's part of what makes this festival an original. Competitions are held for fantasy films and new directors. The other cool aspect is the selection of tributes and retrospectives, which have included the work of Monty Python, Jean Cocteau, David Cronenberg, and Luis Buñuel. Organizers say one of the goals here is to "dignify Portuguese cinema and encourage film production in Portugal," and part of the way the festival succeeds is by programming a lot of American offal, which makes the Portuguese entries that much more dignified by comparison.
Major Award Winners Best Film: *Bound,* by the Wachowski Brothers; Best Actor: Juan Inciarte, *Solo Se Muere Dos Veces*; Best Actress: Jennifer Tilly, *Bound*; Best Screenplay: Julian Richards, *Darklands*; Best Short Film: Richard Wright, *L'Echanteur*; Special Jury Award: *Children of the Wilderness*
Films 400 feature and short films
Noteworthy Celebrity Sightings David Lynch, Luc Besson
How to Enter Send VHS copy and entry form to:
Oporto International Film Festival
Cinema Nova Multimedia Centre
Rua da Constitutaçao, 311
4200 Porto
Portugal
Telephone 011.351.507.3830
Fax 011.351.255.08210
E-mail fantas@caleida.pt
Web www.caleida.pt/fantasporto
Entry Deadline December

Fantastic'Arts

Where Gérardmer, France
When First week of February
Background The only French festival devoted to "fantastic" films—encompassing horror, science fiction, and fantasy—Fantastic'Arts recently paid tribute to such artists as master of bombast Ken Russell and Andrzej Zulawski and has also held a retrospective of Dracula films, from Tod Browning's 1931 *Dracula* to Mel Brooks's 1995 *Dracula: Dead and Loving It*. This is hardly a serious festival (anything that dedicates valuable festival screen time to the Michael Jordan/Bugs Bunny vehicle *Space Jam* or calls on Rutger Hauer to serve as president of its jury is immediately suspect), but one can have little argument with a festival that allows one to relax in the beautiful confines of Gérardmer while watching Wes Craven's *Scream* on the big screen. About 40,000 attend the five-day festival.

Major Award Winners Grand Prix: *El Día de la Bestia*, by Alex de la Iglesia; Prix Spécial du Jury: *Mute Witness*, by Anthony Waller; Prix Premiere di Public: *Powder*, by Victor Salva; Trophée Fun Radio: *Nadja*, by Michael Almereyda
Films About 15 features, plus shorts
Noteworthy Celebrity Sightings John Carpenter, Walter Hill, Claude Chabrol, Peter Coyote
How to Enter For more information contact:
    Telephone 011.33.46.40.55.55
    Fax 011.33.47.38.10.10
    E-mail publics@imaginet.fr
Entry Deadline Not applicable

Fantastisk Film Festival

Where Malmö, Sweden
When Five days in late September
Background "Scandinavia's only festival devoted to films of the fantastic." While this is a dubious distinction, this festival has an eye for the weird and out-there, showing such films as *Dark City*, *Atomica*, and best of all, both Tetsuo films. Expect lots of monsters, gore, and eyes widened in shock and/or pain, God bless 'em.
Major Award Winners Noncompetitive
How to Enter For more information contact:
    Fantastisk Film Festival
    Norra Neptunigatan 5
    211 18 Malmö
    Sweden
    Telephone 011.46.40.12.4666
    Fax 011.46.40.12.2264
    E-mail info@fff.se
    Web www.fff.se
Entry Deadline August

Festival de Cine de Alcalá de Henares

Where Alcalá de Henares, Spain
When One week in mid-November
Background Held in Madrid, this festival (which recently celebrated its 30th birthday) has recently grown in reputation both in Spain and throughout Europe. The festival provides a good overview of Spanish cinema and European as well, having recently honored such directors as Raúl Ruiz and the Taviani brothers. In other years, the festival has focused on specific aspects of filmmaking including soundtracks and cinematography.
Major Award Winners Best Film (600,000 ptas): *Solo Amor*, by José Rodríguez
How to Enter Send VHS dub and entry form to:
    Festival de Cine de Alcalá de Henares
    Plaza del Empecinado, 1
    28801 Alcalá de Henares (Madrid)

Spain
Telephone 011.34.1.881.39.34
Fax 011.34.1.881.39.06
Entry Deadline Not available

Festival de Cine IberoAmericano

Where Huelva, Spain
When One week in late November
Background Screening at Huelva's Columbus Center, with its quartet of pavilions, and at the Gran Teatro, the Emperador Cinema, and the Rabida Cinema, the festival shows a wide array of films in a variety of categories. Outside of the main competition, the festival spotlights particular Spanish-speaking countries (e.g., a recent tribute to Venezuelan films), and the best of modern Spanish cinema, European Visions (showing a broader scope of foreign films), alongside plenty of tributes. These have included homages to the work of Tomás Gutiérrez Alea and Arturo Ripstein. Films that have premiered here include Alain Tanner's *Fourbi* and *The Other Side of Sunday*.
Major Award Winners Colón de Oro Jury Prize (3,000,000 ptas): *Sicario*, by José Ramón Novoa
Films About 75
How to Enter Send VHS dub and entry form to:
  IberoAmerican Film Festival
  Casa Colón
  Plaza del Punto
  21003 Huelva
  Spain
  Telephone 011.34.59.21.01.70
  Fax 011.34.59.21.01.73
  E-mail de@omnuba.otd.es
  Web www.festicinehuelva.com
Entry Deadline September

Festival des Trois Continents

Where Nantes, France
When One week in late November
Background Founded in 1989, the festival was created to highlight films from Africa, Latin and black America, and Asia. Screening at Nantes's Gaumont, UGC Apollo, and Cinématographe Theaters, the festival has presented retrospectives of 1940s and 1950s Argentinian melodramas and Shanghai cinema, along with photography exhibits.
Major Award Winners Grand Prize: *After Life*
Films About 70 features
Tickets 30 Fr per individual screening; 80 Fr for three screenings; 220 Fr for 10 screenings
How to Enter Send VHS dub and entry form to:
  Festival des Trois Continents

19a, Passage Pommeraye
BP 43302
44033 Nantes
France
Telephone 011.33.40.69.74.14
Fax 011.33.40.73.55.22
E-mail f3c@franceplu.com
Web www.infocomnantes.net/f3c99
Entry Deadline October

Festival Internacional de Cinema de Muntanya Vila de Torello

Where Torello, Spain
When Two weeks in mid-November
Background Founded in 1983, the festival focuses on films related to mountain sports: mountaineering, expeditions, climbing, spelunking, skiing, hang gliding, mountain biking, and rafting. Located in a town of 12,000 inhabitants about 50 miles north of Barcelona, the festival offers the opportunity for festivalgoers to engage in the very sports depicted in the festival's films, which have included Leo Dickinson's *Grappling with the Ogre* and Jan Bocek's *In the Icy Embrace of the River Tashenshini*. Except in special circumstances, films screened are less than an hour long. The Grand Prize (Vila de Torello), edelweiss of gold, and 500,000 ptas is offered for the best film. Edelweiss of silver and 200,000 ptas for the best mountaineering film. Edelweiss of silver and 200,000 ptas for the best mountain sports film. Edelweiss of silver and 200,000 ptas for the best mountain environment film.
Films About 40 films
Tickets 5,000 ptas purchases entry to all events
How to Enter Send copy of film and entry form to:
Festival de Cine de Montaña
P.O. Box 19
Anselm Clavé
08570 Torello (Barcelona)
Spain
Telephone 011.34.93.859.28.99
Fax 011.34.93.859.30.00
Entry Deadline October

Festival International du Film d'Animation

Where Annecy, France
When Last week of May
Background Long known as the most important animation festival in the world, the Annecy fest was born in 1956 as a noncompetitive section of the Cannes Film Festival. During the Annecy fest, more than 4,000 animation professionals descend on France to watch films and attend an animation marketplace that is held simultaneously with the festival.

Major Award Winners Best Animated Short: *The Old Lady and the Pigeons*, by Sylvain Chomet; Special Jury Prize: *The Mermaid*, by Alexander Petrov; Best First Film: *Under the Waxing Moon*, by Hans Spillaert; Best Animated Feature: *James and the Giant Peach*, by Henry Selick; Best Animated TV Program: *Famous Fred*, by Joanna Quinn; Prix du Public: *A Close Shave*, by Nick Park
Films About 250 features and shorts
How to Enter Send VHS dub and entry form to:
    Annecy Fest
    6, avenue des Iles
    BP 399
    74103 Annecy
    France
    Web www.annecy-animation-festival.tm.fr
Entry Deadline January

Festival International du Film des Métiers d'Art à Namur

Where Namur, Belgium
When Last weekend of January
Background Founded in 1998 by the World Crafts Council and the Cultural Service of Namur, the festival spotlights feature films and shorts about arts and crafts and concentrates specifically on films that depict artists at work. All arts and crafts are eligible except food crafts. The festival hopes to gain an audience of art critics, journalists, curators, and teachers. The festival is held in Namur's Maison de la Culture.
Major Award Winners None as of yet
How to Enter Send VHS dub and entry form to:
    International Arts and Crafts Film Festival
    Maison de la Culture de la Province de Namur
    Avenue Golenvaux 14
    5000 Namur
    Belgium
    Telephone 011.32.81.229.014
    Fax 011.32.81.221.779
Entry Deadline October

Festival International du Film et Reportage Moteur

Where Stavelot, Belgium
When One week in mid-July
Background Cars are the theme here, and this festival holds competitions in still and motion photography of automobiles and car-related areas. So in addition to a bunch of ads for cars, there are also a lot of fun car movies here. Over the year these have included Dennis Hopper's *Easy Rider*, Francis Ford Coppola's *Tucker*, Charlie Chaplin's *Modern Times*, John Carpenter's *Christine*, Lee Hatzin's *LeMans*, and, perhaps one day soon, Adam Langer's *The Story of a 1988 Ford Escort*.
Major Award Winners Noncompetitive
How to Enter For more information contact:

F.I.F.R.M.
Haute Levée 30
4970 Stavelot
Belgium
E-mail mettraux@euregio.net
Entry Deadline Not applicable

Festival International du Film Francophone

Where Namur, Belgium
When Ten days in late September and early October
Background Founded in 1985, the festival screens films from France, French
Canada, and French-speaking African nations. Recent premieres have included
Claire Denis's *Nenette et Boni*, the French-Belgian-Algerian coproduction *Salut
Cousin!*, and *Y'Aura-t-ilde la Neige a Noël?* The festival has also featured tributes to
Jean-Pierre Melville, Michel Simon, and Ousmaane Sembene.
Major Award Winners Golden Bayard for Best Film (50,000 BF): *Douce France*, by
Malik Chibane
Films About 120 films
Noteworthy Celebrity Sightings Alain Delon
How to Enter Send VHS dub and entry form to:
    Festival International du Film Francophone
    Rue des Brasseurs 175
    5000
    Namur
    Belgium
    Telephone 011.32.81.24.12.36
    Fax 011.32.81.22.43.84
Entry Deadline August

Festival International du Film Maritime et d'Exploration

Where Toulon, France
When One week in mid-November
Background Held at the 800-seat Palais Neptune and the 250 Cinema Ariel in
Toulon, this is perhaps the most extensive festival for the seagoing tar in all of us.
Films such as *Mahi-Mahi Hunters, Island Memories, 1,000 Meters Under the Jungle*,
and *Divers in Troubled Waters* have screened here. It's been around since 1954.
Major Award Winners Ancre d'Or: *Ils N'ont Pas Marche sur la Lune*, by Serge DeCleer
and Jacques Van Koekenbeeg; Ancre d'Argent: *La Grand Peche des Imraguens*, by
Nicolas Jouvin; Ancre de Bronze: *Fous d'Animaux: Mission Lamantin*, by Jean-Albert
Lievre
Films About 130 films
How to Enter Send VHS dub and entry form to:
    Festival International du Film Maritime et d'Exploration
    743, Chemin de la Batterie Basse du Cap-Brun
    83000 Toulon
    France

Telephone 011.33.04.94.41.06.78
Fax 011.33.04.94.03.48.45
Entry Deadline Not available

Festival International du Film Ornithologique

Where Ménigoute, France
When One week in late October
Background The temptation is to quip that this festival is for the birds. But although ornithology is in the festival's title, the festival does also screen films that deal with natural history in general and with the environment. Founded in 1984, this "rendez-vous tout naturel" presents films in a breathtaking natural environment where visitors can watch birds along with films. Film titles have included *Bowerbird: Playboy of the Australian Forest, The Grizzly Summer, Lions of the Kalahari*, and *The 4,000 KM Migration of Common Cranes*. You get the idea. A number of seminars on protecting nature are held in conjunction with the festival. About 30,000 attend each year.
Major Award Winners Noncompetitive
Films 40 films from 14 countries
How to Enter Send video copy of film, entry form, and (here's the hard part) a copy of the script with every species discussed in the film translated into its Latin name to:

Festival International du Film Ornithologique
Residence la Fontaine
Rue de Saint Maixent
BP5
79340 Ménigoute
France
Telephone 011.33.49.69.9009
Fax 011.33.49.69.9725
Entry Deadline July

Festival International du Premier Film

Where Annonay, France
When Ten days in late February and early March
Background Situated within an hour's drive from Saint-Étienne and Lyon (try the quenelles at the Vieux Forneau—I don't know what the hell it is, but it's delicious), the festival has served since 1988 to highlight the works of first-time directors. First works are shown alongside noncompetitive showcases of features and shorts as well as a tribute to either a filmmaker of some note (e.g., Tomie Marshall, Margarethe von Trotta) or a film genre (e.g., Iranian cinema). A number of noteworthy films have made their debuts here, including *La Promesse, Ponette, Beautiful Thing*, and *Welcome to the Dollhouse*.
Major Award Winners Prize of the Jury (22,000 Fr): *Flame*, by Ingrid Sinclair; Special Prize of the Jury (8,000 Fr): *Miel et Cendres*, by Nadia Fares
Films 30 features and 10 shorts
Noteworthy Celebrity Sightings Nathalie Baye, Jean-Louis Trintignant

How to Enter Send VHS dub and official entry form to:
Festival International du 1er Film d'Annonay
Avenue Jean Jaurés
07100 Annonay
France
Telephone 011.33.475.32.40.80
Fax 011.33.475.32.40.81
Entry Deadline December

Festival Videoart de Locarno

Where Locarno, Switzerland
When One week in mid-August
Background This festival of videos, founded in 1980, screens the latest in multimedia technology and also holds seminars and panel discussions. A decent variety of exhibitions and installations are featured in conjunction with the festival.
Major Award Winners Grand Prix de la Ville de Locarno: *Videovoid Text*, by David Larcher, and *Urbino Memoriale*, by Cristiano Carloni and Stefano Franceschetti
Films About 250 videos
How to Enter Send $20 entry fee and work sample to:
VideoArt Festival
Via Varenna 45
P.O. Box 146
6604
Switzerland
Telephone 011.41.9331.2208
E-mail avart@tinet.ch
Web www.tinet.ch/videoart
Entry Deadline July 15

Film Art Fest of Slovenia

Where Ljubljana, Slovenia
When Two weeks in early November
Background Although there's something mildly depressing about the fact that if you travel all the way to Slovenia, you still might wind up seeing *Trainspotting*, this is nevertheless the major festival of Slovenia. Screening in four separate theaters including the Komuna, Kompas Cinema, and the Slovenian Cinematheque, the festival screens documentaries (*Looking for Richard*, *The Battle over Citizen Kane*), country focus features (Scandinavian cinema), American indies (*Safe*, *Clerks*, *Trees Lounge*), and the best of groovy Euro-cinema (*Les Voleurs*, *Drifting Clouds*). *Dead Man*, *Flirt*, and *Land and Freedom* have had their Slovenian premieres. And so has *Trainspotting*.
Major Award Winners Noncompetitive
Films About 65 features
How to Enter Send VHS dub and entry form to:
Film Art Fest

Presernova 10
1000 Ljubljana
Slovenia
Telephone 011.386.61.176.7150
Fax 011.386.61.22.4279
Entry Deadline Not available

Filmfest Emden

Where Emden, Germany
When One week in mid-June
Background It may not be well known for much else, but Emden sure knows how to put on a pretty good film festival. Founded in 1990, the festival has offered recent features on British cinema, a tribute to Neil Jordan, spotlights on new Arab and new German cinema, animation, and a children's film fest. It also premiered the first *Beavis and Butt-head* feature, but we won't hold that against it.
Major Award Winners Best Feature Film: *Left Luggage*s, by Jeroen Krabbé; Best Short Film: *Deviant*, by Eoin Clarke
Films About 100
How to Enter Send VHS dub and entry form to:
International Film Festival Emden
Postfach 2343
26703 Emden
Germany
Telephone 011.49.121.915.533
Fax 011.49.30.2195.591
Web www.filmfest-emden.de
Entry Deadline March

Filmfest Hamburg

Where Hamburg, Germany
When One week in late September and early October
Background In the grand scheme of things, the Hamburg fest is no doubt a very strong one—comprehensive, well-programmed, respectable. But given all the great European festivals, one would have hoped that Hamburg would be a little more adventurous in its film selection than it has been of late. Though a great number of films appear here, they are mostly of the mainstream variety and amount to little more than a condensed and intensified series of sneak previews of the coming season from major American and European distributors. Films are screened in the following categories: European Masters (e.g., Greenaway's *The Pillow Book*, von Trier's *Breaking the Waves*), Young Cinema, Hollywood and Beyond (Altman's horrific *Kansas City*, the Coen Brothers' *Fargo*), and United States Independents (Steve Buscemi's *Trees Lounge*, Edward Burns's *She's the One*). Recent spotlights have focused on Latin American, Asian, and Australian cinema. The festival awarded the 1999 Douglas Sirk Award to Jim Jarmusch. There is also a children's film festival and a festival of short films that, by its nature, tends to be more eccentrically and intriguingly programmed. I have no quarrel with the festival's excellent selection of venues: the

Abaton (Allende Platz 3), the Alabama (Jarerestr. 20), the Fama (Luruper Haupstr. 247), the Holi (Schlankreye 69), Metropolis (Dammtorstr. 30A), Streit's (Jungfernstieg 38), 3001 (Schanzenstr. 75-77), and the Zeise Kinos (Friedensallee 7-9). Clint Eastwood recently received a lifetime achievement award here.

Films About 200 features and shorts

Noteworthy Celebrity Sightings Jodie Foster, Cate Blanchett, Clint Eastwood, Woody Harrelson, Alan Parker, Sting, Oliver Stone, Monika Treut

Tickets 12 DM per individual screening

How to Enter Send VHS dub and entry form to:
Filmfest Hamburg
Friedensallee 44
22765 Hamburg
Germany
Telephone 011.49.40.39919.000
Fax 011.49.40.39826.211
E-mail filmfest-hamburg@t-online.de
Web www.filmfesthamburg.de

Entry Deadline June

Filmfestival Internazionale Montagna Esplorazione Aventura

Where Trento, Italy

When Ten days in late April and early May

Background For the mountaineer in all of us, or perhaps for the voyeur too frightened by the concept of actually climbing one of those damned things, this festival, founded in 1942 and promoted by the city of Trento and the Italian Alpine Club, presents one of the most impressive collections of mountain- and adventure-related cinema. Documentaries, not surprisingly, are the focus here, and most of them relate to some aspect of mountaineering, mountain environment, or, at least, regions that have mountains in them. There are films about penguins, films about otters, films about mountain climbers, films about trains that run through mountains, films about icy rivers that flow through mountain ranges, films about planes that fly over mountains, and films about bears that live in the mountains. Most of them come from various European countries. But the festival also provides cool retrospectives of mountain-related cinema and has shown such classics as *Nanook of the North* and *Lost Horizon*.

Major Award Winners Best Film: *Bergkristall*, by Gerhard Baur; Best Film by an Italian Director: *Sotto la Giungla il Fiume*, by Claudio Norza; Best Photography: *Hightops of Scotland*, by Manuel Hinge; Best Film of Ethnographic Interest and Scientific Value: *Karsha*, by Jean Boggio Pola; Best Film on Exploration and/or Environmental Conservation: *Mountain Gorilla: A Shattered Kingdom*, by Bruce Davidson; Best Film on Mountains: *Alambics ou le Dernier Défi de la Marraine*, by Pierre Beccu; Best Fiction or Documentary Film: *Wie die Zeit Vergeht*, by Joseph Vilsmaier; Best Film on Alpinism: *La Zone de la Mort*, by Claude Andrieux

Films About 100

How to Enter Send VHS dub and entry form to:
Festival Office
Centro S. Chiara-Via S. Croce, 67

Trento TN
Italy
Telephone 011.46.1.238.178
Fax 011.46.1.986.120
Entry Deadline March

Filmfestival Max Ophüls Preis

Where Saarbrücken, Germany
When One week in late January
Background Named for director and hometown Saarbrücken boy Max Ophüls (1902–1957), who moved to the United States during World War II and directed many noteworthy films including *Letter from an Unknown Woman*, *Caught*, and *The Reckless Moment* before moving to France, where he directed the classic *Lola Montes*, the festival has been called the Sundance Film Festival of German cinema. In the past, the festival has focused on the works of German filmmakers and those from German-speaking countries. Along with the excellent selection of German features and shorts, the occasional strange U.S. film shows up inexplicably in an unnecessary Saarbrücken premiere (e.g., Barbara Streisand's *The Mirror Has Two Faces*). Retrospectives have included the work of Daniel Schmid and focus on Young German-Language Cinema, New Dutch Cinema, and Saarbrücken premieres, and, of course, every year there is a revival of an Ophüls film. Filmmakers compete for the Max Ophüls Preis (30,000 DM) and many other honors. Films are screened at the Kino im Filmhaus (Mainzer Strasse 8), UT Kinos (Saarcenter), Kino 8½ (Nauwieserstrasse 19), the Passage-Kino (Bahnofstasse 82), and Le Garage (Bleichstrasse). About 20,000 attend annually.
Major Award Winners Max Ophüls Preis for Best Film: *Müde Weggefahreten*, by Zoran Solomon; Filmpreis des Saarland: *Honig und Asche*, by Nadia Fares; Publikfilmpreis: *Lea*, by Ivan Fila
Films About 250 features and shorts
Noteworthy Celebrity Sightings Volker Schlondorff
Tickets 10 DM per individual screening
How to Enter Send VHS dub and official entry form to:
Filmfestival Max Ophüls Preis
Mainzer Strasse 8
66111 Saarbrücken
Germany
Telephone 011.49.681.39452
Fax 011.49.681.905.1943
Entry Deadline September

Filmfest München

Where Munich, Germany
When One week in late June and early July
Background It may not be quite the event that Berlin is, but even so, this festival is *huge*. Screening hundreds of films in a variety of categories, the fest has deserved the right to (rather pompously) declare itself "El Dorado for Film Fans." Recent

festival premieres have included mainstream fare such as *Clockers*, *Antonia's Line*, and *Georgia*. But on the more interesting side have been the stunning tributes to John Milius, Max Linder, Jules Dassin, and others. There is always a great selection of American and European independents here and a focus on young filmmakers. There are also special sections for animation and children's cinema. Recently the festival has paid tribute to the work of Susan Sarandon and Robert Wise.

Major Award Winners Noncompetitive

Films About 300

Noteworthy Celebrity Sightings Susan Sarandon, Robert Wise

How to Enter Send VHS dub and entry form to:

> Filmfest München
> IMF GmbH
> Kaiserstrasse 39
> 80801 Munich
> Germany
> Telephone 011.49.89.3819.040
> Fax 011.49.89.3819.0427

Entry Deadline April

FilmKunstFest Schwerin

Where Schwerin, Germany

When One week in mid-May

Background One of the lesser-known film festivals in Germany, this still offers a really cool array of retrospectives, premieres, and strange features. Along with premieres of films like Volker Koepp's *Kalte Heimat* and Trueba's *Belle Epoque*, the festival has screened a retrospective of Herbert Achternbuch's films, a tribute to Spanish film, a series of Jimi Hendrix concert films, and even an erotic film festival. Also, there are programs of shorts and children's cinema.

Major Award Winners Best Film: *Engelchen*, by Helke Misselwitz; Prix du Public: *Der Boxherer II*; Best Short: *The Wheel*, by Heike Wasem

Films About 100 features plus additional programs of shorts and cartoons

How to Enter Send VHS dub and entry form to:

> FilmKunstFest Schwerin
> Bleicher Ufer 5
> 19053 Schwerin
> Germany
> Telephone 011.49.385.557.4512
> Fax 011.49.385.447.4514
> Web www.filmkunstfest.i24.de

Entry Deadline Not available

Flanders International Film Festival

See Best of the Fests

Florence Festival dei Populi Review of Social Documentary

Where Florence, Italy
When Ten days in late November and early December
Background Founded in 1959 by a group of social scientists and film professionals, the festival has been a great source for interesting retrospectives and features. Recent screenings have included a retrospective of Jean-Luc Godard's work including *Two or Three Things I Know About Her* and the Florence premiere of *JLG by JLG*, as well as programs on Cinema and Art and Cinema and Music. Other films that have screened here recently include Werner Herzog's *Gesualdo* and Nicolas Roeg's *Performance*, along with a tribute to the films of Abbas Kiarostami.
Major Award Winners Best Documentary Film (20,000,000 L): *Middle of the Moment*, by Nicolas Humbert and Werner Penzel
Films About 100 films
How to Enter Send VHS dub and entry form to:
    Festival dei Popoli
    Via Castellani 8
    50122 FI
    Italy
    Telephone 011.39.55.294.353
    Fax 011.39.55.213.698
    E-mail mega@mega.it
Entry Deadline September

Freiburg Gay and Lesbian Film Festival

Where Freiburg, Germany
When One week in mid-April
Background With the huge number of gay and lesbian film festivals that have sprouted up in the past 20 years, this isn't a particularly enormous one, but it does offer a decent collection of new and classic works of gay cinema. Recent screenings have included *The Boys in the Band*, *Madagascar Skin*, *Lie Down with Dogs*, and *Cabaret*.
Major Award Winners Noncompetitive
Films About 20 features plus programs of shorts
How to Enter Send VHS dub and entry form to:
    Schwule Filmwoche Freiburg
    Luisenstrasse 7
    79098 Freiburg
    Germany
    E-mail ludwigamm@aol.com
Entry Deadline Not available

Galway Film Festival

Where Galway, Ireland
When A week in mid-July
Background Founded in 1981 as part of the Galway Arts Festival, which is noteworthy for its international street theater presentations, the so-called Galway Film

Fleadh presents the latest in Irish cinema, offering about 12 world premieres per year. Among these have been Tommy McArdle's *Angela Mooney Dies Again*, starring Mia Farrow. Also part of the festival are screenings of new Irish shorts, new Irish animation, and films from different world regions including New African cinema and European New Wave features. About 100 attend annually. Screenings are held at the Town Hall Theater in the Omniplex Cinema.

Major Award Winners Noncompetitive

Films About 60 features plus programs of shorts and cartoons

Noteworthy Celebrity Sightings Gabriel Byrne, Roddy Doyle, Caryl Phillips, Patrick McCabe

How to Enter Contact:
    Galway Film Festival
    Cluain Mhuire
    Monivea Road
    Galway
    Ireland
    Telephone 011.353.91.751.655
    Fax 011.353.91.770.746
    E-mail galfilm@ist.ie

Entry Deadline April

Geneva Film Festival

Where Geneva, Switzerland

When One week in late October

Background This is known cheesily as the "Stars of Tomorrow" film festival, which, though it may bring to mind images of *Soul Train* or *Star Search*, is actually a name for an adventurous film fest showing a decent array of films mainly from Europe, although the occasional American or African film shows up as well.

Major Award Winners International Jury Award (20,000 Fr): *Salto al Vacio*, by Daniel Calparsoro; *Limita*, by Denis Evstigneev; and *Manneken Pis*, by Frank Van Panel

How to Enter Send VHS dub and entry form to:
    Geneva Film Festival
    Case 35, rue des Bains
    CP 5615
    1211 Geneva
    Switzerland
    Telephone 011.41.22.809.9450
    Fax 011.41.22.809.9444

Entry Deadline August

Giffoni Children's Film Festival

Where Giffoni, Italy

When One week in late July and early August

Background Although this is a children's film festival, it does not merely offer garden-variety kids' fare but tries to stretch the definition of what is suitable for younger audiences. This doesn't mean that the Giffoni festival shows *Pulp Fiction* to five-year-olds, but it does have the advantage of not treating children like morons. The festival, founded in 1970, is geared to the intelligent 12-year-old. An official competition of 14 films is held as filmmakers vie for a winning lottery ticket.

Major Award Winners Silver Gryphon Award Winner for Best Film: *Clockwork Mice*, by Jean Vadim

Films About 14

How to Enter Send VHS dub and entry form to:

Giffoni Film Festival
Piazza Umberto, 1
84095 Giffoni Valle Piana SA
Italy
Telephone 011.39.89.868.544
Fax 011.39.89.866.111
E-mail gff@ph.itnet.it

Entry Deadline Not available

Gijon International Film Festival

Where Gijon, Spain

When Last week of November

Background This Spanish film festival, located in the north of Spain in a town of 300,000, is subtitled "a festival for young people," which explains a recent tribute to the work of Gregg Araki and Derek Jarman but not the tribute to classic American film director Robert Aldrich. Nevertheless, in keeping with its otherwise youth-oriented spirit, the festival offers a Young Jury Prize, in which the best feature film is voted upon by 60 16- to 26-year-olds. Outside the official selection of films, Gijon has featured a spotlight on "Radical Cinema" as well as a grab bag of Spanish shorts and children's flicks. Films recently premiered here include Adrienne Shelley's *Sudden Manhattan*, Mary Harron's *I Shot Andy Warhol*, and, uncharacteristically, Simon Wincer's *The Phantom*.

Major Award Winners Best film: *Orphans*; Best Director: Clara Law, *Floating Life*; Best Actor: Gary Lewis, *Orphans*; Best Actress: Dina Panozzo, *Fistful of Flies*

How to Enter Contact:

Festival Internacional de Cine de Gijon
Paseo de Begoña
24-entlo
33205 Gijon
Spain
Telephone 011.34.98.534.3739
Fax 011.34.98.535.4152
E-mail festcine@las.es
Web www.las.es/gijonfilmfestival

Entry Deadline September

Golden Knight International Amateur Film and Video Festival

Where Malta

When One weekend in late November

Background Founded in 1961 by the Malta Amateur Cine Circle, this film and video festival is divided into categories for amateur filmmakers, student filmmakers, and filmmakers who might want a little more remuneration and notoriety than is afforded by appearing at the Malta festival.

Major Award Winners Golden Knight: *Must-Have Artifact*, by Alejandra Siquot; Silver Knight: *Nee*, by Klaus Werner Voss; Bronze Knight: *The Lift*, by Chris Armstrong

Films Nine films (three from each category)

Noteworthy Celebrity Sightings None to speak of

How to Enter Send entry fee ($17 for student filmmakers, $34 for amateur filmmakers, and $56 for all other categories) plus official entry form to:

The Secretary of the Golden Knight Festival
Malta Amateur Cine Circle
P.O. Box 450
Valletta CMR 01
Malta
Telephone 011.356.222.345
Fax 011.356.225.047
E-mail maxx@global.net.mt

Entry Deadline September

Goldfish International Children's Animation Festival

Where Nizhny Novgorod, Russia

When One week in September

Background Founded in 1996 in conjunction with the annual fair in this town 250 miles east of Moscow, the festival invites a large selection of Russian and Western European film professionals to this screening of animated shorts. And any festival that gives out a golden poisson as its grand prize can't be all bad.

Major Award Winners Noncompetitive

How to Enter Send VHS dub and entry form to:

Goldfish
Russia
127000 Moscow
Koroleva 12 office 3-6
Goldfish
Telephone 011.7.95.217.71.09
Fax 011.7.95.978.54.16

Entry Deadline May

Göteborg Film Festival

Where Göteborg, Sweden

When One week in late January, early February

Background Founded in 1977, this Swedish film festival boasts the heaviest festival program of any other international film festival, which not only means that it spends a lot of money on promotion, but that it has a hell of a lot of films to promote. The folks at the festival are fond of calling it the biggest and most important in northern Europe. Although there is a strong focus on Scandinavian cinema, the selection of international films rivals that of any other festival in Europe, and retrospectives are usually unusual and interesting-witness a retrospective of Hungarian filmmaker Paul Fejos. One must say, though, that the selection of American films (*She's the One*, *Don't Be a Menace to South Central While Drinking Your Juice in the Hood*) is both idiosyncratic and questionable. On a more high-minded and worthy note, the Göteborg Film Festival has also started a fund-raising program to build a fully equipped cinema in the Tuzla region of Bosnia-Herzegovina to bring movies to an area that is certainly not as cinematically blessed as Sweden. And hell, who's going to quibble with a festival that has Ingmar Bergman as president of its honorary board?

Major Award Winners Nordic Film Prize: *Hunting the Kidney Stone*, by Vibeke Idsøe; Great Film Award: *The Hunters*, by Kjell Sundvall; Swedish Film of the Year: *The Christmas Oratorio*, by Kjell Andersson

Films 160 features and documentaries and 160 shorts (no video)

How to Enter You can't. The festival is by invitation only. Although you may feel free to "suggest a film" by sending a copy to:

Göteborg Film Festival
Box 7079
402 32 Göteborg
Sweden
Telephone 011.46.31.41.0546
Fax 011.46.31.41.0063
E-mail goteborg@filmfestival.org
Web www.goteborg.filmfestival.org

Entry Deadline December

Grand Ücran National Festival of Animation

Where Marly-le-Roi, France

When One weekend in mid-October

Background Founded in 1986 by the French Association of Animated Cinema, the festival holds a competition for 35 mm and 16 mm animated films. About 2,000 attend the festival, which takes place at the 400-seat cinema Institute National de la Jeunesse et de L'Education Populaire in Marly-le-Roi, a suburb of Paris. Recent homages have included the work of Paul Grimault and Raymond Maillet. In conjunction with the festival, art exhibits are held, which have included "Athanse Kircher and the Magic Lantern."

Major Award Winners Grand Prix: *La Petite Jeune Fille de Paris*, by Lys Flowerday; Best First Work: *L'Amour Est un Poisson*, by Eric Vaschetti; Best Animation: *Une Mission Ephémère,* by Piotr Kamler

Films About 100 films including 52 shorts and nine first features.

How to Enter Send VHS dub and entry form to:

Grand Ücran National Festival of Animation
48, Chemin Perdu
78310 Maurepas
France
Telephone/Fax 011.33.130.50.1957

Entry Deadline Not available

Grenzland Film Days

Where Wunsiedel, Germany
When Last week of April
Background Founded in 1978, this midsized festival offers a decent range of by-now-familiar European cinema (Kieslowski's *Trois Couleurs* trilogy and *Camera Buff*) in addition to the usual array of shorts, animated films, documentaries, experimental films, and music videos.
Major Award Winners Noncompetitive
Films About 100 films
Tickets 8 DM per individual screening, 32 DM for five screenings; 50 DM for 10 screenings
How to Enter Send VHS dub and entry form to:
Grenzland Film Days
Postfach 307
95622 Wunsiedel
Germany
Telephone 011.49.923.24770
Fax 011.49.923.24710
E-mail office@grenzland-filmtage.de
Web grenzland.filmtage.de
Entry Deadline January

Györ Media Wave

Where Györ, Hungary
When Last week in April
Background Founded in 1991 by the Visual Workshop of Györ, this festival, held about a hundred miles west of Budapest, screens a vast collection of films and videos. The festival pays particular attention to works dealing with ethnic and folkloric themes, including films about dance and gender issues, and erotic cinema. The Media Wave Festival holds concerts and exhibitions in conjunction with the film screenings. There is also a series of screenings called "Dusty Reels," which focuses on films that have not been screened for political reasons.
Major Award Winners Best Feature Film: *Surprise*, by Veit Helmer; Best Documentary: *Kanehsatake*, by Alanis Obomsawin; Best Pseudo-documentary: *Growing City*, by Sandor Kardos; Best Dance Film: *The Dream of Creation*, by András Veszprémi.
Films About 200
How to Enter Send VHS dub and entry form to:
Györ Media Wave
Mediawave Foundation
Györ
Soprani ut 45.
9028
Hungary
Telephone 011.36.96.449.444
Fax 011.36.96.449.445
Entry Deadline December

Hamburg International Short Film Festival

Where Hamburg, Germany
When One week in mid-June
Background This festival gets special mention for its creativity in coming up with categories of short films. Embracing low-budget and no-budget films, the festival screens "three-minute quickies" and digital video shorts. Among the coolest aspects of the festival is the way it turns up the first short works of major directors, including shorts by Tarkovsky, Michael Radford, Terry Gilliam, and Walter Vontz of Woody Woodpecker fame. Screening at six venues, the festival also offers a Trash Night, boasting the motto, "The Depths of Drivel Know No End." A short film market is held in conjunction with the festival.
Major Award Winners Noncompetitive
Tickets 10 DM per individual screening; 90 DM for admission to all screenings
How to Enter Send VHS dub and entry form to:
    Hamburg Short Film Agency
    Friedensallee 7
    22765 Hamburg
    Germany
    Telephone 011.49.40.3982.6122
    Fax 011.49.40.3982.6123
Entry Deadline March

Helsinki International Film Festival

Where Helsinki, Finland
When One week in mid-September
Background Also known by its more groovy title, "The Love and Anarchy Film Festival," this Finnish fest founded in 1988 hosts a variety of Finnish and international films, though its focus seems to be on the offbeat, underground, and controversial. It recently guested director Lodge Kerrigan (Claire Dolan). It's also a festival where films by Jean-Luc Godard and Edward Burns can share the spotlight. The festival was founded in 1988 and organized by Image Arts and Culture magazine and most recently has been run by the independent film distributor Cinema Mondo. About everything that screens here is a Finnish premiere. Screenings are held in five theaters in Helsinki (Savoy, Athenaeum, and Kino Engel 1-3).
Major Award Winners Popular vote: *Surrender Dorothy*, π
Films About 100
Tickets 30 Fmk per individual screening; 300 Fmk (about $60) for admission to 11 screenings, plus a free catalog
How to Enter Send VHS dub and entry form (no fee) to:
    Helsinki Film Festival
    Unioninkatu 10
    00130 Helsinki
    Finland
    Telephone 011.358.0.629.578
    Fax 011.358.0.631.450

Entry Deadline July

Holland Animation Festival

Where Utrecht, Netherlands
When Five days in late November
Background Founded in 1985, this biennial festival attempts to merge the worlds of industrial and artistic animation, holding competitions for publicity and promotional films, music videos, and educational movies. The festival started out in a Utrecht art house showing a bizarre array of promotional cartoons and even a program of erotic animation. Later festivals featured retrospectives of the works of animation masters such as Norman McLaren and screenings of classics including *Yellow Submarine*. Alexander Petrov's *Dream of a Ridiculous Man* premiered here.
Major Award Winners Best Educational Film: *When Life Departs*, by Karsten Külerich; Best Music Video: *Buttmeat*, by Run Wrake; Best Commercial: *Russian Sugar: Tea Party*, by Yury Norshtein; Grand Prix: *Wind der Stiller Wird*, by Vuk Jevremovic
Films About 150 animated features, shorts, and others in assorted categories
How to Enter Send VHS dub and entry form to:
Holland Animation Festival
Hoogt 4
3512 GW Utrecht
Netherlands
Telephone 011.31.30.233.17.33
Fax : 011.31.30.233.10.79
E-mail haff@knoware.nl
Entry Deadline September

Huesca Film Festival

Where Huesca, Spain
When Ten days in mid-June
Background Featuring a "sample of European cinema" and an international short film competition, the midsize Huesca festival, founded in 1973, does an excellent job of blending vital premieres with worthy tributes and retrospectives and related museum exhibitions. Though a great deal of Spanish features and shorts are shown here, there is a decidedly international flavor along with a wide variety of tributes and retrospectives, which in recent years have included an homage to the deservedly lauded National Film Board of Canada, a retrospective of films based on books by Blasco Ibáñez, a good sampling of Latin American cinema, a children's festival, tributes to German Hanna Schygulla, and the Budapest Academy of Drama Film and TV. Lifetime achievement awards were recently given to María Rojo, Manuel Gutiérrez Aragón and José Luis Borau.
Major Award Winners Gold Dancer Award: *In the Mirror of the Sky*, by Carlos Salces; Silver Dancer: *I Move, so I Am*, by Gerrit van Dijk; Bronze Dancer: *Chainsmoker*, by Maria von Heland
How to Enter Send VHS dub and entry form to:

Festival de Cine de Huesca
Avda, Parke
1 piso
22002 Huesca
Spain
Telephone 011.34.74.21.25.82
Fax 011.34.74.21.00.65
E-mail huescafest@fsai.es
Web www.huesca-filmfestival.com
Entry Deadline April

Imagina

Where Monte Carlo, Monaco
When Three days in mid-February
Background You wanna get dressed up in a tuxedo to watch the premiere screening of the *Gulliver's Travels* miniseries starring Ted Danson? Be my guest. Hell, would you expect anything different from this snooty gambling mecca? The festival, founded in 1961, is attended by the movers and shakers of the TV world (BBC, Canal +, and more), and it is here that one dresses up in sleek evening attire or froufrou dresses to cocktail one's way along the French Riviera and check out all the latest in TV technology, computer graphics, and special effects. There's a contest called the "Dancing Baby Championship" in which teams of CGI techs work for 24 hours straight to produce an animated short. About 8,000 attend each year, chowing down on hors d'oeuvres and listening to panel discussions on such topics as "Learning How to Become the New Columbus of the Virtual World" and "From Virtual Banks to Cyber Casinos." Join the virtual throng.
Major Award Winners Best Film: *Bunny*
How to Enter For more information contact:
Imagina
BP 300
MC 98006
Monaco
Telephone 011.377.93.15.93.94
Fax 011.377.93.15.93.95
E-mail
imagina@imagina.ina.fr
Web www.ina.fr/imagina
Entry Deadline December

Incontro Internazionale di Cinema de Donne

Where Florence, Italy
When First week in July
Background A festival of women's cinema that spotlights specific regions and trends in the field. A recent festival focused on German filmmakers including Helke Sander, Helma Sanders-Brahms, Jutta Brückner, and Margarethe von Trotta.

Major Award Winners Noncompetitive
How to Enter Send VHS dub and entry form to:
Laboratorio Immagine Donna
Via S. Gallo, 32
50129-Firenze FI
Italy
Telephone 011.39.55.474.680
Fax 011.39.55.461.159
Entry Deadline Not available

Innsbruck International Film Festival Cinematograph

Where Innsbruck, Austria
When One week in early June
Background Founded in 1992, the festival screens in the 90-seat Innsbruck Cinema, featuring Austrian premieres of films from Africa, Latin America, and Asia. Edward James Olmos's *American Me* premiered here. The festival has offered tributes to Tomás Gutiérrez Alea, Julio García Espinosa, and Raoul Peck.
Major Award Winners Best Film: *Swaham*
Films About 40 features
Noteworthy Celebrity Sightings Ousmane Sembene
How to Enter Send VHS dub and entry form to:
International Film Festival Cinematograph
CineVision
Museumstrasse 31
6020 Innsbruck
Austria
Telephone 011.43.512.580.723
Fax 011.43.512.581.762
E-mail cinema@nomad.transit.or.at
Entry Deadline Not available

International Festival of Amateur Films

Where Ebendorf, Austria
When First week of September
Background Founded in 1987, the "Festival des Nichtkommerziellen Films," as its name suggests, devotes itself solely to short amateur films (20 minutes and less) in Super-8, 16 mm, Video VHS, and Super VHS formats.
Major Award Winners Noncompetitive
How to Enter Send $15 and very rudimentary entry form to:
Paul Kraiger
Buchhalm 42
9141 Ebendorf
Austria
Entry Deadline August

International Festival of Cinematographic Art of Barcelona

Where Barcelona, Spain
When One week in mid-January
Background The festival prides itself on unusual cinema, sponsoring both a national and international competition as well as a noncompetitive generic section. The festival also sponsors a European marketplace to seek out European audiences for films in all formats and genres. It is housed in the Maremagnum complex, five minutes from the center of Barcelona. The coolest aspect of the festival is the so-called Wild Fest, where anyone who shows up with a movie less than 15 minutes long in their grasp can screen on a first-come, first-served basis.
Major Award Winners Noncompetitive
Films About 30 features and 30 shorts
How to Enter Send VHS dub and entry form to:
    Barcelona Film Festival
    Baluard, 79
    08003 Barcelona
    Spain
    Telephone 011.343.221.31.95
    Fax 011.343.221.31.95
    E-mail jungla@teclata.es
    Web www.teclata.es/jungla
Entry Deadline November

International Festival of Fantastic Films

Where Manchester, England
When Three days in early September
Background New and old material in a festival that spans 100 years of sci-fi movies. Shows such classics as *The Day of the Triffids*, *It Came from Outer Space*, and *Werewolves on Wheels*. Premiered *Halloween H₂0* as well as a recent Corman masterpiece *A Very Unlucky Leprechaun*. All that plus Boris Karloff double features and a panel discussion on the rise and fall of the British horror film make this one of the better geek fests around.
Major Award Winners Best Independent Feature: *The Alchemist and the Virgin*, by Zoltán Kamondi; Best Independent Short: *Succubus: The Motion Picture*, by Harry Weinmann
Films Around 35 films
How to Enter send entry form to:
    International Festival of Fantastic Films
    33 Barrington Road
    Altrincham
    United Kingdom
    WA14 1HZ
    Telephone 011.44.161.929.1067
    Fax 011.44.161.929.1067
    E-mail hnad@globalnet.co.uk
    Web fantastic-films.com/festival
Entry Deadline July

International Festival of Free Flight

Where St.-Hilaire du Touvet, France (known as the Mecca of Free Flight)
When One week in mid-September
Background Founded by the appropriately named Icarus Festival Organization, this is perhaps the only known cinema festival that combines moviemaking with the art of hang gliding. The festival presents, along with aerial shows, balloon flights, and paper plane competitions, a three-day festival of films on video concerned with hang gliding, skydiving, ballooning, kiteflying, muscular flight, bungee jumping, and so forth. This is the only known festival that is overshadowed by balloon flights, skydiving performances, and boomerang competitions. Those with either acrophobia or agoraphobia should avoid the St.-Hilaire du Touvet funicular, built in 1924, which holds the world record for railway and tunnel inclination as it skyrockets from the depths of Montfort's Gresivaudan Valley up to the heights of St.-Hilaire.
Major Award Winners Noncompetitive
Noteworthy Celebrity Sightings More than 600,000 pilots annually
Tickets 150 Fr gains admission to all festival events, including film screenings
How to Enter Send VHS- or Beta-formatted video dub along with entry form and a photo from the film to:

> Festival International du Film de Vol Libre
> Office du Tourisme
> 38660 St. Hilaire du Touvet
> France
> Telephone 011.476.08.33.99
> Fax 011.476.97.20.56

Entry Deadline July

International Hofer Filmtage

Where Munich, Germany
When One week in late October
Background Founded in 1967 by Heinz Badewitz and then-up-and-coming filmmakers Werner Herzog and Wim Wenders, this is a rather small festival but has a respectable array of familiar films. The main focus is contemporary German and independent European and American cinema. *Palookaville*, *Shine*, and *Jude* have all premiered here, as has Jim Wilson's *Head Above Water*. A recent tribute focused on the works of director Clara Law. Screenings are held in four rooms of the Central Theater.
Major Award Winners Noncompetitive
Films About 50 features and 50 shorts
Tickets 7 DM per individual screening
How to Enter Send VHS dub and entry form to:

> International Hofer Filmtage
> Loth Str. 28
> 80335 Munich
> Germany
> Telephone 011.49.89.129.7422
> Fax 011.49.89.123.6868
> E-mail hofer-filmtage@media-online.de

Entry Deadline September

Italian Film Festival

Where Glasgow and Edinburgh, Scotland
When Ten days in late April
Background Not just the bunch of Fellini and Rosselini flicks that you might expect from an Italian film fest in Scotland, this festival has offered tributes to Marcello Mastroianni, Carlo Mazzacurati, and Carlo Verdone. In addition to the tributes, though, there are screenings of New Italian cinema and a festival of Italian TV programs.
Major Award Winners Noncompetitive
Films About 25 films
How to Enter Send VHS dub and entry form to:
    Italian Film Festival
    82 Nicolson Street
    Edinburgh
    United Kingdom
    EH8 9EW
    Telephone 011.44.131.668.2232
    Fax 011.44.131.668.2777
Entry Deadline February

Karlovy Vary International Film Festival

Where Karlovy Vary, Czech Republic
When Ten days in early July
Background The world's third-oldest film festival, founded in 1946, the Karlovy Vary fest is nothing if not eclectic, having in recent years featured a retrospective of films with Holocaust themes side by side with a series of John Woo-style Hong Kong action pics and a tribute to Antonin Artaud. Held in this West Bohemian spa town, the festival holds competitions for features and documentaries and presents films out of competition in the following categories: Horizons (featuring allegedly major films, such as a recent screening of Oliver Stone's yawn-o-rama *Nixon*, Julian Schnabel's *Basquiat*, and Clint Eastwood's *Absolute Power*), Czech Films, Independents, Student Films, and Another View, which basically allows the jury to choose films they like that don't fit into the previous categories. Special features have included a tribute to Australian cinematography and retrospectives of the works of Alexander Sokurov and Nick Broomfield. Festival screenings take place in six separate halls of the Thermal Hotel and in the Cas, Lazne III, and Drahomira Cinemas. About 118,000 attended the most recent festival.
Major Award Winners Crystal Globe for Best Film: *Yana's Friends*, by Arik Kaplun; Special Jury Prize: *Show Me Love*, by Lukas Moodysson; Best Director: Alexander Rogozhkin, *Checkpoint*; Best Actress: Evlyn Kaplun, *Yana's Friends*; Best Actor: Hilmar Thate, *Paths in the Night*; Audience Prize: *Show Me Love*, Lukas Moodysson
Films About 250
Noteworthy Celebrity Sightings John Landis, Woody Harrelson, Max von Sydow, Bruce Beresford, John Schlesinger, Leonardo DiCaprio, Mia Farrow, Gina Lollobrigida, Britt Ekland, Mika Kaurismaki, Errol Morris, Robert Wise, Christopher Walken

Send VHS dub and entry form to:
Karlovy Vary International Film Festival Foundation
Panská 1
110 00 Prague 1
Czech Republic
Telephone 011.420.2.24.23.5412
Fax 011.420.2.24.23.3408
E-mail foundation@iffkv.cz
Web http://www.iffkv.cz
Entry Deadline April

La Baule Festival of European Cinema

Where La Baule, France
When Last week in June
Background Founded in 1990 in this lovely coast town with its comfy beaches, this festival showcases films that have had difficulty getting distribution in France. Nevertheless, one of the most ballyhooed events at recent festivals has been the premiere of *Christopher Columbus* starring Gerard Depardieu, which, if there were a just God, would have had trouble getting distribution anywhere. Features and spotlights focus on a particular country's film industry, including in recent years Belgian and Icelandic cinema. The festival screens at eight theaters including the Cinéma Gulf Stream (52, avenue du General de Gaulle). The festival also has held tributes to Belgian cinema and major French actor star/stud Jean Gabin. Films premiered here include *Moll Flanders*, by Pen Densham, and *Food of Love*, by Serge Poliakoff.
Major Award Winners Grand Prize: *The Waltz with Rogitze*, by Kaspar Rostrup; Jury Prize: *The Northerners*, by Alex von Womerdorn; Best Actress: Patricia Piccininni, *The Peaceful Air of the West*; Best Actor: José Airosa, *Sinais de Fogo*
Films About 40 features
Noteworthy Celebrity Sightings Sean Connery, Jacqueline Bisset, Gina Lollobrigida
How to Enter Send VHS dub and entry form to:
La Baule European Film Festival
97, rue Raumur
75002 Paris
France
Telephone 011.33.2.40.41.04.54
Fax 011.33.2.40.26.54.78
Entry Deadline Not available

La Rochelle International Film Festival

Where La Rochelle, France
When Early July
Background Founded in 1973, this festival offers a number of truly fascinating retrospectives and discoveries. Seemingly lost films are shown alongside the screenings of art fare such as *Some Mother's Son* and *Prisoner of the Mountains*. Most interesting have been a tribute to American 1920s burlesque comedian Max Davidson and homages to the work of Jacques Rozier, Valentin Vaala, and Dina Menichelli.

Screenings are held at La Coursive and the Cinema le Dragon.
Major Award Winners Noncompetitive
Films About 100 features
Tickets 35 Fr per individual screening; 270 Fr for 10 screenings; 470 Fr gains entry to all screenings
How to Enter Send VHS dub and entry form to:
    La Rochelle International Film Festival
    16, rue Saint Sabn
    75011 Paris
    France
    Telephone 011.33.1.48.06.16.66
    Fax 011.33.1.48.06.15.40
Entry Deadline May

Leeds International Film Festival

Where Leeds, England
When Two weeks in mid-October
Background Founded in 1983, this festival is one of the most challenging in Great Britain, boasting a political and social awareness that is rarely found in your garden-variety bread-and-circuses film fest. Combining entertainment with a profound sense of social justice, the Leeds fest recently featured a great thematically linked series of films called *The Crucified World*, curated by a vicar from the church of England, which explored the relationship between religious faith and cinematic art. Films as diverse as *The Exorcist III*, *Pornostar*, *Stop Making Sense*, Nicolas Roeg's *Eureka,* and a documentary on Atom Egoyan were shown. Of equal social and artistic value was another retrospective called *War Zone*, which explored the treatment of war on film from Gene Barry's *War of the Worlds* to Stanley Kubrick's *Full Metal Jacket*, also including films about war in Bosnia. Leeds' Social Studies series explored sex, race, and gender-based conflicts in films ranging from Jean Renoir's *La Regle du Jeu* to Ken Loach's *Family Life*. Other special sections of the Leeds fest have focused on Spanish cinema, women directors, and gay and lesbian cinema. Films that have received Leeds premieres have included *Fanny and Elvis*, *East is East*, and *The Darkest Light*. Screenings are held at Hyde Park Picture House (Brudnell Road), Odeon Cinema (The Headrow), MGM Cinema (Vicar Lane), Civic Theatre (Cookridge Street), Leeds City Art Gallery (The Headrow), Showcase Cinema Centre (27 Gelderd Road, Birstall), and the Brunswick Theatre (Leeds Metropolitan University).
Major Award Winners Noncompetitive
Films About 200 features and shorts
Noteworthy Celebrity Sightings Pete Postlethwaite, Mark Herman (Brassed Off), Jimmy McGovern
Tickets About £3.50 per screening
How to Enter Send VHS dub and entry form to:
    Leeds International Film Festival
    The Town Hall, The Headrow
    Leeds
    United Kingdom
    LS1 3AD

Telephone 011.44.1132.478.398
Fax 011.44.1132.478.397
E-mail filmfestival@leeds.gov.uk
Web www.leedsfilm.com
Entry Deadline June

Leipzig International Festival for Documentary and Animated Film

Where Leipzig, Germany
When One week in late October
Background Back in 1955, the first documentary film festival was held, honoring all the aspects of life that would make Leni Riefenstahl proud: the beautiful homeland and sports, educational science films, puppet films, and cartoons. Come the Berlin Wall and the raising of the Iron Curtain, the film festival became uniquely intertwined with foreign policy, dedicating itself to the goal of raising "the international standing of the GDR." These days, the festival promises that it has become more normal, presenting a selection of cartoons and documentaries chosen for their artistic merit rather than their political or nationalistic philosophy.
Major Award Winners Golden Dove (9,000 DM) for best feature-length film: *Better and Better*, by Alfredo Knuchel and Norbert Wiedmer; Silver Dove (5,000 DM) for feature-length film: *We Wanted to Be Heroes*, by Barbara Metselaar-Berthold; International Mercedes Benz Grant for Best Young Documentary Film (20,000 DM): *The Unconquerable*, by Arvid Sinha; Egon-Erwin Kirsch Prize for Best Journalistic Production (5,000 DM): *Noel Field—The Imaginary Spy*, by Werner Schweizer; Prize for Environment, Conservation, and Reactor Safety: *Alpine Ballad*, by Erich Langjahr; Prize of the City of Leipzig: *Lost in Mississippi*, by Jim Chambers
How to Enter Send VHS copy of film and entry form to:
Dokfestival Leipzig
Elsterstrasse 22-24
04109 Leipzig
Germany
Telephone 011.49.341.980.4828
Fax 011.49.341.980.6141
Entry Deadline July

Limerick Irish Film Festival

Where Limerick, Ireland
When One week in mid-April
Background Founded in 1993, this relatively small film festival offers screenings of new films by Irish filmmakers. Screening at the Savoy Cinema and the Belltable Arts Center, the festival has featured a retrospective of the work of Patrick Carey; a premiere of *Dusk Till Dawn*, about the Irish jazz scene; and a revival of David Lean's *Ryan's Daughter*.
Major Award Winners Noncompetitive
Films About 15 features plus programs of shorts

Tickets £3 per individual screening.
How to Enter Send a letter addressed to the festival director to:
Limerick Film Festival
3 Upper Hartstonye Street
Limerick
Ireland
Telephone 011.353.61.318.150
Fax 011.353.61.318.152
E-mail bmadden.rsl@rtc-limerick.ie
Entry Deadline Not available

Locarno International Film Festival

See Best of the Fests

London Film Festival

Where London, England
When Three weeks in November
Background Founded in 1956, this claims to be the largest noncompetitive film festival in the world, and though size is a matter of opinion, it's a pretty big one nonetheless, and it is noncompetitive, though the audience does vote for a winner. Films that have received their London premieres here over the years are Sam Mendes's *American Beauty*, Steven Soderbergh's *The Limey*, Martin Scorsese's *Casino*, Patrice Leconte's *Ridicule*, and Terence Ryan's *The Brylcreem Boys*. Among recent retrospectives was a tribute to Spanish cinema. Although this is quite a big and reasonably comprehensive festival, the only quibble one might have is that it is not particularly daring in its programming and tends to show films that have already premiered in other countries and at other festivals. Which is great if you don't go to a lot of other festivals or if there are a lot of movies you'd like to see again.
Major Award Winners Critic's Award: *Boys Don't Cry*
Films About 175 features and 70 shorts
Noteworthy Celebrity Sightings Spike Lee, Mike Leigh, Brad Pitt, Tim Robbins, Bernardo Bertolucci, Dennis Hopper, Carl Franklin, Helena Bonham Carter
Tickets $10–$13 per individual screening.
How to Enter Send VHS dub and entry form (no fee) to:
London Film Festival
South Bank
Waterloo
London
United Kingdom
SE1 8XT
Telephone 011.44.171.815.1323
Fax 011.44.171.633.0786
E-mail jane.ivey@bfi.org.uk
Web www.iff.org.uk
Entry Deadline August

London Raindance Film Showcase

Where London, England
When One week in mid-October
Background Patterned after the New York Independent Feature Market, Raindance is both a marketplace and a showcase for filmmakers along with a ton of seminars, pitch sessions, and panel discussions. Boasting one of the best attitudes of the European film festivals, this ragtag but ultra-cool festival/market has premiered the works of Michael Corrente, Matthew Harrison, John Covert, and this author. Discussion topics have included "The Bucks Start Here: Getting Movie Money" and "Guerilla Filmmaking—Tales from the Trenches." There is an aspect of poseur city to this festival—folks who sit around and wear shades in the dark and say, "Wot do yew think about Tarantino?" and, "We all share the same language: the language of film." And like at many festivals, audiences consist largely of filmmakers, their casts, and their buddies. But at least you're in London.
Major Award Winners Raindance Spirit Award (£500): *Plan 10 from Outer Space*, by Trent Harris
Films About 24 features
Tickets £10 for a day pass; £40 gains admittance to all events for the week
How to Enter Send VHS dub and entry form to:
> Raindance Film Showcase
> 81 Berwick Street
> London
> United Kingdom
> W1V 3PF
> Telephone 011.44.171.287.3833
> Fax 011.44.171.439.2243
> Web www.ftech.net/n.ind
Entry Deadline August

Mannheim International Film Festival Mannheim-Heidelberg

Where Mannheim, Germany
When One week in mid-October
Background What I like best about this film festival is either its greatest strength or its biggest liability: the fact that it is willing to take risks on unknown or little-known films. The festival almost exclusively shows films by new directors and awards nearly $70,000 in prizes. There is a category called International Discoveries, a Focus on South Korea, documentaries, and short films, as well as the official competition. But the discoveries are everywhere, particularly in the selection of American indies, many of which have been overlooked stateside. There is also a children's fest held alongside the major fest. Approximately 40,000 attend the festival.
Major Award Winners Best Fiction Film: *Understanding Jane*, by Caleb Lindsey; Best Documentary: *Fatherless*, by Yoshiya Shigeno; Best Short Film: *The Son*, by Ketil Kern; Rainer Werner Fassbinder Award (for film with most unique narrative structure): *Weekend Lover*, by Lou Ye; Audience Prize: *Girls Under Investigation*, by Pete Bayer
Films About 100, 25 in competition
Noteworthy Celebrity Sightings Agnes Varda, Wim Wenders, Volker Schlondorff

How to Enter Send VHS copy and entry form to:
Internationales Film Festival Mannheim-Heidelberg
Collini-Center-Galerie
68161 Mannheim 1
Germany
Telephone 011.49.621.102943
Fax 011.49.621.291564
E-mail ifmh@mannheim-filmfestival.com
Web www.mannheim-filmfestival.com
Entry Deadline July

Marseille Vue sur les Docs

Where Marseille, France
When One week in mid-June
Background Founded in 1987 and held along the docks in the old port of
Marseille, where chugging tour boats give tours of the Count of Monte Cristo's
notorious Château d'If, this international documentary film festival plays host to
about 20,000 spectators and thousands more professionals in the documentary
film industry. Competitions are held for the best French documentary, and there
are social programs as well, featuring a program of international docs focusing on
Eastern Europe and the Mediterranean. Retrospectives of nondocumentary film-
makers including Robert Kramer and Krzysztof Kieslowski have also been held.
Screenings are held daily from 10 A.M. to midnight at the 900-seat Palais de Pharo
and the movie theater complex Cinma le Paris. About 20,000 attend.
Major Award Winners Noncompetitive
Films About 100
Tickets 25 Fr per individual screening; 210 Fr grants access to all screenings
How to Enter Send VHS dub and entry form to:
Vue sur les Docs
2, Square Stalingrad
13001 Marseille
France
Telephone 011.33.491.8440.17
Fax 011.33.491.84.3834
E-mail vue.sur.docs@hol.fr
Web www.film-fest-marseilles.com
Entry Deadline June

Midnight Sun Film Festival

Where Sodankylä, Finland
When Five days in mid-June
Background They say, "Time has no meaning here," since the sun shines as much on
the midnight screenings as it does upon the noon programs. Founded in 1986, this
festival, where movies screen in three venues 24 hours a day, prides itself on its unpre-
tentiousness, quirkiness, and lack of bureaucracy. Although many premieres by
Finnish filmmakers are shown here, the festival pays special attention to screenings of

silent films with live musical accompaniment. Perhaps coolest of all are the 3-D movies shown under the big top of a circus tent. As one might expect from the bizarreness of it all, the deadpan Kaurismaki brothers had a hand in founding this fest.

Major Award Winners Noncompetitive
Noteworthy Celebrity Sightings Abbas Kiarostami, Francesco Rosi, Costa Gavras
Films About 70 features.
Tickets About $7 per screening
How to Enter Send VHS copy and entry form to:
    Midnight Sun Film Festival
    Malminkatu 36
    100 Helsinki
    Finland
    Telephone 011.358.9.685.2242
    Fax 011.358.9.694.5560
    Web www.msfilmfestival.fi
Entry Deadline March 30

Moscow International Film Festival

Where Moscow, Russia
When Ten days in mid-July
Background The festival had its start in 1959 and is fast becoming an impressive international showcase for new unsung films and highly regarded international cinema. Woody Allen's musical *Everyone Says I Love You* and Peter Duncan's *Children of the Revolution* recently had their Russian premieres here. Retrospectives have included tributes to Milos Forman and Andrei Konchalovsky and a spotlight on Music and Cinema, featuring Russian and American musicals and a concert of Dmitry Shostakovich's film scores, conducted by his son Maxim with his grandson Maxim Shostakovich as a piano soloist. Mika Kaurismaki's *Condition Red* premiered here.
Major Award Winners Statuette of Saint George: *A French Woman*, by Regis Wargnier
Films About 22 features
How to Enter Send VHS dub and entry form to:
    Interfest
    Russia
    109028 Moscow
    Khokhlovswki Pereulok 10/1
    Interfest
    Telephone 011.7.95.917.8628
    Fax 011.7.95.916.0107
Entry Deadline Not available

Mostra Internazionale del Cinema Libero

Where Bologna, Italy
When One week in late June and early July
Background A festival of restored films, the Mostra Internazionale has one of the most impressive series of unearthed and rediscovered flicks. Screenings in recent years have included Chaplin's *The Kid*, Losey's *Im Barroa Mezzanotte*, Luis Morat's *Le*

Juif Errant, Albert Parker's *Eyes of Youth*, Alfred Hitchcock's *The Lodger*, and King Vidor's *Family Hour*. Murnau's *Faust* has screened here accompanied by a new score.
Major Award Winners Noncompetitive
Films About 50 features
How to Enter For more information contact:
  Mostra Internazionale del Cinema Libero
  Via Galliera, 8
  40121-Bologna BO
  Italy
  Telephone 011.39.51.237.088
  Fax 011.39.51.261.680
Entry Deadline Not Applicable

Namur Festival International du Court Métrage

Where Namur, Belgium
When One week in mid-November
Background Founded in 1994, this incredibly vast festival of short films organized by the province of Namur and the ministry of French community focuses primarily on films from French-speaking countries, although a few from other countries including Russia and the United States show up as well. Most of the films here are by newcomers, and such directors as Mathieu Kassovitz (*La Haine*) were first introduced to the Belgian public here. Films are screened at Namur's Maison de la Culture.
Major Award Winners Grand Prix de la Province de Namur (100,000 F): *Carnet Noir*, by Benjamin Ntabundi, Jacques Faton, and Michel Castellain; Grand Prix de la Communauté Française de Belgique (100,000 F): *Vacance*, by Ines Rabadan; Prix de la Sabam (50,000 F): *Dites-le Avec les Mains*, by Daniel Hiquet; Best Children's Film: *Bernois Family*, by Luc Otter; Prix du Public: *Saturday Night Sugar*, by Sandrine Lambiotte
Films More than 300 shorts
Noteworthy Celebrity Sightings Daniel Hiquet
How to Enter Send entry form and VHS dub to:
  Festival International du Court Métrage
  Avenue Golenvaux 14
  5000 Namur
  Belgium
  Telephone 011.32.81.24.12.36
  Fax 011.32.81.22.43.84
Entry Deadline August

Netherlands Film Festival

Where Utrecht, Netherlands
When Last week of September
Background Tributes have focused on American director Alan Pakula, Dutch writer Jan de Hartog, and the Amsterdam-based Studio Nieuwe Gronden. In conjunction

with the film festival, the Holland Film Meeting is held, at which Dutch filmmakers attend seminars and try to find international distributors for their films.

Major Award Winners Golden Calf for Best Film: *Flying Liftboy*, by Ben Sombogaart; Best of the Fest: *Turnes Bakc*, by Kazimierz Kutlz; Best Director: Roel Reiné, *The Delivery*; Best Actress: Willeke van Ammelrooy, *Antonia's Line*; Best Actor: Rijk de Gooyer, *Hoogste Tijd*; Best Dutch Film of the Century: *Turkish Delight,* by Paul Verhoeven

Noteworthy Celebrity Sightings Rutger Hauer, Paul Verhoeven, Jeroen Krabbé

How to Enter For more information contact:
Netherlands Film Festival
P.O. Box 1581
3500 BN Utrecht
Netherlands
Tel. 011.31.30.232.26.84
Fax 011.31.30.231.32.00
E-mail nedfilmfest@artnet.xshall.nl
Web www.nethlandfilm.nl

Entry Deadline July

Noir Film Festival

Where Courmayer, Italy

When One week in early December

Background As the title suggests, the Italian festival devotes itself to the rather broadly defined genre of film noir, which can mean anything from your standard Raymond Chandler fare (for whom one of the festival's awards is named) to Scorsese's *Bringing Out the Dead* to John Sayles's *Lone Star*, which is more of a beige than a noir, but when the movies are as good and varied as the ones shown here, it's really difficult to mind too much. The festival, in addition to a competition of contemporary noirs, screens a retrospective of Italian noirs (a recent series featured 1960s Italian films under the title "The Violent City") and a thematically linked chain of international noirs (e.g., the festival's recent "Noirs from Other Worlds," which focused on Philip K. Dick-style films).

Major Award Winners Mystery Award for Best Film: *Justino, un Asesino de la Tercera Edad*

How to Enter For more information contact:
Noir Film Festival
Via Tirso, 90
00198 RM
Italy
Telephone 011.39.6.8848.030
Fax 011.39.6.8840.450
E-mail noir@noirfest.com
Web www.noirfest.com

Entry Deadline Not available

Nordic Film Days

Where Lubeck, Germany
When Four days in early November
Background Founded in 1956, this festival does an excellent job of presenting a comprehensive portrait of contemporary Nordic cinema including Scandinavian and Icelandic cinema. Along with screenings of children's movies, shorts, documentaries, and experimental works, recent retrospectives have focused on the films of the Kaurismaki Brothers. *Cold Fever* was one film premiered here.
Films About 125 total films
How to Enter Send VHS dub and entry form to:
Filmpalast Stadthalle
Mühlenbrücke 11
23552 Lübeck
Germany
Tel: 011.47.0451.122.5742
Fax 011.47.0451.122.5745
E-mail janina.proseek@filmtage.luebeck.de
Web www.luebeck.de/filmtage
Entry Deadline Not applicable

Nordic Glory Film Festival

Where Jyväskylä, Finland
When Five days in mid-February
Background Here in the country that probably has the most festivals per capita comes this relatively recent collection of films by female Nordic directors and seminars related to women's roles in the cinema world. Recent seminars have included the topic "Is There Such a Thing as a Camera Woman?" and screenings have included the premieres of Annette Olsen's *They Don't Burn Priests, Do They?* and Susanna Edwards's *Sunshadow,* as well as works by Mai Zetterling and Liv Ullman. Recent tributes have featured the likes of Glory Leppanen, an early female Finnish director. Screenings are held at the Fantasia (Jyvaskeskus, Kauppakatu 31) and the Kampus Kino (Kekussairaalantie 2).
Major Award Winners Among films honored at recent festivals: *Morketid; They Don't Burn Priests, Do They?; Gracious Curves,* and *Sin*
Films About 60 films
Noteworthy Celebrity Sightings Liv Ullman, Kiti Luostarinen
Tickets 25 Fmk per individual screening; 120 Fmk for entrance into all competition films.
How to Enter Send VHS dub and entry form to:
City of Jyväskylä
Office for Cultural Affairs
Vaupaudenkatu 39-41
Telephone 011.358.1462.4815
Fax 011.358.1462.4802
E-mail leena.laaksonen@jkl.fi
Entry Deadline October

Norwegian International Film Festival

Where Haugesgund, Norway
When One week in late August
Background With fjords, the North Sea, and mountains all around, this modern seaport and fishing town serves up a heaping helping of international cinema along with its selection of Norwegian flicks. Founded in 1973, the festival hosts a screening of 30 films in its main program, along with a selection of new Norwegian films, new Nordic films, a director's choice of films chosen by the Norwegian Filmworkers Association, focuses on specific countries (France, Italy, and Canada have been among recent choices), a children's fest, and a program of Norwegian shorts. Films that have received their Norwegian premiere here include James Mangold's *Heavy*, David Cronenberg's *Crash*, Hal Hartley's *Flirt,* and Jon Turteltaub's *Phenomenon* ["He (John Travolta?!)'s way off the charts! I don't think he's testable!"]. A recent festival opened with *Misery Harbor* and featured David Cronenberg's *Existenz* and Atom Egoyan's *Felicia's Journey*. Screenings are held, among other places, at the 126-seat cinema in the Maritim Hotel.
Major Award Winners Andreas Prize: *It All Starts Today*, by Bertrand Tavernier; Best Norwegian Film: *Zero Kelvin*, by Hans Peter Moland; Best Actor: Bjørn Sundquist, *The Other Side of Sunday*; Best Actress: *Rut Tellefsen*, Kristin Lavransdattere
Films About 70
Noteworthy Celebrity Sightings John Badham, Liv Ullman, Sven Nykvist, Billie August, Ettore Scola, Roger Moore (weirdly enough), Alan Alda
How to Enter Send VHS dub and entry form to:
The Norwegian International Film Festival
P.O. Box 145
5501 Haugesgund
Norway
Telephone 011.47.52.73.4430
Fax 011.47.52.73.4420
E-mail info@filmfestivalen.no
Entry Deadline June

Norwegian Short Film Festival

Where Grimstad, Norway
When One week in late August
Background Founded in 1978, the festival concentrates on shorts produced by Norwegian filmmakers and has a really cool, eccentric attitude, challenging viewers rather than just showing them a bunch of films. One of my favorites of its recent retrospectives was a program called "Isn't It?" featuring what the Grimstadians call "fake films," or films that challenge traditionally held notions of truth. Very cool. Another excellent feature was a lecture on how to turn 35 mm films into 16 mm and 8 mm films using a sewing machine and surgical tools.
Films About 75
Noteworthy Celebrity Sightings German filmmaker Ulrike Ottinger, Dutch photographer Anton Corbin
How to Enter Send VHS dub and entry form to:
Norwegian Short Film Festival

Storengvn 8B
1432 Jar
Norway
Telephone 011.47.22.47.4646
Fax 011.47.22.47.4690
Entry Deadline March

Nyon International Documentary Film Festival

Where Nyon, Switzerland
When One week in late April
Background Held in a quaint resort town on the shores of Lake Geneva, the Nyon festival has already become one of the most significant documentary film festivals in the world. The festival shows about 20 documentaries in its international competition and also screens films in the following sections: Regards Neufs, a competitive showcase of first films by self-taught filmmakers and film students (the films are judged, coolly enough, by a jury of their peers—film students and autodidactic filmmakers); Les Incontournables, a noncompetitive panorama of international documentaries; and Etat des Lieux, focusing on a particular trend or individual in documentary filmmaking (which recently screened a series of films by Canadian documentarian Mike Holboom, including *Shooting Blanks*, in which he decried filmic sex and violence by juxtaposing clips from horror, action, and pornographic films; *Dear Madonna*, in which he deconstructed a Madonna video; and *Frank's Cock*). One of the most fascinating aspects of the Nyon Festival is a category titled Atelier, in which a filmmaker screens works in process to stimulate discussion. Films are screened in Nyon's cultural center, a former gas factory. About 50,000 attend.
Major Award Winners Visions du Réel First Prize Winner for Best Film (15,000 Fr): *Nobody's Business*, by Alan Berliner; First Prize for Feature Film (5,000 Fr): *Sabbath in Paradise*, by Claudie Heuermann, and *The Winners*, by Paul Cohen; Best Short Film (5,000 Fr): *Bliss*, by Vitaly Mansky; First Prize of Regards Neufs (2,500 Fr): *Outsider*, by Yann Olivier Wicht, and *Negative Nights*, by Susanne Schule, Istvan Imreh, and Robert Laatz
Films Around 200 features and shorts
How to Enter Send VHS dub and entry form to:
Visions du Réel Festival International du Cinèma Documentaire
CP 593
18, rue Juste-Livier
1260 Nyon
Switzerland
Telephone 011.41.22.361.60.60
Fax 011.41.22.361.70.71
E-mail docnyon@prolink.ch
Entry Deadline January

Oberhausen Short Film Festival

Where Oberhausen, Germany
When One week in early May

Background Founded in 1954, this short-film festival boasts that it was bridging the gap between East and West Germany long before the wall came down. With its early 1960s motto "Way to the Neighbor," the festival has long prided itself on breaking down international barriers. Retrospectives have focused on such topics as Japanese video art, and showcases highlighting the best of multimedia work have focused on Peter Gabriel (of all people), among others. The festival offers many prizes, but perhaps the strangest is the Alexander S. Scotti Prize, given each year to the filmmaker who deals best with the subject of old age and death. Following close behind in the strangeness department is the 5,000 DM prize given to the filmmaker who does the best job dealing with the harmony among man, flora, fauna, and technology.

Major Award Winners Grand Prize: *Crystal Aquarium*, by Jayne Parker; First Prize: *Chronic*, by Jennifer Reeves and Hubart Robert, and *A Fortunate Life*, by Alexander Sokurov; Honorable Mention: *Anpoore*, by P. Balan

Films More than 200 from more than 50 countries

Tickets 8 DM

How to Enter Send VHS copy and entry form to:
International Short Film Festival
Grillostrasse 34
46045 Oberhausen
Germany
E-mail info@kurzfilmtage.de
Web www.kurzfilmtage.de

Entry Deadline January

Odense International Film Festival

Where Odense, Denmark

When One week in mid-August

Background Although the screenings of new material here are far from ground-breaking (*Speed 2*, *Everyone Says I Love You*, *Ponette*, *Mr. Magoo*), the OIFF's strong point is its excellent series of retrospectives. A recent tribute to silent cinema featured the work of John Barrymore, Charlie Chaplin, and Douglas Fairbanks, Jr. Alain Resnais's *Night and Fog*, Norman McLaren's shorts, and the works of Lindsay Anderson have also been screened here recently.

Films About 100 features

Major Award Winners Grand Prize: *Silence*, by Orly Yadin and Silvie Bringas; Most Surprising Film: *Todo Día Todo*, by Flavio Frederico

How to Enter Send VHS dub and entry form to:
Odense International Film Festival
Vindegade 18
5000 Odense C
Denmark
Telephone 011.45.6.613.13.72
Fax 011.45.6.591.43.18
E-mail filmfestival@postodkomn.dk
Web www.filmfestival.dk

Entry Deadline April

Oldenburg International Film Fest

Where Oldenburg, Germany
When Five days in September
Background They sure like Frank Oz out here, so much so that they recently devoted a tribute to him while screening the German premiere of *The Indian in the Cupboard*. The New York independent scene has been spotlighted here, as has director Alex Cox. And one of the more creative screenings here was the tribute to Alan Smithee, the legendary pseudonym of countless directors who have not wanted their name associated with work they felt to be inferior. German premieres here have included *Romeo Is Bleeding* and Spike Lee's *Crooklyn*.
Films About 70 features
Notable Celebrity Sightings Matthew Modine, Asia Argento
How to Enter Send VHS dub and entry form to:
    Oldenburg International Film Festival
    Gottorpstrasse 6
    26122 Oldenburg
    Germany
    Tel: 011.49.441.25.659
    Fax 011.49.441.26.155
    E-mail ritter@filmfest-oldenburg.de
    Web www.filmfest-oldenburg.de
Entry Deadline None stated

Oulu Children's Film Festival

Where Oulu, Finland
When One week in mid-November
Background "Children count the days to the international Oulu Children's Film Festival." At least that's what the folks at the Oulu Children's Film Festival say, and given the diversity of programming and the opportunities afforded children in the weeklong fest, it's probably true. Designed like a traditional adult fest, Oulu presents 15 new children's features, a competition, a panorama of world children's films, a focus on Finnish children's films, and retrospectives, which have included the work of actress Elina Salo and a tribute to a centennial of Finnish cinema. A jury of children awards a prize of 3,000 ecus and the Kaleva newspaper's Starboy figurine to the director of the best film in the competition.
How to Enter Send VHS dub and entry form to:
    Torikatu 8
    90100 Oulu
    Finland
    Telephone 011.358.981.314.1732
    Fax 011.358.981.314.1730
Entry Deadline September

Pesaro Film Festival

Where Rome, Italy

When Ten days in mid-June
Background Founded in 1965, this festival, also known as the International Exhibition of New Cinema, combines showcases of new film directors with retrospectives of old masters and specific countries. Previous retrospectives have included Arab, Chinese, Spanish, Japanese, South Korean, and Latin American cinema, as well as the works of Nagisa Oshima, Raul Ruiz, and Philippe Garrel. Also, Pesaro presents a retrospective of an Italian cinematic genre, which has in previous years focused on Italian fascist cinema, neorealism, and the cinema of the 1970s. The festival also publishes beautifully designed and edited scholarly guidebooks to supplement the films shown. In conjunction with the festival, the International Conference on Film Language is held. One recent festival featured the premiere of *Contours of the Void*.
Major Award Winners Noncompetitive
Films About 100 features and shorts, plus very extensive retrospective and tribute screenings
How to Enter Send VHS dub and entry form to:
Pesaro International Festival of New Cinema
Via Villafranca, 20
00185 RM
Italy
Telephone 011.39.6.491.156
Fax 011.39.6.491.163
E-mail pesarofilmfest@mclink.it
Entry Deadline March

Pordenone-Le Giornate del Cinema Muto

See Best of the Fests

Prague International Film Festival

Where Prague, Czech Republic
When Two weeks in June
Background Founded in 1995, the festival offers a showcase of international cinema and spotlights on Czech and indie cinema as well as a focus on the best of cinematography.
Major Award Winners The Golden Golem for Best Picture: *Things I Never Told You*, by Isabel Coixet; Best Actress: Jana Preissova, *The Order*; Best Actor: Miki Manojlovik, *Someone Else's America*; Best Director: Christine Carriere, *Rosine*
How to Enter Send VHS dub and entry form to:
The Prague International Film Festival
V Haji 15
170 00 Prague 7
Czech Republic
Telephone 011.420.2.66795.421
Fax 011.420.2.66795.405
Entry Deadline April

Rassegna di Palermo

Where Palermo, Italy
When One week in mid-October
Background Also known as the International Sport Film Festival, a retrospective here recently honored sports documentaries made in the United States and France between 1901 and 1911. Anything that deals with some sort of outdoor activity or sport can be screened here. Recent screenings have included Ron Shelton's *Cobb*, John Badham's *Drop Zone*, and *The River Wild,* starring Meryl Streep.
Major Award Winners Golden Paladino for Best Sports Film (1.5 million L): *A Quoi Revent les Boxeurs*, by F. Laffont; Silver Paladino: *Dreams of Gold*, by G. Butt
Films About 30 features.
How to Enter Send VHS dub and entry form to:
    Rassegna Citta di Palermo
    Via Notarbartolo, 1
    90141 PA
    Italy
    Telephone 011.39.91.611.4968
    Fax 011.39.91.611.4986
    E-mail sporfife@mbox.vol.it
Entry Deadline July

Riga Arsenals International Film Forum

Where Riga, Latvia
When One week in mid-September in even-numbered years
Background Screening films from nearly 50 countries, this festival is noteworthy for the creativity it shows in creating categories in which to screen films. Aside from spotlights on Asian and Russian cinema and showcases of American indies, the Latvian fest also screens in the following categories: Sex and Arguments, Spiritual Emigration, Fiction of Reality, and Adaptation of the Idiot.
Major Award Winners Magic Crystal Winner for Best Film ($10,000): *The Story of a Young Accordion Player*, by Satybaldy Narymbetov; FIPRESCI Award: *The Shoe*, by Laila Pakalnina; Special Mention: *Ayneh*, by Jafaf Panahi
Films More than 200 features
How to Enter Send a letter describing the project to:
    Arsenals International Film Forum
    Marstalu 14
    Riga 1047
    Latvia
    Telephone 011.371.722.1620
    Fax 011.371.782.0445
    E-mail arsenals@latnet.lv
    Web www.cip.laatnet.lv/Arsenals
Entry Deadline June

Riminicinema

Where Rimini, Italy
When Five days in late September
Background Founded in 1988, the festival has always attempted to bridge cultural gaps by juxtaposing seemingly unrelated films from diverse cultures. What can one say about a festival that has paid tribute to classic Mexican horror films, Israeli documentary filmmaker Amos Gitai, Wayne Wang, Hong Kong Fantasy cinema, American filmmaker Mario Van Peebles, Iranian director Abbas Kiarostami, and 1950s 3-D movies? Outside of competition, the festival screens its patented mixture of the respectable and the bizarre, placing a "White Africa· Black Heart" festival of South African films featuring works by Athol Fugard and many others alongside screenings of trashy scary flicks under the heading "Necroeroticon" (*The Lovers of Dr. Jekyll, Dracula vs. Frankenstein*, and *The Diabolical Dr. Satana*). One of the most recent people to receive a lifetime achievement award here was Roberto Benigni.
Major Award Winners Federico Fellini Award: director Kathryn Bigelow; Golden 'R' and 15 million L: Wan Jen, *Chao Ji Da Kuo Min*; Silver 'R' and 5 million L: Saeed Akhtar Mirza, for *Naseem*
Films About 100 features
How to Enter Send VHS dub and entry form to:
Riminicinema
Via Gambalunga, 27
47037-Rimini RN
Italy
Telephone 011.39.541.22627
Fax 011.39.541.24227
E-mail cinema@commun.rimini.it
Web www.comune.rimini.it
Entry Deadline June

Rotterdam International Film Festival

See Best of the Fests

Rouen Nordic Film Festival

Where Rouen, France
When Two weeks in mid-March
Background Founded in 1988, the festival offers screenings of a dozen films in competition, shorts, cartoons, student films, and films produced in Nordic countries.
Major Award Winners Best Film: *Eggs*, by Bent Hamer; Best Actor: Johan Widerberg, *Beauté des Choses*; Best Actress: Ulla Henningsen, *Carmen et Adrian*; Grand Prize of the Jury: *Hamsun*, by Jan Troell
Notable Celebrity Sightings Sophie Marceau
How to Enter Send VHS dub and entry form to:
Nordic Film Festival
22, rue de la Champesie

76000 Rouen
France
Telephone 011.33.35.98.28.46
Fax 011.33.35.70.92.08
Web w3.crihan.fr/cinemanordique
Entry Deadline December

San Sebastián International Film Festival

Where San Sebastián, Spain
When September
Background By now almost 200,000 attend this nearly 50-year-old festival, which that is almost always marked by controversy. (Why is it that only Europeans boo the selections of international film juries?) Anyway, aside from the extensive selection of Spanish and international cinema, San Sebastián also offers some of the coolest retrospectives around. Recent ones have included a Tod Browning retrospective and, most interestingly, a Red Nightmare section, including McCarthy-era films from the United States and Spanish flicks from the Franco era. Past jury members have included Laura Esquivel and the ubiquitous Bertrand Tavernier.
Major Award Winners Best Film: *C'est Quoi la Vie*, by Francis Dupeyron; Best First or Second Feature: *Johns*, by Scott Silver; International Critics' Prize: *Soft Fruit*, by Christina Andreef; Best Actress: Norma Aleandro, *Autumn Sun*; Best Actor: Jacques Dufillio, *C'est Quoi la Vie*
Films About 200 features
Tickets $4.25 per individual screening
How to Enter Send VHS dub and entry form to:
San Sebastián International Film Festival
Plaza de Oquendo s/n
20004 San Sebastián Guipúzcoa
Spain
Telephone 011.34.43.48.12.12
Fax 011.34.43.48.12.18
E-mail ssiff@mail.ddnet.es
Web www.ddnet.es/san_sebastian_film_festival
Entry Deadline Late July

Sheffield International Documentary Festival

Where Sheffield, England
When One week in late October
Background Founded in 1994, the United Kingdom's only documentary festival has fast become a major fest notable for its programming diversity, choosing films that range from the bluntly political to the pleasantly goofy to the eccentric. Some of the more intriguing screenings in recent years have included Rivka Hartman's *The Mini-Skirted Dynamo* ("Dora Bialestock: world-renowned pathologist, champion of children's rights, airplane pilot. But what kind of mother was she?") and Jonathan Schell's *Picasso Would Have Made a Glorious Waiter* (concerning the struggles of artists working for a New York catering company). A recent retrospective paid

tribute to quirky American documentarian Errol Morris. The festival dedicates itself to exploring the question of "authorship," holding seminars and conferences on the separations between individual and collective voice.

Tickets £3–£4

Films About 75 documentaries and shorts

How to Enter Send VHS dub and entry form to:
Sheffield International Documentary Festival
The Workstation
15 Paternoster Tow
Sheffield
United Kingdom
GB51 2BX
Telephone 011.44.114.276.5141
Fax 011.44.114.272.1849
E-mail shefdoc@fdgroup.co.uk

Entry Deadline Not available

Short Film Festival of Drama

Where Drama, Greece

When One week in November

Background Founded in 1978 by the Cinema Club of Drama (Drama the city, not necessarily drama the concept), the festival is the only major festival of short films in Greece. The festival presents films in the categories of narrative features, documentaries, and animated films. A recent festival highlighted Japanese short films.

Films 38 films

How to Enter Send VHS dub and entry form to:
Short Film Festival of Drama
Ag. Barbaras 9
661 00 Drama
Greece
Telephone 011.30.5.2147.575
Fax 011.30.5.2133.526
E-mail drama-festival@hyper.gr

Entry Deadline Not available

Showcase of Independent Video and Interactive Phenomenae

Where Barcelona, Spain

When First week of July

Background Founded in 1993 and held at the Barcelona Center for Contemporary Culture (Montalegre, 5), this noncompetitive showcase features a wide array of cutting-edge video screenings, open video, interactive works, and work in digital formats (such as *Quicktime* and *AVI*). Organized by OVNI (Observatori de Video No Identificat) and La 12 Visual Independent Video Association, the festival is unique in that it encourages the art of video and multimedia artists not only by showcasing their work but by paying them for their contributions as well. The film organizes its screenings around a particular theme. One recent example was identity as juxtaposed with themes of madness, pain, and the intimate. This all went under the heading of "Dark Night of the Soul." The showcase also features tributes including one recent one dedicated to William Burroughs, featuring works about or inspired by Burroughs, Francis Ford Coppola, Gus Van Sant, and many others.

Major Award Winners Noncompetitive

Films About 100 works in a variety of formats

Tickets Free to the public

How to Enter Send sample of work to:

    Centre de Cultura Contemporania de Barcelona

    Montalegre, 5

    08001 Barcelona

    Spain

    Telephone 011.34.3.306.41.00

    Fax 011.34.3.306.41.04

Entry Deadline March

Sitges International Fantasy Film Festival

Where Barcelona, Spain

When Ten days in early October

Background Yet another fantasy festival, a concept that has yet to find its way to the United States but probably should. Recent premieres in the self-explanatory fest have included Stuart Gordon's *Space Truckers*.

Major Award Winners Best Film: *Cube*; Best Director: Michael Disacomo, *Animals*; Best Actor: Jarred Harris, *Trance*

Noteworthy Celebrity Sightings Roger Corman, Quentin Tarantino

How to Enter For more information contact:

    Sitges International Fantasy Film Festival

    Rosello, 257 3-E

    08008 Barcelona

    Spain

    Telephone 011.34.3.415.39.38

    Fax 011.34.3.237.65.21

    E-mail cinsit@sitgestur.com

    Web www.sitges.com/cinema

Entry Deadline August

Snow, Ice, and Adventure Film Festival

Where Autrans, France

When Five days in early December

Background It took 95 years to found a film festival here, but it's the thought that counts. A mountain-climbers club began here in 1889, and, although the festival did not start until 1984, the spirit of the climbers club is preserved with numerous screenings of mountain, nature, and skiing films. The first film shown here in 1984 was Apocalypse Snow, which should give the general idea. But unlike festivals in American ski towns where the idea is to watch art films and ski with Dennis

Hopper, here the skiing and the nature are primary and the films merely add to the ambience. Many are documentaries, but others, such as Fridrik Thór Fridriksson's *Cold Fever*, that take place in an appropriately Arctic atmosphere are included as well. Titles in recent years have included *Ski Bums*, *Alaska*, *Death Zone*, and *The Spirit of the Mountain*. Getting the idea? The festival also features and holds a competition for thematically appropriate commercials.

Major Award Winners Grand Prix du Festival: *Schlafes Bruder*, by J. Vilsmaier, and *A Glorious Way to Die*, by R. Dennison; Prix Fiction Télévision: *Crime à l'Altimetre*, by José Giovanni; Young Director's Prize: *Reines d'un Jour*, by P. Magnin; Best Environmental Film: *Chronique de la Foret des Vosges*, by F. Chilowicz; Best Snow and Ice Film: *Erhard Loretan, L'écume des Cimes*, by P. A. Hiroz and B. Aymon; Best Ethnological Film: *Karsha*, by J. Boggio Pola

Films About 50 features and shorts

Noteworthy Celebrity Sightings Werner Herzog, Thierry L'Hermitte

Tickets Contact Autrans Tourism Office: 011.33.76.95.30.70

How to Enter Send VHS dub and entry form to:
Festival International du Film d'Autrans-Neige et Glace Aventure Evasion
Centre Sportif Nordique
38880 Autrans (Vercors)
France
Telephone 011.33.76.95.30.70
Fax 011.33.76.95.38.63
E-mail autrans@alpes-net.fr

Entry Deadline September

Solothurn Film Festival

Where Solothurn, Switzerland

When One week in late January

Background Founded in 1966, the festival is devoted to promoting Swiss cinema, screening Swiss features, shows, children's movies, and shorts. The festival takes place in six Solothurn cinemas.

Films More than 100 films, 70 or so videos

Major Award Winners Best Short Film: *Pastry, Pain and Politi*, by Stina Werenfels; Prix du Public: *Zuppa Tartaru*, by Karin Gernperle; Prix de Promotion: *Wolde*, by Björn Kurt; and *Soir de Fête*, by Helene Fauchere

Films About 107 films and 56 videos

How to Enter For more information contact:
Solothurner Film Tage
Postfach 140
4504 Solothurn
Switzerland
Telephone 011.41.32.625.80.80
Fax 011.41.32.623.64.10
E-mail filmtage@cuenet.ch
Web www.filmtage-solothurn.ch

Entry Deadline October

St. Petersburg International Film Festival of Festivals

Where St. Petersburg, Russia

When June

Background Founded in 1993, the "Festival of Festivals" is held during the "White Nights" of St. Petersburg and screens the best work from other international festivals and in the following categories: New Cinema of Russia, Master Class (works of world-renowned filmmakers), Special Screenings (experimental work), and assorted retrospectives.

Major Award Winners Grand Prize: (tie) *Breaking the Waves*, by Lars von Trier, and *Spiklenci Slasti*, by Jan Svankmajer; Audience Prize: *The Pillow Book*, by Peter Greenaway; Prize of Creative Support (Director of Photography): Alexey Fyodorov, *Mother and Son*: Prize of Creative Support (Best Actor): Alexey Ananishnov, *Mother and Son*

Films About 100 features

Noteworthy Celebrity Sightings Sally Potter, Sandrine Bonnaire

How to Enter Send VHS dub and entry form to:
St. Petersburg International Film Festival of Festivals
Russia
197101 St. Petersburg
10 Kamennoostrovsky pr.
St. Petersburg International Film Festival of Festivals
Telephone 011.7.812.237.03.04
Fax 011.7.812.394.58.70

Entry Deadline May

Stockholm International Film Festival

Where Stockholm, Sweden

When Ten days in November

Background Founded in 1990, the festival is now a year-round operation, running the Stockholm Film Club for free outdoor film screenings along with the festival itself. The festival also operates CINEMA, Sweden's largest film magazine, which has published essays by Pedro Almodóvar and Krzysztof Kieslowski. More than 40,000 attend. The 1999 festival raised quite a fuss when its program of sexually explicit films including *Sex, The Annabel Chong Story*, and *The Girl Next Door* incited boycotts from the Green Party and from other groups as well.

Major Award Winners Bronze Horse for Best Picture: *Pretty Villages Pretty Flames*, by Srdjan Dragojevic; Best Directorial Debut: *Fistful of Flies*, by Monica Pellizzari; Best Cinematography: Jane Castle, *Fistful of Flies*. Best Script: *Un Héros Tres Discret*; by Alain Henry and Jacques Audiard; Best Actress: Lili Taylor, *I Shot Andy Warhol*; International Critics' Jury Prize: *Fistful of Flies* and *Breaking the Waves*

Films About 125

Noteworthy Celebrity Sightings Rod Steiger, Frances McDormand

How to Enter For more information contact:
Stockholm International Film Festival
Box 3136
103 62 Stockholm

Sweden
Telephone 011.46.8.677.5000
Fax 011.46.8.200.590
E-mail program@cinema.se
Web www.filmfestivalen.se
Entry Deadline June

Stuttgart Animation Film Days

Where Stuttgart, Germany
When One week in late March and early April
Background Founded in 1988, this is one of the hugest animated film festivals in the world. Generously sponsored by Mercedes Benz and other well-heeled concerns, the festival screens films in the following categories outside of competition: International Panorama (featuring animated works from every conceivable country, with the possible exception of Burundi), Young Animation (featuring the works of newcomers on the animation scene), and a Night Festival, which features creepy shit that you wouldn't show the kids in the audience during the day. These include Dave Borthwick's nightmarish *The Secret Adventures of Tom Thumb* and a selection of erotic cartoons including *Safesex: The Manual*. The festival also features many retrospectives, which have included films related to paintings (e.g., Joan Grat's *Mona Lisa Descending a Staircase*) and spotlights on specific filmmakers, including Bill Plympton, Phil Mulloy, and Joanna Priestley. Films are screened in four locations, including the Alte Reithalle of the Hotel Maritim (Forststrasse 2), Treffpunkt Rotebühlplatz (Rotebühlplatz 28), Haus der Wirtschaft (Willi-Blecher-Strasse 19), and the Filmakedemie of Baden-Wurttemberg (Mathildenstrasse 20).
Major Award Winners State of Baden-Wurttemberg Award (15,000 DM): *How Wings Are Attached to the Backs of Angels*, by Craig Welch; State Capital Stuttgart Award (15,000 DM): *Pink Doll*, by Valentin Olschwang; Suddeutscher Rundfunk Audience Award First prize (15,000 DM): *Death and the Mother*, by Ruth Lingford; Second Prize (10,000 DM): *The Devil Went Down to Georgia*, by Mike Johnson
Films More than 400 features and shorts.
Tickets 10 DM per individual screening; 35 DM for a day pass
How to Enter Send VHS dub and entry form to:
Internationales Trickfilm-Festival Stuttgart
Teckstrasse 56
70190 Stuttgart
Germany
Telephone 011.49.7.11.262.2699
Fax 011.49.7.11.262.4980
E-mail info@itfs.de
Web www.itfs.de
Entry Deadline December

Tampere Short Film Festival

Where Tampere, Finland
When One week in early March

Background Don't ask me why Finland has the coolest film festivals around, but it seems to be true. In addition to screening a great collection of shorts, Tampere also has featured great series of retrospectives and homages. In recent years, these have focused on the work of Tex Avery, Jacques Tati, Wim Wenders, Chuck Jones, Alain Resnais, Nagisa Oshima, Agnes Varda, and Jules Verne. The festival, founded in 1971, has also debuted a new score for Fritz Lang's *Metropolis*, performed by the Tampere Philharmonic.

Major Award Winners Best Short Film: *The Quiet Harbour*, by Mariusz Malec; Best Film in National Competitions: *Gracious Curves*, by Kiti Luostarinen; Best film in International Competition: *Jojo's Cafe*, by Nicolas Cuche

Films About 200

How to Enter Send VHS dub and entry form to:
Tampere Short Film Festival
Box 305
33101 Tampere
Finland
Telephone 011.358.3.213.0034
Fax 011.358.3.223.0121
E-mail filmfestival@tt.tampere.fi
Web tampere.fi/festival/film

Entry Deadline January

Taormina International Film Festival

Where Taormina, Italy

When One week in July

Background Any festival that has both maligned artist Andres Serrano and maligned film director Michael Cimino on its board has to be up to something good. Leaving aside the rather predictable American efforts that have graced Taormina's screens since it opened in 1971 (*Speed 2?!*), a great panorama of European, African, and American films is screened here over the course of the festival. Recent years have seen the premieres of Alain Resnais's *Smoking/No Smoking* and homages to Gilles Deleuze, Victor Erice, and Curtis Harrington. Several oddities here, including David Lynch's commercials.

Major Award Winners Best Film: *The Saltmen of Tibet*

Noteworthy Celebrity Sightings Andres Serrano, Alain Robbe Grillet, Michael Cimino

Tickets 17,000 L per individual screening

How to Enter Send VHS dub and entry form to:
Taormina International Film Festival
Via Pirandello, 31
98039-Taormina ME
Italy
Telephone 011.39.942.21142
Fax 011.39.942.23348
E-mail aast@taormina-ol.it

Entry Deadline June

Thessaloníki Film Festival

Where Athens, Greece

When Twelve days in mid-November

Background The oldest film festival in Greece, originally devoted to Greek filmmakers alone, it now is international in scope, offering rather generous prizes to first and second-time filmmakers. Films are screened in the recently renovated Olympia Theater beneath its arcaded walkways in downtown Athens. Special film series have focused on Balkan cinema, and tribute programs have included such directors as Nagisa Oshima, Charles Burnett, Bernardo Bertolucci, David Cronenberg, and Nanni Moretti, as well as prominent figures in the Greek film industry. The festival has also held artistic exhibits of famous directors including Sergei Eisenstein and Peter Greenaway.

Major Award Winners The Golden Alexander, which offers a cash prize of 12.5 million Dr ($50,000): *Shower*, by Zhang Yang; Silver Alexander, 7.5 million Dr ($30,000): *Garage Olimpio*, by Marco Bechis; Best Director: Justin Kerrigan, *Human Traffic*

Films About 150

Noteworthy Celebrity Sightings Atom Egoyan, John Waters, Michelangelo Antonioni

How to Enter Send VHS dub and entry form to:
Thessaloníki International Film Festival
Sina 36
106 72 Athens
Greece
Telephone 011.30.1.3601.0418
Fax 011.30.1.3621.1023

Entry Deadline October

Thriller Film Festival of Cognac (Festival du Film Policier)

Where Cognac, France

When Four days in early April

Background Hardly a serious festival for the cineaste, the Cognac fest is nevertheless one of the most charming and engaging festivals in Europe. Housed in the middle of liqueur country near Bordeaux, films are projected on buildings right smack in the middle of town. One can quibble little about a vacation spot that affords the opportunity to watch great old silent and other classic thrillers while sipping the cognac and Cointreau that are made nearby. The festival holds a competition for about seven thrillers and presents seven others out of competition. There have also been retrospectives of the film work of Robert Duvall and Catherine Deneuve and screenings of classics such as *The Killing*, *The Pink Panther*, *The Thomas Crown Affair*, *Die Hard with a Vengeance* and more Agatha Christie films than one would care to dignify by naming. A recent festival featured Pedro Almodóvar's *All About My Mother* and Ed Radtke's *Dream Catcher*. More than 25,000 attend the festival.

Major Award Winners Grand Prix: *The Last Supper*, by Stacy Title; Prix Special du Jury: *Things to Do in Denver When You're Dead* and *Copycat*

Noteworthy Celebrity Sightings Jacqueline Bisset, Charles Bronson (!), Gregory Peck, Keith Carradine

Tickets Contact: 202.857.0060
How to Enter Send VHS dub and entry form to:
 Cognac International Thriller Film Festival
 36, rue Pierret
 92200 Neuilly
 France
 Telephone 011.33.1.41.34.20.33
 Fax 011.33.1.41.34.20.77
 E-mail jlasserre@le-public-systeme.fr
 Web www.cognac-france.com
Entry Deadline March 13

Turin International Festival of Young Cinema

Where Turin, Italy
When One week in mid-November
Background Dedicated to "young cinema" and directors in the dawns of their careers, the Turin festival has also grown to include retrospectives of directors such as Jerzy Skolimowski and Mohsen Makhmalbaf. Founded in 1983, the Turin festival now attracts annual crowds of 45,000 to the home of the famous shroud.
Major Award Winners Best Feature Film: *Wushan Yunyu*, by Zhang Ming; Special Jury Award: *Pedar*, by Majid Majidi; Screenplay Award: *After Life*
Films About 270 short and feature films
Noteworthy Celebrity Sightings Ornella Muti
How to Enter Send VHS dub and entry form to:
 Turin Festival of Young Cinema
 Via Monte di Pieta 1
 10121-Tunn TO
 Italy
 E-mail ficg@webcom.com
Entry Deadline September

Umea International Film Festival

Where Umea, Sweden
When One week in mid-September
Background Founded in 1986, the festival is one of Scandinavia's largest and pays particular attention to specific regions (New Zealand, Spain) as well as screening a decent number of films by women directors.
Major Award Winners Noncompetitive
Films About 100 features and shorts
How to Enter Send VHS dub and entry form to:
 Umea International Film Festival
 P.O. Box 43
 901 02 Umea
 Sweden
 Telephone 011.46.90.133.388
 Fax 011.46.90.777.961

E-mail film_festival@ff.umea.se
Web www.ff.umea.se
Entry Deadline August

Uppsala International Short Film Festival

Where Uppsala, Sweden
When One week in late October
Background Founded in 1982, this Swedish festival screens an incredibly intriguing variety of contemporary and aged shorts in a variety of categories. Screening at the 1914 Slottsbiografen, the festival screens short horror movies, children's movies, shorts from the "four corners of Europe," and a section of nondialogue-driven experimental films called "More than Words."
Major Award Winners Best Short Film: *Trêve*, by Emmanuel Paulin; Best Children's film: *Thirty Five Aside*, by Damien O'Donnell; Best Documentary: *Ouraki*, by Galina Leontieva; Best Short Fiction Film (less than 20 minutes): *The Short Walk*, by Jonathan Hacker; Best Medium-Length Fiction Film (between 20 and 60 minutes): *Le Bonheur à Cloche-Pied*, by Jacqueline Surchat
Films About 150 shorts
Noteworthy Celebrity Sightings Nicholas Goodman, James Frey, Bill Tomlinson
How to Enter Send VHS dub and entry form to:
Uppsala International Short Film Festival
Box 1746
751 47 Uppsala
Sweden
Telephone 011.46.18.1200.25
Fax 011.46.18.1213.50
Web www2.passagen.se/opulus.com/film/film.htm
Entry Deadline August

Valladolid International Film Festival

See Best of the Fests

Venice Film Festival

See Best of the Fests
Fact: The Venice region has more spas than anywhere else in the world. Forget the movies.

Vevey International Comedy Film Festival

Where Vevey, Switzerland
When Five days in mid-October
Background Founded in 1981 and dedicated to Charlie and Oona Chaplin, the festival, as one might expect, focuses on comedy in cinema, but it takes a more unpre-

dictable slant than the usual fare of Jerry Lewis and Stooges flicks. One of the most recent festivals paid tribute to Indian comedy. Films are divided between short comedies and feature-length comedies and are screened at the Rex and Astor cinemas.

Major Award Winners Golden Cane Award for Best Comedy: *Funny Bones*, by Peter Chelsom

How to Enter Send VHS dub and entry form to:
Vevey International Comedy Film Festival
La Grenette
CP 421
1800 Vevey
Switzerland
Telephone 011.41.21.922.20.27
Fax 011.41.21.922.20.24

Entry Deadline September

Viennale-Vienna International Film Festival (Internationale Filmfestwochen Wien)

Where Vienna, Austria

When Last two weeks of October

Background Hip, unpretentious, and dutiful, the Vienna festival prides itself on presenting "difficult films" and has given particular emphasis to strange low-budget U.S. indies as well as bizarre Asian cinema while also paying homage to contemporary Eurocinema. According to Westdeutscher Rundfunk, "The festival is not dominated by the million-dollar deals of Cannes or the almost-industrial trade-show mojo of Berlin but by metropolitan coolness." Special tribute programs have been dedicated to the works of André Techiné, Ken Loach, and Mike Leigh. The festival has also offered a number of midnight horror, sex, and action films, as well as a retrospective of Hollywood films from 1929–1934 before the censorship code (*Scarface*, *Little Caesar*, and more). One recent retrospective honored Australian cinematographer Christopher Doyle, who shot *Temptress Moon*. More than 50,000 attend annually. Films are screened at the Urania, Gartenbau, Stadtkino, Metro, and Kunstlerhaus cinemas.

Major Award Winners Fipresci Award: *Nordrand*, by Barbara Albert; Best Documentary: *Freedom on My Mind*

Films About 100 films

Noteworthy Celebrity Sightings Nick Broomfield, Illeana Douglas, Mohsen Makhmalbaf

How to Enter Send entry form to:
Viennale
Stiftgasse 6
1070 Vienna
Austria
Telephone 011.431.5265.947
Fax 011.431.5234.172
E-mail office@viennale.or.at
Web www.viennale.or.at

Entry Deadline August

Viper Festival

Where Lucerne, Switzerland
When One week in late October
Background Not only a film festival, Viper is a forum for debates on media and screens multimedia projects, video art, and installations.
Major Award Winners Best Film: *The Smell of Burning Ants*, by Jay Rosenblatt, and *Drift* by Chris Welsby
Films About 250 films and videos
Tickets 24 Fr for a day pass
How to Enter Send VHS dub and entry form to:
Viper-International Film Video and Multimedia Festival
P.O. Box 4929
6002 Lucerne
Switzerland
Telephone 011.41.1.450.6262
Fax 011.41.1.450.6261
E-mail viper@sial.eunet.ch
Entry Deadline February

Viva 8

Where London, England
When One week in early February
Background For four days, the London Filmmakers Co-op becomes home to a festival of Super-8 and 8 mm video, showing films and hosting panel discussions about the future of Super-8.
Major Award Winners Noncompetitive
How to Enter Send VHS dub and entry form to:
London Filmmakers Co-op
12-18 Hoxton Street
London
United Kingdom
N1 6NG
Telephone 011.44.171.739.7132

Welsh International Film Festival

Where Aberystwyth, Wales
When Ten days in mid-November
Background Known also as the "Gwyl Ffilm Ryngwladol Cymru" [clear throat now], the Welsh fest was founded in 1989 and over the years has premiered such films as Tarantino's *Reservoir Dogs*, Lynch's *Twin Peaks*, Kenneth Branagh's *In the Bleak Midwinter*, Peter Greenaway's *Prospero's Books,* and P. J. Hogan's *Muriel's Wedding.* Luckily, though, not all of the festival's films have been so middle-of-the-road. Aside from the fairly familiar collection of New International Cinema, the fest also screens a program of shorts, a "bumper crop" of films from Welsh filmmakers, and

a comprehensive look at Irish cinema. It has spotlighted various film cities, most recently New York. A recent retrospective featured the work of Richard Attenborough, which not only allowed audiences to see his excellent work in *Brighton Rock* and *Seance on a Wet Afternoon* but also permitted them to forget his less-than-stellar career as a director (*In Love and War*). Other retrospectives have included tributes to Martin Scorsese, Steven Spielberg, and horror movies (*Frankenstein, Phantom of the Opera*). The festival also presents Late with Attitude, a festival of midnight screenings programmed by the editor of *Film Threat* and a competition for short films (The D. M. Davies Award), which at £25,000 pounds is the biggest short-film prize in Europe. Films are screened at the Commodore Cinema. About 10,000 attend annually.

Major Award Winners D. M. Davies Award Winners for Best Film (£25,000): *Up the Valley*, by Sara Sugerman, and *Life in the Bus Lane*, by Justin Kerrigan; Runners-up: *Sunday Stories*, by Euros Lyn; *The Animator*, by The Catlow Sisters; and *Bound*, by Karen Rees

Films About 50 features, plus a very extensive program of short films

Noteworthy Celebrity Sightings Julie Christie

Tickets £3 per individual screening

How to Enter Send VHS dub and entry form to:
Welsh International Film Festival
6G Science Park
Cefn Llan
Aberystwyth
Aberystwyth
United Kindgom
SY23 3AH
Telephone 011.44.122.249.0034
Fax 011.44.122.248.5728
E-mail wff995@aber.ac.uk
Web www.iffw.co.uk

Entry Deadline September

World Festival of Animated Film

Where Zagreb, Croatia

When One week in mid-June

Background Founded in 1984, this Croatian fest was, strangely enough, one of the first to advertise over the Net, and now the fest offers information on "fingervision" Web kiosks carefully placed throughout the city of Zagreb. In the past, the festival has screened special features on British and Macedonian animation, Warner Brothers and Hanna-Barbera cartoons, and the early abstract animated work of artists including Man Ray.

Major Award Winners Grand Prize: *Mermaid*, by Alexander Petrov; Best First Films: *Major's Nose*, by Mikhail Lisovoj, and *Pink Doll*, by Valentin Olshvan; Internet Favorite: *A Close Shave*, by Nick Park; Most Erotic Film: *Oh Julie*, by Frances Lea

Films About 80 films

How to Enter Send VHS dub and entry form to:
Koncertna Direkcja Zagreb

Animafest
Kneza Nislava 18
10000 Zagreb
Croatia
Telephone 011.385.1.461.18.08
Fax 011.385.1.461.18.07
E-mail kdz@zg.tl.hr
Web animafest.hr
Entry Deadline February

World Festival of Underwater Films

Where Antibes Juan-les-Pins, France
When Five days in late October and early November
Background Founded in 1974 by the Spondyle Club, one of France's largest underwater diving clubs, this underwater festival not only presents the best in underwater films but also holds competitions for underwater photography, music inspired by the depths, and books of underwater photography. It gives an award for "Miss France Plongée" and even a rather specialized award, the French Association of Conchology Prize, for the best slide or print that "increases our knowledge of the still-sometimes-mysterious world of shellfish." Representative film titles include *Underwater Marvels*, *Titanic: The Investigation*, *The Human Fish*, *The Diving Archeologist*, and *Private Life of Seahorses*. This is an incredible festival for the Jacques Yves Cousteau in all of us. Screenings are held at the Palais des Congrés de Juan-les-Pins, starting at 9 in the morning and going nearly until midnight. One of the more recent editions of the festival dedicated itself to "the International Year of the Oceans" and also paid tribute to underwater filmmakers such as Marcel Isy-Schwart, Folco Quilici and Ramon Bravo. The festival also gives award for Underwater CD-ROMs and a "Music and the Sea" prize.
Major Award Winners Palme d'Or: *Iris et Onris*, by Sylvie DeParnay and Robert Ranc; Palme d'Argent: *Incredible Suckers*, by BBC Natural History Unit; Palme de Bronze: *Sperm Whales-Back from the Abyss*, by BBC Natural History Unit; Prix du Public: *L'Oeil de la Mer*, by Jean-Yves Collet; Prize for the Best Animal Documentary: *Les Chasses du Dauphin Roi*, by Bertrand Loyer; Prize for Best Historical Documentary: *La Septiéme Merveille du Monde*, by Yves Pellisier, Jean-Marie Heckmann, and Rene Heuzey
Films About 75 splishy-splashy movies
Noteworthy Celebrity Sightings A cornucopia of underwater diving photography stars
Tickets 30 Fr for one day's admission fee; 350 Fr gains admittance to all events
How to Enter Send VHS dub, 150 Fr entry fee, and entry form to:
Festival Mondial de l'Image Sous-Marine
62, avenue des Pins du Cap
06160 Antibes Juan-les-Pins
France
Telephone 011.33.193.61.45.45
Fax 011.33.193.67.34.93
E-mail spondyle@riviera.fr
Entry Deadline September

More European Festivals

These are not complete listings. For more information on any of these festivals, write or call for details.

Agrofilm Festival
Wenzigova 15
120 00
Praha 2
Czech Republic
Annual festival taking place in August.

Ale-Kino International Festival of Children's Films
Ale Kino
SW Marcin 80/82
61-809
Poznan
Poland
Telephone 011.48.61.5360.90
Fax 011.48.61.52.85.80

All Russian Festival
Russia
123056 Moscow
Vasilievskaya 3
All Russian Festival
Telephone 011.7.0950.254.70.56
Fax 011.7.0950.251.02.20
A weeklong festival in April.

Amateur ARSfilm Festival
Dum kultury, ARSfilm-Ivo Hanak
Tovacovskeho 2828
767 01 Kromeriz
Czech Republic
Telephone 011.42.634.23.827
Fax 011.42.634.921.557
Entry Deadline September

Amiens International Film Festival
MCA Place, Leon Gontier
80000 Amiens
France
Telephone 011.33.22.71.35.70
Fax 011.33.22.92.53.04
E-mail amiensfilmfestival@burotec.fr
Annual festival held for a week in early November.

Amnesty International Film Festival Amsterdam
P.O. Box 1968
1000 BZ Amsterdam
Netherlands
Telephone 011.31.20.626.44.36
Fax 011.31.20.624.08.89
E-mail filmfestival@amnesty.nl
Web www.dds.nl/amnestyfestival
Biennial film and video festival centering on human rights themes in September.
Entry Deadline April 1

Amsterdam Cinekid Film Festival
Weteringschaus 249
1017 Amsterdam
Netherlands
Telephone 011.31.20.624.71.10
Fax 011.31.20.620.99.65
Annual festival held for 10 days in mid-October.

Animascience Festival
Mediathèque
Cite des Sciences et de l'Industrie
30, avenue Corentin Cariou
75930 Paris France
Annual festival taking place in October and November.

Antenna Cinema Festival
Palazzo Sarcinelli
Via XX Septembre, 132
31015-Conegliano TV
Italy
Telephone 011.39.438.411007
Fax 011.39.438.32777
Annual festival held in March and April.

Antwerp Action and Adventure Film Festival
1104 Kortrijksesteenweg
9051 Ghent
Belgium
Telephone 011.32.9.331.8946

Fax 011.32.9.221.9074
E-mail filmfestival@infoboard.be
Web www.rug.ac.be/filmfestival/
  Welcome.html

Antwerp International Film Festival
Antwerpse Film Stichting
Theatercentrum
Theaterplain 1
2000 Antwerp
Belgium

Archeofilm Fest
Associazione Culturale Athena File
c/o A.B.A.C.O.
Via Sigismondo Marchesi, 12
47100-Forli FO
Italy
Telephone 011.39.543.35494
Fax 011.39.543.35805
Entry Deadline July 1
Festival held in mid-September.

Arctic Light Film Festival
Box 234
981 24 Kiruna
Sweden
Telephone 011.46.1980.177.69
Fax 011.46.1980.828.01
E-mail Arcticlight.Filmfestival@
  kiruna.se
Annual festival held for a week in mid-
November. The festival recently
screened Allan Piper's *Starving Artists*.

Arles Multimedia and Animation Festival
E-mail Animagiques@provnet.fr
Web www.provnet.fr/Animagiques
Annual festival held for a week in late
July and early August. Films that have
premiered here include *Asterix et le
Coup de Menhir* and Hayao Miyazaki's
Porco Rosso.

Armed Forces and People Film Festival
Rassegna Cinematografica
Internazionale
Eserciti e Popoli
Via A. Catalani, 31
00199 Rome RM

Italy
Entry Deadline September

Artek Children's International Film Festival in Artek
Artek Children's International Film
Festival in Artek
Russia
129226 Moscow
Artek Children's International Film
Festival in Artek
Telephone 011.7.095.181.0451
Fax 011.7.095.181.1841
Annual festival taking place for a week
in August.

The Art Film Biennial
Direction des Manifestations et
Spectacles
Centre Georges Pompidou
75191 Paris
France
Telephone 011.33.1.44.78.4722
Fax 011.33.1.44.78.1644
Entry Deadline May
Festival of films on art held in even-
numbered years.

Asolo International Animation Festival
c/o Amministrazione Provinciale
31100 Treviso TV
Italy
Annual festival held in May.

Athens Film Festival
Banaki 5
152 35 Athens
Greece
Telephone 011.30.1.6061.363
Fax 011.301.6014.137
One week in September.

Augsburg Children's Film Festival
Filmbüro Augsburg
Schroekstr. 6
86152 Augsburg
Germany
Telephone 011.49.821.153.079
Fax 011.49.821.349.5218
Annual festival taking place for two
weeks in November.

Augsburg Days of Independent Film
Filmbüro Augsburg
Schroeckstr. 6
86152 Augsburg
Germany
Telephone 011.49.821.349.1060
Fax 011.49.821.349.5218
E-mail filmbuero@t-online.de
Annual festival held for a week in
late March.

Avoriaz Film Festival
c/o Unifrance
4, Villa Bosquet
75007 Paris
France
Telephone 011.33.147.53.27.41
Fax 011.33.147.05.96.55
Annual festival taking place for a week
in January.

Baltic Pearl International Festival of Film Actors
Baltic Pearl International Festival of
Film Actors
Russia
123825 Moscow GSP
3 Vasilievskaya
Baltic Pearl International Festival of
Film Actors
Telephone 011.7.312.32.0026
Fax 011.7.312.21.1918
Annual festival of films in August.

Belgrade International Film Festival
Sava Center
Milentija Popovica 9
11000 Belgrade
Yugoslavia
Telephone 011.381.11.622.555
Fax 011.381.11.222.1156
Annual festival held in late January and
early February.

Bellaria Film Festival
Viale Paolo Guidi 108
1-47041
Bellaria, Italy
Telephone/Fax 011.39.541.347.186
Annual festival held for a week in June.

Bergamo Film Meeting
Via Giovanni Reich, 49
24020-Torre BG
Italy
Telephone 011.39.35.36.3087
Fax 011.39.35.34.1255
E-mail bfm@alasca.it
Web http://www.alasca.it/bfm
Annual festival held in Bergamo for a
week in early March.

Berlin Lesbian Film and Video Festival
Feurigstrasse 61
D-10827
Berlin, BRD
Telephone 011.49.30.788.5884
Fax 011.49.30.788.6487
E-mail anne@contrib.com or
jo@contrib.com

Bite the Mango: Black and Asian Film Festival
National Museum of Photography, Film,
and Television
Bradford BD1 1NQ
UK
E-mail c.sawhney@nmsi.ac.uk
Web http://www.nmsi.ac.uk/nmpft/
Entry Deadline August
Annual festival taking place for ten days
in late November.

Bradford Film Festival
National Museum of Photography, Film
and Television
Pictureville
Bradford
United Kingdom
BD1 1NQ
Telephone 011.44.1274.773.399
Fax 011.44.1274.770.217
E-mail c.fell@nmsi.ac.uk
Web www.bradfordfilmfestival.org.uk

Bratislava Danubefilm Festival
Internatonal TV Fest of Children's and
Youth Programs
Mlynska dolina
845 45 Bratislava
Slovakia

Telephone 011.42.7.772.7448
Fax 011.42.7.772.9440
An international festival of programs for children's and youth Television taking place for a week in late September.

Bremen Underground Film Festival
Am Dobben 147
28203 Bremen
Germany
Telephone 011.49.421.323.136
E-mail haynes@zfn.uni-bremen.de
Underground festival of short amateur and semi-professional films held in September.

Brief Encounters
Brief Encounters
P.O. Box 576
Bristol
United Kingdom
BS99 2BD
Tel: 011.44.117.922.4628
Fax 011.44.117.922.2906
E-mail brief_encounters@
    dial.pipex.com
Web www.brief-encounters.org.uk
Entry Deadline July 31
A festival of short films held in late November.

British Short Film Festival
Room 313, Threshold House
65-69 Shepherd's Bush Green
London
United Kingdom
W12 7RK
Telephone 011.44.181.748.8000
Fax 011.44.181.740.8549
Annual festival taking place for a week in late September.

Brynmawr Film Festival
Blaenau Gwent Arts
Development Office
Beaufort Theatre
Beaufort
Ebbw Vale
United Kingdom
NP3 5QQ

Telephone/Fax 011.44.1495.308996
Annual festival taking place for a week in mid-November.

Cádiz International Video Festival
Pl. España
Edf. Roma
11071 Cádiz
Spain
Entry Deadline September
Annual festival in November.

Cergy-Pontoise Cinema Festival
Theatre des Arts de Cergy-Pontoise
Centre d'Action Culturelle
Place des Arts
BP 307
95027 Cergy
France
Annual festival taking place in January.

Certamen de Cine Amateur
Area de Cine
Delegación Municipal de Cultura
Juan R. Jiménez, 11
29600 Marbella (Málaga)
Spain
Entry Deadline March
Annual festival taking place in March.

Certamen de Cine y Video Etnológico de las Communidades Autónomas
Apartado do Correso, 159
22080 Huesca
Spain
Annual festival taking place the first week of April.

Certamen Internacional de Cine Amateur
Apartal 378
08700 Igualada Barcelona
Spain
Entry Deadline July

Certamen Internacional de Curmetrages i Video
Apartado de Correos 286
08911 Barcelona
Spain
Entry Deadline September

Cherbourg British Film Festival
15, Passage Digard
50100 Cherbourg
France
Telephone 011.33.33.93.38.94
Fax 011.33.33.01.20.78

Chichester Film Festival
Westlands, Mainroad, Hunston
Chichester
United Kingdom
PO20 6AL
Telephone 011.44.1243.784.441
Fax 011.44.1243.539.853
Annual festival taking place for a week
in August.

Cinédécouvertes
Rue Ravenstein 23
1000 Brussels
Belgium
Telephone 011.32.2.506.83.70
Fax 011.32.2.513.12.72
Annual festival taking place in July and
August.

Cinema JOVE
Festival Internacional de Video
Institut Valencia de la Joventut
Jeroni de Monsoriu, 19
46022 Valencia
Spain
Telephone 011.34.96.398.59.26
Fax 011.34.96.398.59.69

Cinema Mediterraneen Montpellier
6, rue Vielle-ai Guillerie
34000 Montpellier
France
Telephone 011.33.467.66.36.36
Fax 011.33.467.66.36.37
Held for 10 days in late October and
early November.

Cinémemoire
Cinémathèque Française
Palais de Chaillot
Paris
France
Tel.:011.33.56.26.01.01

Annual festival of rare and restored
French films held in November and
December.

**Cinemusic International Music and Film
Festival**
Chalet Rialto
Postfach 382
3780 Gstaad
Switzerland
Telephone 011.41.33.748.83.38
Fax 011.41.33.748.83.39

Deutsches Kinderfilm und Fernseh Festival
Postfach 166
07052 Gera
Germany
Telephone 011.49.365.800.4878
Fax 011.49.365.800.1344
E-mail gold-spa@geraweb.de
Annual festival taking place for a week
in mid-March.

Diagonale Festival of Austrian Films
Stiftgasse 6
1070 Vienna
Austria
Telephone 011.431.526.33.23
Fax 011.431.526.6801
E-mail afilmco@ping.at
Annual festival taking place for a week
in mid-March.

Diamond Film Experience
Boulevard du Centenaire 20
1020 Brussels
Belgium
Telephone 011.32.2.478.04.50
Fax 011.32.2.478.78.40
Annual festival taking place for a week
in August in Brussels.

Duisburger Filmwoche
am Konig-Heinrich-Platz
47049 Duisburg
Germany
Telephone 011.49.203.283.4171
Fax 011.49.203.283.4130
Festival taking place for a week in mid-
November.

Espoo Cine
P.O. Box 95
Ahertajankwa 4
02100 Espoo
Finland
Telephone 011.358.9.466.599
Fax 011.358.9.466.458
E-mail espoocine@cultnet.fi
Web www.espoo.fi/cine
Entry Deadline May 31
Annual festival held for 10 days in late
August.

Europacinema Festival
Via Giulia, 66
00186 Rome RM
Italy
Fax 011.39.6.6880.5417
Entry Deadline July

Europäischen Schulerfilmfestival
Bundesweites Schuler Film und
Videozentrum, e.v.
Postfach 19
Lizter Platz 67
30019 Hanover
Germany

**European Festival of Rural and Fishing
Cinema**
Apartado de Correos, 74
33430 Candas (Asturias)
Spain
Telephone 011.34.85.87.10.21
Fax 011.34.85.88.47.11
Annual festival taking place in July and
August.

European Media Art Festival
Hasestrasse 71
Postfach 1861
49008 Osnabruck
Germany
Telephone 011.49.541.216.58
Fax 011.49.541.283.27
Web www.emaf.de

Fantafestival
Via Palestro, 78
00185 Rome
Italy

Annual fantasy film festival taking place
for a week in June.

Festival Internacional de Cinema do Algarve
P.O. Box 8091
1801 Lisbon Codex
Portugal
Entry Deadline March 31
Annual festival taking place a week in
late May.

Festival Internacional de Curtas Metragens
Auditorio Municipal-Praga da
Republica
4480 Vila do Conde
Portugal
Telephone 011.351.52.641.644
Fax 011.351.52.642.871
International festival of short films tak-
ing place for a week in June.

**Festival International du Court Métrage de
Mons**
Rue de Arbalestries
7000 Mons
Belgium
Tel: 011.32.65.31.81.75
Fax 011.32.65.31.30.27
Entry Deadline February
Annual festival of short films for a week
in mid-March.

**Festival International du Film d'Art et
Pédagogique**
FIFAP
Bureau 2.16
UNESCO
7, Place Fontenoy
75352 Paris 07 SP
France
Telephone 011.33.145.68.16.58
Fax 011.33.149.24.98.45

Festival International du Film sur l'Art
K Comme Communication
Chausée de Louvain 30
1030 Knokke
Belgium
Telephone 011.322.218.10.55
Fax 011.322.218.66.27
Annual festival held for a week in early
April in Knokke, Belgium.

Festival of Films about Love
Festival Internationale du Film
d'Amour
Rue du 11 Novembre
7000 Mons
Belgium

Festival of Nations
Festival der Nationen
Gaumbergstrasse 82
4060 Linz
Austria
Telephone 011.43.6133.80.16
Entry Deadline April 1
This festival awards gold, silver and
bronze bears as well as awards for best
experimental films. The festival is limit-
ed to films under 30 minutes.

Festival of New Film and Video in Split
Zagrebacka 35
APO Box 244
21000 Split
Croatia
Telephone/Fax 011.385.21.525.925
E-mail split.filmfest@st.tel.hr
Web www.st.carnet.hr/split-filmfest
Annual festival held for a week in
October.

Festival of Sailor's Films
Center for Technical Progress
Ul. Buczka 1b, Skr. Poczt. 454
40-95 Katowice
Poland
Annual festival taking place in
December.

FIFREC International Film and Student Directors Festival
BP 7144
30913 Nîmes
France
Telephone 011.33.72.02.20.36
Annual festival held in Nîmes for a
week in May.

Figueira da Foz Festival Internacional de Cinema
Apartado dos Correios 50407
1709 Lisbon Codex
Portugal

Telephone 011.351.812.6231
Fax 011.351.812.6228
Annual festival held for 10 days in early
September.

Frankfurt am Main International Film Fest for Children and Young People
Deutsches Filmmuseum
Schaumainkai 41
60596 Frankfurt am Main
Germany
Telephone 011.49.69.2123.8835
Fax 011.49.69.2123.7881
Annual festival held for two weeks in
mid-September.

French Film Festival
French Institute
13 Randolph Crescent
Edinburgh
United Kingdom
EH3 8TX
Telephone 011.44.131.243.3601
Fax 011.44.131.220.2443
Annual festival of French Cinema held
in Glasgow and Edinburgh for ten days
in late November and early December.

Fribourg Film Festival
Rue de Locarno 8
1700 Fribourg
Switzerland
Telephone 011.41.26.322.22.32
Fax 011.41.26.322.79.50
Web www.worldcom.ch/counter.
     count$smart/fribourg.html
Annual festival held for a week in
mid-March.

German Fantasy Film Festival
German Fantasy Film Festival
Rosebud Entertainment
Herzog-Wilhelmstr. 27
80331 Munich
Germany

Golden Frame International Festival of Independent Film and Video
Federazione Nazionale
Cinevideoautori, Via Giove Tonante, 10
Caselle Postale 368
47100-Forli FO

Italy
Telephone/Fax 011.39.543.25678
Web www.cvc.fo.it/associazioni/fotoro

Golden Rose of Montreux
Case Postale 234
1211 Geneva
Switzerland
Telephone 011.41.22.708.85.99
Fax 011.41.22.781.52.49
E-mail buchergabrielle@7sr.srg.ssr.ch

HIV Positive Film Fest
c/o Ovegylet Alapitvany
Budapest
Zichy Jeno u. 291.
1066
Hungary
Telephone 011.36.1.131.2589
Fax 011.36.1.312.5844
E-mail dcrp@zpok.hu
Entry Deadline September
Noncompetitive festival concerned with issues relating to people carrying HIV.

Hungarian Film Week
Magyar Filmunio
Budapest
Varosligeti Saso 38.
1068
Hungary
Annual festival held in the first week of February.

International Celtic Film and Television Festival
1 Camelot Court
Alverton Street
Penzance
United Kingdom
TR18 2QN
Telephone 011.44.1736.333.151
Fax 011.44.1736.333.153
One week in mid-March.

Internationale Filmwochenende
Gostbertsteige 2
97082 Würzburg
Germany
Telephone 011.49.931.414098
Fax 011.49.931.416279

Ten days in late January and early February.

International Exhibition of Documentary Films on Art
Associazione Culturale Francescana
Mostra Internazionale del Documentario sull'Arte
Via S. Francesco, 61
35100-Padova PD
Italy
Entry Deadline April
Annual festival taking place in May.

International Festival of Comedy Films
P.O. Box 104
5300 Gabrovo
Bulgaria
Entry Deadline March 1
Annual festival taking place in May.

International Festival of Documentary Films about Parks
Assessorato Cultura-Commune di Sondrio
Piazza Campello, 1
23100 Sondrio SO
Italy

International Festival of Film Schools
c/o IMF GmbH
Kaiserstrasse 39
80801 Munich
Germany
Telephone/Fax 011.49.8938.1904
Annual student film festival taking place for a week in late November.

International Festival of Films on Architecture
Artimage Austria
Katziannergasse 3
8010 Graz
Austria
Telephone 011.43.316.82.95.13
Fax 011.43.316.82.95.11
Annual festival taking place the last weekend in November. Holds a competition for features, shorts, and animation that deal with the philosophical and political implications of architecture.

International Festival of Films on Art

"Asolo Art Festival, Antennacinema Arte"
Palazzo Sarcinelli
Via XX Settembre, 132
31015 Conegliano TV
Italy

International Festival of Films on Energy

Chemin de Mornex 6
Case Postale 674
1001 Lausanne
Switzerland
Telephone/Fax 011.41.21.310.30.90

International Festival of Maritime Documentaries

Instituto delle Civita del Mare
Piazza E. Llussu, 4
80820 San Teodoro (NU)
Italy
Entry Deadline April

International Festival of Non-Professional Films

Hauptplatz 11
9100 Volkermakt/Karnten
Buchalm 42
P141 Eberndorf
Austria
Annual festival takes place in September.

International Festival of Scientific and Technical Films

Centre Universitaire de Film Scientifique de L'Université Libre de Bruxelles
Avenue F. D. Roosevelt 50 (CP 1065)
1050 Brussels
Belgium
Telephone 011.32.2.650.3110
Fax 011.32.2.650.4225
E-mail adepauq@resulb.ulb.ac.be

International Festival of Scientific Films

Drustovo "Nikola Tesla"
Kneze Milosa 10
11000 Belgrade
Yugoslavia
Biennial festival in February of even years.

International Film and Student Directors Festival

FIFREC
B.P. 7144
30913 Nîmes
France

International Film and Video Festival

24c West Street
Epson
United Kingdom
KT18 7RJ
Entry Deadline January

International French Film Festival

Friedrichstrasse 11
72072 Tübingen
Germany
Telephone 011.49.70.713.2828
Fax 011.49.70.713.1006
E-mail 1@t-online.de
Held in the last week of June.

International 9.5 mm Film Festival

BP 39
Place St. Cecile
81000 Albi
France

International Science and Documentary Film Festival

Sovinterfest
Russia
109028 Moscow
Khokhlovsky Pereulok 10
Sovinterfest
Annual festival taking place in January.

International Short Film Festival of Kraków

Miedzynarodowy Festival Filmow Krotkometrazowych
c/o PIF "Apollo-Film"
Ul. Pychowicka 7
30-364 Kraków
Poland
Telephone 011.48.12.267.2340
Fax 011.48.12.267.1552
Entry Deadline January 31
Annual festival of short films held for a week in late May and early June.

International Sports Film Festival Budapest
Budapest
Rosenberg HP 1
1054
Hungary
Telephone 011.36.11.316.936
Annual festival held in November.

International Super-8 Festival
Club Super-8
34, rue Fournirue
57000 Metz
France
Entry Deadline September

International Tourfilm Festival
Via Germanico, 66
00192 Rome
Italy
Annual festival taking place for a week in October.

International TV and Film Festival for Youth and Children
International TV and Film Festival for Youth and Children
Russia
101000 Moscow
Christoprudny 12-A
International TV and Film Festival for Youth and Children
Annual festival taking place in March.

International Week for Education and Teaching Films
"ICEM Festival"
Landesbidstelle Berlin
Zentrum für Audio-Visuelle Medien
Wikingerufer 7
1000 Berlin 21
Germany
Telephone 011.49.30.3909.2247

Internationale Duisburger Amateur Film days and Youth Video Forum
Welkerstrasse 4
47053 Duisburg 1
Germany
Entry Deadline May 10
Annual festival held in mid-June.

Internationales Festival der Filmhochschulen München
International Festival of Film Schools
Kaiserstrasse 39
80807 Munich
Germany

Italian Comedy Film Festival
Piazza Einaudi, 2
25041 Boario Terme BS
Italy
Annual festival held in October.

Kaliningrad Film Festival
Kaliningrad Film Festival
Russia
236000 Kalingrad
Ploschad Pbedny 1
Kaliningrad Film Festival
Telephone 011.7.0112.21.8926
Fax 011.7.0112.21.1677
Festival held in the last week of June.

Kidscreen
Rue Royale St. Marie 2
1030 Brussels
Belgium
Telephone 011.32.2.219.48.96
Fax 011.32.2.219.58.60
Festival held one week in late October and early November.

Kiev International Film Festival
International Film Festival Molodist
6, Saksagansky
Kiev
252033 Ukraine
Telephone/Fax 011.380.44.22.74557
Annual festival held for 10 days in mid-October.

Laon International Film Festival for Young People
BP 526 Maison des Arts
Maison des Arts
BP 526
02001 Laon
France
Telephone 011.33.03.20.38.61
Fax 011.33.03.20.28.99
Festival held for 10 days in mid-March.

London Jewish Film Festival
South Bank
Waterloo
London
United Kingdom
SE1 8XT
Telephone 011.44.171.815.1322
Fax 011.44.171.633.0786
E-mail jane.ivey@bfi.org.uk
Annual festival held for 10 days in mid-June.

London Lesbian and Gay Film Festival
South Bank
Waterloo
London
United Kingdom
SE1 8XT
Telephone 011.44.171.815.1322
Fax 011.44.171.633.0786
Annual festival held for 10 days in mid-March.

London Low-Budget Film Festival
19 College Crescent
London
United Kingdom
NW3 5LL
Telephone 011.44.7654.519.493
Fax 011.44.171.916.1091
E-mail alf@worldviewpictures.co.uk
Entry Deadline July 1

Madrid International Festival of Science Fiction and Fantasy Films
Gran Vía, 62-80
28013 Madrid
Spain

Madrid International Film Festival
Gran Vía, 62
8th Floor
28013 Madrid
Spain
Telephone 011.34.1.541.37.21
Fax 011.34.1.542.54.95

Magdeburg International Film Festival
Coquistrasse 18a
39104 Magdeburg
Germany

Telephone 011.49.3914.8668
Festival held for five days at the end of September.

Magyar Filmszemi
Filmunion Hungary, VI
Budapest
Varosligeti fasor 28.
Hungary
Telephone 011.38.351.7760
Annual festival of Hungarian films held in February.

Manchester Festival of Fantastic Films
33 Barrington Road
Altrincham
Cheshire
United Kingdom
WA14 1H2
Telephone 011.44.161.929.1423
Fax 011.44.161.929.1067

Medikinale International Hannover
Fuchswinkel 37
3100 Celle
Germany
Entry Deadline July

Minimalen Short Film Festival
P.O. Box 1083
Lademoen
7030 Trondheim
Norway
Telephone 011.47.73.52.2757
Fax 011.47.73.53.5750
E-mail perf@interlink.no
Annual festival held for a weekend in mid-March.

Mons International Film Festival
Festival International du Cinema a Mons
Rue des Arbalestriers 106
7000 Mons
Belgium

Montpellier Jewish and Israeli Film Festival
500, Boulevard d'Antigone
3400 Montpellier
France
Telephone 011.33.67.15.08.76

Fax 011.33.67.15.08.72
Festival held 10 days in late November and early December.

Mostra de Valencia
Plaza del Arzobispo
2 Bajo
46003 Valencia
Spain
Telephone 011.346.392.15.06
Fax 011.346.391.15.56
Annual festival held for a week in mid-October.

Munich International Documentary Film Festival
Troger Strasse 46
81675 Munich
Germany
Telephone 011.49.89.470.3237
Fax 011.49.89.470.6611
Annual festival held for 10 days in late April and early May.

Nancy Festival of Underground Film
Faculté de Lettres
23 BD Albert Ier
54000 Nancy
France

New Visions International Festival
P.O. Box 1269
Glasgow
United Kingdom
G3 60A
Telephone 011.44.141.552.3436
Fax 011.44.141.553.2660

North Devon Film Festival
The Plough
Fore Street
Torrington
United Kingdom
EX38 8HQ
Annual festival taking place in June.

Nottingham Shots in the Dark Mystery and Thriller Film Festival
Broadway Media Centre
14 Broad Street
Nottingham

United Kingdom
NG1 3AL
Telephone 011.44.115.962.6600
Fax 011.44.115.952.6622
E-mail broadway@bwymedia.
demon.co.uk
Entry Deadline March 28
Annual festival held for 10 days in early June. Started in 1991, this festival pays tribute (unsurprisingly) to crime films. One recent festival feted Elmore Leonard, showing films that he wrote or that were adapted from his works (*Out of Sight*, *Jackie Brown*, *Touch*, *Hombre*, *Cat Chaser*). Other films that have screened here include *Blackboard Jungle*, *Bunny Lake is Missing*, and *Badlands*. Special features and retrospectives have featured Jean Gabin and Alma Reville.

Okomedia International Ecological Film Festival
Okomedia Institute
Habsburgerstr. 9
79104 Freiburg
Germany
Entry Deadline July 31

Open Russian Film Festival Kinotaur
Open Russian Film Festival Kinotaur
Russia
121835 Moscow
Arbat 35
Open Russian Film Festival Kinotaur
Telephone 011.7.095.248.0911
Fax 011.7.095.248.0966
Annual festival held for three weeks in Moscow in late May and early June. Held in Black Sea resort town and dedicated to "Revival of Cinema."

Oslo Film Days
P.O. Box 1584 Vika
0118 Oslo
Norway
Telephone 011.47.22.42.71.54
Fax 011.47.22.33.39.45
Festival held annually in February.

Oslo Gay and Lesbian Film Festival

P.O. Box 6838 St. Olav's Plaza
0130 Oslo
Norway
Telephone 011.47.22.36.19.48
Fax 011.47.22.36.28.03

Oslo International Film Festival

Ebbellsgate 1
0182 Oslo
Norway
Telephone 011.47.22.20.07.66
Fax 011.47.22.20.18.03
E-mail filmfestival@login.eunet.no
Web www.wit.no/filmfestival

Ourense Film Festival

Apartado 664
32080 Ourense
Spain
Telephone/Fax 011.34.88.21.58.85
E-mail rey@bitmailer.net
Web www.sister.ed/ourense.htm
Festival held annually during a week in
November.

Outdoor Short Film Festival

4, rue Hector Berlioz
38000 Grenoble
France
Telephone 011.33.76.54.4351
Fax 011.33.76.51.2443
Web www.alpes-net/envu
Festival held annually during a week in
mid-July.

Parnu Visual Anthropology Festival

Parnu I.V.A. Society
P.O. Box A
3600 Parnu
Estonia
Telephone 011.372.44.43869
Fax 011.372.44.30774
Entry Deadline April 1
Annual festival held for a week in July.

Reinaert Film Festival

Baljuwweg 1
9080 Lochristi
Belgium
Telephone 011.32.9.355.71.14

E-mail pin00974@ping.be
Annual film festival held for a weekend
in April in Lochristi, Belgium.

Rencontres d'Annecy

Bonlieu Scene Nationale
1, rue Jean Jaures
BP 294
74007 Annecy
France
Telephone 011.33.50.33.44.00
Fax 011.33.50.52.82.09
Annual festival of Italian cinema held in
Annecy France, for a week in early
December.

Rennes Traveling Film Festival

Association Clair
Rennes 2 Villejean 6
Avenue Gaston Berger
3500 Rennes
France
Telephone 011.33.299.13.11.43
Held for a week in January in Rennes,
France, this "traveling" festival high-
lights a different city every day. Over
the years, these have included London,
Rome, Madrid, Montreal, and other
expected burgs.

Retina International Film and Video Festival

Retina Workshop
Szigetvar
Deak ter 21.
7900
Hungary

Reykjavik Film Festival

Gimli, Laekljargotu
P.O. Box 88
101 Reykjavik
Iceland
Festival held every other year in
October.

Romantic Film Festival

Mons, Belgium
Telephone 011.32.065.36.34.99
Annual festival of romantic films held
just in time for Valentine's Day.

Sarlat International Film and Video Festival
BP 163
24205 Sarlat
France

Slavic and Orthodox People Film Festival
Slavic and Orthodox People Film
Festival
Russia
123825 Moscow
Vasiilyevskaya 17
Slavic and Orthodox People Film
Festival
Telephone 011.7.095.254.2646
Fax 011.7.095.177.2264

Sochi International Film Festival
Sochi International Film Festival
Russia
121835 Moscow
Arbat Street 35
Sochi International Film Festival
Annual film festival taking place in May
and June.

Southampton Film Festival
Harbour Lights Cinema
Ocean Village
Southampton
United Kingdom
SO15 2RZ
Telephone 011.44.1703.635.335
Fax 011.44.1703.234.444
Annual festival held in late February
and early March.

Southport North West Film Festival
3 Barrington Road
Altrincham
United Kingdom
WA14 1H
Telephone 011.44.161.929.1423
Fax 011.44.161.929.1067

Sportfilm Festival
16 Bajo
48013 Bilbao (Vizcaya)
Spain
Telephone 011.34.4.441.27.04
Fax 011.34.4.441.39.32
Annual festival taking place in March.

St. Petersburg "Message to Man" Documentary Film Festival
St. Petersburg "Message to Man"
Documentary Film Festival
Russia
St. Petersburg 19011
Karavannaya 12
St. Petersburg "Message to Man"
Documentary Film Festival
Telephone 011.7.812.230.2200
Fax 011.7.812.235.3995
Entry Deadline May 1.
Annual festival of short documentaries
and animated films held the first week
of July.

Titaniac International Filmprescence Festival
Toldi, C. Bajcsy-Zsilinszky ut 36-38.
Budapest, Hungary
Telephone 011.36.1.39.311.2809
Annual festival of cult films held in
October.

Troia International Film Festival
Forum Luisa Todi
Avenue Luisa Todi, 65
2900 Setubal
Portugal
Telephone 011.351.6.654.4121
Fax 011.351.6.654.4162
Annual Portuguese festival taking place
for 10 days in early June.

Tromse Film Festival
Georgemes Verft 3
5011 Bergen
Norway
Telephone 011.47.55.32.75.90
Fax 011.47.55.32.37.40
Annual festival held in January in
Norway.

Turin Festival of Gay and Lesbian Cinema
Festival Internazionale de Film con
Tematiche Omosessuali
Piazza San Carlo, 161
10123-Turin TO
Italy
Telephone 011.39.11.535.406
Fax 011.39.11.535.796
E-mail glfilmfest@assioma.com

One of the best of the gay film fests, featuring works of Marco Bellocchio, Ettore Scola, Pasolini, and Visconti. Also known as Da Sodoma a Hollywood. Held for a week in mid-April.

Turin International Women's Cinema Festival
Corso Raffaello, 5
10125-Turin TO
Italy
Telephone/Fax 011.39.1.669.0824

Tyneside International Film Festival
10 Pilgrim Street
Newcastle-upon-Tyne
United Kingdom
NE1 6QG
Telephone 011.44.91.232.8289
Fax 011.44.91.221.0535

Verzaubert
Herzog Wilhelm Str. 27
80331 Munich
Germany
Telephone 011.49.260.22.838
Fax 011.49.260.22.839
Festival of gay and lesbian films held in Munich, Cologne, and Stuttgart in November and December.

Video Festival of Catalan Countries
Maire Place Sant Julia

66800 Estavar
France
Telephone 011.33.68.04.09.91
Fax 011.33.68.04.02.56

Warsaw Film Festival
P.O. Box 816
00-950 Warsaw 1
Poland
Telephone/Fax 011.48.22.644.11.84
E-mail mientowy@toto.ternet.pl
Held for two weeks in October.

Wildscreen Festival
15 Whiteladies Road
Bristol
United Kingdom
BS8 1PB
Telephone 011.44.117.973.3082
Fax 011.44.117.923.9416
Festival held in odd-numbered years in mid-October. Attended by Prince Philip and the Duke of Edinburgh.

World Festival of Short Films
Festival Mondial du Cinema de Courts Metrages
Rue E. Vandervelde 15
4520 Wanze
Belgium
Telephone/Fax 011.32.85.21.78.29
Festival of shorts held in Belgium in late October.

4 Asian Film Festivals

The Few and Far Between

Bangkok Film Festival

Where Bangkok, Thailand

When Ten days in late September

Background Unlike a lot of foreign fests, this one doesn't just serve as a screening room for American blockbusters; it truly focuses on the international and the independent. Premieres have included *One Step on a Mine*, *It's All Over* and *Konjon*. *Mystery Men*, *Three Seasons*, and *Oscar and Lucinda* also screened here.

Major Award Winners Golden Elephant Award: *Nang Nak*, by Nanzee Nimibutr; Silver Elephant: *Mr. Zhao*, by Zhao Xiangsheng; Best Cinematography: Arunrat Sawatayanon, *Beyond*; Best Documentary: *Red, White and Yellow*, by Mark Littman and Marshall Dostal

Films More than 150 features and shorts

How to Enter

    Bangkok Film Festival

    4 Sukhumvit Soi 43

    Bangkok 10110

    Thailand

    Telephone 011.66.2.259.3112

    Fax 011.66.2.259.2987

    E-mail film@nation.nationgroup.com

    Web www.nationmultimedia.com/filmfest

Entry Deadline July

Chiba Electronic Cinema Festival

Where Chiba, Japan

When Five days in late May and early June

Background For years, we've been hearing acronyms like HDTV bandied about, and sure, we get glimpses of the technology in films such as *Until the End of the World.* But it's one of the only opportunities one can get to actually see the stuff in action when this Japanese city—known as a "High Vision City," according to the Japanese Ministry of Posts and Telecommunications—presents the most cutting-edge of HDTV projects. The festival awards an Astrolabium Award, named for the astrolabe, which was used by ancient scientists and seafarers in predicting the future and guiding ships. The festival offers awards in the following categories: dramas, documentaries, sports, current affairs, music videos, music and dance, commercial advertising, science education and industry, and interactive films.

Major Award Winners Best Drama: *The Last Bullet*, by NHK; Best Documentary: *Alone Together*, by Faralla Films; Best Music and Dance Film: *No More Play*, by NPS; Mayor's Award for Best Use of HDTV: *War Love Story*, by NHK; Lifetime Achievement Award: Elizabeth M. Daley, Dean of the School of Cinema Television at the University of Southern California

How to Enter For more information contact:
Electronic Cinema Festival
c/o Sogo Vision
5-24, Akasaka 9 chome
Minato-ku,
Tokyo
107 Japan
Telephone 011.81.3.3408.4111
Fax 011.81.3.3408.4112

Entry Deadline March

Hiroshima International Animation Festival

Where Hiroshima, Japan

When One week in late August

Background As much a symposium as a festival, this "Love and Peace Animation Fest," in addition to screenings, offers seminars and panel discussions on the societal benefits that can be reaped through the art of animation. Recent screening series have included features on Brazilian animation, fine-art animation, children's cartoons, and British animation. The festival accents cartoons that stress peace in what the festival organizers term, quite rightly, an "international city of culture."

Major Award Winners Grand Prize: *Old Lady & the Pigeons*, by Sylvain Chomet; Hiroshima Prize: *Mermaid*, by Alexander Petrov; Debut Prize: *Busby*, by Anna Henckl-Donners-Marck

How to Enter Send VHS dub and entry form to:
Hiroshima International Animation Festival
4-17, Kakomachi
Naka-ku
Hiroshima

730-0812 Japan
Telephone 011.81.82.245.0245
Fax 011.81.82.245.0246
E-mail hiroanima@city.hiroshima.jp
Web www.urban.ne.jp/home/hiroanime
Entry Deadline Late April

Hong Kong International Film Festival

Where Kowloon, Hong Kong
When First two weeks of April
Background Organized by the Urban Council of Hong Kong, the festival, founded in 1977, screens films in the following categories: International Cinema, Hong Kong Panorama, Asian Cinema, and Hong Kong Cinema Retrospective. There still is some controversy about the changing of the political guard here: only a couple of Chinese films show up every year, while many rough-and-tumble films from South Korea, Taiwan, Japan, and, of course, Hong Kong turn up. One interesting recent retrospective feature focused on documentaries made by filmmakers better known for narrative features, such as Masahiro Shinoda and his 1975 *The Ondeko-Za on Sado*, a documentary about Japanese drummers.
Major Award Winners Noncompetitive
Films About 200 features and documentaries
How to Enter Send entry form, VHS copy synopsis, and director's biography to:
Hong Kong International Film Festival
Festival Office
Level 7
Administration Building
Hong Kong Cultural Centre
10 Salisbury Road
Tsimshatsui
Kowloon
Hong Kong
Telephone 011.852.2734.2903
Fax 011.852.2366.5206
Entry Deadline December

Japan Wildlife Festival

Where Toyama, Japan
When One week in August
Background Held in odd-numbered years in this northern Japanese town, the festival promotes wildlife film production in Asia and holds photo exhibits, seminars, workshops, and even puppet shows along with a great number of nature documentaries.
Major Award Winners Best of Festival: *The Riddle of the Sands*, BBC; Best Cinematography: *Arctic Kingdom: Life at the Edge*, National Geographic; Best Environmental Conservation Award: *Tyto the Barn Owl*; Special Award of the Jury: *Parrots: Look Who's Talking*

Films About 10
How to Enter For more information contact:
 Japan Wildlife Festival
 Toyama Organizing Office
 Omachi Building
 3rd Floor
 3-14, Jinzu Honmachi 1 chome
 Toyama City
 Toyama
 930 Japan
 Telephone 011.81.764.45.5460
 Fax 011.81.764.41.2144
Entry Deadline Not available

Pusan International Film Festival

Where Pusan, Korea
When Ten days in mid-October
Background Founded in 1996, this is the first film festival ever to be held in Korea, screening a whole mess of films in downtown Pusan in Nampo-Dong and at an open-air screening facility (something that's all too rare stateside) at the Pusan Yachting Center. More than 150,000 attended the first festival here to laze along Pusan's beaches and rub shoulders with the cast and crew of Mike Leigh's *Secrets and Lies*. Screenings emphasize Asian cinema and are held in the following categories: A Window on Asian Cinema, World Cinema, Korean Panorama, Korean Retrospective, New Currents, Wide Angle, and Special Programs. Korean premieres here have included *Shanghai Triad* and *The Pornographer*.
Fact The Pusan Festival shows films on the world's largest screen at an outdoor theater in Haeundae
Films About 170 from 31 countries
Noteworthy Celebrity Sightings Mike Leigh, Brenda Blethyn, Marianne Jean-Baptiste
Tickets 3,000 won for individual screenings
How to Enter Send VHS dub and entry form to:
 Pusan International Film Festival
 Room 208
 1393 Wool-Dong
 Haundae-GU
 Pusan G12-021
 Korea
 Telephone 011.82.51.747.3010
 Fax 011.82.51.747.3012
 E-mail webmaster@piff.org
 Web www.piff.org
Entry Deadline August

Shanghai International Film Festival

Where Shanghai, China
When Biennially in late October and early November
Background Founded in 1993, the festival is the only international film festival in China, awarding Golden Cup awards and selecting films from India, Europe, North America, Southeast Asia, and Hong Kong, as well as other countries. Films that have received their premieres here include Leonid Gorovets's *Coffee with Lemon* and Wolfgang Panzer's *Broken Silence*.
Major Award Winners Golden Cup for Best Film: *Broken Silence*, by Oogst van de Stitte; Best Director: Erik Clausen, *My Childhood*; Best Actor: Jean Pierre Marielle, *Les Milles*; Best Actress: Guo Keyu, *Red Cherry*
Films 19 features
Noteworthy Celebrity Sightings Oliver Stone, Hector Babenco, Paul Cox
How to Enter Send VHS dub and entry form to:
    SIFF
    651 Nanjing Road
    Shanghai 200041
    Telephone 011.86.21.628.01780
    Fax 011.86.21.625.52000
    E-mail office@siff.com
    Web www.siff.com
Entry Deadline August 31

Singapore International Film Festival

Where Singapore
When Two weeks in April
Background Focusing primarily on Asian cinema, screenings here have also featured cult films that had previously been banned in Singapore, including Peter Bogdanovich's underrated *Saint Jack*, and special features have included a tribute to the cinema of Malaysia.
Major Award Winners Best Feature Film: *The Hole*, by Tsai Ming-Liang; Young Cinema Award: *The Adopted Son*, by Aktan Abdikalikov; Special Jury Prize: *Connection by Fate*, by Wan Jen; Best Director: *The Hole*, Tsai Ming Liang; Best Actress: Yang Kuei-Mei, *The Hole*; Best Actor: Joe Abeywickrama, *Death on a Full Moon Day*; Best Short Film: *Datura*, by Abdul Nizam
Films About 150 features and more than 80 shorts
Tickets Ticket hotline: 011.65.435.2600
How to Enter Send VHS dub and entry form to:
    Singapore International Film Festival
    291 Keong Salk Road
    Singapore 089146
    Telephone 011.65.738.7567
    Fax 011.65.738.7578
    E-mail filmfest@pacific.net.sg
    Web filmfest.org.sg
Entry Deadline January

Taipei Golden Horse Festival

Where Kao-hsiung, Taiwan
Background Established in 1962, the Taiwanese film festival devoted to Chinese-language cinema has recently begun to include mainland Chinese films in its competition as well.
Major Award Winners Best Film: *In the Heat of the Sun*; Best Director: Jiang Wen, *In the Heat of the Sun*; Best Actor: Xia Yu, *In the Heat of the Sun*; Best Screenplay: Zhang Zeming, *Foreign Moon*; Best Actress: Josephine Siao, *Hu-Du-Men*
How to Enter Send VHS dub and entry form to:
Taipei Golden Horse Film Festival
Floor 7, No. 45
Chilin Road
Taipei
Taiwan ROC
Telephone 011.886.2.567.5861
Fax 011.886.2.531.8966
E-mail tghffcff@ms14.htnet.net
Web www.goldenhorse.org.tw
Entry Deadline August

Tokyo International Film Festival

Where Tokyo, Japan
When Ten days in early October
Background Founded in 1985, the well-heeled festival (boasting a budget of approximately $5.6 million) offers an International competition (in which such films as Michel Winterbottom's *Jude* and Alex Cox's *Death and the Compass* have competed), and a Young Cinema competition as well as screenings of what jurors determine to be the best of the Asian films. Even in the Young Cinema competition, in which first-time directors and directors under the age of thirty-five with fewer than thirty-five features compete, the prize is up to $186,000. The festival also hosts Nippon Cinema Classics, a retrospective of classic Japanese films. All films are shown with English subtitles.
Major Award Winners Best Film: *Kolya*, by Jan Sverák; Special Jury Prize: *In Full Gallop*, by Krzysztof Zanussi; Best Director: Wu Tian-Ming, *King of Masks*; Best Actress: Hildegunn Riise and Marje Thiesen, *The Other Side of Sunday*; Best Actor: Zhu Xu, *King of Masks*; Asian Film Award: *Darkness and Light*
Notable Celebrity Sightings Phil Collins
Tickets $13 per individual screening
How to Enter For more information contact:
Tokyo International Film Festival
4th Floor
Ginza Building II, 1-6-5
Ginza, Cho-ku
Tokyo
104 Japan
Telephone 011.81.3.3563.6305
Fax 011.81.3.3563.6310

Web www.tokyo-filmfest.or.jp
Entry Deadline July

Tokyo International Gay and Lesbian Film Festival

Where Tokyo, Japan
Background Founded in 1992, the festival raises money through its friendship club. Donate a little, you get a SMILE. Donate a lot, you get a KISS. Screening at the Aoyama Spiral Hall, the festival has premiered *Beautiful Thing* and *The Celluloid Closet*.
Films About 70 features
Tickets 1,300 yen per individual screening; 4,800 yen for four screenings; 8,800 yen for eight screenings
How to Enter Send VHS dub and entry form to:
Tokyo International Gay and Lesbian Film Festival
5-24-16 No. 1601 Nakano
Nakano-ku
Tokyo
164 Japan
Telephone 011.81.3.5380.5760
Fax 011.81.3.5380.5767
E-mail efaison@msn.com
Entry Deadline Not available

Yamagata International Documentary Film Festival

Where Japan
When One week in late October
Background Founded in 1989, the Yamagata Festival, held about 250 miles northeast of Tokyo, holds a competition for 15 international documentaries, which in recent years have included Japanese premieres of Frederick Wiseman's *La Comedie Française*, Barbara Hammer's *Tender Fictions*, and Jon Jost's *London Brief*. Outside of competition, retrospectives have been held in the following categories: New Asian Currents (films by emerging Asian documentarians), The Pursuit of Japanese Documentary (a retrospective of Japanese documentary history), and Cinema and the Greater East Asia Co-prosperity Sphere (focusing on World War II Japanese propaganda cinema).
How to Enter Send VHS dub and entry form to:
Yamagata International Documentary Film Festival
Kitagawa Building
4th Floor
6-42 Kagurazaka
Shinjuku-ku
Tokyo
162 Japan
Telephone 011.81.3.3266.9704
Fax 011.81.3.3266.9700
E-mail yidff@bekkoame.or.jp
Entry Deadline March

More Asian Film Festivals

These are not complete listings. For more information on any of these festivals, write or call for details.

Asia-Pacific Film Festival
8F No. 116 Hang Chung Street
Taipei
Taiwan
Annual festival taking place in December.

Beijing International Children's Film Festival
Juvenile Dept. BTV
No. 2A Zaojunmiao
Haidian District
100086 Beijing
China
Annual festival taking place in May.

Beijing International Scientific Film Festival
Organizational Committee of the ISFF
China Film Export/Import Corporation
25 Xin Wai Street
Beijing
China
Annual festival taking place in November.

Bombay International Film Fest for Documentary, Short, and Animation Films
Khan Market
New Delhi 110003
India
Telephone 011.91.11.615.953
Fax 011.91.11.694.920

Calcutta Film Festival on Mountains
81 Biren Roy Road W
Calcutta 700061
India
Entry Deadline December
Annual festival held for one week in January.

China International Sports Film Festival
Chinese Olympic Committee
9 Tiyuguan Road
Beijing
China
Annual festival taking place in June.

Dhaka International Short Film Festival
Festival Office
46 New Elephant Road
Dhaka-1205
Bangladesh
Entry Deadline November
Annual festival taking place for one week in January.

Festival Sinatron Indonesia
Sekretariat Pantap
Kedoya Center, Jalan Perjuangan
Blok II, No. 1, Kebon Jeruk
Jakarta 11063
Indonesia
Annual festival held in November.

Filmotsav Documentary Film Festival
Federation of Film Societies of India
No. 3, Northend Complex
R K Ashram Marg
New Delhi 110001
India

Fukuoka International Film Festival
1-8-1 Tenjin
Cho-ku
Fukuoka
810 Japan
Telephone 011.81.9.2733.5170
Fax 011.81.92.733.5595
Annual festival held for 10 days in mid-September.

Hiroshima International Amateur Film and Video Festival
c/o Chugoku Broadcasting Co.
Department of Business Promotion
21-3 Motomachi
Naka-ku
Hiroshima
730 Japan
Telephone 011.81.82.222.1133
Fax 011.81.82.222.1319
E-mail eizo@hiroken.or.jp
Entry Deadline February

International Film Festival for Children and Young People
Films Division Complex
24 G. Deshmukh Marg.
Bombay 400026
India
Entry Deadline August
Annual film festival held in November.

International Film Festival of India
Directorate of Film Festivals, Ministry of Information and Broadcasting
4th floor, Lok Nayak Bhavan
Khan Market
New Delhi 110003
India
Telephone 011.91.11.461.5953
Fax 011.91.11.462.3430
E-mail ffsi@ifson.org
Entry Deadline November
Annual festival held for 10 days in January.

International Nature Film and Television Festival
12th Cross
Rajmahal Vilas Extn.
Bangalore 560080
India
Telephone 011.91.80.334.5595
Fax 011.91.80.334.1674

International Science and Technology Film and Video Festival
Japan Science Foundation
2-1 Kitanomaru-koen
Chiyoda-ku
Tokyo
102 Japan
Entry Deadline October 15

Japan International Film and Video Festival of Adventure and Sports
Jifas Organizing Committee
7025 Hokujo
Hakuba-mura, Kitaazumi-gun
Nagano-ken
Japan

Osaka European Film Festival
530 Osaka
Japan
Telephone 011.81.6.341.9181
Fax 011.81.6.341.3166
Annual festival held the first week of November.

Seoul International Film Festival for Children and Youth
202 Jinsung Building
736-8 Yoksam-dong
Kangnam-gu
Seoul 165-080
Korea
Telephone 011.82.34.49.72.0215
Fax 011.82.34.49.71.9687
E-mail kiffoc@ik.co.kr
Held for one week in late May.

Surprise International Short Film Festival
4th Floor, No. 13, Alley 9, Lane 131,
Chao-Hou Road
Ta-Li
Taiwan
Telephone/Fax 011.886.4.495.0786
Annual festival taking place in Taichung City, Taiwan, for one week in early April.

Tokyo International Fantastic Film Festival
5H Asano Building No. 3 2-4-19
Ginza, Chuo-ku
Tokyo
104 Japan
Entry Deadline June
Annual festival in September and October.

Tokyo International Festival of Film Students
Tokyo Agency, Inc.
4-8-18, Akasaka
Minato-ku
Tokyo
Japan
Entry Deadline July

Tokyo Video Festival
1-7-1 Shinbashi
Minato-ku
Tokyo
105-0004 Japan
Telephone 081.3.3289.2815
Fax 081.3.3289.2819
Entry Deadline October
One-day video festival in February.

5 African and Middle Eastern Film Festivals

Big Continent, Small Festivals

Cairo International Film Festival

Where Cairo, Egypt

When Two weeks in late November and early December

Background Founded in 1977, this festival should get some kind of honor for having the coolest awards of any festival worldwide. Aside from Golden and Silver Pyramids for best and runner-up films, the festival offers a model of a statue of the princess Baket Atoon for best actress; a model of the Imhoteb Engineer, designer of the step pyramid, for best actor, a statue of King Akhenaton (Philip Glass would be proud) for best director, a statue of Naguib Mahfouz for best script, and a statue of the Egyptian Script Old Kingdom for a director's best first or second work. In addition to the awards, Cairo also hosts retrospectives, tributes, and a film marketplace where Egyptian filmmakers attempt to link up with international distributors.

Major Award Winners Golden Pyramid Award for Best Film: *The Terrorist*, by Santosh Sivan; Best Actor: Stephen Rea; Best Actress: Nora Auror; Best Director: Severo Pérez, *And the Earth Did Not Swallow Him*; Best Screenplay: Chris Gerolmo

Films 200 features and shorts

How to Enter For more information contact:

Festival Cairo International Film Festival
17 Kasr el Nil Street
Cairo
Egypt
Telephone 011.20.2.392.3562
Fax 011.20.2.393.8879
E-mail info@cairofilmfestival.com
Web www.cairofilmfestival.com

Entry Deadline October

Fajr Film Festival

Where Tehran, Iran
When Ten days in early February
Background Much as one tends to see Iran stereotyped in the media, this is a rather impressive festival. Founded in 1982, the Fajr fest screens in the following categories: Festival of Festivals (a sampling of the best of other international film fests), Islamic countries, and reconstructed films and classics. There are also tributes, which in recent years have featured the works of Kenji Mizoguchi, Charlie Chaplin, and Sergei Eisenstein.
Notable Celebrity Sightings Abbas Kiarostami
Films About 60 features
How to Enter Send VHS dub and entry form to:
    Fajr Film Festival
    Farhang Cinema
    Dr. Shariati Avenue
    19139 Tehran
    Iran
    Telephone 011.98.21.256.088
    Fax 011.98.21.267.082
Entry Deadline January

FESPACO Pan-African Film and Television Festival of Ouagadougou

Where Ouagadougou, Burkina Faso
When Late February through early March
Background Founded in 1969, the largest festival of African film and filmmakers is held in conjunction with the International African Film and Television Market. Held in Burkina Faso, which declares as its motto that it is "the country of upright people," the festival is devoted to aiding distribution of African films and films from less-developed countries. The festival reaches out to some of the poorer areas of the country with its open-air screenings. Films are shown in the following categories: TV and video, a competition of African films, and children's cinema. There is also a marketplace devoted to finding international distribution for African cinema.
Major Award Winners Grand Prize *Budd-Yam*, by Gaston Kabore; Special Jury Prize: *Taafe Fanga*, by Adama Drabo; Best Actor: Belgacem Hadjaj, *Machano*; Best Actress: Amina Keita, *Mere de Sable*
How to Enter For more information contact:
    Ministry of Information and Culture
    01 BP 2505
    Ouagadougou 01
    Burkina Faso
    Telephone 011.226.307.538
    Fax 011.226.312.509
    E-mail mkab@fespaco.bf
Entry Deadline December in even years

Haifa Film Festival

Where Haifa, Israel
When A week in September
Background Sukkoth isn't the likeliest holiday for a film festival (though it is probably the best holiday invented), especially if you're gonna be showing Stanley Kubrick's *Eyes Wide Shut*. Along with that bizarre choice for the famous tent and schach holiday, screenings have included *Much More Than a Dream*, by Amir Gera, and a great deal of films that addressed the eternal Israeli-Palestinian struggle.
How to Enter For more information check out their web site at www.haifaff.co.il

Istanbul International Film Festival

Where Istanbul, Turkey
When Last two weeks of April
Background Founded by the Istanbul Foundation for Culture and Arts in 1982, the festival has grown from six films to more than 100 from 40 countries attended by 125,000 people. There has been a focus of late on Turkish filmmaking as well as Turkic republics Azerbaijan, Turkmenistan, Kazakhstan, Kyrgyzstan, and Uzbekistan. The festival shows a breathtakingly diverse array of films in the following categories outside of the main competition: Arts and the Movies (e.g., Louis Malle's *Vanya on 42nd Street*), Cinema Looks at Cinema (e.g., Rob Epstein and Jeffrey Friedman's *The Celluloid Closet*), From Literature to Silver Screen (e.g., Darrell Roodt's *Cry the Beloved Country*), Centenary of the Cinema (e.g., Ingmar Bergman's *The Seventh Seal*), Young Stars of the World Cinema (Frank van Passel's *Mannekin Pis*), the Best Films from World Festivals (Hal Hartley's *Flirt*), Winds from Far-East (Wu Kui's *The Wooden Man's Bride*), That Mystery Called Sexuality (*Erotique*, by Lizzie Borden, Monika Treut, and Clara Law), as well as a children's fest and a lot of tributes, which have included Claude Chabrol, Jean Renoir, Jim Jarmusch, Stanley Kwan, and Robert Wise.
Major Award Winners Golden Tulip for Best Film: *Ayneh*, by Jafar Panahi
Films About 150
How to Enter For more information contact:
Istiklal Cad.
Luvr Apt. 146
Beyoglu
80070 Istanbul
Turkey
Telephone 011.90.212.2933.1334
Fax 011.90.212.2497.771
E-mail film.fest@istfest-tr.org
Web www.istfest.org
Entry Deadline December

Jerusalem Film Festival

Where Jerusalem, Israel
When Ten days in July

Background Founded in 1984, the festival has been better at bridging religious and cultural gaps than the country's administration itself, screening both Israeli and Palestinian films and inspiring meaningful exchange. Even so, various Arab nations still won't allow their films to be shown here because of the festival's location in the disputed capital of Jerusalem. Films are screened at the left-leaning Jerusalem Cinematheque.

Major Award Winners Best Feature: *Yana's Friends*, by Arik Kaplun

Films About 150 features

Noteworthy Celebrity Sightings Bob Hoskins

How to Enter Send VHS dub and entry form to:
Jerusalem Film Festival
P.O. Box 8561
Derech Hebron
Wolfson Gardens
91083 Jerusalem
Israel
Telephone 011.972.2.724.131
Fax 011.972.2.733.076
E-mail jer-cine@inr.net.il
Web www.jer.zine.org

Entry Deadline April

Kelibia International Festival of Amateur Film

Where Kelibia, Tunisia

When One week in early August

Background Composed primarily of 16 mm and Super-8 shorts, this Tunisian festival, dedicated to promoting the careers of directors who have yet to hit the big time, features a good selection of films from countries whose films aren't usually seen stateside: Tunisia, Iraq, Iran, Libya, Algeria, and so forth. At the same time, a decent number of mainstream European and American shorts turn up as well. Filmmakers vie for the grand prize of $1,500 and, best of all, a Golden Falcon.

Films About 70 short films

How to Enter Send VHS dub, entry form, a photo of the shooting, and a photo of the director to:
International Festival of the Nonprofessional Film of Kelibia
B.P. 116-1015
Tunis RP
Tunisia
Telephone/Fax 011.216.1.832.152

Entry Deadline May

Out in Africa Film Festival

Where Cape Town, Durban, Johannesburg, and Pretoria, South Africa

When The month of November

Background I get a kick out of this festival. Maybe it's just because it showed a short film describing a fictional amorous encounter between noted French critic Michel

Foucault and Tennessee Williams titled *You Taste American*. Or maybe it's because it raised money by raffling off a 42-piece cutlery set. That aside, the festival does an excellent job of mixing the mainstream (*Boys Don't Cry*, *Velvet Goldmine*) and irreverent (*Killer Condom*) with the hard-hitting and political and manages to screen some fascinating little-known gems of gay cinema, such as Wolfgang Petersen's *The Consequence* (Petersen, before he became known for *Das Boot*, *In the Line of Fire*, and *Air Force One*, directed this story of an actor who was imprisoned for an illicit sexual encounter). Alongside these finds, there is a strong selection of films from the usual customers: Bruce LaBruce, Gregg Araki, Patricia Rozema, Monika Treut, and so on.

Films About 60 features plus special screenings
Tickets 20 R per individual screening.
How to Enter Send VHS dub and entry form to:
South Africa Gay and Lesbian Film Festival
P.O. Box 15707
Cape Town
8000
South Africa
Telephone 011.27.21.241532
Fax 011.27.21.247377
E-mail info@oia.co.za
Web www.oia.co.za
Entry Deadline Not available

Zimbabwe International Film Festival

Where Harare, Zimbabwe
When Twelve days in mid-September
Background A very interesting, eclectic mix of films that makes the "international" in the fest's title more than merely window-dressing. Films shown include Thom Fitzgerald's *Hanging Garden*, Woody Allen's *Celebrity*, Ana Kokinos's *Head On*, Spike Lee's *He Got Game,* and Nils Malmros's *Barbara*.
Major Award Winners Best Director: Niki Caro, *Memory and Desire*
Entry Information Zimbabwe International Film Festival
P.O. Box A4
Avondale
Harare
Zimbabwe
Telephone 011.263.4.794.355
Fax 011.263.4.707.852
E-mail djawitz@usa.net
Web www.zimbabwe.net/ziff
Entry Deadline July

More African and Middle Eastern Film Festivals

These are not complete listings. For more information on any of these festivals, write or call for details.

Alexandria International Film Festival
9 Oraby Street
Cairo
Egypt
11111
Telephone 011.20.2.574.1112
Fax 011.20.2.576.8727
Annual festival taking place for a week in April.

Ankara Film Festival
Bulten Sk.
Kavaklidere 13
06680 Ankara
Turkey
Telephone 011.90.312.468.7140
Fax 011.90.312.468.7139

Cape Town International Film Festival
University of Cape Town
Private Bag
Rondebosch
7700
South Africa
Telephone 011.27.21.238.257
Fax 011.27.21.242.355
E-mail filmfest@hiddingh.uct.az.za
Annual festival taking place for three weeks in April and May.

Carthage International Film Festival
c/o The JCC Managing Committee
P.O. Box 1029-1045
Tunis RP
Tunisia
Telephone/Fax 011.21.61.260323
Annual festival held for 10 days in mid-October.

Damascus Film Festival
Send VHS dub and entry form to:
National Film Organization
Rawam Takriti
Damascus
Syria

Durban International Film Festival
University of Natal
King George V Avenue
Durban
4001
South Africa
Telephone 011.27.31.8113978
Fax 011.27.31.2617107
Annual festival taking place for one week in January.

Haifa International Film Festival
142 Hanassi Avenue
 34633 Haifa
Israel
Entry Deadline July

Ismailia International Film Festival
Culture Development Fund, Ministry of Culture
Opera House Area
El Gezira
Cairo
Egypt
Telephone 011.20.2.340.7001
Fax 011.20.2.340.6759

Jerusalem Film Festival—Festival of Festivals
P.O. Box 8561
Jerusalem 91083
Israel
Entry Deadline May 15
Annual festival held in July.

Johannesburg Film Festival
Hallmark Towers, 8th Floor
54 Siemert Road
P.O. Box 16427
Doornfontein
2028
South Africa
Telephone 011.27.11.402.5477
Fax 011.27.11.402.6646

Kine International Film Festival
Kine Centre
Box 580
Harare
Zimbabwe
Entry Deadline March 31
Annual festival taking place the first
week of June.

The Mail and Guardian International Film Festival
139 Smit Street
Johannesburg
2001
South Africa
Entry Deadline July 31
Annual festival in September and
October.

Morocco International Festival
Commune Urbaine Moulay Youssef
Poste 228
Casablanca
Morocco
Telephone 011.21.22.22.1216
Fax 011.21.22.29.9474
Entry Deadline Last week of September

Roshd International Educational Film Festival
Semnan Lane
Bahar Avenue
Tehran
Iran

Tehran International Video Exhibition
The Season Group of Companies
27 Magnolia Street
Tehran
15886
Iran
Annual festival held for 10 days in
November.

6 Australian Film Festivals

Going Over the Land Down Under

Auckland International Film Festival

Where Auckland, New Zealand
When Last two weeks of July
Background Although a passel of film festivals are held in New Zealand, this is the largest and most prestigious of them, presenting a host of New Zealand premieres (it won't accept anything that's not) in the noted Civic Theater. The festival has been around in one form or another for the past 50 years, having started life in the Workers' Educational Association building, where films such as *The Cabinet of Dr. Caligari* and *Battleship Potemkin* were screened. Along with its program of premiere features, the festival in recent years has also devoted itself to a number of intriguing series and retrospectives including spotlights on Douglas Sirk, animation, Spanish filmmakers, dance in film, and the earliest works of New Zealand silent filmmakers. Recent screenings included Carlos Saura's excellent *Tango*, *Touch of Evil*, and Bertrand Tavernier's *It All Starts Today*. Silent features (a major component of this festival) have included tributes to Buster Keaton and Aki Kaurismaki's overwrought *Juha*.
Major Award Winners Noncompetitive
Films More than 100 features, although few are accepted that are not attached to distributors, and about 50 shorts
Tickets $9.50
How to Enter Do not send copy of film unless specifically asked to do so. Merely send official entry form to:

New Zealand Film Festival
P.O. Box 9544
Marion Square
Wellington 6001
New Zealand
For short films:

Moving Image Centre
P.O. Box 106 097
Auckland
New Zealand
Telephone 011.64.4.385.0162, 011.64.9.373.2772 (short films)
Fax 011.64.4.801.7304, 011.64.9.373.4830 (short films)
E-mail enzedff@actrix.gen.nz
Web www.enzedff.co.nz
E-mail mic@mic.orh.nz
Entry Deadline April

Australian Documentary Conference

Where Various places in Australia
When November through December
Background Sponsored in part by the Discovery Channel, the documentary confer-
ence is not just a convention for folks involved in the professional documentary
filmmaking business; it also hosts a well-attended festival of documentary films.
Hoop Dreams, for example, received its Australian premiere here. The conference
also sponsors an Australian tour of the festival's highlights hitting theaters in
Sydney (Chauvel Cinemas), Brisbane, Cairns, Adelaide, Perth, and Hobart.
How to Enter For more information contact:
Australia Documentary Conference
The George Cinema Complex
135 Fitzroy Street
St. Kilda
Australia
Telephone 011.61.3.9686.7166
Entry Deadline October

Beatfilm: International Festival of Music on Film

Where Sydney, Australia, and Amsterdam, the Netherlands
When One week in early January in Australia; one week in mid-September in
Amsterdam.
Background Although it takes place in only two places around the globe, it represents
a concept that is worth repeating elsewhere. Devoted solely to music films (music
documentaries, concert movies, musicals, rare videos, and so on), this is a music
nut's dream. Screening at Sydney's Bondi Pavilion and at Westergas Fabriek in
Amsterdam, the festival has featured a number of cool categories of screenings,
including Rock and Roots (*Let the Good Times Roll* and assorted Elvis flicks); Jazz,
Blues, and Soul (*Lady Sings the Blues*); Pop Beginnings (*The Harder They Come*, *Gimme
Shelter*); Great Concerts (*Celebration at Big Sur*, *The Last Waltz*); Sex and Excess (*Rod
Stewart and the Faces*, *Purple Rain*); and of course, Greatest Hits (*This Is Spinal Tap*).
Films About 100 assorted films, documentaries, TV programs, and videos
How to Enter Not applicable
Telephone 011.61.2.9266.7242
Fax 011.61.2.9262.4774

E-mail flickerf@tmx.com.au
Web www.media.com.au/fearless/beatpix.html
Entry Deadline Not applicable

Brisbane International Film Fest

Where Brisbane, Australia
When Eleven days in late July and early August
Background Founded in 1992, the festival, subtitled "Inspiration and Imagination," hosts one of the most intriguing competitions out there: the Fast Film Competition, which offers a prize of $2,000 to the best film that is less than five minutes long and features a set of wings in the opening or closing credits. "Bird, plane, butterfly, any wings will do," the festival organizers tell us. Aside from quick flights of fantasy, the festival also holds retrospectives on great old filmmakers (e.g., Herbert Brenon) and not-so-great contemporary ones (Dennis Hopper) as well as series called "Dazzling Debuts" and "Artificial Nights." The festival also sponsors the Chauvel Award for greatest contribution to Australian feature filmmaking. Winners have included George Miller, Gillian Armstrong, Fred Schepisi, and Paul Cox. Yes, Brisbane has moved light years ahead from the time, more than 150 years ago, when it was founded as a penal colony for some of the more difficult convicts housed in Australia.
How to Enter Send VHS dub and entry form to:
Brisbane International Film Festival
GPO Box 909
Brisbane, QLD 4001
Australia
Telephone 011.61.7.3220.0333
Fax 011.61.7.3220.0400
E-mail brisfilm@thehub.com.au
Web biff.thehub.com.au
Entry Deadline July

Melbourne International Film Festival

Where Melbourne, Australia
When Two weeks in late July and early August
Background This is a pretty extensive festival, screening films in the following categories: Regional Focus (a recent spotlight focused on Hong Kong films), Australian Showcase, Spotlights (e.g., films made in Spain post-Franco), Director Tributes (most recently Greece's Theo Angelopoulos), Retrospectives (Sergio Leone was recently honored), The Bug (multimedia), and All That Jazz (focusing on jazz music in cinema) as well as tributes to studios and exhibitions of multimedia technology. Screenings are held in the 680-seat Capitol Theatre (across the street from Melbourne Town Hall) and the 25-year-old State Film Theatre (Treasury Place, opposite Parliament Station). The 1999 fest featured films from around the world with scenes set at December 31, 1999, as well as a series of "High Voltage" music documentaries and a documentary titled *Mozart: Mad and Marvelous.*

Major Award Winners Grand Prix: *Baka*, by Thierry Knauf
Films About 180 features
Tickets $A6 per individual screening; $A185 silver pass gains admission to all screenings except opening and closing nights
How to Enter Send VHS dub, entry form, and $A20 to:
    Melbourne International Film Festival
    P.O. Box 2206
    Fitzroy Mail Center
    Melbourne, VIC 3065
    Australia
    Telephone 011.61.3.9417.2011
    Fax 011.61.3.9417.3804
    E-mail miff@netspace.net.au
    Web www.melbournefestival.com.au
Entry Deadline April

Melbourne Super-8 Film Festival

Where Melbourne, Australia
When One weekend in late November
Background Also known as Naked 8, the festival is dedicated to keeping alive that wonderful but rapidly disappearing art of Super-8 moviemaking. Screenings have included Reid O'Beirne's *One More Fine Line Facsimile*, Tim Block's *Burger Bastard*, and Steven Ball's *Receiver*. A recent tribute has focused on the work of Pat and Richard Larter. The festival is sponsored by the Melbourne Super-8 Film Group. The group holds monthly screenings of low- and no-budget Super-8 films in Melbourne.
Films About 45
How to Enter Send VHS dub and entry form to:
    Super-8 Film Fest
    P.O. Box 2033
    Fitzroy MDC
    Melbourne, VIC 3065
    Australia
    Telephone 011.61.3.9417.3402
    Fax 011.61.3.9417.3804
    E-mail super8@netspace.net.au
    Web www.cinemedia.net/super8
Entry Deadline October

Noosa International Film Festival

Where East Sydney, Australia
When One week in early September
Background International competitive fest screening features, shorts, and documentaries. Programs include Visions of Asia (avant-garde Asian filmmaking), World Cinema (duh), and Women and Film (double duh). Offers awards in sponsored

categories such as the Sheraton Screenwriting Award and the Polo Ralph Lauren Best Director Award.

How to Enter Send entry form to:
Noosa International Film Festival
218 Crown St., Suite 1
East Sydney, NSW 2010
Australia
Telephone 011.61.2.9360.6384
Fax 011.61.2.9360.7893
E-mail noosafilmfest@ozemail.com.au
Web www.noosafilmfestival.com
Entry Deadline June

Sydney Film Festival

Where Sydney, Australia
When Two weeks in mid-June
Background Founded in 1954, this is the major film festival in Australia, playing host to more than 100,000 every year. Films are screened in the magnificent 1929 State Theatre and in the Pitt Centre Cinema 3. In addition to competitions of features, shorts, and documentaries, the festival offers an excellent series of retrospectives. Recent ones have included a program of Roberto Rossellini's films, a series of popular Indian films, and a tribute to Mike Leigh.
Major Award Winners Best Fiction Films: *My Name is Joe*, by Ken Loach, and *Children of Heaven*, by Majid Majidi; Best Documentaries: *Genghis Blues*, by Roko Belic, and *Punitive Damage*, by Annie Goldson; Best Short Films: *Original Schtick*, by Maciej Wszelaki, and *Pentuphouse,* by Cate Shortland
Films 144 features and 90 shorts
Noteworthy Celebrity Sightings Marcel Ophuls, Kenneth Anger
Tickets $4.50 per individual screening; $170 for a pass to all screenings
How to Enter Send VHS dub, $15 entry fee, and entry form to:
Sydney Film Festival
P.O. Box 950
Glebe, NSW 2037
Australia
Telephone 011.61.2.660.3844
Fax 011.61.2.692.8793
E-mail info@sydfilm-fest.com.au
Web www.sydfilm-fest.com.au
Entry Deadline February

Sydney Mardi Gras Film Festival

Where Sydney, Australia
When Two weeks in mid-February
Background Truly international in its scope, this gay and lesbian film festival presented the Australian premieres of *Trick* and *Beefcake*, while also focusing on such categories as Queer Asian Cinema. The festival screens at the Pitt Centre and the Roxy.

Major Award Winners Steven Cummins Award for Best Film: *Personals*, by Jane Shadbolt and Sonja Vivienne
Films About 75 features
Tickets $A12 per individual screening; $A105 for 10 screenings
How to Enter Send VHS dub and entry fee to:
    Mardi Gras Film Festival
    Queer Screen
    P.O. Box 1081
    Darlinghurst, NSW 2010
    Australia
    Telephone 011.61.2.332.4938
    Fax 011.61.2.331.2988
    E-mail info@queerscreen.com.au
    Web wwwqueerscreen.com.au
Entry Deadline Not available

Tropicana Short Film Festival

Where Darlinghurst, Australia
When One night in late February
Background Founded in 1993 in Darlinghurst's Cafe Tropicana by Sydney actor/director John Polson, the Australian festival screens shorts that are no longer than seven minutes. Films are shown pretty much in the middle of Victoria Street on screens outside cafés and such. About 18,000 attend annually.
Major Award Winners First Prize: *Deadline*; Second Prize: *Rust Bucket*; Third Prize: *Indulgence*; Tropicana Award: *Not on the Road*; Best Actress Award: Tania Lacey; Best Actor Award: Rowan Woods
Films More than 200 shorts
Noteworthy Celebrity Sightings Nicole Kidman, Jane Campion, John Polson, Bryan Brown
Tickets Free
How to Enter Send VHS dub, $A10 entry fee, and entry form to:
    The Tropicana Short Film Festival
    24/2a Bayswater Road
    Kings Cross, NSW 2011
    Australia
    E-mail info@tropfest.com.au
    Web www.tropfest.com.au
Entry Deadline January

Wellington Gay and Lesbian Film Festival

Where Wellington, New Zealand
When Ten days in late May
Background Founded in 1996, this is, if you'll forgive the pun, a pretty straightforward festival: gay and lesbian features, shorts, the occasional experimental work. Films that have premiered here include Bruce LaBruce's *No Skin off My Ass*, Derek Jarman's *Sebastiane*, Kelli Herd's *It's in the Water*, Alessandro de Gaetano's *Butch*

Camp, and Andrea Weiss's *A Bit of Scarlet*. Screenings are held at the Paramount Cinema (Courtenay Place) and the City Cinema (City Gallery in Civic Square).
Films About 50 films and programs of shorts
Tickets $9.50 per individual screening; $8.50 per shorts program
How to Enter Send VHS dub and rudimentary entry form to:
Reel Queer Inc.
P.O. Box 12 201
Wellington
New Zealand
Telephone 011.64.4.388.5211
Fax 011.64.4.474.3127
E-mail richard.king@natlib.govt.nz
Web wwwnz.com/nz/queer/reelqueer/
Entry Deadline January

Western Australian Gay and Lesbian Film Festival

Where Northbridge, Western Australia
When One week in mid-October
Background Staged by Fanny Cruise Productions, the small festival screens the best of Australian gay and lesbian cinema at Cinema Paradiso in Northbridge. The festival also schedules a program of local films (*I'll Say Wot I Like*) and shorts especially targeted to gay men (*Bend Me Over Backwards*) and lesbians (*Tie Me Up and Lick Me*).
Films 10 feature films and 4 programs of short films
How to Enter Send VHS dub and entry form to:
Cinema Parardiso
James Street
Northbridge
Australia, WA
Entry Deadline September

More Australian Film Festivals

These are not complete listings. For more information on any of these festivals, write or call for details.

Brisbane Animation Festival
P.O. Box 1361
Fortitude Valley
Brisbane, QLD 4006
Australia
Telephone 011.61.7.3216.0808
Web www.visualeyes.net.au/qa
Entry Deadline August
Founded by the Queensland Animators Group, the festival, also known as

"Celluloid Briefs," showcases everything from traditional cel and stop-motion animation to computer-generated styles.

Metro Super-8 Fest
242 Canning Highway
East Freemantle
Perth, WA 6158
Australia

Metropolis Super-8 Fest
Super-8 Film Festival
Fish Studios
24 Batman Ave.
West Melbourne, VIC 3003
Australia

Moomba International Amateur Film Festival
P.O. Box 286
Preston, VIC 3072
Australia

Wellington Film Festival
P.O. Box 0544
Wellington 6001
New Zealand
Telephone 011.64.4.385.0162
Fax 011.64.4.801.7304
Entry Deadline May
Held for two weeks in mid-July.

7 South American Film Festivals

A Handful of Fests

Cartagena International Film Festival

Where Cartagena, Colombia
When One week in early March
Background Founded in 1960, the festival is now under the direction of Gabriel García Márquez. The festival has screened in the following categories: Latin American shorts; Iberian-Latin American film; spotlights on French, Hindu, Italian, and Spanish cinema; and Colombian made-for-TV films and advertisements. David Cronenberg's *Crash* had its South American premiere here.
Noteworthy Celebrity Sightings Edward James Olmos, Gabriel García Márquez, Maria Conchita Alonzo
How to Enter Send VHS dub and entry form to:
    Cartagena International Film Festival
    Calle San Juan de Días, Baluarte
    San Francisco Javier
    1834 Cartagena
    Colombia
    South America
    Telephone 011.57.5.660.0966
    Fax 011.57.5.660.0970
    E-mail spyder@escape.com
Entry Deadline Not available

International Festival of New Latin American Cinema

Where Havana, Cuba
When Ten days in early December

Background The largest festival of its kind in Latin America, the festival, founded in 1978, does have Latin film as its focus but also showcases films from other countries, including recent spotlights on Spanish, Italian, Japanese, Danish, and Cambodian cinema. Even U.S. indies are featured. Tributes have been given to Cuban director Tomás Gutiérrez Alea, German director Werner Herzog, and Britain's Ken Loach.

Major Award Winners First Prize for Best Film: *El Callejón de los Milagros*, by Arturo Ripstein; Second Prize: *Bajo la Piel*, by Francisco Lombardi; Third Prize: *Corisco & Dada*, by Rosemberg Cariry

Films About 180 feature films and 200 videos

How to Enter Send VHS dub and entry form to:
International Festival of New Latin American Cinema
Calle 23 No. 1155
Vedado
CP 10600 Havana
Cuba
Telephone 011.53.7.552.841
Fax 011.53.7.334.273
E-mail festival@icaic.inf.cu
Web www.cult.cu/cine

Entry Deadline Late September

It's All True International Documentary Film Festival

Where São Paulo, Brazil

When Ten days in early April

Background Taking its name from the ill-fated Orson Welles documentary, this festival of documentary films, founded in 1986, offers screenings of Brazilian and international films and has also presented a retrospective of the work of Marcel Ophüls.

Major Award Winners Best Film: *We Were Waiting for You*, by Marcelo Masagão; Special Mention: *Divorce, Iranian Style*, by Kim Longinotto, and *Sons of the Soil*, by Elisabeth Lauvrey.

Films About 25 films

How to Enter Send VHS dub and entry form to:
International Documentary Film Festival
Rue Cristiano Viana, 907
São Paulo-SP Brazil
05411-001
Telephone/Fax 011.55.11.852.9601
E-mail itstrue@ibm.net
Web www.kinoforum.org

Entry Deadline January

Mar del Plata International Film Festival

Where Mar del Plata, Argentina

When Ten days in late November

Background The first festival was held here in 1954 during the reign of Juan Perón, and had he known that Alan Parker would make a movie of Evita, he might have had second thoughts about hosting a film fest. Even so, this has been one of the more star-studded festivals in recent memory, surviving changes in the government and the film industry. The ghosts of past visitors such as Errol Flynn, Mary Pickford, Joan Fontaine, and Trevor Howard loom over the festival, which is now organized by the Argentine Cinema Foundation. Held 400 kilometers from Buenos Aires in this beachfront town, the festival offers midnight screenings, Ibero and Latin American features, and unreleased films from great Spanish directors including Carlos Saura. Tributes have included the work of Gabriel Figueroa and María Luisa Bemberg.

Major Award Winners Best Film. *The Dog in the Major*, by Pilar Miró; Best Director: Zhang Yuan, *Dong Gong Xi Gong*; Best Actress: Renee Zellweger, *The Whole Wide World*; Best Actor: Silvio Orlando, *My Generation*

Films 125 features

Noteworthy Celebrity Sightings Jean-Claude Carriere, Milos Forman, Maria Callas (a while ago), Cantinflas (also a while ago), John Mills, Hayley Mills, Andrzej Wajda

Tickets $3 per individual screening

How to Enter For more information contact:
    Internacional de Cine de Mar del Plata
    Argentina Auditorium
    Boulevard Maritimo 2280
    7600 Mar del Plata
    Buenos Aires
    Argentina
    Telephone 011.54.223.493.6001
    Fax 011.54.1.383.9091
    E-mail info@incaa.com
    Web www.incaa.gov.ar

Entry Deadline Not available

Rio de Janeiro International Short Film Festival

Where Rio de Janeiro, Brazil

When Ten days in late November

Background Defining itself as the most important short-film program in Rio, this festival showcases Brazilian cinema but also has a fair number of spotlights on other countries as well. Recent festivals have featured Japanese, Russian, and Israeli shorts and, thankfully for the filmmaker on the cheap, a focus on No Budget films. The festival has also featured what it refers to as "Great Directors in Small Doses," which has treated audiences to rarely seen shorts by the likes of Ettore Scola, Martin Scorsese, and Pier Paolo Pasolini.

Films 30 films in the Brazilian program; 100 in national panorama

How to Enter Send entry form and video dub to:
    Mostra Curta Cinema
    Praia de Botafogo, 210-Sala 1103
    Rio de Janeiro-RJ Brazil
    22250-040

E-mail arempre@ax.apc.org
Web www.curtaciinemasffest.com
Entry Deadline Late October

São Paulo International Film Festival

Where São Paulo, Brazil
When Last two weeks of October
Background Founded by the Associação Brasileira Mostra de Cinema in 1977, the Brazilian film festival presents both a new filmmakers (those who have made no more than three) competition and an international perspective (a showcase of international films, as well as a recent tribute to the late Akira Kurosawa).
Major Award Winners Best Film: *Happiness*, by Todd Solondz; Audience Award for Best Film: *Train of Life*, by Radu Mihaileanu. Award winners take home not only the Bandeira Paulista Trophy, but also a flag of Sao Paulo stylized by artist Tomie Ohtake.
Noteworthy Celebrity Sightings Jim Sheridan, Peter Gothar, and Jeffrey Wright
How to Enter Send video copy of film and entry form to:
ABMIC-Mostra Internaçional de Cinema
Alameda Lorena 937-cj. 303
Sao Paolo SP Brazil
01424-001
Telephone 011.55.11.883.5137
Fax 011.55.11.853.7936
E-mail info@mostra.org
Web www.mostra.org
Entry Deadline September

São Paulo International Short Film Festival

Where São Paulo, Brazil
When Ten days in late August
Background Probably the largest festival of short films in South America, the SPISFF screens at four major cinemas and has a quirky sense of humor in coming up with categories. The festival screens shorts in the following categories: Brazilian Panorama, Little Perversions and Sex, Football, and Rock 'n' Roll.
Films About 270 films from 52 countries
How to Enter Send VHS dub and entry form to:
SPISFF
Simão Alvarez 784/2
São Paulo-SP Brazil
05417-020
Telephone/Fax 011.55.11.852.9601
E-mail info@kinoforum.org
Web www.kinoforum.org
Entry Deadline May

More South American Film Festivals

These are not complete listings. For more information on any of these festivals, write or call for details.

Divercine Children's International Film Festival
Lorenzo Carnelli 1311
11200 Montevideo
Uruguay
Telephone 011.598.2.408.24.60
Fax 011.598.2.409.45.72
E-mail cinemuy@chasque.apc.org
Web www.cinemateca.org.uy
Entry Deadline May
Young adult and children's festival in mid-July.

Ecuador Indigenous Film Festival
CONAIE
Los Granados 2553 y 6 de Dicembre
Casilla 17-17-1235
Quito
Ecuador
Telephone 011.593.2.248.930
Fax 011.593.2.442.271
E-mail ccc@conaie.ec
Entry Deadline October
The only festival in Ecuador, the EIFF screens at 16 separate cinemas throughout Ecuador. Held for a week in mid-December.

Gramado Film Festival
Avenue das Hortensias 2029
Gramado-RS Brazil
95670-000
Telephone/Fax 011.55.54.286.2335
E-mail festival@pro.via-rs.com.br
Annual festival held for a week in mid-August.

International Short Film Festival
Internacional de Cortometrajes de Santiago
Avenida Vicua Mackenna 836 of. 43
Santiago
Chile
Telephone 011.56.2.665.2732
Fax 011.56.2.635.5737

E-mail santiago@fics.cl
Web www.fics.cl.espanol.htm
Entry Deadline July
This annual festival takes place in Santiago, Chile, during the last week of August.

International Women's Film Festival
Equis-Intec
Ap. Postal 342-9
Zona 2
Santo Domingo
Dominican Republic

Jornada Internacional de Cinema da Bahia
Prédio da Biblioteca Central
Rue Barão de Geremoabo s/n
Campus de Ondina
Salvador-BA Brazil
40170-290
Telephone/Fax 011.55.71.235.4392
Entry Deadline August
Annual festival and marketplace held in Brazil for a week in mid-September.

Montevideo Film Festival
Cinemateca Uruguaya
Lorenco Carnelli 1311
11200 Montevideo
Uruguay
Annual festival held for a week in March.

One-Minute Kids World Festival
P.O. Box 11022
São Paulo- SP Brazil
05422-970
Telephone/Fax 011.55.11.30.612
Web www.2.uol.com.br/1minuto

Rio Cine International Festiva
Rue da Laranjeiras 219
Rio de Janeiro-RJ Brazil
22240-001
Telephone 011.55.21.553.2118
Fax 011.55.21.553.0130

Rio de Janeiro Film Festival
Rue Voluntarios de Patria 97
Botafogo-RJ Brazil
22270-000
Telephone 011.55.21.286.8505
Fax 011.55.21.286.4029
Web www.estacao.com.br

Santafé de Bogotá Festival
Calle 26 No. 4-92
Santafé de Bogotá
Colombia
Telephone 011.57.1.282.5196
Fax 011.57.1.342.2872

Uruguay International Children's Film Festival
Lorenzo Carnelli 1311
11200 Montevideo
Uruguay
Entry Deadline May
Two weeks in July.

Videobrasil International Video Festival
Rue Conego Eugenio Leite 920
São Paulo-SP
Brazil 05414-001
Entry Deadline September
Biennially held in November and December.

8 A Guide to the Best Places to See Movies in More than 100 Cities

When a Festival Isn't in Town

These are listed alphabetically by city.

Akron, Ohio

Civic Theatre
182 S. Main Street
Local Telephone 330.535.3179

Albany, New York

Spectrum 7 Theaters
290 Delaware Avenue
Local Telephone 518.449.8995
Decent program of art house and off-beat features (*Bad Lieutenant*, *Brassed Off*, *Ulee's Gold*).

Albuquerque, New Mexico

Guild Cinema
3405 Central N.E.
Local Telephone 505.255.1848
Art house screening American indies and mainstream foreign fare (*When the Cat's Away*, *My Favorite Season*).

Lobo Theater
3301 Coors N.E.
Local Telephone 505.265.4759
Art house cinema featuring first-runs on the order of *Kolya* and *Shine* and good midnight fare such as Kubrick's *The Shining*.

Amsterdam, Netherlands

Tuschinski Cinema
Reguliersbreestrat 26
Local Telephone 011.31.20.626.2633
Mainstream art house fare screened in elegant art deco auditorium.

Ann Arbor, Michigan

Michigan Theater
603 E. Liberty
Local Telephone 313.997.9324

Arcata, California

Minor Theatre
1036 G Street
Local Telephone 707.822.3456

Athens, Greece

Radio City-Assos Odeon
Odos Patission 240
Local Telephone 862.4055
Art house cinema closed during the summer, when the open-air cinema reigns supreme in the Grecian capital.

Atlanta, Georgia

High Museum of Art
1280 Peachtree Street
Local Telephone 404.733.4570

Good summer film series ("It Takes a Thief," featuring such flicks as *The Usual Suspects*).

Lefont Plaza Theatres
1049 Ponce de Leon Avenue
Local Telephone 404.873.1939
Comfortable first-run art house and revival cinema (*Kolya*, *Pink Flamingos*) featuring $5 screenings.

Toco Hills Theatre
3003 N. Druid Hills
Local Telephone 404.325.7090
Art house cinema featuring first-runs (*When the Cat's Away*).

Auckland, New Zealand

Hollywood Cinema
St. George's Road 20
Local Telephone 828.8393
Silent film series (Buster Keaton's *The General* and Lon Chaney in *The Phantom of the Opera*).

Austin, Texas

Texas Union Theater
UT-Austin, Texas Union Building
Local Telephone 512.471.3434
Excellent university film series mixing first-run art house flicks (*Irma Vep*) and classics (*Badlands*, *Charlotte's Web*).

Village Cinema Art
2700 Anderson
Local Telephone 512.416.5700, ext.3815
Art house cinema featuring first-runs (*Dream with the Dishes* and *Shall We Dance*).

Baltimore, Maryland

Mansion Theater
4201 York Road
Local Telephone 301.435.3604
Everything from Super- and Regular 8 to 16 mm, videos, and filmstrips, housed in a rehabbed funeral home.

Orpheum Cinema
1724 Thames Street
Local Telephone 301.732.4614
$4.50 double features with excellent revivals featuring such films as *Detour*, *Out of the Past*, *All about Eve*, and *Clash by Night*.

Barcelona, Spain

Filmoteca de la Generalitat de Catalunya
Avda. de Sarria, 33
Local Telephone 011.343.436.5004
Art house featuring often bizarre double features.

Berlin, Germany

Berliner Kinomuseum
Grossbeerenstrasse 57
Located in Kreuzberg, a bizarre little 25-seat house featuring occasionally lousy prints of excellent historical items such as *The Golem*, *The Gold Rush*, and *Die Verlorene Strasse*.

Filmmuseum Potsdam
Schlossstrassse 1
Local Telephone 011.49.30.31.23.675
Classic German films and Hollywood classics.

Zeughaus Kino
Deutsches Historisches Museum
Unter den Linden 2
Local Telephone 011.49.30.215.020
An excellent selection of classic films (Billy Wilder's *One, Two, Three*; Hitchcock's *The Lady Vanishes*) that almost makes you forget the dearth of popcorn.

Boise, Idaho

The Flicks
646 Fulton Street
Local Telephone 208.342.4222
Screens typical Miramax-style fare in the tradition of *Il Postino* and *The Picture Bride*. Also the occasional local-interest production, such as *Not This Part of the World*, a production featuring Boise talent and directed by a faculty member at Boise State University.

Boston, Massachusetts

Coolidge Corner
290 Harvard Street (Brookline)

Local Telephone 617.734.2501
Mostly art house fare, but many intriguing surprises show up on off-nights (Alloy Orchestra's original, brilliant score to Fritz Lang's *Metropolis*; *The Four Corners of Nowhere*; *The Isle of Wight* concert film; and more).

Museum of Fine Arts
465 Huntington Avenue
Local Telephone 617.267.9300, ext. 300
Good museum film series featuring classic and new features (a festival of new Chinese cinema).

Boulder, Colorado

Boulder Almost-Free Outdoor Cinema
Boulder Museum of Contemporary Art
1745 14th Street
Local Telephone 443.2122
An open-air cinema featuring screenings of such films as *Little Shop of Horrors* for a suggested donation of $5.

Chatauqua Silent Film Series
9th and Baseline
Local Telephone 303.545.6924
Screenings of classic silents, such as *The Phantom of the Opera* and *Faust* starring Lon Chaney, in an 1898 auditorium.

Colorado University International Film Series, University Film Society
Muenzinger Auditorium on Boulder campus
Local Telephone 303.492.1351

Bratislava, Slovakia

Charlie Centrum
Spitalska 4
Four-screen art house cinema named after Charlie Chaplin.

Film Club Nostalgia
Starohorska 2
Good variety of off-the-beaten-path art house screenings.

Brussels, Belgium

Actors' Studio
Petite Rue des Bouchers 16

Local Telephone 512.1696
Good selection of art house flicks in fairly unimpressive surroundings, yet near an all-important Internet café.

Arenberg Galeries
Galerie de la Reine 26
Local Telephone 512.1696
Very comfy seats in high-class (and usually empty) theater near the Grand Place. Recent screening: Moretti's *Aprile*.

Movy Club
Rue des Moines 21
Local Telephone 011.32.2.537.6954
Classic American films screened in a vintage music hall.

Musée du Cinema
Palais des Beaux Arts
Local Telephone 011.32.2.507.8370
Features an excellent selection of revivals, including classic German and American silent films. Recent showings featured an excellent series on the "double" in film, including Jacques Rivette's *Noirot*.

Passage 44
Boulevard du Jardin Botanique 44
Local Telephone 217.6054
Art house and revival cinema featuring animated, science fiction, and cult classics (*Last Tango in Paris*).

Budapest, Hungary

Blue Box
Kinizsi utca 28.
Local Telephone 218.0983
Wide array of screenings held in a former hot nightspot.

Metro
Terez korut 62.
Local Telephone 353.4266
Art films, popular Hungarian flicks in vintage theater.

Orokmozgo Filmmuzeum
Erzsebet korut 39.
Local Telephone 342.2167
Incredibly varied selection of art house classics and offbeat films.

Cambridge, Massachusetts

Brattle Theater
40 Brattle Street
Local Telephone 617.876.6837
Arguably the top repertory cinema in the country featuring an excellent array of offbeat, exclusive first-runs (*Irma Vep*) and great double bills of classics (*La Dolce Vita* and *The Big Picture*, old Tarzan flicks, Antonioni films).

Harvard Film Archive
Carpenter Center for the Visual Arts
24 Quincy Street
Local Telephone 495.4700
One of the best university film series with more choices than the local art house video store (Dreyer's *Ordet*, *Blow-up*, films by Murnau, Eisenstein, and more).

Kendall Square Cinema
1 Kendall Square
Local Telephone 617.494.9800
One of the better art house malls in the country, screening Miramax fare in comfortable surroundings (*Brassed Off*, *The Van*, *The Designated Mourner*).

Canterbury, England

Canterbury Arts Center
Worcester Street and Rolleston Avenue
Local Telephone 011.44.1223.578.937
Classic cinema selected by the Canterbury Film Society.

Cape Town, South Africa

Labia Theater
69 Orange Street
Yet another theater claiming to be the world's oldest independent repertory art house. Two theaters here, one seating about 250, the other about 70. A predictable but respectable series of screenings (*Bad Lieutenant*, *Shine*).

Carmel, California

Crossroads Cinemas
18 Carmel Center
Local Telephone 408.624.8682
Excellent series of $3 matinees of classic films.

Chapel Hill, North Carolina

Carolina Theater
108 E. Columbia Street
Local Telephone 919.935.8684
Decent series of art house double bills (*Swingers*, *Secrets and Lies*).

Chelsea Theater
1129 Weaver Dairy
Local Telephone 919.968.3005
Standard art house cinema with all of the expected offerings from major "independents" (*Looking for Richard*, *Big Night*).

Chicago, Illinois

Chicago Filmmakers
1543 W. Division
Local Telephone 773.384.5533
Imaginatively programmed series of experimental and underground 16 mm and 8 mm work.

Documentary Film Group
Ida Noyes Hall
University of Chicago
1212 E. 59th Street
Local Telephone 773.702.8575
One of the best university film series nationwide (*Jeanne Dielman* and *La Chinoise*).

Facets Multimedia
1517 W. Fullerton
Local Telephone 773.281.4114
A questionable sound system aside, this is the most inventively programmed of the local cinemas, featuring revivals (*Mickey One*), tributes (Francesco Rosi and Robert Bresson), foreign films that are difficult to see anywhere else (obscure works of Maurizio Nichetti), and art house flicks that can't find audiences elsewhere (*The Darien Gap* and *Sudden Manhattan*).

Film Center of the Art Institute
Columbus and Jackson
Local Telephone 312.443.3733
Very well-programmed selection of revivals (French New Wave features),

art house flicks (*Who Shot Pasolini*, *Irma Vep*), retrospectives (the works of Peter Lorre and Alan Bennett), and premieres (*Viridian*, *The Blank Page*, and *Waiting for the Man*).

Fine Arts
418 S. Michigan Avenue
Local Telephone 312.939.3700
Mainstream Miramax and major distributors' art house flicks, many of which are in the Merchant Ivory mold. Good flicks (*The Horseman on the Roof*, *Traveler*), mediocre popcorn.

Music Box Theater
3733 N. Southport
Local Telephone 773.871.6604
Excellent art house fare in one beautiful restored cinema and one newly built garage of a movie theater. Great foreign flicks (*Gabbeh*, *La Promesse*, *Haut Bas Fragile*) and weekend 11:30 A.M. series (*The Fallen Idol*, *The Blue Angel*, *The Seventh Seal*).

Patio Theater
6008 W. Irving Park
Local Telephone 773.545. 2006
You could keep most of the dreck that screens here (*Space Jam*, *Mission Impossible*, *Con-Air*), but it's hard to argue with the beautiful restored theater or the price—all screenings $2.

Cincinnati, Ohio

Mariemont Theater
6905 Wooster Pike
Local Telephone 513.272.2002
Decent program of American independents (*Traveler*) and revivals (*The Garden of the Finzi-Continis*).

The Movies Repertory
719 Rave Street
Local Telephone 513.381.3456
First-run art house cinema (*Gray's Anatomy*, *The Quiet Room*).

Cleveland, Ohio

Cedar Lee Theater
Cedar and Lee Streets

Local Telephone 216.321.8232
Art house cinema featuring first-runs in the Miramax, Sony Classics tradition (*Love Serenade*, *Shall We Dance*, *Ulee's Gold*).

Columbus, Ohio

Drexel Theater
2254 E. Main Street
Local Telephone 231.9518
Best aspect of this theater is its annual 24-hour science-fiction movie marathon.

Wexner Center
Ohio State University
1871 N. High Street
Local Telephone 292.2354
Great program of revivals (*The Night of the Hunter*) and art house flicks (*From the Journals of Jean Seberg*).

Corvallis, Oregon

Avalon Cinema
160 N.W. Jackson
Local Telephone 541.752.4161
Sixty-nine-seat cinema founded in 1997 and dedicated to the goal of "exploiting art films for money." Features excellent out-of-the-mainstream art flicks (*Forever Mozart*, *Death and the Compass*) and amusing double bills (*Mrs. Brown* and *Mr. Universe*).

Costa Mesa, California

Edwards South Coast Village
1561 W. Sunflower (across the street from South Coast Plaza)
Local Telephone 714.540.0594
Comfortable art house cinema featuring excellent first-runs such as the Iranian feature *Gabbeh*.

Dayton, Ohio

Little Art Theater
Route 68, Yellow Springs, Ohio
Local Telephone 937.767.7671
Web www.littleheart.com

New Neon Movies
130 E. Fifth Street
Local Telephone 937.222.SHOW

Features 1:00 P.M. weekend screenings of classics (*How the West Was Won*).

Denver, Colorado
Mayan Theatre
110 Broadway
Local Telephone 303.744.6883

Detroit, Michigan
Landmark Main Art Theatre
118 Main Street
Local Telephone 248.542.0180
Decent art house featuring Sony Classics, Miramax, and the like (*Love, Valour, Compassion!*, *Ulee's Gold*).

Dresden, Germany
Hauptbahnhof
Wiener Platz
Local Telephone 011.49.351.471.0532
Attached to a 100-year-old railroad station, this art house shows cult and contemporary European and American features in their original language.

Dublin, Ireland
Irish Film Centre
6 Eustace Centre
Local Telephone 011.353.1.679.4377
Theater plus film archive, library, and film-related bookshop. Features frequent screenings of *Flashback*, a documentary about the history of Irish cinema.

Edinburgh, Scotland
Filmhouse
Lothian Road
Local Telephone 011.44.31.228.2688
Excellent art house fare (Kieslowski's *Trois Couleurs* trilogy) and revivals (*Mamma Roma*, *The Spiral Staircase*).

Edmonton, Alberta, Canada
The Princess Theatre
10037 82nd Avenue
Local Telephone 403.439.6600
Art films (*Shine*) shown in a restored 1915 cinema.

Eugene, Oregon
Bijou Art Cinemas
492 E. 13th Street
Local Telephone 541.686.2458

Freiburg, Germany
Kommunales Kino
Urachstrasse 40
Excellent series of contemporary features, revivals, and retrospectives (tributes to Emma Thompson, and the German silents of Fritz Lang).

Frankfurt, Germany
Filmtheater Valentin
Windthorstr. 84
Local Telephone 011.49.69.308.6925
Excellent art house and revival cinema (Japan animation, *The Flower of My Secret*, *Harold and Maude*, *Killing Zoe*, *Mrs. Dalloway*).

Franklin, Tennessee
Franklin Cinema
419 Main Street
Local Telephone 615.790.7122

Glasgow, Scotland
Glasgow Theatre
Rose Street
Local Telephone 011.44.41.332.8128
Excellent revival series featuring grand cineasts such as Hitchcock and Woody Allen.

Guttenberg, New Jersey
Galaxy Theatre
7000 Boulevard East
Local Telephone 201.854.6540
Cinema offering $4 screenings hosts the Black Maria Fest and features a silent-film series with live organ music.

Hartford, Connecticut
Cinestudio
Campus of Trinity College
Local Telephone 860.297.CINE
An excellent re-creation of a 1930s movie theater. Features mainstream art house flicks and revivals (*2001: A Space Odyssey*, *M*, *La Promesse*).

Helsinki, Finland
Illusion Cinema
Mannerheiminitie 5
Local Telephone 011.348.0.131.1925
Mainstream art house cinema (*Gabbeh*).

Honolulu, Hawaii

Academy Theatre
9000 S. Beretania Street
Local Telephone 808.532.8768
Cheap ($4) screenings of art house fare
(*Celestial Clockwork*).

LCC Cinematheque
Leeward Community College
Room BE-103
Local Telephone 254.5328
A surprisingly good art film series at
Leeward Community College
(*Combination Platter*, *Moonlighting*).

Movie Museum
3566 Harding Avenue
Local Telephone 808.735.8771
Excellent series of revivals (*Long Day's
Journey into Night*, *Great Expectations*) in
comfortable intimate cinema with vinyl
reclining chairs.

Houston, Texas

Greenaway 3
5 Greenaway Plaza
Local Telephone 713.626.0402
Art house cinema featuring first-runs
(*Mrs. Brown*, *When the Cat's Away*).

Houston Museum of Fine Arts
1001 Bissonet
Local Telephone 713.639.7300
A good program of art films (festival of
Kieslowski films).

River Oaks 3
2009 W. Gray Street
Local Telephone 713.524.2175
Art house cinema featuring exclusive
screenings of first-runs (*Shall We Dance*,
Ponette, *Heavy*, *Celestial Clockwork*).

Innsbruck, Austria

Open Air Kino in Zeughaus
Museumstrasse 31
Outdoor screenings in a beautiful setting
between two beautiful arcaded buildings
where bleachers are set up. Screenings
range from classics (*To Have and Have
Not*, *The Last Metro*) to goofy modern
stuff (*Wallace and Gromit*, *Fargo*).

Ithaca, New York

Cinemapolis
Ithaca Commons
Local Telephone 607.277.6115
Not particularly scenic mall-ish theater
with decent mainstream art house flicks
(*Brassed Off*, *The Pillow Book*, *Ulee's
Gold*).

Fall Creek Pictures
1201 N. Tioga St.
Local Telephone 607.272.1256
Very cool neighborhoodsy theater. A
throwback to the days of *The Last
Picture Show*.

Jersey, Channel Islands

Jersey Arts Centre
Local Telephone 011.44.1534.855.546
One of the best possible places to find
oneself if stranded on the Channel
Islands (I don't envy you). Great retro-
spectives and revivals (*Bonnie and Clyde*,
Kagemusha, *The Lady Vanishes*).

Jerusalem, Israel

Cinematheque
Local Telephone 011.972.2.6274.131
Politically controversial cinema featur-
ing first-run art films and revivals (*My
Dinner with Andre*, *Breaking the Waves*).

Kansas City, Missouri

Fine Arts Theatre
5609 Jackson Drive
Local Telephone 816.262.4446
Art house screening facility (*A Month
by the Lake*).

Larkspur, California

The Lark
549 Magnolia
Local Telephone 415.924.3311
Run by the film institute of Northern
California featuring revivals (*Contempt*)
and first-runs (*Ponette*, *Female
Perversions*, and *Cats Don't Dance*).

London, England

Electric Cinema
191 Portobello Road

Local Telephone 011.44.71.792.2020
Oldest running and first black-owned cinema in London.

Everyman Cinema
Holly Bush Vale, Hampstead
Local Telephone 011.44.71.435.1525
Calling itself the oldest repertory cinema in the world, the Everyman features amazing revivals and frequent triple bills featuring the works of great directors (David Lynch, Wim Wenders, and Jean Renoir).

National Film Theatre
South Bank
Local Telephone 928.3232

Los Angeles, California
Laemmle's Sunset 5
8000 Sunset Boulevard (West Hollywood)
Local Telephone 310.848.3500
Excellent series of offbeat and classic midnight movies (*Heidi Fleiss: Hollywood Madam* and *Taxi Driver*).

Los Gatos Cinema
41 N. Santa Cruz Avenue
Local Telephone 213.395.0203

New Beverly Cinema
7165 W. Beverly Boulevard
Local Telephone 938.4038
Bills itself as Los Angeles's only independent repertory theater, featuring excellent slate of double bills (*Five Easy Pieces* and *The Last Picture Show*).

Silent Movie
611 N. Fairfax
Local Telephone 213.653.2389
Silent movie series accompanied by live organ (Harold Lloyd's *Safety Last*, *The Volga Boatmen*).

USC Taper 202
3501 Trousdale Parkway
Local Telephone 213.740.2666
Excellent university film series, which features classics to inspire students (Akira Kurosawa's *Dreams*, *Murder My Sweet*). Often great directors turn up to discuss their work.

Louisville, Kentucky
Baxter Avenue Filmworks
Mid City Mall and Baxter
Local Telephone 502.459.2288
Cheap matinees, new art house fare, and revivals ($1.50-$5), including *Ponette*, *Ulee's Gold*, and *Lawrence of Arabia*.

Vogue Theater
3727 Lexington Road
Local Telephone 502.893.3646
Art house cinema (*The Designated Mourner*, *Temptress Moon*).

Luxembourg City, Luxembourg
Cine Utopia
Avenue de la Faiencerie 16
Local Telephone 011.352.472.109
Mainstream art house fare.

Luzern, Switzerland
Atelier Kino
Theater Street 5
Local Telephone 011.41.41.210.1230
Excellent series of art house premieres and revivals (Woody Allen film festival).

Madison, Wisconsin
Majestic Theater
115 King Street
Local Telephone 608.225.6698
Aside from art house flicks (*Il Postino*), also offers the occasional evening of classic silent movies with live accompaniment (Hitchcock's *Blackmail*).

Madrid, Spain
Alphaville
Martín de los Heros, 14
Local Telephone 011.34.1.559.3686
Art house cinema named after the Godard film, not the 1980s band that sang "Big in Japan."

Cine Dore
Santa Isabel, 3
Local Telephone 011.34.1.369.1125
Cinema complex featuring two art house cinemas, a bar, restaurant, and book shop.

Marseille, France

Le Cesar
4, Pl. Castellane
Local Telephone 011.33.1491.37.1280
Decent art house showing flicks such as
A Taste of Cherry and *Ernesto Guevara:
El Che.*

Melbourne, Australia

Village Rivoli
200 Camberwell Road, E. Hawthorn
Local Telephone 011.61.3.9982.1221
Mainstream art house fare (*For
Roseanna, Sling Blade*).

Miami, Florida

Alcazar Cinematheque
235 Alcazar Avenue
Local Telephone 305.446.7144
Art house cinema that has featured
exclusive screenings of *Temptress Moon*
and *A Chef in Love.*

Alliance Cinema
927 Lincoln Road
Local Telephone 305.531.8504
Art house cinema with intriguing
revivals and exclusive screenings that
have included *Gay Cuba* and Buñuel's
Los Olvidades.

Astor Art Cinema
4120 Laguna Street
Local Telephone 305.443.6777
Art house fare with lesser known newer
films that have included *The Slave* and
Guantanamera.

Milwaukee, Wisconsin

Times Cinema
5906 W. Vliet
Local Telephone 414.453.2436
Revivals and midnight shows (*I Walked
with a Zombie* and *Repo Man*).

Minneapolis/St. Paul, Minnesota

Oak Street Cinemas
309 S.E. Oak Street
Local Telephone 612.331.3134
Revival house screening excellent off-
beat classics (*Nashville, The Long Voyage
Home*) with first-run art house fare.

Red Eye Theater
15 W. 14th Street
Local Telephone 612.870.0309
Very cool series of specialty screenings
and revivals. One recent event featured
a new live musical accompaniment by a
member of the Afghan Whigs played to
a D. W. Griffith classic.

Riverview Theater
38th Street and 42nd Avenue
Local Telephone 612.729.7369
Decent series of midnight screenings
based on a particular theme (Hong
Kong cinema).

St. Paul Student Center
2017 Buford Street
Local Telephone 625.9794
Humble but well-programmed university film series featuring the usual colle-
giate classics (*The Seven Samurai*).

University Film Society
17th and University Avenue
Local Telephone 612.627.4430
Another university film series featuring
first-run art house flicks (*The Garden*
and *Ponette*).

Montreal, Quebec, Canada

Bar Camera
2071 St. Catherine W.
Local Telephone 514.933.0169
Excellent showcase for new indie films
in jazz surroundings.

Café Cine-Lumière
5163 Boul St. Laurent
Local Telephone 514.495.1796
The only place I know where you can
watch classic 1930s and 1940s films,
listen through infrared headphones,
and stay until 2 A.M. sipping an espres-
so or dining on a plate of moules.

Cinéma du Parc
3575 Park Avenue
Local Telephone 514.287.7272
Excellent revival series (*The Garden of
the Finzi Continis, The Graduate,
Midnight Cowboy*).

Cinémathèque Québecoise
335 Maisonneuve Boulevard E.
Local Telephone 514.842. 9678
Excellent revival series featuring films
on the order of *Bringing Up Baby*, *Funny
Face*, *The Graduate*, *Midnight Cowboy*,
and *Le Jour Se Leve*. Sometimes shows
five features in a day.

Moscow, Russia
Rossiya Movie Theater
Pushkinskaya Place
Located on the grounds of a former
monastery; shows a bizarre but intriguing selection of films dubbed by a
solemn male voice into Russian. Films
have included Billy Wilder's *The
Apartment*.

Munich, Germany
Filmmuseum
St. Jakobsplatz 1
Local Telephone 011.49.89.233.22348
Very good series of revivals (*Night and
Fog*) and contemporary art house flicks
(*Haut Bas Fragile*) in 165-seat house.

Kunstpark Ost Open Air
Grafingerstr. 6
Local Telephone 011.49.89.34.0500
Outdoor cinema featuring cult favorites
and classics (*Ben Hur*).

Neues Arena
Hansa-Sachs Str. 7
Local Telephone 011.49.89.260.3265
Mainstream art house and cult films
(*The Lovers of Pont-Neuf*).

Nashville, Tennessee
Belcourt Twin
2102 Belcourt Avenue
Local Telephone 615.333.FILM, ext. 765
First-run cinema featuring mainstream
art house flicks (*Shall We Dance*, *Ulee's
Gold*, *Mrs. Brown*).

New Orleans, Louisiana
Jane Pickens
48 Touro Street
Local Telephone 504.846.5252
First-run cinema featuring art house
flicks (*Female Perversions*, *Waiting for
Guffman*).

Movie Pitchers
3941 Bienville Street
Local Telephone 504.488.8881
Good program of offbeat art house
flicks (*Grosse Fatigue*, *The Last Good
Time*).

New York, New York
Angelika Film Center
Houston and Mercer streets
Local Telephone 212.995.2000
One of the best mall-style screening
facilities for Miramax-style mainstream
"indies." Home of the Independent
Feature Film Market.

Film Forum
Houston west of Sixth Avenue
Local Telephone 212.727.8110
One of the best series of revivals
(*Contempt*), new films (Caribbean film
fest), and great double bills (*The Line-
Up* and *The Riot in Cell Block 11*).

Lincoln Plaza Cinemas
63rd and Broadway
Local Telephone 212.752.2280
Good concessions (try the sandwiches)
and mainstream art house flicks (*The
Flower of My Secret*).

Walter Reade Theater
165 W. 65th Street
Local Telephone 212.857.5600
Features very intriguing movie series,
including Cinerock collection of great
rock 'n' roll flicks.

Oakland, California
Paramount Theatre
2625 Broadway
Local Telephone 465.5400

Parkway Theater
1834 Park
Local Telephone 510.814.2400
Can't beat the price here ($3 per screen-
ing), and the selection of offbeat cult
flicks ain't bad either (*The Celluloid
Closet*, *Sid and Nancy*, *Robocop*).

Old-time cinema featuring classic films, cartoons, news reels, and Wurlitzer organ accompaniment.

Oklahoma City, Oklahoma

Burg Auditorium
2501 N. Blackwelder
Local Telephone 405.946.4891
Pretty good university screening center at Oklahoma City University, of all places (*And the Earth Did Not Swallow Him*, *Gallipoli*).

Oklahoma Historical Society
2100 Lincoln Boulevard
Local Telephone 405.522.5244
Free screenings of oldies at the Wiley Post Historical Building (*Empire of the Rising Sun* and *Target: Pearl Harbor*).

Orlando, Florida

Enzian Theater
1300 S. Orlando
Local Telephone 407.644.4662
Cool old movie house.

Palo Alto, California

Stanford Theatre
221 University Avenue
Local Telephone 415.324.3700
This is a 1925 theater owned by Stanford Theatre Foundation featuring screenings of great classics (*Lives of a Bengal Lancer*, *Gunga Din*, and *Beau Geste*).

Paris, France

Accatone
20, rue Cujas
Local Telephone 011.33.1.46.33.8686
Absolutely amazing selection of art house flicks and retrospectives (tributes to Alain Resnais, Robert Bresson, Jean-Luc Godard, and more).

Action Écoles
23, rue des Écoles
Local Telephone 011.33.1.43.25.7207
Mainstream art house fare and excellent tributes (tribute to Humphrey Bogart featuring *Key Largo*, *Dark Passage*, and *The Barefoot Contessa*).

Le Champo
51, rue des Écoles
Local Telephone 011.33.1.43.54.51.60
Excellent late-night concert flicks (*Janis*, *The Harder They Come*, and *Monterey Pop*) and tributes (Woody Allen, David Lynch, and Katherine Hepburn).

Le Cinéma des Cinéastes
7, av. de Clichy
Local Telephone 5342.4020
Excellent presentations of cinema from around the world.

Denfert
24, Place Denfert Rochereau
Local Telephone 011.33.1.43.21.4101
Very elaborate screening series from mainstream art house movies (*Trainspotting*, *Nennette et Boni*), to classics (*La Dolce Vita*), to tributes (the work of Jacques Demy).

Images d'Ailleurs
21, rue de la Ciel
Local Telephone 011.33.1.45.87.1809
Excellent selection of mainstream art house flicks (*For Ever Mozart*, *Land and Freedom*, *La Promesse*).

Quartier Latin
9, rue Champollion
Excellent first-run art house flicks (*The Pillow Book*) and retrospectives (Robert Bresson, Krzysztof Kieslowski).

Philadelphia, Pennsylvania

Film Forum
509 S. Broad Street
Local Telephone 215.732.7704
Excellent program of revivals (*Rocking House Winner*).

International House
3701 Chestnut
Local Telephone 215.895.6542
Web www.libertynet.org/~ihouse
Excellent collection of offbeat features and shorts programs (*Mondo Plympton*, *Children of Lumiere*).

Penn Film Society
Third and Spruce streets
Local Telephone 215.898.5000

Good university film series featuring revivals and art house flicks (*Orlando*) in Penn's Irving Auditorium.

Ritz Bourse
4th above Chestnut
Local Telephone 215.925.7900
First-run art house cinema (*La Promesse* and *The Pillow Book*).

Pittsburgh, Pennsylvania
Carnegie Museum of Art
4400 Forbes Avenue
Local Telephone 412.622.3212
Excellent selection of revivals (*The General*, *My Darling Clementine*, *Metropolis*).

Orgone Cinema Archive
2238 Murray Avenue
Local Telephone 412.521.3714

Pittsburgh Filmmakers
809 Liberty Avenue
Local Telephone 412.471.9700
Art house fare and local specialty screenings. Home of the gay and lesbian film fest.

The Rex
1602 E. Carson Street
Local Telephone 412.381.2200
An excellent revival and first-run cinema featuring classics (*The Graduate*), not-so-classics (*Grease*), and newer flicks (*Love and Other Catastrophes*).

Portland, Oregon
Cinema 21
616 N.W. 21st Avenue
Local Telephone 503.223.4515
Excellent program of mainstream and offbeat revivals (Hong Kong cinema, *Contempt*, *Woman in the Dunes*).

Prague, Czechoslovakia
Dlabacov Cinema
Belohorská 24
Art house cinema featuring mainstream flicks and revivals.

Ponrepo Cinema
Narodni Trida 40

Art house cinema for members of film club.

Providence, Rhode Island
Avon Cinema
260 Thayer Street
Local Telephone 401.421.3310
First-run cinema featuring mainstream art house flicks (*Les Voleurs*, *Female Perversions*).

Raleigh-Durham, North Carolina
The Camel Lounge
Hillsborough Street (Raleigh)
Local Telephone 919.833.8090
Monday-night series of local filmmakers' screenings: "Comet Movie Night."

Griffith Film Theater
Freewater Films
Bryan Center (Durham)
Local Telephone 919.684. 2911
In a town where little else is going on, one is thankful for this excellent university film series on the Duke campus (*The Killing*, *Frantic*, and *Trainspotting*).

Reading, Pennsylvania
Berks Filmmakers
Albright College Center for the Arts
Local Telephone 610.921.7713
Shows excellent series of new flicks and revivals (retrospective of German experimental cinema, Lina Wertmuller's *Seven Beauties*) and allows local filmmakers the opportunity to showcase their films.

Rochester, New York
The Little Theatre
240 East Avenue
Local Telephone 716.258.0444

Rome, Italy
Cinema Pasquino
Vicolo del Piede, 19A
Local Telephone 011.39.6.580.3622
The only English-language cinema located in Rome.

San Lorenzo Sotto le Stelle
Villa Mercede

Via Tiburtina, 113
Outdoor evening series of screenings.

Sacramento, California
The Crest Theater
1013 K Street
Local Telephone 916.44.CREST
Web www.thecrest.com
Film series accompanied by popcorn
and draft beer. Midnight movies feature
fare on the order of James Bond festivals
and Pee Wee Herman movies.

Salt Lake City, Utah
Trolley Square Cinemas
5th South and 7th East
Local Telephone 801.521.9877
A good cinema featuring Miramax-y
films (*Beautiful Thing*).

Utah Film And Video Center
20 S. West Temple
Local Telephone 801.534.1158
Interesting program of films and experi-
mental video (*Four Dreams* from Robert
Holman).

San Antonio, Texas
Crossroads
Loop 410 and Fredericksburg
Local Telephone 210.333.3456
Art house cinema.

San Diego, California
Ken Theater
4061 Adams
Local Telephone 619.283.5909
Decent art film series (*Sling Blade* and
One False Move).

San Francisco, California
Castro Theater
429 Castro
Local Telephone 415.621.6120
Great local cinema featuring revivals
(Fassbinder festival) and groovy first-
runs (*Irma Vep*).

Pacific Film Archive (Berkeley)
2625 Durant
Local Telephone 510.642.1124
Very good program of first-run art

house flicks and revivals (Fassbinder
festival, *Contempt*).

Red Vic
1727 Haight
Local Telephone 415.668.3994
Excellent program of revivals (*Latcho
Drom*, *Saturday Night Fever*, and *Paris,
Texas*).

Roxie Theater
3117 16th Street
Local Telephone 415.863.1087
Groovy program of first-run flicks (*The
Watermelon Woman*) and shorts program
(*Mondo Plympton*).

UC Theater (Berkeley)
2036 University and Shattuck
Local Telephone 510.843.6267
Groovy cinema with excellent programs
of double bills (*Mean Streets* and
Goodfellas, *Devil in a Blue Dress* and
Chinatown, and films of S. Ray).

San Jose, California
Agenda Restaurant
399 S. First Street
Local Telephone 408.287.3991
Very cool 16 mm film series on
Thursday nights featuring classics and
oddities (*Nanook of the North*, *The
Odyssey*, Gerald McDermott's anima-
tion).

Towne Theatre
1433 Alameda
Local Telephone 408.287.1433
Excellent series of offbeat fare (Hong
Kong cinema), art house flicks (*Kolya*),
and excellent silent films with organ
accompaniment (*The Lost World*,
Nosferatu).

Santa Fe, New Mexico
CCA Cinematheque
1050 Old Pecos Road
Local Telephone 505.473.4154
Located in the Center for
Contemporary Arts, screens mainstream
art house flicks (*Irma Vep* and *The Pillow
Book*).

Scottsdale, Arizona

Camelback 3
7033 E. Camelback Road
Local Telephone 520.949.5200
Excellent wide-screen projections of art
house films (*Brassed Off, Temptress Moon*).

Seattle, Washington

Fremont Outdoor Cinema
Fremont Avenue N. and 34th N.
Local Telephone 206.632.0287
Web www.glamorama.com/cinema
A wonderful tonic from the usual slate
of summer trash that usually shows up
at outdoor screens and drive-ins.
Screens an excellent series of classics
(*Who's Afraid of Virginia Woolf, The
Treasure of the Sierra Madre*).

The Grand Illusion
1403 N.E. 50th Street
Local Telephone 206.523.3935
One of the best independent movie theaters in the country and the only indie
theater in Seattle. Owned by the Northwest Film Forum, the humble little
space screens an incredible variety of
revivals tied to specific themes. A
"Road Movie Marathon" featured *Wild
Strawberries*; *Paris, Texas*; *Weekend*;
Leningrad Cowboys Go America; and
O Lucky Man. For the price ($4.50–
$6.50), you can't beat it.

911 Media Arts
117 Yale Avenue
Local Telephone 206.682.6552
Web www.011media.org
Videos, Super-8 and 16 mm flicks.

Spokane, Washington

Magic Lantern
123 S. Wall Street
Local Telephone 509.838.4919

St. Louis, Missouri

Esquire
6706 Clayton Road
Richmond Heights
Local Telephone 314.781.3806

Hi-Pointe Cinema
1001 McCausland
Local Telephone 314.781.0800
There's a $5 admission to art house
movie fare, such as *Smilla's Sense of
Snow*.

St. Louis Art Museum
1 Fine Arts
Local Telephone 314.721.0072
Features previews of the St. Louis Film
Festival selections and specialized
series, such as a retrospective of Italian
cinema.

Tivoli Theater
6350 Delmar
Local Telephone 314.862.1100
Art house films on the order of *Kama
Sutra* and *Prisoner of the Mountains* and a
Thursday classic-film matinee series with
excellent oldies such as *The Big Sleep*.

Webster University Film Series
Winifred Moore Auditorium
470 E. Lockwood
Local Telephone 314.968.7487
Excellent year-round university film
series featuring classics and little-
known contemporary features, including *Ma Saison Preferée, The Man by the
Shore*, and *Ollie's Army*.

Stockholm, Sweden

Saga Theater
Kungsgatan 24
Local Telephone 011.46.8.789.6060
Good art house cinema (*A Great Day in
Harlem, Breaking the Waves*).

Strasbourg, France

Star Cinema
27, rue du Jeu des Enfants
Local Telephone 011.33.3.88.32.4497
Multiplex featuring a number of main-
stream art house features (*Jude,
Surviving Picasso*).

Sydney, Australia

Chauvel
Oatley Road and Oxford Street

Local Telephone 011.61.2.9361.5398
Web www.eg.com.au/chauvel
Excellent collection of classic movies on Monday nights (*Metropolis*, *The Shape of Things to Come*, *Betty Blue*).

Greater Union Pitt Centre
232 Pitt Street
Local Telephone 011.61.2.9264.1694
Art house cinema featuring excellent first-runs (*Different for Girls*, *The Well*, Deepa Mehta's *Fire*).

Syracuse, New York

Landmark Theatre
362 S. Salina Street
Local Telephone 315.475.7980
Offering $3 screenings of reasonably good arty features (*The Last Emperor*).

Manlius Art Cinema
Off the Seneca Turnpike, Route 173
Local Telephone 682.9817
Art house fare and revivals (*Pink Flamingos*).

Syracuse Cinephile Society
Celebrity Den Restaurant
435 N. Salina Street.
Local Telephone 637.8985
Classic films shown Monday nights at 7:30 P.M.

Tel Aviv, Israel

Tel Aviv Museum
27, Shaul Hamelech Boulevard
Local Telephone 695.7361
Art house cinema (*Gabbeh*, *A Moment of Innocence*)

Tokyo, Japan

Bunkamurare Cinema
Local Telephone 011.81.3.3477.9264
Mainstream art house fare (*Kolya*).

Cinema Qualite
Local Telephone 011.81.3.3354.5670
Art house featuring intriguing retrospectives and revivals (Audrey Hepburn fest including *Roman Holiday* and *Funny Face*).

Toronto, Ontario, Canada

Bloor Cinema
506 Bloor
Local Telephone 416.532.6677
Aside from housing various film fest screenings, the Bloor Cinema doubles as a mainstream art house and revival cinema (*Platoon*, *The Usual Suspects*).

Carlton Theater
20 Carlton Street
Local Telephone 416.598.2309
Art house cinema featuring offbeat and mainstream first-runs (*La Seconda Volta*, *Floating Life*, *Zero Kelvin*, *The Other Side of Sunday*, *When the Cat's Away*).

Cinematheque Ontario
Jackman Hall
317 Dundas W.
Local Telephone 416.968.FILM
Excellent revival cinema. Among recent features was a comprehensive series devoted to the work of Rainer Werner Fassbinder (*Despair*, *Rio das Mortes*).

Tucson, Arizona

The Loft Cinema
3233 E. Speedway
Local Telephone 520.795.7777
Art house fare plus revivals (Sick and Twisted Animation Festival, *Moving the Mountain*).

The Screening Room
127 E. Congress Street
Local Telephone 520.622.2262
Asking a $4 entrance fee for excellent slate of double bills (Marlon Brando festival included *A Streetcar Named Desire* and *The Wild Ones*).

Vancouver, British Columbia, Canada

Edison Electric
1435 Commercial Drive
E-mail panic@istar.ca
A concept that should explode in the twenty-first century: storefront cinemas. Screens avant-garde and cult films.

Pacific Cinematheque
1131 Howe

Local Telephone 604.688.FILM
Decent art house cinema.

Ride Theatre
3131 Arbus
Local Telephone 604.738.6311
Good art house featuring relatively new films (*Gabbeh*, *Guantanemara*, *Irma Vep*).

Vienna, Austria

Burgkino
Opernring 19
Local Telephone 011.43.1.587.8406
Screenings of classic features (Carol Reed's *The Third Man*).

Filmmuseum
Augustinerstr. 1
Local Telephone 011.43.1.533.7054
Excellent revival house featuring classic films (*A Night at the Opera*, *Birth of a Nation*).

Stadtkino
Schwarzenbergplatz 8
Local Telephone 011.43.1.712.6276
Art house and experimental features and shorts.

Washington, D.C.

American Film Institute
Kennedy Center
Local Telephone 202.785.4600
Aside from hosting events honoring cinema's greats, also offers an excellent program of classics (David Lean festival: *Great Expectations*, *A Passage to India*, and *Hobson's Choice*).

Key Theater
1222 Wisconsin Avenue NW
Local Telephone 202.333.5100
Good series of artsy features (*The Journey of August King* and *The White Balloon*).

Windsor, Ontario, Canada

Windsor Theatre
2135 Wyandotte W.
Local Telephone 519.969.4494
Fairly decent collection of mainstream art house releases (*Lost Highway* and *Waiting for Guffman*).

Winnipeg, Manitoba, Canada

Cinématheque
100 Arthur Street
Local Telephone 204.942.6795

Worcester, Massachusetts

Jefferson Academic Center
Main and Downing Streets
Local Telephone 508.793.7477
Clark University screening series featuring revivals and art house flicks (*Crumb* and *Belle de Jour*).

Zurich, Switzerland

Kino Xenix
Helvetiaplatz
Kanzleistrasse 56
Local Telephone 011.41.1.242.0411
Excellent art house and repertory cinema (a tribute to Stanley Kubrick featuring *Spartacus*, *Killer's Kiss*, and *Lolita*).

Submission Calendar

This index will help you plan your submissions throughout the year.

January

Atlanta Film and Video Festival
Balticum Film and TV Festival
Brussels International Festival of Fantasy, Thriller, and SF Films
Fajr Film Festival
Festival International du Film d'Animation
Film Fest New Haven
Grenzland Film Days
Hispanic Film Festival
Inside/OUT Lesbian and Gay Film and Video Festival of Toronto
International Film and Video Festival
International Short Film Festival of Kraków
It's All True International Documentary Film Festival
Los Angeles Independent Film Festival
New York Underground Film and Video Festival
Newport Beach International Film Festival
Nyon International Documentary Film Festival
Oberhausen Short Film Festival
Philadelphia Festival of World Cinema
Philadelphia Independent Film and Video Festival
Singapore International Film Festival
Tampere Short Film Festival
Taos Talking Picture Festival
Tropicana Short Film Festival
United States Super-8 Film and Video Festival
Wellington Gay and Lesbian Film Festival

February

Ann Arbor 16 mm Film Festival
Arizona International Film Festival
Athens International Film and Video Festival
Canyonlands Film and Video Festival
Carolina Film and Video Festival
Chicago Latino Film Festival
Festival International du Court Métrage de Mons
Filmfest DC
Florida Film Festival
Gen Art Film Festival
Hiroshima International Amateur Film and Video Festival
Humboldt International Film and Video Festival

Italian Film Festival
Minneapolis/St. Paul International Film Festival
Moomba International Amateur Film Festival
Movies on a Shoestring
Rough and Ruined Film Festival
Saguaro Film Festival
San Francisco International Lesbian and Gay Film Festival
Sydney Film Festival
Toronto Jewish Film Festival
USA Film Festival
Victoria Independent Short Film and Video Festival
Viper Festival
World Festival of Animated Film
WorldFest Houston

March

Asian American International Film Festival
Boston International Festival of Women's Cinema
Cannes Film Festival
Certamen de Cine Amateur
Charlotte Film and Video Festival
Chiba Electronic Cinema Festival
Cinémas d'Afrique
Festival Internacional de Cinema do Algarve
Filmfest Emden
Filmfestival Internazionale Montagna Esplorazione Aventura
Global Africa International Film and Video Festival
Hamburg International Short Film Festival
Hometown Video Festival
Hudson Valley Film Festival
International Festival of Comedy Films
Kine International Film Festival
Laguna Beach Film Festival
Maui Film Festival
Midnight Sun Film Festival
Mountainfilm in Telluride
Native American Film and Video Festival
Norwegian Short Film Festival
Nottingham Shots in the Dark Mystery and Thriller Film Festival
Outfest: Los Angeles Gay and Lesbian Festival
Palm Beach International Film Festival
Pesaro Film Festival
San Francisco Jewish Film Festival
Seattle International Film Festival
Showcase of Independent Video and Interactive Phenomenae
Thriller Film Festival of Cognac (Festival du Film Policier)
Yamagata International Documentary Film Festival
Yorkton Short Film and Video Festival

April

Amnesty International Film Festival Amsterdam
Art Film Festival
Auckland International Film Festival

Avignon/New York Film Festival
Cascadia Festival of Moving Images
Chicago Underground Film Festival
Festival of Nations
Filmfest München
Galway Film Festival
Hiroshima International Animation Festival
Hot Springs Documentary Film Festival
Huesca Film Festival
International Exhibition of Documentary Films on Art
International Festival of Maritime Documentaries
Jerusalem Film Festival
Karlovy Vary International Film Festival
Maine International Film Festival
Melbourne International Film Festival
Montreal/New York International Nouveau Festival
Nantucket Film Festival
New Zealand Film Festival
Newark Black Film Festival
Odense International Film Festival
Parnu Visual Anthropology Festival
Philadelphia International Gay and Lesbian Film Festival
Prague International Film Festival
Sinking Creek Film and Video Festival
Slice of Life Film and Video Showcase
Wine Country Film Festival

May

Black Harvest Film Festival
Cambridge International Film Festival
Cattolica International Mystery Film Festival
Dances with Films
Divercine Children's International Film Festival
Edinburgh International Film Festival
Espoo Cine
Festival Cine Latino
Goldfish International Children's Animation Festival
Great Plains Film Festival
International Duisburger Amateur Film Days and Youth Video Forum
Internet Festival of Crud
Jackson Hole Wildlife Film Festival
Jerulsalem Film Festival—Festival of Festivals
Kelibia International Festival of Amateur Film
Locarno International Film Festival
Margaret Mead Film Festival
Marion County National Film Competition
Mill Valley Film Festival
Palm Springs International Short Film Festival
La Rochette International Film Festival
São Paulo International Short Film Festival
St. Petersburg "Message to Man" Documentary Film Festival
St. Petersburg International Film Festival of Festivals
Téléscience

UFVA Student Film and Video Festival
Uruguay International Children's Film Festival
Wellington Film Festival

June

AFI Los Angeles International Film Festival
Atlantic Film Festival
Border Film Festival
Boston Jewish Film Festival
Breckenridge Festival of Film
Chicago International Children's Film Festival
Cinewomen Film Festival
Cologne Feminale Women's Film Festival
Copenhagen Film Fest
Dublin Lesbian and Gay Film Festival
Filmfest Hamburg
Gravity-Free Film and Video Competition (Lucille Ball Festival of
    New Comedy)
Hawaii International Film Festival
Hollywood Film Festival
Indiana Film and Video Festival
Leeds International Film Festival
Long Island Film Festival
Marseille Vue sur les Docs
Noosa International Film Festival
Northampton Film Festival
Norwegian International Film Festival
Riga Arsenals International Film Forum
Riminicinema
Rocky Mountain Women's Film Festival
St. John's International Women's Film and Video Festival
St. Louis International Gay and Lesbian Film Festival
Silver Lake Film Festival
Stockholm International Film Festival
Taormina International Film Festival
Tokyo International Fantastic Film Festival
Toronto International Film Festival
Valladolid International Film Festival
Venice Film Festival
World Population Film/Video Festival

July

Archeofilm Fest
Aspen Film Fest
Bangkok Film Festival
Birmingham International Film and TV Festival
Boston Film Festival
Brief Encounters
Brisbane International Film Fest
Central Florida Film and Video Festival
Certamen Internacional de Cine Amateur
Chicago Lesbian and Gay International Film Festival
Cinéma Tout Écran

Cinemagic International Film Festival for Young People
Columbus International Film and Video Festival
Cork International Film Festival
Dallas Video Festival
Deauville Festival of American Films
Empire State Film Festival
Festival de Cinema Ste.-Thérèse/Ste.-Adéle
Festival International du Film Ornithologique
Festival Videoart de Locarno
Film Arts Festival
Fort Worth Film Festival
Haifa International Film Festival
Heartland Film Festival
Helsinki International Film Festival
International Festival of Fantastic Films
International Festival of Free Flight
International Short Film Festival
Leipzig International Festival for Documentary and Animated Film
London Low-Budget Film Festival
MadCat Women's International Film Festival
The Mail and Guardian International Film Festival
Mannheim International Film Festival Mannheim-Heidelberg
Medikinale International Hannover
Montreal World Film Festival
Netherlands Film Festival
New Orleans Film and Video Festival
New York Expo and Video
New York Film Festival
New York Independent Feature Film Market
Okomedia International Ecological Film Festival
Ottawa International Animation Festival
Rassegna di Palermo
San Sebastian International Film Festival
Tacoma Tortured Artists Film Festival
Telluride Film Festival
Tokyo International Festival of Film Students
Tokyo International Film Festival
Vancouver International Film Festival and Trade Forum
Virginia Film Festival
Zimbabwe International Film Festival

August

African Diaspora Film Festival
American Indian Film Festival
Amsterdam International Documentary Film Festival
Austin Film Festival
Barcelona International Exhibition of Gay and Lesbian Films
Bite the Mango: Black and Asian Film Festival
Brest Short Film Festival
Brisbane Animation Festival
Brno 16
Chicago International Film Festival
Cinanima International Animation Film Festival

Cinefest: The Sudbury Film Festival
Fantastisk Film Festival
Festival International du Film Francophone
Flanders International Film Festival
Geneva Film Festival
Hamptons International Film Festival
Hollywood Black Film Festival
H. P. Lovecraft Film Festival
International Festival of Amateur Films
International Film Festival for Children and Young People
Jornada Internacional de Cinema da Bahia
Kudzu Film Festival
London Film Festival
London Raindance Film Showcase
Louisville Film and Video Festival
Namur Festival International du Court Métrage
New York Gay and Lesbian Experimental Film and Video Festival
New York International Independent Film and Video Festival
Northern Lights International Film and Video Festival
Northwest Film and Video Festival
Ohio Independent Film Festival
Olympia Film Festival
Pusan International Film Festival
St. Louis Film Festival
San Juan Cinemafest
San Luis Obispo International Film Festival
Shanghai International Film Festival
Short Attention Span Film and Video Festival
Sitges International Fantasy Film Festival
Super Super-8 Fest
Taipei Golden Horse Festival
Umea International Film Festival
Uppsala International Short Film Festival
Viennale-Vienna International Film Festival (Internationale Filmfestwochen Wein)
West Virginia International Film Festival

September

Abbitibi-Temiscaminique International Film Festival
Amateur ARSfilm Festival
Armed Forces and People Film Festival
Banff Mountain Film Festival
Bilbao Festival of Documentary and Short Films
Cádiz International Video Festival
Camerimage
Cartoombria International Festival of Animation Film
Certamen Internacional de Curmetrages i Video
Festival de Cine IberoAmericano
Filmfestival Max Ophüls Preis
Florence Festival dei Populi Review of Social Documentary
Fort Lauderdale International Film Festival
Gijon International Film Festival
Golden Knight International Amateur Film and Video Festival
Herland Film Festival

HIV Positive Film Fest
Holland Animation Festival
Idyllwild International Film Festival
International Festival of New Latin American Cinema
International Health and Medical Film Festival
International Hofer Filmtage
International Super-8 Festival
Lo-Con Short Film Festival
Morocco International Festival
Oulu Children's Film Festival
San Francisco International Asian American Film Festival
São Paulo International Film Festival
Shorts International Film Festival
Snow, Ice, and Adventure Film Festival
Turin International Festival of Young Cinema
Vevey International Comedy Film Festival
Videobrasil International Video Festival
Welsh International Film Festival
Western Australian Gay and Lesbian Film Festival
World Festival of Underwater Films
WorldFest Flagstaff

October

Belfort International Film Festival
Brussels International Film Festival
Cairo International Film Festival
Cancún Film Festival
Cinequest San Jose Film Festival
CineVegas Las Vegas Film Festival
Clermont-Ferrand Short Film Festival
Ecuador Indigenous Film Festival
Festival des Trois Continents
Festival Internacional de Cinema de Muntanya Vila de Torello
Festival International du Film des Métiers d'Art à Namur
Filmfront National Student Film and Video Festival
International Festival of Films on Art
International Science and Technology Film and Video Festival
Melbourne Super-8 Film Festival
Nordic Glory Film Festival
Portland International Film Festival
Rio de Janeiro International Short Film Festival
Rotterdam International Film Festival
Solothurn Film Festival
Sundance Film Festival
Thessaloníki Film Festival
Tokyo Video Festival
Two Rivers Native Film and Video Festival

November

Berlin International Film Festival
Black Maria Film and Video Festival
Brandon Film Festival
Brussels Animated Film and Cartoon Festival

Cinéma du Rèel
Cleveland International Film Festival
Dhaka International Short Film Festival
Dortmund Women's Film Festival
Dublin Film Festival
Education Local Heroes International Screen Festival
European First Film Festival of Angers
International Festival of Cinematographic Art of Barcelona
International Film Festival of India
Miami International Film Festival
Palm Springs International Film Festival
Portland Jewish Film Festival
San Diego Film Festival
Santa Clarita International Film Festival
Slamdance Film Festival

December

Aspen Shorts Festival
Bermuda Film Festival
BUFF Children's Film Festival
Calcutta Film Festival on Mountains
Créteil International Festival of Women's Films
Fantasporto
FESPACO Pan-African Film and Television Festival of Ouagadougou
Festival International du Premier Film
Göteborg Film Festival
Györ Media Wave
Hong Kong International Film Festival
Human Rights Watch International Film Festival
Imagina
Istanbul International Film Festival
N.A.P. Video Festival
Nashville Independent Film Festival
Rainy States Film Festival
Rouen Nordic Film Festival
San Francisco International Film Festival
Santa Barbara International Film Festival
Stuttgart Animation Film Days
SXSW Film Festival
Texas Film Festival
U.S. Comedy Arts Festival

Index